Why Ireland Starved:

A Quantitative and Analytical History of the Irish Economy, 1800–1850

Why Ireland Starved:

A Quantitative and Analytical History of the
Irish Economy, 1800–1850

JOEL MOKYR

Professor of Economics and History,
Northwestern University, Evanston, Illinois

London
GEORGE ALLEN & UNWIN
Boston   Sydney

George Allen & Unwin (Publishers) Ltd,
40 Museum Street, London WC1A 1LU, UK

George Allen & Unwin (Publishers) Ltd,
Park Lane, Hemel Hempstead, Herts HP2 4TE, UK

Allen & Unwin Inc.,
9 Winchester Terrace, Winchester, Mass. 01890, USA

George Allen & Unwin Australia Pty Ltd,
8 Napier Street, North Sydney, NSW 2060, Australia

First published in 1983

British Library Cataloguing in Publication Data

Mokyr, Joel
   Why Ireland starved.
1. Ireland–Economic conditions
I. Title
330.9415′081   HC260.5
ISBN 0-04-941010-5

Library of Congress Cataloging in Publication Data

Mokyr, Joel.
   Why Ireland starved.
Bibliography: p.
Includes index.
1. Ireland–Economic conditions. 2. Ireland–Rural conditions.
3. Poor–Ireland–History. 4. Ireland–Famines–History. I. Title.
HC260.5.M64 1983 330.9415′081   82–24508
ISBN 0-04-941010-5

Set in 10 on 11 point Times by Fotographics (Bedford) Ltd,
and printed in Great Britain by Mackays of Chatham

Contents

Acknowledgements   *page* ix
 1 Introduction   1
 2 A Poverty-Stricken Economy?   6
 3 The Problem of Population: Was Malthus Right?   30
 4 Land, Leases, and Length of Tenure   81
 5 The Economics of Rural Conflict and Unrest   112
 6 The Problem of Wealth   151
 7 The Human Factor: Entrepreneurship and Labor   197
 8 Emigration and the Prefamine Economy   230
 9 The Great Famine: the Economics of Vulnerability   261
10 Explaining Irish Poverty   278
Bibliography   295
Index   317

Dedicated to
NACHUM T. GROSS
WILLIAM N. PARKER
and
JONATHAN R. T. HUGHES
Mentors, colleagues, friends

Acknowledgements

During the research and writing which led to this book, I have accumulated more debts than I can ever hope to repay. Financially, I am deeply grateful to the Northwestern University Research Committee which financed the project in its earliest stages. The bulk of the research was financed by a generous grant from the National Science Foundation (SOC 78-06710). The manuscript was completed thanks to a fellowship from the John Simon Guggenheim Foundation. The views expressed in this book are, of course, my own and do not necessarily reflect those of the institutions which provided me with financial support.

I further wish to acknowledge permission to reprint portions of my earlier articles, "Industrialization and poverty in Ireland and the Netherlands", *Journal of Interdisciplinary History*, vol. X, no. 3 (Winter 1980), pp. 429–58 (copyright 1980, by MIT Press); "The deadly fungus: an econometric investigation into the short-term demographic impact of the Irish famine", *Research in Population Economics*, vol. II (1980), pp. 237–77 (copyright 1980, by JAI Press); "Malthusian models and Irish history", *Journal of Economic History*, vol. XL, no. 1 (March 1980), pp. 159–66 (copyright 1980, by the Economic History Association).

Much of the quantitative work on which the study is based would not have been completed without the diligent labors of my research assistants. I have been singularly fortunate to have been aided by a number of talented and responsible RAs, who often had to assume the functions of proof-readers, counselors, and testing-grounds for half-baked ideas. In the early stages of the project, Michael Waks helped me to create the data basis. Other assistants at various stages include Louis Bryniarski, Jaclyn Gier, Nancy Kroc, and Janet Reddy (at Northwestern); Chris Sanders (at Stanford); and Mrs Marian Becker (in Dublin). Above all, Paul Zawa and Evelyne Seebauer fought and won many hard battles against the recalcitrant Northwestern University computer and against my often impenetrable prose. Mrs Barbara Karni edited and corrected the final manuscript with great skill. My secretary, Mrs Ann Roth, who typed most of the manuscript, has shown a diligence and devotion rare even among the Jewish Mothers of Skokie, Illinois.

The list of colleagues and friends who have helped and encouraged me in this project is long and covers four continents. The largest debt of all I owe to Dr Cormac Ó Gráda of University College, Dublin. Throughout the work on this book I have had the privilege of drawing upon his vast knowledge of Irish Economic History. During my visits to Ireland, I also benefited from conversations with Dr David Dickson, the late Professor E. R. R. Green, and Dr J. M. Goldstrom. The Economic and Social Research Institute of Dublin, and in particular Mr Brendan Dowling and his family, have shown me warm hospitality. The staff of the library of the Royal Irish Academy, led by Mrs Bridget Dolan and the staff of the National Library of Dublin supplied all my needs in terms of books and periodicals. The director of the National Library, Mr Alf Mac Lochlainn, provided me with much-needed help at a crucial moment. Dr Leslie Clarkson generously supplied me with a prepublication copy of the *Festschrift* in honor of K. H. Connell, which he coedited with J. M. Goldstrom.

My colleagues in the Economics Department of Northwestern University have enriched this study with their understanding and insights. Many of them contributed important ideas, while in other cases they helped relegate some of my own to well-deserved early graves. Especially Karl DeSchweinitz, Gregory Duncan, Gerald Goldstein, Robert J. Gordon, Craig Hakkio, Jonathan Hughes, and Aba Schwartz, should be mentioned. Louis Cain of Loyola University and Elizabeth Hoffman of Northwestern read the entire manuscript and made so many valuable comments that I cannot imagine how I can in good faith absolve them of remaining errors. Eric L. Jones, formerly of Northwestern University and at present at Latrobe University, Melbourne, has for many years been providing me with the support and encouragement no scholar can do without. F. Michael Scherer's contribution to this work is larger than reciprocity would demand.

During my year at Stanford many insights stemmed from the inexhaustible minds of Paul A. David and Warren C. Sanderson. Without them and their students David Weir and Tom Mroz, the demographic parts of this book would never have been completed. Two visitors at Stanford, Jacob Metzer and Frank Lewis, read preliminary chapters and made many excellent suggestions. Among the many others who have placed me in their debt are Eric Almquist, Reuven Brenner, James Donnelly, Stanley Engerman, Stefano Fenoaltea, Kim McQuaid, Frederic Mishkin, N. Eugene Savin, T. W. Schultz, Gavin Wright, and Harold R. C. Wright.

EVANSTON, ILLINOIS
June 1982

Famine is in thy cheeks
Need and Oppression starveth in thine eyes,
Contempt and beggary hang upon thy back;
The world is not thy friend nor the world's law:
The world affords no law to make thee rich

Romeo and Juliet

Chapter 1

Introduction

This book is not a general survey of the economic history of Ireland between the Union and the famine. It is not intended as such and should not be read for the purpose of an introduction to the subject. It is true that no up-to-date work has tried to supersede O'Brien (1921) as a general textbook covering the period. There is perhaps a reason for that absence: modern scholarship has revised and criticized many of the positions taken by nineteenth- and early twentieth-century writers, but disagreements among scholars persist and many revisionist positions find themselves subject to the same degree of criticism their proponents have raised against earlier scholarship. It may be appropriate to post-pone the writing of more definitive work which synthesizes modern research until the dust has settled on current controversies.

My purpose in this work is to answer one question which is central to Irish economic history: why was Ireland poor? No pretense is made here to provide an overall picture of all aspects of the prefamine economy. To be sure, there are many other interesting research topics in the economic history of prefamine Ireland besides poverty: the emergence of the Belfast linen industry, the rise of the commercial economy which channeled Irish agricultural products to Britain, and the slow rise of a small urban bourgoisie. But what is most striking about this country is that most of the people who lived in Ireland in this period were poor, poorer than in comparable economies in Europe. Poverty was not con-fined to the proverbially wretched conditions in the Irish West: it was bad in the cottages of Armagh, in the grazing farms of the midlands, and in the Wicklow mountains. It was almost synonymous with life in Ireland. But why?

Answering questions concerning causation in economic history is always controversial. It is not possible to prove anything beyond reason-able doubt. All we can do is to employ *a priori* reasoning to formulate and test hypotheses and then try our best to test these hypotheses. Both parts of this procedure invite criticism. First, the hypotheses to be tested have to be derived either from some kind of deductive economic reasoning (neoclassical or other), or from the opinions and judgements of contemporaries. The pitfalls in this procedure are obvious: deductive economic reasoning makes *a priori* assumptions such as "a class structure exists" or "the aggregate production function is of the Cobb–Douglas type" which, if accepted, could yield testable hypotheses. But should such assumptions be accepted? If a hypothesis based on absurd assumptions is found consistent with the data, do we thereby gain any historical insight? Secondly, the testing procedure is by definition hazardous. In a rigorous statistical test we find that a hypothesis is consistent with the data. By that we mean that the likelihood that the test statistic generated by the data was obtained fortuitously is less than some critical value. Many hypotheses concerning causal relations in economic history do not permit very sophisticated tests due to data constraints. It is even harder to discriminate between one plausible model and another as historical data are so often consistent with a whole array of interpretations. None the less, deficient as this methodology is, it is the best available.

The strategy followed in this book is simple: a list of possible explanations of Ireland's poverty can be made, based on observations of contemporaries, on theories proposed by historians, or on models which are based on modern economic analysis and social thought. Once that list is complete, an attempt will be made to examine each of these hypotheses critically. Some of these hypotheses will be criticized primarily on *a priori* bases, but as a rule a deliberate and explicit attempt will be made to confront the argument with data which have the capacity to falsify the hypothesis. Hypotheses that are not falsifiable by any means will not be analyzed since they are for that very reason of little interest. What is important is that the final list does not have to be reduced to one single cause: some hypotheses could be rejected in a weak form in the sense that the "factor" may be shown to have been relatively unimportant although not entirely without effect. What will be attempted is to evaluate the relative importance of the causal factors in Irish economic history. The factors of importance to be examined can be divided into the following groups, which to some extent overlap.

(1) *Geographical factors*   Ireland lacked two of the critical resources which played such a central role in the Industrial Revolution in Great Britain and Belgium: coal and iron. The quality of its soil, especially in the west, has also been viewed as inherently inferior. It could be maintained that Ireland's ability to pull itself out of the poverty trap of preindustrial economy was reduced by these natural resource deficits.

(2) *Political and institutional factors*   Many historians place the responsibility for Ireland's economic backwardness squarely upon Britain, either directly or indirectly. The wholesale confiscation of land in the seventeenth century ultimately led to the Irish Land Question which was to play a central role in British politics in the closing decades of the nineteenth century. In the decades before the famine the character of the Land Question had become economic rather than political. Other arguments which belong in this category are the effects of the mercantilist measures and penal codes adopted over 1667–1705, and the effect of the Union with Britain of 1800.

(3) *Social and ethnic factors*   Many contemporary observers believed that the characteristics of the "average" Irishman were inconsistent with the requirements of economic growth. While some of these statements amount to little more than racial and religious prejudice, it is not absurd to think that interregional, international,

and interreligious differences in tastes, attitudes, and customs *could* have affected the rate of economic development.

(4) *The population factor* Classical political economy viewed Ireland as an example of overpopulation. This view is still widely accepted among modern historians, and is consistent with the revival of Malthusian models in modern economic history.

(5) *Capital formation factors* The accumulation of capital, in industry, in agriculture, and in transportation and other social overhead capital was a strategic element in the economic development of the European economies in the nineteenth century. The factors which determined the rate of accumulation were of two kinds: those that determined the rate of saving in the economy and those that determined how much of that saving would become available for investment projects which were instrumental in the modernization process. If it is found that Ireland's economy suffered from a lack of capital, it will be necessary to examine both the total supply of savings and the form that investment took.

(6) *Entrepreneurial factors* These hypotheses place the responsibility for Ireland's backwardness on the absence of economic agents who could take advantage of economic opportunities rather than on the absence of such opportunities themselves. The widespread lamentations about the absenteeism of Irish landlords belong in this category, although the argument is not limited to the agricultural economy.

(7) *The emigration factor* The mass exodus of Irishmen and Irishwomen from Ireland predates the famine by half a century. As a result, the history of Ireland is the history of a residual population. The effect of emigration on those who stayed behind has not received sufficient recognition among historians, but could go a long way in explaining the difficulty the Irish had in following the economic path taken by countries which received immigrants or countries in which emigration was quantitatively insignificant.

These classes of causal factors will be analyzed in detail in the following chapters. All factors share one property: all are *prima facie* legitimate and sensible explanations of Irish backwardness. But not everything that *could* serve as an explanation was necessarily of importance; we are interested in what *was* true, not what *could have been* true. While historians can never be certain about causation, the challenge of the New Economic History is to distinguish between the possible and the probable.

Rigorous tests require numbers and theoretically sound and consistent reasoning. Much of this book is devoted to quantitative analysis in an attempt to build the data base to be utilized in the testing procedure. Because of the obvious limitations of quantitative history, however, semi-quantitative and qualitative evidence is indispensable to this type of study. Much attention will be paid to the writings and testimonies of contemporaries, and their opinions and views of the roots of Ireland's economic conditions will have to be taken into consideration. Quantitative and qualitative evidence serve different ends and should be viewed as complements, not substitutes. They can also be combined to yield suggestive, though not always unambiguous, quantitative indices of qualitative information. The idea of content analysis of qualitative information is pursued in several instances because the Irish sources lend themselves well to it. It is more persuasive to support an argument with the fact that a majority of contemporaries stated a particular opinion or believed something to be the case than, as is so often done, to cite isolated examples, implying that these represent a majority view. Some hypotheses, of course, do not lend themselves readily to any kind of quantitative test: consider, for example, the widespread opinion that the Irish Catholics were lazy (or, to use a modern technical phrase, had a high preference for leisure). While a test of this argument is not completely inconceivable, it is not very practicable in this case.

In a recent review article L. A. Clarkson (1980) noted with some relief that present work in Irish economic history was "a trifle old fashioned, with the bewitching voices of the social sciences muted and statistical wizardry missing. Consequently Irish economic history is generally readable, if not always profound". Wizardry or not, economic history without the social sciences and statistics is becoming increasingly unthinkable. Recent work by Ó Gráda, Almquist, and Clark, among others, incorporates both quantitative sophistication and sound social theory, without suffering in terms of readability. Clarkson's implicit exhortation is, however, observed here: the detailed derivation of data and some complex technical arguments are deferred to appendices, to facilitate the reading.

This study makes no claim to being an exhaustive survey of all sources of Irish Economic History in the first half of the nineteenth century. The length of the period covered and the attempt to analyze the entire economy rather than a region would make any such attempt futile. The backbone of the information used to test the hypotheses comes from the British *Parliamentary Papers*. Three sources play a central role in any study of prefamine Irish history: the 1841 Census (Great Britain, 1843, Vol. XXIV), the Poor Law Commission Report (Great Britain, 1836b, Vols XXX–XXXIV), and the Devon Commission Report (Great Britain, 1845a, Vols XIX–XXII; see also Kennedy, 1847). Other parliamentary reports and investigations complement these three monumental sets of data and information. Furthermore, writings of contemporaries on Ireland provide unusually good coverage of economic and social history and are available for the earlier part of the period as well. The *Parochial Survey* edited by Mason (1814–19); the *Statistical Surveys* commissioned by the Dublin Society; and the massive efforts of individuals such as Wakefield (1812), Hall and Hall (1825–40), Kane (1845), and Foster (1847), as well as the many foreign travelers who visited Ireland, all constitute the source material from which the data to test the hypotheses will be drawn.

No deliberate attempt to rely on unpublished source material has been made. The *a priori* preference some historians still have for *sources manuscriptes* over *sources imprimées* seems especially absurd in view of the enormity of the underutilization of the printed sources, especially the *Parliamentary Papers.* Estate papers, private correspondence, firm accounts, and similar material have not been used, and vast amounts of material still await many historians to confirm or reject the conclusions put forward in this book. Rather than sample from the vast array of manuscript material available,[1] I have tried to restrict the use of manuscript sources to those directly relevant to the questions posed. Among these, the New York Harbor Passengers Lists, from which the sample of emigrants used in Chapter 8 was drawn, figures prominently. Other extensively used sources were the O'Brien Rentals, which provided the data on land tenure used in Chapter 4, the Ordnance Survey manuscripts, the Constabulary Survey of 1846, and the microfilm collection of Irish parish records in the National Library of Dublin. These sources were chosen either because they provided direct quantitative information or because their coverage was sufficiently complete to avoid the dangers of unrepresentativeness, which always looms large in surviving microdata.

Chapter 2 presents a more exact description of the phenomenon of Irish poverty and how (as opposed to why) it came about. In Chapter 3 the view which placed overpopulation at the center of the stage is examined. Chapter 4 takes a closer look at the Land Tenure Hypothesis, and Chapter 5 contains an attempt to understand the economic background of social conflict and the connection between agrarian unrest and poverty. Chapter 6 deals with the issues of the scarcity of resources and capital, and Chapter 7 looks at the "human side" of the underdevelopment problem, namely, labor and entrepreneurship. In Chapter 8 the impact of emigration on the Irish economy is examined. Chapter 9 deals with the consequences of Irish backwardness, and Chapter 10 contains some concluding reflections on the ability of the economic historian to "explain" Irish poverty.

Note: Chapter 1

1 Consider, for instance, the amount of unpublished material listed by Donnelly (1975, pp. 387–92), who has studied only one county, Cork.

Chapter 2

A Poverty-Stricken Economy?

"In some ways", writes one historian (Freeman, 1957, p. 10), "the story of prefamine times resembles a tragedy rising to its devastating climax". Irish economic history in the four or five decades before the famine seems in retrospect to lead almost inevitably to disaster. It is tempting to argue that the occurrence of the Great Famine was an inexorable consequence of poverty, overpopulation, and an overdependence on potatoes. But, as I have argued elsewhere (Mokyr, 1980c), such inferences are dangerous. Poverty does not lead inevitably to disaster, and disasters do not require a necessary precondition of poverty. At the most, we can hypothesize that poverty reduced the resilience of the economy and increased its vulnerability to exogenous shocks. The nexus between poverty and vulnerability is not self-evident, however, and requires careful testing.

The poverty of prefamine Ireland was unambiguously described by contemporary writers. Foreign and British travelers such as Kohl (1844), Walter Scott (1935), Beaumont (1839), de Tocqueville (1958), Lavergne (1855), Foster (1847), and Inglis (1835) were unanimous on this subject. They followed the example of Berkeley (1953, p. 237) in comparing the Irish peasant unfavorably to black slaves, Russian peasants, and Indian savages, and clearly believed that the material condition in Ireland was vastly inferior to that in their own countries. While the Irish west was obviously regarded as the worst off, the negative verdict held for Ireland as a whole. Kohl (1844, p. 5) noted, for example, that "until one has seen the west of Ireland he has no idea that human beings can live in a state of greater misery than in the fertile environs of Dublin or that a peopled and cultivated land can look wilder than the corn-abounding plains of Meath, Kildare, and Westmeath". The occasional Irishman abroad made similar observations. A. H. Lynch (1839, p. 86) wrote that "an Irishman travelling through Belgium cannot refrain from asking himself, why is it that Ireland is wretched whilst Belgium is flourishing?" The British government, too, was very much aware of the inferior economic situation in Ireland. During 1801–45 they launched a large number of major investigations into the problem of Irish poverty. Some of these investigations, to be sure, stemmed from some specific problems such as the absence of a poor law in Ireland. There was, however, a growing realization in Britain that Ireland was not sharing in the growth and development of the British economy, and recommendations designed to reverse this process were made repeatedly.

In spite of such unanimity among contemporary observers, the classification of Ireland as one of the poorest nations in Europe should not be accepted without qualifications. Serious objections can be raised against an overly pessimistic view of the Irish economy. The judgements of contemporaries were clearly tainted by their preconceived notions of what consumption patterns should look like. The most dramatic descriptions, often overblown, were reserved for the low quality of housing and clothing in Ireland. Foster (1847, p. 57) maintained, for instance, that two-thirds of all Irishmen never wore shoes. Colorful descriptions of the filth and squalor of the smoke-filled Irish cabins in which pigs and human beings cohabited fill many pages in the descriptions of contemporaries. It is possible, however, that these observations conceal a gigantic "index number problem" caused by the fact that the rural Irish simply consumed a *different* bundle of consumption goods from the French, the Germans, or even the inhabitants of Dublin. When comparing the economic well-being of two situations or societies in which radically different combinations of goods are being consumed, it is difficult or impossible to determine what part of these differences were due to any one of three potential causes: different levels of income, different relative prices, or different tastes. A "ranking" of degrees of poverty or a welfare comparison might thus be unwarranted.

As far as energy supplies were concerned, Ireland seems to have been well off. The Irish diet, while monotonous and perhaps tasteless, was probably richer than all but the most advanced regions of Europe. Although potato harvests were becoming more volatile after 1810, and were possibly becoming more risky than cereals even before 1845, there were no truly major famines in Ireland during 1750-1845.

The central pillar of the Irish diet was the potato. Total acreage of potatoes on the eve of the famine was approximately 2·1 million statute acres (Mokyr, 1981a). We can compute the total energy value of the potato crop by assuming a mean gross output figure of 6 ton of potato per acre (Bourke, 1968; 1969; Ó Gráda, 1980c). As a pound of potatoes contains about 317 calories (Burton, 1968, p. 173; see Crawford, 1978, p. 63, for a higher estimate), the total gross output of calories per annum was about $8{,}947 \times 10^9$ calories. Bourke estimated that 47 percent of the potato crop was directly consumed by humans. To that we have to add the amount consumed indirectly through potato-fed animals, but since meat or pork were not a daily fare of most Irish peasants, most of the 33 percent of the potato crop fed to animals must be considered exports. All in all, it is reasonable to assume that the potato crop alone provided the Irish with at least $4{,}200 \times 10^9$ calories per year, which is equivalent to 1,400 calories per capita per day. These averages conceal much higher potato dependencies in some regions, but they demonstrate the enormous value of the potato in the supply of energy. Bourke (1968, p. 76) estimated the adult male diet to be at least 12 lb a day, implying a calorific intake of over 3,800 calories per day, sufficient for all but the most physically exerting occupations (Davidson and Passmore, 1965, pp. 27–8). The potato diet was complemented by dairy products, oatmeal, and in some regions fish and eggs. Connell (1950a, p. 155), Burton (1968, pp. 170–82), and Crawford (1978) have all concluded that the prefamine diet was sufficient in vitamins, proteins, and minerals.

Davidson and Passmore (1965, p. 285) note that the potato is the only single cheap food that can support life when fed as the sole article of diet. It is possible, however, that during 1815–45 there was some deterioration in the diets of the poorest classes.

The second source of energy in the Irish economy was peat, which supplied a constant and almost ubiquitous source of fuel for home heating and cooking. Its cheapness and widespread availability may have contributed to the shoddiness of the Irish house and clothes. Contemporaries noted the intensive use of peat in households and pointed out that people took it almost for granted. Weld (1832, p. 78) observed that people living as little as 4 miles away from a source of turf already considered themselves inconvenienced. Some areas such as southern Antrim or Limerick were gradually depleting their peat reserves, and this caused considerable suffering to the population. But in most of Ireland the situation was one of abundance of fuel, although few were as well off as Co. Clare where a laborer could cut as much turf as his family needed for a year in two days, and carry it home (Dutton, 1808, p. 175). Elsewhere the cutting and carrying of turf was a time-consuming activity, and considered as important as the harvesting of corn (Wakefield, 1812, Vol. 1, p. 623).

The abundance of high-calorie food and other forms of energy were in part responsible for the peculiar basket of consumer goods consumed in Ireland. Irish consumption patterns differed from those in most other Western European countries. At least some of the hyperbolical and dramatic descriptions of contemporaries may be attributed to this difference. But there is more: measures of national income per capita are misleading as indices of welfare. Some items, such as leisure and large families, while obviously consumer goods bearing positive prices, are not included. Comparison among economies which have considerable differences in leisure consumption or average family size may therefore be highly misleading. Contemporary writers pointed out that the condition of the laboring poor seemed wretched but that they were neither discontented, nor unhappy, and that the Irishman's simple form of life made him "experience a delight unknown to his superiors" (Townsend, 1815, Vol. 1, p. 90). Foster (1847, p. 288) stated with no little condescendence that "The Celtic peasant's . . . contentment has made him rest satisfied with shelter and turf fire, and potatoes and water to live upon . . . and is happy so long as he can get them, and he strives for nothing better". Beaumont (1839, Vol. 2, pp. 19–20) observed that the Irish "seem contented with the mere display of their wretchedness, and are almost insensible of their wants".

One indication of the fact that the Irish economy was different from but not necessarily poorer than other Western economies of the time is the reputed physical strength and good health of the Irish. Evidence for this point is not easily interpreted. High birth rates and high infant-mortality rates tend to produce a residual adult population which is hardier and more resistant to disease than would be the case with low-fertility rates. In addition, six-sevenths of the Irish population lived in rural areas in 1841, which helps to explain the healthiness of the Irish people. The potato, obviously, was another major factor. Arthur Young (1892, Vol. 2, p. 43) noted in 1779 that the potato was largely responsible for the healthiness of the Irish: "when I see [their] well formed bodies . . . their men athletic and their women beautiful, I know not how to believe them subsisting on an unwholesome food." A few years earlier Adam Smith had made the same observation when he wrote his famous sentence on the nutritional value of the potato, citing as evidence that the strongest men and the most beautiful women in London were mostly drawn from "the lowest rank of people in Ireland, who are generally fed with this root". Half a century later the vast majority of the parochial surveys edited by Mason (1814–19) reported that the inhabitants were healthy, vigorous, and robust. Of the seventy-nine surveys, forty-two reported on the health of the inhabitants, with thirty-nine reporting that the population was healthy or words to that effect. The Halls (1825–40, Vol. 1, p. 129) and Smyth (1844–9, Vol. 3, p. 37) maintained that a finer or hardier race of peasantry could not be found in the world, for which they credited the potato. Kane (1845, pp. 400–1) reported that the average height of the Irish was 70 inches, compared to 68·5 inches for the English and 68 inches for the Belgians. The average physical strength of an Irishman, measured by pulling the stem of a spring dynamometer was 432 lb, compared to 403 lb for the English and 339 lb for the Belgians. These data were obtained from experiments conducted on university students in the 1870s and should be interpreted with caution, but Kane buttressed his conclusions by data obtained from unskilled laborers in London.

The supply of food and fuel was not only abundant, it was also relatively stable and reliable. This statement may seem strange in view of the disaster of 1845–50, but it is simply a fact that there was nothing in the Irish experience between 1740–1 and 1845 to deserve the title of general famine. One contemporary wrote in 1802 that "it is a happy circumstance that the food of the majority of the inhabitants of this country consists of potatoes which are more certain in produce and less liable in injuries, and that wheat is an article of commerce rather than of food" (Tighe, 1802, p. 191). In the 1820s and 1830s this ranking was possibly reversed (Mokyr, 1981b), but ten years before the Great Famine witnesses before the Poor Law Commission emphasized that potato scarcities occurred in some areas for a few months each year, but that cases of serious harvest failure were unknown (Great Britain, 1836b, Vol. XXXII, pp. 11, 35). The main complaints concerning scarcity and famine were of a seasonal nature: potatoes did not keep after early summer, while the new crop was not harvested until September. A Leitrim witness explained (ibid., p. 4) that "we have never experienced the distress which so often occurs in the West of Connaught where the degree of misery and starvation may be measured by the period which separates the old and the new potatoes". Still, the potato has rather ambiguous implications for the welfare of those who depended on it for diet, some of which are explored elsewhere (Mokyr, 1981a; Hoffman and Mokyr, 1981).

The picture that emerges from these observations is not one of a poor society in the traditional sense. Rather, it is one of a society which is comparatively well fed and well heated, but poorly housed and clad. Healthy and, as we shall see in Chapter 6, not significantly less well educated than most other Europeans, the Irish appear to have chosen a different point on the ubiquitous "butter vs guns" tradeoff between different groups of commodities. Still, choices had to be made, and the opportunities varied considerably within Ireland. Inconsistent as it may seem with our earlier remarks on the difficulties in interpreting aggregate income statistics, it is important to construct a set of numbers that captures the mean income of the various counties of Ireland. Such estimates would be more valuable for internal variation than for international comparisons.

The income estimates used in this study are based on the estimates provided by the witnesses testifying before the 1836 Poor Law Commission, complemented by data from the 1841 Census and the Poor Law and Government Valuations. The estimates are from the income rather than the output side and should be viewed as personal rather than national income, since they do not capture any profits plowed back into farms or businesses. The fact that the estimates are derived largely from a sample of witnesses estimating local incomes in their district is clearly regrettable, but there is no serious alternative.[1] Some details on the methods used are presented in an appendix to this chapter. The results, broken down by province, are presented in Table 2.1.[2] Since the data were derived from sources dating over 1836–45, no precise date can be affixed to these estimates except that they are for the period which can best be dubbed "the eve of the famine". The province-by-province data are consistent with the qualitative impression ranking Connaught as the poorest part of Ireland and Leinster as the least poor. The county-by-county data are also reasonably consistent with what we know from other sources.

Table 2.1   *Annual Income and Income per Capita, circa 1841*

Province	Income (£ million)	Population (million)	Income per capita (£s)
Ulster	39·03	2.386	16·36
Leinster	39·26	1·974	18·37
Munster	34·10	2·396	14·23
Connaught	15·00	1·419	10·57
Ireland	124·39	8·175	15·22
Great Britain	452	18·5	24·43

Source: Ireland: see text.
Great Britain: Deane and Cole, 1969, p. 166.

The county with the highest income per capita in Ireland was Dublin, which is explained by the higher prices in the city as well as the administrative and commercial role the city played. Among the other counties, incomes of £17 and above were measured in counties Down,

Antrim, Wicklow, Wexford, Kildare, and Meath. Income per capita was less than £13 in Galway, Roscommon, Clare, Leitrim, Sligo, and Mayo.

The total figure of an annual personal income of about £125 million is consistent with Ó Gráda's (1980c) estimate of Irish agricultural output of about £43 million. In 1841 64 percent of all Irish families defined themselves as "chiefly employed in agriculture" (Great Britain, 1843, Vol. XXIV, p. xvi). In societies in which the proportion of the labor force employed in agriculture is about two-thirds, the contribution of the agricultural sector to Gross Domestic Product is slightly more than one-third.[3] Moreover, even those who classified themselves as employed in agriculture typically had considerable earnings from cottage industry, activities ancillary to agriculture, peat-cutting, and in some areas fishing. It is thus reasonable that agriculture, while the mainstay of two-thirds of the population, contributed only about one-third of national income. In any event, if these figures even only roughly approximate the true level of income in Ireland, they would place Ireland considerably behind Great Britain, the Netherlands, and Belgium, but would not indicate a degree of poverty and backwardness consistent with Beaumont's vivid descriptions of "wretchedness".

While it thus appears that from some points of view Ireland's poverty on the eve of the famine was less severe than has been thought, it still does not follow that we can reject the position that Ireland was in 1845 in an economic position which was significantly inferior to other European countries. This belief rests on two arguments. The first is that Ireland's economy was definitely not improving and was probably deteriorating over 1815–45. The second argument is that the traditional definition of poverty is misleading in the case of Ireland as it is in all preindustrial societies, and that a proper definition of terms will allow us to obtain a better understanding of the Irish prefamine economy.

Turning to our first argument we run into the difficulty that the absence of hard quantitative information on Irish conditions around the end of the Napoleonic Wars makes any statement about change during 1815–45 hazardous. Literary evidence can be very misleading here. Sir Walter Scott, who visited Ireland in 1825, wrote that

> to talk of the misery of Ireland at this time is to speak of the illness of a malade imaginaire. *Well* she is not, but she is rapidly becoming so . . . Everything is mending . . . the country is rapidly improving . . . the younger people are all more decently dressed and the new huts which are arising are greatly better than the old pigsties. (Scott, 1935, Vol. IX, pp. 196, 201, 202)

Other indirect evidence, however, seems to contradict this rosy view. It is quite unmistakable that the Irish diet was undergoing profound changes in the first half of the nineteenth century. Eighteenth-century diets, the ever-growing importance of the potato notwithstanding, seem to have been supplemented by a variety of vegetables, dairy products, and even pork and fish (Cullen, 1981a, pp. 140–71). Although glowing reports of the Irish cuisine in the eighteenth century must be deemed unrepresentative since they pertain to the shrinking class of well-to-do farmers, things were clearly worsening in the nineteenth. There was some across-the-board deterioration of diets due to the reduction of certain supplies, such as dairy products, fish, and vegetables, but the main reason was the relative decline of the number of people who could afford to purchase decent food. The dependency on potatoes, while it cut across all classes, was most absolute among the lower two-thirds of the income distribution. Potatoes were still abundant, but the tastier varieties such as the Apple, the Minion, and the Red, were gradually being replaced by the abundant but watery and bland variety known as "lumpers". While the Mason *Surveys* of 1814–19 do, on the whole, convey an impression of satisfaction with the Irish diet, twenty years later the dependency of large segments of the population on lumpers elicited disgusted comments such as "just try it for six months and you'll never want another" (Great Britain, 1836b, Vol. XXXII, p. 6).

More systematic evidence on perceived economic change in Ireland before the famine can be obtained from the tabular appendices to the Poor Law Commission in which all witnesses were asked specifically whether the condition of the poor had improved or deteriorated since 1815. While such subjective evaluations cannot have more than suggestive value, they are consistent with the hypothesis that the material condition of Ireland was deteriorating. Of the 1,590 witnesses tabulated, 1,362 replies could be used. Those witnesses who specifically said that their experience did not go back to 1815 were excluded, but it is quite clear that many of the witnesses who did not admit ignorance on this point based their judgements on hearsay rather than on experience. None the less the analysis is revealing. If we utilize a simple scoring technique assigning the value of –2 to "much deteriorated", –1 to "deteriorated", 0 to "unchanged", 1 to "improved", and 2 to "much improved", we obtain an index which we can term the "subjective economic change index". The mean value for all of Ireland turns out to be –0·432. Only in two counties, Wexford and Wicklow, which in many ways were atypical, does the index take on a positive value. The most severe judgement was passed on Co. Mayo (–1·10) which was also the poorest in terms of personal income. But apart from Mayo, the correlation between the "subjective economic change index" and personal income breaks down: the Ulster counties score the lowest on the Poor Law data (–0·661), while the least deterioration was thought to have occurred in Munster (–0·221). Connaught as a whole does almost as poorly as Ulster (–0·620) but some of the poorest Connaught counties, such as Galway and Leitrim, score relatively well. Statistical analysis on such subjective indices is hazardous, but it is interesting to note that the "subjective economic change index" shows a negative and significant correlation with variables measuring the importance of domestic industry (these coefficients are around –0·50, and are significant at the 1 per cent level).

A second indication of a malfunctioning in the Irish economy can be found in the nonagricultural sector. The malaise of rural domestic industries was nothing exceptional. Everywhere in Europe during

1815–45 the rural spinsters, weavers, nailmakers, cutlers, and similarly occupied experienced increasing economic hardship due to the decline in the prices of the goods they produced. But in most of these economies other industries emerged which could absorb, if not always the displaced cottage-industry workers themselves, at least their sons and daughters. While hardship and at times disaster occurred almost everywhere, the ultimate result was that these economies emerged with a strong modern industrial sector, which formed the core around which increasing prosperity was generated by continuing capital accumulation. In Ireland, a small region around Belfast excepted, such industrialization did not occur. The overall picture, albeit fuzzy and almost entirely lacking in quantitative detail, is in no way consistent with an economy undergoing a process of industrialization in the crucial years 1815–45. These are the years in which the British Industrial Revolution surged forward at full speed, the years in which Belgium, Switzerland, Alsace, French Flanders, and the German Rhineland laid the foundations for industrial prosperity.

Whether there was actual deindustrialization of Ireland in the first half of the nineteenth century has been in dispute, and a definitive study on the subject has not yet been produced. L. Cullen (1972, p. 124) has attempted to minimize the severity of the difficulties, arguing that the industrial crisis was confined to textiles other than linen, and that outside textiles there was no crisis. Cullen bases his conclusion largely on the rise in the number of people classifying themselves as being occupied in manufacturing in 1831–41. The comparison between the two Censuses is, however, almost entirely meaningless. To be sure, the proportion of families chiefly employed in "Manufacturing, trade, etc." rose from 18 to 24 percent in 1831–41, but as the 1841 Census explains, the classification procedure was different in the two Censuses. As a result, the proportion of individuals engaged in "Other pursuits" fell from 18 percent in 1831 to 10 percent in 1841. As "Other pursuits" were likely to contain mostly nonagricultural occupations, the increase in manufacturing employment is a statistical mirage. Occupational data from the three Censuses are presented in Table 2.2. Such data are far from easy to interpret from an economic point of view even when they have been collected in a consistent fashion. The comparability among the three Censuses leaves a lot to be desired, and for most practical purposes the 1831 Census is useless. Comparing the 1821 and 1841 figures we can say with some certainty that the data do not indicate any significant progress in industrialization in Ireland between these years. Whether they confirm the hypothesis of *actual* deindustrialization or not depends entirely on the degree of credence we can attach to the 1821 data. Clearly, the 1821 Census has to be enormously off the mark if the conclusion of a decline in industrial-commercial activity is to be reversed.

A large amount of other evidence, most of it admittedly indirect and circumstantial, seems to support the view that, with a few exceptions, deindustrialization was widespread, and not confined to textiles other than linen. The Railroad Commission reported, not without smugness, that under the system of bounties and protective duties, many industries had emerged which "not being the natural growth of circumstances favourable to their establishment . . . gradually disappeared as soon as the undue encouragement was withdrawn" (Great Britain, 1837–8, Vol. XXXV, p. 482).

Table 2.2   *Occupational Breakdown of Irish Population, 1821–41*

	1821		1831		1841	
	Total	*Percentage*	*Total*	*Percentage*	*Total*	*Percentage*
Agriculture	1,138,069	40·1	1,226,887	65·7	1,854,141	52·8
Industrial					1,071,303	30.5
Commercial	1,170,044	41·2	640,711	34·3	44,269	1·3
All others	528,702	18·6			542,147	15·4
Total occupied	2,836,815	100·0	1,867,598	100·0	3,511,860	100·0
Population	6,801,827		7,767,401	100·0	8,175,124	
Percentage occupied in population	41·7		24·0		43·0	

Source: 1821: Great Britain, 1824, Vol. XXII, p. 817.
       1831: Great Britain, 1833, Vol. XXXIX, p. 405.
       1841: Great Britain, 1843, Vol. XXIV, p. 440.

The Commissioners pointed to food-processing industries as Ireland's true comparative advantage, and claimed that "from North to South indications of progressive improvement are everywhere visible". Some historians have doubted these improvements (O'Brien, 1921, p. 376; Green, 1969, p. 95). It is not quite clear whether the growth in the exports of some processed foods could compensate for the decline in victualing industries in Co. Cork after 1815 and the increased shipping of live cattle and pigs across the Irish Sea after 1825. Distilleries and breweries did much better, but in the late 1830s Father Mathew's temperance campaign resulted in serious hardship for these industries (Donnelly, 1975, pp. 34–5; Lynch and Vaisey, 1960, p. 88). In the city of Dublin manufacturing fell on very hard times after 1815. Shipbuilding and silk almost completely disappeared, while coachmaking, glass, and tanneries declined severely (Webb, 1913, pp. 81–92). Wool output in Dublin declined by more than half over 1821–36 (Great Britain, 1837–8, Vol. XXXV, pp. 481–2). Other towns—Belfast excepted—followed Dublin's sad example. A Select Committee in 1830 concluded that the worst distress was found in Dublin and other towns due to "the influx of paupers from agricultural districts and the diminished profits of manufacturing industry" (Great Britain, 1830, Vol. VII, p. 15). Artisans and craftsmen in the Irish countryside and smaller towns were probably somewhat better protected against this decline, insulated as they were by transportation costs and the personal nature of local trade networks.

The absence of industrialization and the apparent deterioration of economic conditions throughout the economy are one reason why the pessimistic view of prefamine Ireland cannot be rejected altogether. This conclusion is strengthened by our second argument, which is based on the view that the performance of an economy should not be judged entirely by the level of the consumption basket, but also by the resilience of the economy to exogenous shocks. It was precisely from that point of view that the Irish economy was in a comparatively inferior situation.

The greatest shock of all was, of course, the potato famine. In what sense can we say that prefamine Ireland was poor, and that this poverty was responsible for the horrors of the "hungry forties"? In the traditional definition of poverty in terms of consumption per capita, Ireland was not as well off as most other countries, but the gap was not dramatic, and comparability in any case is made all but impossible by index-number problems. Nevertheless, Irish poverty was real. To understand its nature we have to redefine the concept of poverty in terms that are not independent of the famine. The famine was more than a transitory fall in Irish incomes. It completely altered the course of Irish history, left an indelible mark on the mentality, attitudes, and beliefs of the Irish, and made Ireland into a demographic anomaly which singles it out as a *sui generis* in modern European history.

The argument may be clarified if we use a new definition of poverty. This definition views poverty in terms of famines and their demographic impact. Although the traditional definitions in terms of real income per capita, properly corrected for externalities and nonpecuniary items, remain a sound measure for many purposes, they are clearly insufficient (Sen, 1981, pp. 9–23). One reason, widely mentioned in the literature, is that a rise in income per capita, when accompanied by an increase in the inequality of income distribution, may do little to alleviate the poverty of the vast majority of the population. Even correcting for inequality may not, however, capture all the elements of poverty. Although economic growth in Europe after 1740 may not have raised the overall level of consumption on average, it changed the life of those who lived through it by gradually eliminating the great subsistence crises and catastrophes which struck Europe before and in the early stages of the Industrial Revolution.

As an alternative to the traditional measures, therefore, I suggest a new measure: poverty is measured as the probability of a random individual at a random point in time dropping beneath subsistence. The severity and frequency of subsistence crises thus become a central factor in the measurement of poverty, and the elimination of these crises from the European scene is an indication of the disappearance of poverty by this absolute definition.

A few observations about this new measure are in order. First, the objection that the minimum of subsistence is not directly observed with much accuracy can be ignored. Income per capita, not to mention externalities, is not observed with much accuracy either, but death rates are available for many countries, and sharp increases in death rates ("excess mortality") can be associated with subsistence crises. Secondly, the new measure is positively associated with the traditional measures of poverty. Poverty as defined above, will rise, all other things equal, with a fall in income per capita and with an increase in income inequality. Our definition, however, contains more information, since it also takes into account the variance over time of income, as well as interactions between the variance over time and the cross-sectional variance at any given point of time.

For instance, if we use our definition of poverty to compare a case in which a crisis wipes out 10 percent of everyone's income with a case in which a disaster reduces national income by 10 percent by wiping out the income of the poorest 30 percent, the economy in the latter case would be considered to be poorer. Alternatively, we may consider two cases in which the poorest 30 percent of the population lose all of their income. In one case the remaining 70 percent divert resources to prevent the worst from happening, whereas in the other case the mechanisms of poor relief fail in their task, or the government does not overcome the inherent "free rider" problems plaguing disaster relief efforts. The latter economy, according to our definition, would be said to be poorer.[4] The definition above is useful for the purpose of comparing Ireland with other economies. Demographic data are comparable across different economies; income figures usually are not. As Sen (1981) has recently stressed, poverty has to have an absolute definition; purely relative measures are ultimately unsatisfactory. The definition proposed here, though different from the Sen measure and variants thereof, satisfies this requirement.

Having found the determinants of an economy's *vulnerability* to subsistence crises, however, we cannot simply look at the excess mortality statistics, since we would be then involved in a logical circularity: Ireland starved because it was poor and we know that it was poor from the fact that it starved. What is necessary is to find independent observations on underdevelopment and backwardness as measures of those factors which made Ireland relatively vulnerable. It is therefore *not* very useful to say that we can know that Mayo was more backward than Wicklow from the fact that excess mortality during the famine was higher there, since that simply restates our definition of poverty. Understanding the reasons for the difference requires us to observe that Wicklow had higher income, more capital, a more diversified economy, and so on, and conclude from these facts that it was less likely to be vulnerable to exogenous shocks — clearly a refutable and testable proposition.

What kind of economy are we dealing with? Ireland before the famine was predominantly rural, with six out of every seven persons living in rural areas (defined as settlements of less than 2,000 inhabitants). Its rural society, as we have noted, was losing its nonagricultural basis toward the end of the period and in so far as this resulted in the production of more subsistence crops, it is likely to have involved a partial setback in the commercialization of the Irish economy (Hoffman and Mokyr, 1981). One feature shared by all parts of Ireland is the total absence of a group of peasant-proprietors. Landlords, of whom there were about 8,000 (Pim, 1848, p. 43), could hardly be defined as a class. The vast bulk of Irish society worked on the land but did not own it.

From the point of view of economic geography, it is customary to divide Ireland into three main regions. The eastern, central, and southeastern counties, including Leinster and east Munster, included much of the land in large tenant farms, which used landless laborers and cottagers for their labor supply. In the northern counties, including most of Ulster and north Connaught, farming was combined with rural industry, and smallholders held a large proportion of the land. The west and southwest contained elements of both other regions, and for most parts was more backward and less prosperous than the other two. In all three regions, the potato formed the staple of everybody's diet (though this was somewhat less true for the northeastern counties), but the regions differed in their marketed and export crops. The northern region relied on manufactured goods, while the southern counties exported large amounts of dairy products and provisions. The west exported live animals, both directly and indirectly, after fattening in the meadows of the midlands. Regional specialization should not be overdramatized for these years: most of it was yet to come in the second half of the nineteenth century (Kennedy, 1981).

Turning to factor markets and economic stratification, we definitely come to the end of the easy generalizations on the composition of Irish society. The main source of the complexity is that tenants sublet to each other and worked for each other. The majority of the poor laborers and cottiers were not landless, but cultivated small lots of land, mostly arable products. These lots were rented sometimes from the landlord directly, sometimes from a rentier-middleman, and sometimes from another tenant. Both rich and poor were landholders in Ireland, and terms like "farmer" and "laborer" had become fuzzy. The 1821 Census-takers pointed out that the distinction between farmers and laborers was hard to draw as "most persons who earn the chief part of their subsistence as hired labourers hold also a small portion of land and therefore ... are entitled to the name farmers" (Great Britain, 1824, Vol. XXII, p. 426). Clark (1979, p. 36) points out that the system led to a society in which such distinctions were becoming meaningless since many people "found it difficult to think of themselves either as landlords or as tenants, because they were both". Class structure is thus hard to identify in prefamine Ireland, although by any definition it will be clear that the majority of the populace belonged to a rural proletariat. The occupational tables in the 1841 Census show that 1·1 million males above the age of 15 defined themselves as "servants and labourers ministering to food". If we add to that about 100,000 weavers, about 55 percent of the male population declaring occupations should be viewed as proletariat (Great Britain, 1843, Vol. XXIV, p. 440). The 1831 Census, flawed as it is, tells a similar tale.[5]

One source that can be utilized to analyze the socioeconomic structure of prefamine Ireland is the 1841 Census classification of families "according to their means". The Census-takers (Great Britain, 1843, Vol. XXIV, p. xviii) explain the three classes as follows. Class I contained professional people or heads of families whose means of subsistence allowed them to live without labor. In rural districts this would have included farmers holding 50 acres or more. Class II included artisans possessing some skill and enjoying fixed employment, or farmers holding 5–50 acres. Class III included laborers, smallholders, and other persons "without capital, in either money, land, or acquired knowledge". The Census results are summarized in Table 2.3.

Table 2.3   *Distribution of Families by "Classes" in 1841, in Percentages*

	Class I	Class II	Class III	Not specified	Total
Ulster (rural)	1·8	32·9	64·1	1·2	100·0
Leinster (rural)	2·6	31·6	63·2	2·6	100·0
Munster (rural)	1·6	28·0	68·3	2·1	100·0
Connaught (rural)	1·6	17·5	79·0	1·9	100·0
Total rural areas	1·9	28·3	67·9	1·9	100·0
Urban areas	6·6	49·9	36·4	7·1	100·0
Total	2·6	31·8	62·9	2·7	100·0

Source: Computed from Great Britain, 1843, Vol. XXIV.

Table 2.3 shows clearly that by the Census's classification about two-thirds of rural Irish families should be viewed as "proletarian". The classes designed by the Census commissioners must have corresponded roughly to material welfare, social prestige, and an overall measure of the quality of life. But clearly in a society like rural Ireland, the principal determinant of these matters was how much land one held. Data on farm size before the famine are available from two separate and independent sources. The 1841 Census listed the number of farms by county in its "Tables of the Rural Economy" with three cutoff points: 5, 15, and 50 acres. These data have been criticized by Bourke (1965b), who pointed out that the "acre" used in the tables was understood by some enumerators to mean "statute acre" and by others "plantation (Irish) acre". Since the two relate to each other in the proportion 1:1·64, the possible margin of error created is rather large. In addition, the Census totally omitted holdings below 1 acre (or below 1·64 acre if we follow Bourke in his assumption that Irish acres were mostly used). An alternative source to the Census is the data provided by Ireland's 132 Poor Law Unions at the request of the House of Lords. The data are reproduced in appendix 94 to the Devon Commission Report (Great Britain, 1845, Vol. XXII, pp. 280–3). They include farms smaller than 1 acre, and explicitly denote the acreages in statute acres. The data were arranged by Poor Law Union rather than by county, and were converted using the 1848 agricultural Census (Great Britain, 1849a, Vol. XLIX), which provides the breakdown of farms for each Poor Law Union in each county. Ostensibly then, the Poor Law Union data seem an impeccable source. A summary of the farm size data is presented in Table 2.4.

Table 2.4 shows that the two sources broadly conform to each other. The omission of farms smaller than 1 acre from the Census data distorts in particular the figures for Leinster, where the number of very small farms was quite substantial. In county Dublin 55·3 percent of all farms were smaller than 1 acre, but the small gardens tilled by the inhabitants of the capital accounted for a large number of reported tiny farms. Removing Dublin does not alter the picture dramatically, however, as it causes the percentage of farms of less than 1 acre to decline from 22·5 to 19·2, still significantly above the nationwide average percentage of 14·8. In some Leinster counties the percentages were still amazingly high: in Westmeath, Queen's, Kildare, and Carlow more than a quarter of all persons "holding land" held less than 1 statute acre. Examination of the table suggests that landholding in Ireland followed two quite distinct patterns. In Connaught and Ulster farms were smaller than in Munster and in Leinster, but in the latter two the proportion of very small farms was larger. In Ulster and Connaught a single-peaked distribution of farms existed, whereas in Munster and Leinster the distribution of farms was bimodal, with large numbers of both very small and very large farms. We shall return to the significance of this finding below.

Table 2.4   *Farm Sizes in Prefamine Ireland*

	Ulster	Leinster	Munster	Connaught	Ireland
(a) Census data					
No. of farms	234,999	133,220	162,386	155,204	685,309
Mean farm size (acres)	14·48	29·73	23·86	14·31	19·63
Percentage small farms (under 5 acres)	43·0	36·9	35·1	64·4	44·8
Percentage medium farms (5–15 acres)	42·2	34·2	37·8	29·1	36·6
Percentage small and medium farms under 15 acres	85·2	71·1	72·9	93·5	81·4
(b) Poor Law Union data					
No. of farms	287,909	195,412	221,438	210,754	915,513
Mean farm size (acres)	11·79	20·27	17·50	10·54	14·69
Percentage farms under 1 acre	12·6	22·5	16·2	9·2	14·8
Percentage farms 1–5 acres	18·6	21·5	16·5	23·1	19·7
Percentage farms 5–10 acres	24·0	14·8	13·9	28·3	20·5
Percentage small farms (under 10 acres)	55·2	58·8	46·6	60·6	55·0
Percentage medium farms (10–20 acres)	30·4	15·9	17·4	20·8	20·2
Percentage small and medium farms (under 20 acres)	85·6	74·7	64·0	81·4	75·2

Source: Computed from Great Britain, 1843, Vol. XXIV, pp. 454–5, and Great Britain, 1845a, Vol. XXII, pp. 280–3.

An alternative way to analyze the prefamine economy was proposed by Lynch and Vaisey (1960). Lynch and Vaisey distinguished between two sectors, a modern and monetized sector in the maritime east of Ireland, and a backward subsistence sector in the rest of the country. In this approach the authors follow a tradition in development economics which takes the view that many developing economies have a "dual" structure, in which a modern and a traditional sector coexist and interact to some degree. While dualistic theories of economic development have been found useful to economic historians concerned with modern Europe, their application to Ireland has been criticized as basically unfounded in the facts (Lee, 1966; 1971; Johnson, 1970). The reason why Lynch and Vaisey's dualism has been difficult to accept seems to be that some of the characteristics which they assign to the traditional and subsistence economy could be found in the heart of the maritime cash economy. Moreover, enclaves of commercial farming, specialized retail trade, and actively improving landlords were found in many regions which Lynch and Vaisey seem to designate as parts of the subsistence economy. It seems that one of the sources of criticism against the dualistic hypothesis is the sharpness which Lynch and Vaisey claim for the division, although in the same paragraph they acknowledge in a brilliantly mixed metaphor that "the cash economy extended tentacles into subsistence Ireland, but the penetration was neither deep nor broad" (Lynch and Vaisey, 1960, p. 25). Clearly, the image of a subsistence economy in which smallholders paid their rents with labor, grew their own potatoes, and had very little economic inter-action with each other is an inaccurate picture. Elements of the subsistence economy and the cash economy were combined in different proportions throughout Ireland. The relative importance of the cash economy declined as one moved from east to west, and in fact differed within the east and the west as well. There was no pure cash economy in the east and no pure subsistence in the west. Lynch and Vaisey's basic insight is not invalidated but strengthened by the recognition that the degree of commercialization is a continuous rather than a dichotomous variable.

The concept of a dual economy is a useful one, but it should be reformulated. There were indeed two Irelands, but they were not geographically separate as Lynch and Vaisey suggested. Instead, they were living alongside each other, intertwined and mutually dependent though utterly different in their degrees of commercialization, economic attitudes, agricultural techniques, and so on. (Gibbon, 1975, pp. 136–7, makes precisely the same point.) One Ireland is the Ireland of cash crops and commercial farming, relatively large agricultural units which were either grazing or mixed farms. This sector produced the vast bulk of the live cattle that Ireland exported, as well as most of the cereal crops. It is to these graziers and farmers that Ireland owed the existence of its 5,000 country fairs, which dealt primarily in livestock. Many of these fairs were in the west, including the great fairs in Ballinasloe and Sligo (Ó Gráda, 1980c, p. 5; Freeman, 1957, pp. 257–64). There is no contradiction between the existence of this monetized sector and the observation that the majority of the people lived in a different world. To be sure, the number of persons *completely* insulated from the cash economy was probably negligible.[6] Virtually everyone carried out a few unavoidable cash transactions a year: food had to be purchased in the summer months before the harvesting of the potato crop; some clothes and shoes were bought; tobacco, spirits, tea, and sometimes beer were purchased from local merchants; and religious services from the Catholic priests were also usually paid for in money.

Nevertheless, the subsistence economy was a real enough phenomenon. The cottiers and laborers of Ireland produced most of the goods and the services they consumed. Many cottiers engaged each year in one major barter transaction, namely the exchange of their labor for a cabin and a piece of land rented from a larger farmer on which they grew potatoes and sometimes grazed a cow or a few sheep. In these transactions money often played the role of a unit of account but not of a means of exchange, the labor services being valued at a predetermined rate and subtracted from the rent. Residual balances, where they existed were often settled in cash. In other cases, especially in medium-sized farms (between, say, 10 and 20 acres) the rent was paid in money. The tenants therefore had to receive some income in money, earned in different ways in different areas. To the extent that local employment was possible and paid for in cash, the labor market supported the land market. The sale of pigs, eggs, and butter were other sources of money income. In the north, the cottage industry supplied a welcome cash supplement to the subsistence crop, while seasonal emigration to England and Scotland was increasingly resorted to as the cottage industries declined (Johnson, 1970, pp. 229–38). Except for the payment of rent and a few other occasional transactions, however, the subsistence sector was clearly little commercialized, and the use of money by classes below that of the well-to-do farmers not widespread.

The two economies were thus distinct, but they were not separate, either geographically or economically. The cash sector hired its labor from the subsistence sector and sublet land to it. This generalization, while not uniformly true, is a fairly accurate description of the relation between the two Irelands. Each region and each county can be characterized by its combination of the relative weights of the cash and the subsistence economies. One implication of the coexistence of the grazing and the subsistence sectors is a bimodal size distribution of farms. Grazing farms were large because of scale economies in pasturage. The labor used on these farms for herding, haymaking, and similar jobs, was paid for in terms of very small lots rented out to cottiers, or in terms of conacre land (land rented out by a farmer to a landless laborer for the potato season only). These grazing farms were relatively more important in the midlands and the south than in Ulster and Connaught. In the latter two provinces cottage industry and pigs were the primary sources of cash. The farm-size figures in Table 2.4 confirm the hypothesis that farms in Leinster and Munster had a bimodal distribution with a relatively large number of either very large or extremely small farms, while in Ulster and Connaught the percentage of medium-sized farms was larger.

Following Lynch and Vaisey's (1960) somewhat stylized description of the Irish economy, the issue of the extent to which Ireland was a barter economy has been frequently addressed in the literature (Barrow, 1970; Lee, 1971; Cullen, 1982). The geographical line drawn by Lynch and Vaisey between the two economies does obviously not correspond closely with the historical reality. Table 2.3 shows that one-third of all Irish families belonged to classes I and II. On the whole, farmers corresponded roughly to the class II families of Table 2.3, while cottiers and laborers belonged to class III. Farmers and nonagricultural rural families obviously handled cash frequently. Even in Mayo, close to 16 percent of the population were in these classes. Class III rural families were smallholders, cottiers, and landless laborers, comprising over two-thirds of the rural population (see Table 2.3). In rural Dublin, Wexford, and Wicklow, among the richest agricultural regions in Ireland, the percentages of class III families were respectively 49·8, 57·5, and 61·5 percent. Even in these maritime counties, the majority of the people produced most of the food they consumed, built and repaired their own houses, made and mended their own clothes, and were thus for most practical purposes self-sufficient.[7] Among these people the use of money was rare by European standards, although of course not completely unknown (Barrow, 1970, pp. 84–5).

To support the hypothesis of comparatively low money usage among the lower classes, it is necessary to utilize some nationwide source. The Census data are insufficient to permit any quantitative statement about the comparative frequency of monetized as opposed to barter trans-actions in the land and labor markets. Fortunately, the Poor Law commissioners' massive sample of 1,590 witnesses once more allows us to be somewhat more precise. The Poor Law commissioners were primarily interested in the lower classes, that is, the bottom two-thirds of the income distribution. The commissioners posed two separate questions to the witnesses concerning the factor market, namely, "are wages of labour paid in money, or provisions, or by conacres or in what other way?" and "upon what conditions, exclusive of that, do labourers or cottiers hold their cabins and land? Is it usual to require duty labour, in addition to, or in lieu of rent?" (Great Britain, 1836b, Vols XXXI and XXXII). The number of usable responses to the second question is much smaller because of its awkward formulation. Duty labor, a feudal obligation, was nowhere required in Ireland, and many witnesses responded by denying that any payments other than rent were demanded without specifying whether the rents were paid in cash or in terms of a barter exchange for labor.

The responses confirm that the subsistence and the cash sectors co-existed in an intricate and complex manner. The most frequent bartering of labor for land existed between farmers and cottiers. Cottiers were regarded as permanent laborers, and therefore could be paid in terms of conacre land and cabins. Occasional laborers (or "spalpeens"), who were ranked below cottiers in economic status and social prestige (Thompson, 1802, p. 340), were more often paid in money, although potatoes, turf, and other "provisions" were also used as means of payment. The means of exchange also depended on the nature of the employer: gentlemen, resident landlords, and nonagricultural employers almost always paid for labor with cash, while farmers generally paid in terms of sublet land or commodities. Labor employed in public works, domestic servants, and similar employees also received their wages in cash. In general, cash payments were the rule in or around urban areas, while in more remote rural areas the laborers themselves insisted on being paid in kind and in conacre. Many farmers and other observers declared in their testimony that the form of payment was left to the option of the laborer.[8]

One way of coming to grips with the complicated but important question of the degree of monetization in the Irish economy is to assign a numerical score to the Poor Law Commission witnesses who provided usable responses to the two questions dealing with the means of exchange. The method utilized for this purpose was to assign to each witness a score of 3 points. If only one form of payment was cited, this mode received the full score; if more than one was cited as was predominantly the case—the "points" were allocated according to the judgement of the witness. For instance, if the response to the first question was "mostly money but sometimes provision", 2 points would be allocated to "money" and 1 to "provisions". Needless to say, such scoring techniques are very crude, and the sample is too small to utilize the county-by-county scores in econometric analysis as an "index of monetization". None the less, on the more aggregate level of the province the figures presented in Table 2.5 are suggestive.

Table 2.5   *Monetization and Barter in Factor Markets*

(a) Land market (3 = fully monetized; 0 = completely barter transaction)

Province	No. of witnesses	Total score	Mean score
Ulster	308	346	1·12
Leinster	187	191	1·02
Munster	239	243	1·02
Connaught	82	85	1·04
Ireland	816	865	1·06

(b) Labour market (total score = 3)

Province	No. of witnesses	Wages paid in money	Wages paid in provisions	Wages paid in conacre land	Wages paid in other land	Total
Ulster	488	1·92	0·75	0·26	0·07	3·00
Leinster	409	1·65	0·63	0·55	0·17	3·00
Munster	364	1·24	0·46	0·85	0·45	3·00
Connaught	148	1·31	0·62	0·73	0·34	3·00
Ireland	1,409	1·60	0·63	0·55	0·22	3·00

Source: Computed from Great Britain, 1836b, Vol. XXXI; see text.

Table 2.5 indicates that the variation in practices was not nearly so sharp as Lynch and Vaisey imply. On the whole, Ulster seems to have been more monetized than the rest of Ireland, although considerable internal variation existed within the province. Cavan, Fermanagh, and Monaghan were much less monetized than the coastal counties. The two most monetized counties were naturally the two counties which contained the two largest towns: in Antrim, the rent-monetization index was 1·43 and the wage-monetization index was 2·23, while in Dublin the numbers were 1·46 and 2·69, respectively. In Leinster some of the southern midland counties show very low levels of monetization: Kilkenny, Carlow, and Queen's were all below the nationwide mean by both measurements. The simple east–west dichotomy is clearly an over-simplification. Connaught was not less monetized than Munster by our measures, and by both measures Mayo—traditionally cited as the most backward county in Ireland—scored higher on both monetization indices than Cork, Longford, and Carlow. In the south and the midlands, where graziers and cottiers coexisted, the transactions between them required less cash than in the west and north.

Some caution should be exercised in interpreting the relatively low level of monetization shown for the land market. The Irish landlord received his rent in cash. There was very little demesne agriculture, and a considerable number of landlords were absentee. The proprietors had thus little use for labor in exchange for land, and Table 2.5 should not be interpreted as indicating that the land market was not monetized. The reason that the land market appears from the data to have been less monetized than the labor market is that the "land market" reported on by the witnesses was primarily the *secondary* land market. By 1836, increasing numbers of cottiers and smallholders held land directly from landlords, but others still held land indirectly from middlemen of various kinds. In any event, most of the land was not let to cottiers but to more substantial tenants who would fall outside the confines of the question as posed by the commissioners. It is also possible that the un-avoidable elimination of witnesses providing obscure or irrelevant answers to the awkwardly phrased rent question biased the averages downward.

In spite of the crude method used in evaluating the responses, the data appear consistent with an economy in which at least half the trans-actions between laborer and farmer involved barter deals. In the absence of similar data from other countries it is far from easy to evaluate this finding, but if we assume that Dublin and Antrim were the most "commercialized" counties and were most similar to England, Belgium, or Western Germany, Ireland as a whole was seriously behind the rest of Europe in its commercial and financial development. This backward-ness did not make her necessarily poorer in the sense that it had lower personal income per capita. But surely it must be viewed as a factor responsible for its greater vulnerability to exogenous shocks.

Appendix: the Computation of the Personal Income Data

The core of the personal income estimates for prefamine Ireland was derived from income-related information gathered by the Poor Law commissioners. Appendix D to the report (Great Britain, 1836b, Vol. XXXI) contains the replies of about 1,590 witnesses to questions circulated by the commissioners' "Relative to the condition of agricultural labourers in Ireland". The two questions relevant to the estimation of male labor income were questions 9 and 13. Question 9 was "What are the daily wages of labourers, with or without diet, (specify winter and summer) in your parish", and question 13 asked "What in the whole might an *average* amount of employment, both in day work and in task work, earn in the year, including harvest work and the value of his other advantages and means of living?" (italics in original). The problem with the answers to question 9 are that they cannot readily be converted to annual income figures, since no accounting for seasonal unemployment nor adjustments for payment in kind and land were made.[9] Moreover, many responses to question 9 did not specify whether the wage was inclusive or exclusive of board. Question 13 attempted to take account of these factors and for those reasons was utilized in the calculations. The daily labor income estimates in the responses to question 9 were used as controls and indicate, in the majority of cases, that the number of days worked annually fluctuated over 230–50 days. Such a figure casts some doubt on the basis for the widespread complaints of contemporaries concerning the devastating effects of (mostly seasonally induced) unemployment in Ireland (Foster, 1847, pp. 15–22; see below, Chapter 7). For some observations the estimate of annual income was absurdly high, and was replaced by the response to question 9 using an average between the summer and the winter wage (without diet) and assuming a working year of 300 days.

The earnings of other family members were more difficult to compute. The relevant questions were "What in the whole might his [the laborer's] wife and four children, all of an age to work (the eldest not more than 16 years of age) earn within the year, obtaining . . . an average amount of employment?" (question 14), and "Are women and children usually employed in labour and at what rate of wages?" (question 11). Four children at a working age in one family were, of course, relatively rare. Contradictions between the two responses were rampant.[10] Moreover, the response to question 14 was cited in many cases in terms of a daily rather than a yearly figure, indicating the irregularity of employment for women and children over the growing season. The estimates of labor income of other family members were computed using the following rules. (1) If the wage quoted was specified as a *daily* figure, it was multiplied by a set of employment coefficients reflecting the frequency of employment described in the response to question 11. These coefficients range from 0 ("never employed") to 300 ("always employed"). (2) If the wife's and children's income was specified in annual terms, the number was accepted if it did not exceed £7 per annum. (3) If the reported annual income exceeded £7, it was assumed that the witness had not corrected it for seasonality but simply multiplied the wage earned by women and children when employed by 300 or 312, and the reported figure was accordingly adjusted using the employment coefficients.

Of the 1,590 witnesses who testified, 1,285 testimonies for the male wage and about half that number for the other family members' income could be used. This implies that less than half the country was actually covered, since Ireland contained 2,422 parishes, and some parishes were covered by more than one witness. Almost all the witnesses were intimately familiar with local conditions. Sixty percent were clergymen (either Catholic priests or Church of Ireland vicars) and 35 percent were local gentlemen serving as justices of the peace. Thus, while the procedures used are crude and based on a number of inevitable simplifying assumptions, the county averages should represent a reasonably close reflection of actual earnings. In only two counties were the estimates based on fewer than twenty usable witnesses: Leitrim (twelve) and Sligo (eighteen). Connaught as a whole still provided twenty-seven witnesses per county, its coverage in per capita terms was about two-thirds of that of the entire country (0·97 per 10,000 persons as compared to 1·57 for Ireland as a whole). The coverage of the sample was thus satisfactory, although the use of a sample of this kind for the calculation of national aggregates is inevitably hazardous. The error of the estimate in the aggregation procedure was reduced somewhat by weighting the parish estimates by the population of the parish.[11]

To the earnings of the male head of the family and those of the other members of the family the value of the stock of pigs was added, as the pigs represented a labor-intensive industry generally ignored by the witnesses, and since the turnover period of the stock was about a year. These results are summarized in Table 2.6.

Table 2.6   *Labor Income and its Components*

Province	Number of witnesses	Annual male labor income (£s)	Annual labor income of others (£s)	Income from pigs (£s)	Total (£s)
Ulster	449	10·83	3·66	0·15	14·64
Leinster	376	11·80	3·73	0·23	15·76
Munster	323	8·94	3·23	0·27	12·44
Connaught	137	7·38	1·68	0·15	9·21
Ireland	1,285	9·91	3·21	0·21	13·33

Source: Computed from Great Britain, 1836b, Vol. XXXI; see text.

The basic assumption behind the aggregation of the wage figures is that those peasants who were fully self-employed had an implicit wage which could be approximated by the wages paid to hired labor in the parish.

The two other components of personal income were rent and capital income. Three independent estimates for rent income earned in pre-famine Ireland are available: the Poor Law valuation, the government valuation and a third estimate presented by Crotty in his pioneering but controversial study (Crotty, 1966). None of these three estimates is usable directly, but it is possible to combine the information contained in them to distill a more definitive set of estimates.

The Poor Law valuation (PLV) is clearly a problematic approximation of the rents. The assessments were made by local notables who had been appointed to the board of guardians of each Poor Law Union (Nicholls, 1856, p. 244). Most of the witnesses before the Devon Commission denounced it as highly inaccurate, sometimes even fraudulent. Crotty, in his analysis of the witnesses testifying before the Devon Commission, devised a method to "correct" the Poor Law valuation by assigning numerical values to the witnesses' statements about the relation between true rent and the PLV.

The government valuation (GV), carried out under the supervision of its competent commissioner, Richard Griffith, is on the whole far less subject to error. The problem with this set of estimates is that it is incomplete, since only twenty of the thirty-two counties were surveyed before 1845. Furthermore, while the standard error here is smaller than for the PLV, the GV is clearly biased downward. It deliberately excluded from the valuation all houses and structures whose rent was less than £5 and counted the rest at only two-thirds of their annual rent. The Devon Commission concluded that the GV was biased but presented a "correct relative scale" (Kennedy, 1847, p. 704). Crotty collected from the Devon Commission all remarks pertaining to the relation of the government valuation to the true rent and constructed a correction factor similar to the one for the Poor Law valuation.

A third estimate for the rents in prefamine Ireland was extracted by Crotty directly from the Devon Commission. Of the 1,117 witnesses before the commission, 557 provided direct observations on the level of rents in their area. Of these, 295 were cited on the difference between the true rent and the PLV, so that the Devon Report estimates could be viewed as independent of the PLV. Similarly, of the 316 witnesses from the twenty counties covered by the GV, 186 commented on the relation between rents and GV (most of them noting that the government rent was too low), and 249 presented independent estimates. Hence, it is reasonable to view the estimates prepared by Crotty from the Devon Commission witnesses as a third independent approximation of rents.

A crude but not ineffective way to choose among the three independent measures is to look at the raw ("zero-order") correlation coefficients. If all three variables are independently measured and all three are proxies for an unobserved variable, then if two of the measures are closely correlated with each other but not with the third, it is more likely that the true variable is closer to the two correlated variables. For twenty observations, the correlation coefficient between Crotty's measure and the adjusted PLV and adjusted GV were 0·8235 and 0·8391, respectively, while the correlation coefficient between the latter two was 0·9453. We cannot exclude the possibility that both the PLV and the GV are inaccurate and Crotty's measure is closer to the truth, but it still appears that the new estimate used should be based primarily on information contained in the PLV and the GV estimates. While the PLV, as indicated, is clearly subject to much larger errors, it is complete, and does not suffer from the obvious downward bias of the GV. The procedure followed is thus to utilize the GV for the twenty counties for which it is available, and to generate figures for the twelve remaining counties by a simple least-squares procedure. The downward bias in the GV was then reduced by multiplying all counties by a correction factor based on the PLV totals. A summary calculation of the new rent series, aggregated to the province level, is presented in Table 2.7, and compared with some of the other estimates.

Table 2.7   *Prefamine per Acre Rent, by Province (£s)*

Province	New estimate	Poor Law estimate	Crotty estimate I	Crotty estimate II
Ulster	0·566	0·606	0·817	0·551
Leinster	0·948	0·943	1·045	0·825
Munster	0·614	0·623	1·021	0·632
Connaught	0·374	0·334	0·821	0·458
Ireland	0·629	0·633	0·931	0·619

Table 2.7 reflects further problems with the Crotty estimates: since he dealt with a sample of rents, he had to generate the total rent bill by multiplying the sample means by an acreage figure. Inexplicably, however, he multiplied his mean rents per acre by total area of each county, instead of area under cultivation, thus tending to bias his results upward, as is reflected in Table 2.7. The adjusted "Crotty II" estimate is a correction of his rent estimates and brings their overall order of magnitude into line with the other estimates. It can be tentatively concluded that the three rent series are more or less equivalent and that the income data will not be very sensitive to the choice of rent proxy.

While capital income was probably not an important proportion of national income, it cannot be ignored. The most important components of total capital stock before the famine were animals, land improvement, and houses. As to the latter two, most of the capital income is already included in the rent and wage figures. Livestock figures were collected by the 1841 Census, and there appears to be a consensus that "the essential accuracy of these figures is not in question" (Bourke, 1965b, p. 381). The income from capital in the form of livestock was estimated by applying a uniform net rate of return of 10 percent to the value of livestock reported in the 1841 Census, under the assumption that most other forms of capital were included in the wage and rent income estimates.

Notes: Chapter 2

1   The only figures for nineteenth-century national income in Ireland available until now are those proposed by Larkin (1967). Larkin assumed that Irish income was 15 percent of British total income in 1801, and then fell stepwise one percentage point per decade (relative to Britain) until 1901, when it reached 5 percent of British income. He then used Deane and Cole's (1969) estimates of British national income and divided by population figures. The author's own admission that his method is "somewhat crude" will certainly find wide acceptance.

2   Throughout this study, figures calculated on the county level will be presented aggregated by province or by region. The more disaggregated data are available on tape or printout from the author.

3   According to figures collected by Simon Kuznets for contemporary underdeveloped economies, in countries which had 63·3 percent of their labor force in Kuznets's A-sector, the contribution of this sector to GDP was 36·8 percent. The poorest nations, in which the share of the A-sector in the labor force was on average 80·5 percent, the product share of the A-sector was 48·4 percent (Kuznets, 1971, pp. 111, 203).

4   If we apply this definition to the issue of the standard of living controversy in industrializing nations, the irrelevance of such evidence as the excise yields of hides and skins in London (Hobsbawm, 1975, p. 78) becomes apparent. See Mokyr (1980a) for a more detailed exposition.

5   Of the 1,226,887 families listed by the 1831 Census as employed chiefly in agriculture, only 7·8 percent employed laborers, 46·0 percent were "occupiers not employing labourers", and 46·2 percent were "labourers, employed".

6   Foster (1847, pp. 313–14) illustrates his claim that money was unknown by an anecdote about a Galway peasant pawning a £10 note for a shilling. The fact that this story is repeated by historians (O'Brien, 1921, p. 527; Lynch and Vaisey, 1960, p. 11) does not legitimize it as historical evidence. In recent work Cullen (1981a, p. 16; 1982) has argued for the other extreme position, maintaining that Ireland was poor but highly commercialized, more so, for example, than Scotland or France. Here, too, the evidence is unconvincing.

7   Consider the relatively wealthy county of Wexford. Out of the 56,750 males aged over 15 who listed an occupation, only 461 actually were selling consumer goods "ministering to food", such as butchers, tobacconists, and so on. In Donegal, beyond doubt part of "subsistence Ireland", only 301 out of 78,531 employed sold food or related products. The number of thatchers and slaters in Wexford was 197; in Donegal, 74.

8   Some witnesses (Great Britain, 1836b, Vol. XXXI, pp. 370, 461, 474) claimed that single men preferred to be paid in cash, while married men preferred barter transactions.

9   Question 10 in the same appendix specifically asked at what periods of the year the men were the least employed. The answers indicate that there were two off-seasons, one in the winter (approximately between early December and the end of February) and one in late spring and early summer. It is hard to ascertain to what degree economic activity slowed down in these slack seasons.

10 For example, in the parish of Kilcommon West (Co. Mayo) the witness answered question 11 by saying that women and children were unemployed, but in response to question 14 estimated their income at £20–£24 per annum, more than double the annual earning of the male laborer.

11 The income estimates are the only estimates in this study in which population weights have been applied to the Poor Law commissioners' witnesses. All other estimates using this source are unweighted.

Chapter 3

The Problem of Population: Was Malthus Right?

Irish history is demographic history. In no other European economy has so much attention been paid to population growth, marriage patterns, birth rates, and similar variables. The most influential work in prefamine Irish economic history written in the twentieth century (Connell, 1950a) is in fact entitled *The Population of Ireland*, and was one of the first successful attempts to integrate demographic history with economic history. Since its publication, a constant stream of work, largely supplementary and critical of Connell's seminal piece, has appeared. The reasons for this remarkable interest in demography are quite obvious: Ireland's uniquely high population growth rates before the famine, the catastrophical decline of population during the Great Famine, the continuation of population decline for eight decades until its 1926 low point, the unique demographic pattern combining unusually low propensities to marry with extremely high marital fertility rates, and the enormous impact of emigration on Irish population. All represent issues of unusual interest to the demographic historian.

It is by no means the intention here to provide a complete demographic account of prefamine Ireland. Even if the data allowed such an account, it would lie outside the confines of this book. Rather, I intend to examine only one fundamental issue, namely, what connection was there, if any, between Irish poverty and demographic variables. In order to make progress on that issue, however, it is necessary to examine once more the available data and to demonstrate what can be done with them. Armed with these statistics I shall attempt to conduct a set of tests of the Malthusian hypothesis in its various forms.

(1) A New Look at Prefamine Demographic Statistics

For population data on the macrolevel, the three Censuses taken in Ireland before the famine and especially the 1841 Census (Great Britain, 1843, Vol. XXIV) are indispensable. The Census data have been subject to serious criticism which might raise doubts as to their usefulness. Woodham-Smith (1962, p. 31), for instance, has contended that the 1841 Census seriously undercounted population. While some undercounting cannot be ruled out, observers and historians agree that the 1841 Irish Census was carried out zealously and meticulously by disciplined and well-trained enumerators, with police officers used whenever possible (Connell, 1950a, pp. 43–4; Royle, 1978, p. 119).

None the less, one historian has gone so far as to call the 1841 Census a "statistical trap" which has to be supplemented, if not replaced, by other data (Lee, 1968a, pp. 293–4). Others (for instance, Tucker, 1970) have countered that alternative sources, mainly family reconstitution based on parish records, are, if practicable at all, expensive and time-consuming.

To start with, it will be assumed below that the *total* population figures as reported in the 1821 and 1841 Censuses are accurate. The 1831 Census is a different matter. Thomas Larcom, the commissioner in charge of the 1841 Census, maintained that the enumerators were under the impression that they would be paid proportionately to the numbers surveyed and thus tended to overstate population (Great Britain, 1843, Vol. XXIV, p. viii). That such overstatement indeed happened seems consistent with the quite amazing deceleration of Irish population growth between 1821–31 and 1831–41: the implied growth rate over 1821–31 is 1·33 percent per annum, while the growth rate over 1831–41 is 0·51 percent per annum.[1] It is widely agreed now that Irish population growth was slowing down after 1790. The three Census figures, if taken at face-value, imply that in the 1820s Irish population grew faster than anywhere else in Europe (and faster than in the period 1791–1821), while in the next decade population growth was as slow as in France. Additional evidence casting doubt on the usefulness of the 1831 Census is contained in the religious Census taken in 1834 (Great Britain, 1835d, Vol. XXXIII). This Census used the 1831 returns as its basis, so that its aggregate population estimate is quite close to the 1831 one (it reported a total population of 7,943,940, while the 1831 Census reported 7,767,401). In a number of parishes, however, an "original Census" was taken and in many of those parishes the population figures show a miraculous decline in 1831–4. Some examples are Templepeter (Co. Carlow) which registered a decline from 349 to 284, the parish of Kildersherden (Co. Cavan) in which population according to the 1831 Census was 6,997 and the "original Census" of 1834 recorded only 6,202, the parish of Rathbarry (Co. Cork) in which population declined from 2,748 to 2,533, and the parish of Desertegney (Co. Donegal) for which the figures are 1,890 and 1,779, respectively. These findings confirm Larcom's concerns about the possibility of overenumeration in 1831, although it is difficult to estimate the size of the problem. Jettisoning the 1831 data, thus, we obtain an average annual rate of growth of 0·92 percent over 1821–41.

It has often been argued that the 1821 and 1841 Censuses suffered from severe underenumeration, and that the overenumeration of the 1831 Census may have produced a figure "ironically nearer the truth" (Ó Gráda, 1980b, p. 5). A recent paper by Joseph Lee (1981b) restates this position in strong terms. Lee launches a severe criticism of the Census of 1821 and attempts to rehabilitate that of 1831. There can be no doubt that underenumeration plagued the 1821 Census like all early European Censuses. Lee's opinion that the true population in 1821 was as high as 7·2 million (instead of the 6,801,827 reported, implying an understatement of almost 6 percent) seems to overshoot the mark a bit.

Lee's corrected figures for the other two Censuses restore the intercensal growth rates to more reasonable orders of magnitude (0·93 percent annually for the 1820s, 0·61 percent annually for the 1830s), but they imply an unreasonably high rate of growth for the preceding three decades. Daultrey *et al.* (1981) have revised Connell's 1950 estimate of the 1791 population to about 4·4 million, implying a rate of growth of 1·4 percent annually over the next thirty years. Lee's revised figures imply a 1·6 percent annual rate of growth, which is close to the extraordinarily high estimate of population growth rate for the 1753–91 period (Daultrey *et al.*, 1981, pp. 624–5). Since Lee does not explain exactly how he reached the 7·2 million estimate for 1821 — except for saying (p. 46) that a 5 percent underenumeration is "far from inconceivable" (actually his estimate implies a 5·6 percent underenumeration) — his criticisms do not warrant at present a complete abandonment of the 1821 Census data.

Moreover, many of the problems in the 1821 Census also affected the 1841 Census, and therefore the use of the two Censuses for comparative purposes is not materially affected by underenumeration, in contrast to the use of absolute figures. A similar logic underlies the use of modern Censuses which are known with certainty to be underenumerations (including the 1980 Census of the USA and the 1971 Census of the Republic of Ireland). In fact, it could even be argued that if we knew with certainty that the 1821 and 1841 Censuses were underenumerations whereas the 1831 Census was accurate, most statistical work would still have to be based on the former two, since the latter does not permit the computation of flow variables such as population growth. For our present purposes we need only assume that the rate of underenumeration did not vary dramatically in the three Censuses of 1821, 1841, and 1851. In addition, it must also be assumed that the regional variation in the degree of underenumeration was not too large and does exhibit only random fluctuations over time. Under these assumptions — which appear not unrealistic — the usage of the Censuses can be defended. In any event, as is true about any Census, historical or current, their usage cannot be avoided, lacking serious alternatives.

What happened before 1821 is far more difficult to ascertain. Connell (1950a) used hearth-tax returns to estimate pre-1821 population. His estimate for the average growth rate over 1791–1821 is about 1·2 percent a year, slightly less than the one recently estimated by Daultrey *et al.* (1981). The rate of population growth was thus decelerating slowly between the three benchmark years 1791, 1821, and 1841. It should be added that Daultrey and his collaborators revise *downward* Connell's population estimates for the middle of the eighteenth century, thus implying a higher growth rate during 1753–91, which strengthens the view of a high but decelerating rate of growth in the century before the famine. Clarkson (1981), using a different methodology, argued for a somewhat faster growth between 1791 and 1821, but his estimates imply as well that population growth slowed down after 1791. None the less, the conclusion drawn by Carney (1975), that on the eve of the famine Irish population had reached a stage of stagnation and even decline, implies a discontinuity which is not corroborated by other sources (Lee, 1981b, p. 55).

Gross rates of population growth are, of course, the crudest of demographic indicators. In Ireland this is even more so than elsewhere in Europe before 1845, as emigration from there assumed important proportions before it did anywhere else. Connell (1950a, p. 27) estimated total emigration from Ireland during 1780–1845 to be about 1·75 million. To decompose the rate of growth into birth, death, and migration rates, and to obtain more refined demographic indicators, such as marital-fertility rates and age-specific death and infant-mortality rates, two kinds of information can be used: nationwide Censuses or a large sample of local sources, mainly parish records. The methodology employed here is to extract as much information from the Census as possible, and to verify the assumptions made in processing the Census data by using local sources.

By definition, the change in population in 1821–41 consisted of three components: the crude birth rate, the crude death rate, and the net migration rate. It is enough if we know two of these in order to calculate the third. I shall proceed by, first, estimating the crude birth rates using a rather involved procedure. Given the birth rate, it is possible to estimate death rates and to present a more or less complete demographic picture of Ireland on the eve of the famine.

The Census-takers reported the crude birth rate in Ireland to be 33 per thousand (Great Britain, 1843, Vol. XXIV, p. xl). This estimate has been accepted—with some misgivings—by historians (McDowell, 1957b, p. 5; Connell, 1950a, p. 30; Lee, 1968a, p. 292). And yet it is so clearly an underestimate that one wonders why it has not been challenged more vigorously. A brief calculation shows that a birth rate of 33 per 1,000 implies a death rate of approximately 17 per 1,000.[2] Comparing this figure with other—more developed—European economies reveals its unacceptability. In Belgium, death rates in the years 1840–5 averaged 23 per 1,000, in the Netherlands 24 per 1,000, in Britain 22 per 1,000, and even in Denmark, which was noted for its low death rates, it was still around 20 per 1,000. If the birth rate were to be revised upward, so would the death rate, and the paradox could be settled. The key to the problem is not faulty memories, since people were not directly asked by the enumerators about past births. Rather, it is the confused and inconsistent way in which the Census commissioners computed the birth rates by subtracting reported deaths from existing children, ignoring migration, confusing calendar years and years running 7 June–6 June. These errors are outlined in detailed fashion by Tucker (1970, pp. 268–70) and there is no need to reiterate them here. It is sufficient to say that I accept Tucker's conclusion that birth rates as reported by the 1841 Census cannot be used.

It is, none the less, possible to compute a birth rate from the Census, although the birth figures themselves cannot be used. The details of the computation are presented in Appendix A to this chapter. The results suggest that the average annual crude birth rate for prefamine Ireland can be bounded approximately at 38–40 per 1,000. This implies a revision of the implied death rate to 22–3 per 1,000, which is far more plausible than the previously accepted figures. A summary of various birth-related statistics is provided in Table 3.1.

Table 3.1   *Crude Birth Rates, General, and Marital Fertility Rates (all in per 1,000)*

Province	Crude birth rate		General fertility rate*		Marital fertility rate†	
	Upper bound	Lower bound	Upper bound	Lower bound	Upper bound	Lower bound
Ulster:						
rural	38·3	37·3	187	183	382	373
urban	47·6	47·2	201	200	413	410
total	39·1	38·2	189	185	386	377
Leinster:						
rural	35·8	33·3	169	157	375	349
urban	43·1	40·1	162	151	364	339
total	37·4	34·8	167	155	372	346
Munster:						
rural	41·9	40·2	203	194	396	379
urban	37·2	35·8	143	138	315	303
total	41·1	39·5	191	183	381	366
Connaught:						
rural	40·8	38·0	202	189	365	340
urban	41·1	38·3	168	157	347	323
total	40·8	38·0	200	186	364	339
Ireland:						
rural	39·2	37·4	190	181	381	363
urban	41·8	39·9	163	156	356	339
total	39·9	37·8	186	177	377	360

* Defined as number of births per 1,000 women, aged 17–44.
† Defined as number of births per 1,000 women, married (excluding widows), aged 17–44.
Source: Computed from Great Britain, 1843, Vol. XXIV (see text).

Once we have estimated the crude birth rate, it is easy enough to estimate the total crude death rate residually. It is far more complicated to arrive at county-by-county estimates of the annual death rate. Two alternative sets of figures were estimated, as explained in Appendix A. The decomposition of Irish population growth among its three components is presented in Table 3.2. In terms of crude death rates the similarity on the province level is quite striking: all estimates, except that for Connaught, are within 1 per 1,000 of each other. On the county level the raw correlation coefficient obtained when regressing the two versions on each other is 0·638 for the death rates and 0·643 for the emigration rates.[3]

Two other demographic variables were computed, as they are of considerable importance in the reconstruction of the prefamine population structure, namely, the propensity to marry and infant-mortality rates. The propensity to marry reflects two separate variables, the marriage *rate* (that is, the proportion of the population who ever entered

Table 3.2   *Estimates of Average Annual Death and Migration Rates, 1821–41 (per 1,000)*

Province	Net rate of population change	Birth rate	Death rate, version I	Emigra-tion rate, version I*	Death rate, version II*	Emigra-tion rate, version II
Ulster	8·9	39·1	21·7	8·5	21·8	8·4
Leinster	5·8	37·4	25·5	6·1	25·1	6·5
Munster	10·7	41·1	24·2	6·2	24·6	5·8
Connaught	12·3	41·2	23·6	5·3	22·4	6·5
Ireland	9·2	39·9	23·8	6·9	23·7	7·0

*Computed residually.
Source: Computed from Great Britain, 1843, Vol. XXIV (see text and Appendix A).

matrimony) and the marriage *age* (that is, the age at marriage of those who did marry). Table 3.3 presents some measures of the propensity to marry in prefamine Ireland. The four measures are μ (the proportion of adults ever married, adjusted for different age distributions); HSM (Hajnal's singulate mean age at marriage); the median age at marriage (computed using Coale's nuptiality function); and the highest celibacy age (HCA) which is an adjusted version of HSM.

Table 3.3   *Measures of the Propensity to Marry in Prefamine Ireland*

Province	μ Male	Female	HSM Male	Female	Median Male	Female	HCA Male	Female
Ulster:								
rural	0·571	0·605	29·79	27·10	27·73	25·18	30·18	27·96
urban	0·607	0·607	28·25	26·46	26·26	24·81	28·32	27·00
Leinster:								
rural	0·513	0·586	31·40	27·69	29·32	25·93	31·79	28·48
urban	0·571	0·588	28·82	27·14	26·65	25·16	28·86	27·61
Munster:								
rural	0·553	0·631	30·09	25·17	28·35	24·59	30·50	26·34
urban	0·584	0·594	28·05	26·08	26·61	24·79	28·19	26·78
Connaught:								
rural	0·591	0·669	29·16	24·79	27·46	24·01	29·45	25·78
urban	0·589	0·636	28·84	26·38	26·63	24·62	28·86	26·78
Ireland:								
rural	0·557	0·620	30·11	26·25	28·23	24·88	30·49	27·19
urban	0·584	0·597	28·44	26·59	25·14	24·90	28·52	27·15

Source: Computed from Great Britain, 1843, Vol. XXIV (see Appendix A for methods).

It is also useful for purposes of comparing Irish demographic behavior with that of other countries, to compute some of the measures of marital fertility, nuptiality, and general fertility proposed by Coale (1967). These measures, which are computed with reference to the maximum fertility ever observed (Hutterite fertility), have been calculated for a number of other European countries and, thus, are useful for com-

parative purposes (Table 3.4). Using the upper and lower bounds of our
birth estimates, and the Census data for age-specific marriage proportions, Coale's three measures I_g (marital fertility), I_m (the propensity to
marry), and I_f (general fertility) were calculated.

Table 3.4 *Values of* I_m, I_f, *and* I_g

	I_m	I_f upper bound	I_f lower bound	I_g upper bound	I_g lower bound
Ulster: rural	0·4446	0·3796	0·3705	0·8538	0·8333
urban	0·4271	0·3896	0·3865	0·9122	0·9048
total	0·4427	0·3807	0·3723	0·8600	0·8411
Leinster: rural	0·4027	0·3397	0·3163	0·8436	0·7855
urban	0·4033	0·3251	0·3027	0·8062	0·7507
total	0·4028	0·3358	0·3126	0·8336	0·7762
Munster: rural	0·4633	0·4068	0·3901	0·8780	0·8419
urban	0·4199	0·2931	0·2819	0·6981	0·6714
total	0·4550	0·3850	0·3693	0·8461	0·8117
Connaught: rural	0·5058	0·4086	0·3809	0·8078	0·7530
urban	0·4456	0·3389	0·3158	0·7607	0·7087
total	0·5027	0·4038	0·3764	0·8049	0·7503
Ireland: rural	0·4519	0·3838	0·3659	0·8493	0·8096
urban	0·4163	0·3275	0·3125	0·7867	0·7507
total	0·4460	0·3744	0·3569	0·8395	0·8004

Note: I_m is a nuptiality measure defined as $\Sigma m_i F_i/\Sigma w_i F_i$, where m_i is the number of women
married in cohort i, and w_i is the total size of female cohort i. F_i is the Hutterite
fertility rate as defined above. I_f is a general fertility rate defined as total annual births
divided by $\Sigma w_i F_i$ and I_g, the marital fertility rate, equals births/$\Sigma m_i F_i$. The computations assume that illegitimate births in Ireland were negligible.
Source: All raw data from Great Britain, 1843, Vol. XXIV; Hutterite fertility rates from
Eaton and Mayer, 1953.

Comparison with other European countries shows that Ireland's propensity to marry before the famine was not exceptionally high. It is, to be
sure, considerably higher than in Belgium, where the nationwide average in 1846 was 0·375 (Lesthaeghe, 1977, p. 52). However, the values of
I_m in Ireland, even in Connaught, are below those reported by Van De
Walle for France which are around 0·520 in the 1840s (Van De Walle,
1974, p. 127). The earliest figures for Germany are for 1865, when the
value of I_m was 0·454. For England and Wales, and for Scotland, the
values of I_m in, respectively, 1851 and 1861 were 0·4876 and 0·5830
(computed from raw data provided in Mitchell and Deane, 1971, pp.
14–18). The real difference between Ireland and the rest of Europe is in
their marital fertility, not in their propensities to get married. The Irish
value for I_g of 0·80–0·84 compares with a value of 0·757 for Belgium,
0·531 for France (both for 1845), and 0·649 for England and Wales
(1851). As general fertility I_f is the product of I_m and I_g (ignoring
illegitimacy), it is clear that the high Irish fertility rates should be
attributed to higher marital fertility, not younger and more frequent
marriages. Comparing the mean age at marriage is more difficult, since
here there is little aggregate material available for other countries. Com-

paring the results in Table 3.3 with estimates of the mean age at first marriage from family reconstitution studies affirms the conclusion that Ireland was not significantly different from the rest of Europe in the decades before the Great Famine. The Western European studies summarized by Gaskin (1978) show an average age at first marriage of 25·7 for females (s.d. = 2·00) and 28·1 for males (s.d. = 2·16).The singulate means for Ireland are 26·3 and 29·9 respectively, and indicate that we cannot reject the null-hypothesis that the propensities to marry were the same.

One of the more difficult phenomena to explain is the persistent contemporary opinion according to which the Irish married extremely young. Well-informed contemporaries such as Pim (1848, p. 119) and Foster (1847, p.513) repeated these views. And yet they seem to be based more on myth and prejudice than on facts. One of the observers in the Ordnance Survey memoirs for the parish of Desertegney, Co. Donegal, for example, states (OSM, box 21, file VII) that women in this parish marry "frequently" at age 16. The 1841 Census reported that of the 42,945 married women in Co. Donegal in 1841, only twenty were under 17. For the country as a whole, of the marriages reported in the "Tables of marriages", only 3·3 percent of all marriages involved brides under 17 years. Nor does it seem likely that the high age at marriage in 1841 was a comparatively recent phenomenon, although a slight rise in the 1830s may have occurred. The Hajnal formula is based on cross-sectional data, computing the age at marriage from actually married people who had been wed in the past. Thus, the mean ages computed reflect the age at marriage of women married over a period of three decades and more prior to the Census.

We turn, finally, to the infant-mortality rates. Infant-mortality rates, more than the crude death rate itself, contain interesting information about the population dynamics of any society. The 1841 Census contains a wealth of age-specific mortality data in its appendix entitled "Tables of death". The figures are given for each of the individual years 1830–40, and are broken down by sex, county, and rural vs urban. The conversion of these data into infant-mortality rates is, however, far from immediate. The details of the computation are presented in Appendix A to this chapter. The summary data are presented in Table 3.5.

Table 3.5   *Infant-Mortality Rates, by Province (per 1,000 births)*

Province	Rural		Urban		Total	
	Version A	Version B	Version A	Version B	Version A	Version B
Ulster	188	179	301	291	200	189
Leinster	200	194	321	324	231	227
Munster	225	225	293	310	239	240
Connaught	244	235	373	355	253	243
Ireland	213	207	313	315	224	223

Note: Version A is based on death data from 1840; version B is based on an average of 1838–40.
Source: Computed from Great Britain, 1843, Vol. XXIV; see text.

The infant-mortality data provide an indication of the degree of backwardness of Ireland. Comparing it with other European countries shows unambiguously higher infant mortality in Ireland. In England and France the average number of infants to die in their first year was 150 and 160 per 1,000 live births (1840–5) respectively. In the Low Countries the figures are of the same order of magnitude. Even lower infant-mortality rates were recorded for some Scandinavian countries: in Denmark the rate was 137 per 1,000 for the same years; in Norway, 122. Higher rates were recorded in Austria (246 per 1,000) and Germany (298 per 1,000). The comparability of these figures is at best hazardous, and the German figure in particular looks suspiciously high (all data from Mitchell, 1975, p. 127). The conclusion is confirmed, however, by family-reconstruction studies which show lower infant-mortality rates for the period 1780–1820 in England, France, and Sweden (though again the German figures are higher). The comparability of family-reconstitution data with Census data is risky because of the dangers of unrepresentativeness of small communities to which the family reconstitutions pertain. However, the summarization of a large number of such studies (Flinn, 1981, pp. 92, 132–7) circumvents this problem.[4]

(2)   The Overpopulation Controversy

The data described in Section 1 were generated primarily to shed light on one of the most interesting and hotly debated issues in prefamine Irish economic history, namely, was Ireland poor because it was overpopulated? Overpopulation is, however, notoriously tricky to define. Grigg (1980, p. 11) has proposed three definitions: (1) overpopulation occurs when population pressure reduces the rate of population growth to zero; (2) overpopulation occurs when the size of population exceeds by a significant amount that level which maximizes income per capita; (3) overpopulation occurs when the marginal productivity of labor is zero. Definitions 1 and 3 are quite obviously at variance with conditions in Ireland and the discussion below will be conducted in terms of definition 2, although the demarcation lines between the three definitions cannot be drawn very sharply (note that 3 is really a special case of 2). Since the "optimal" population level cannot be computed directly, the arguments will be presented in a comparative context: was income in Ireland (or some parts of it) lower than elsewhere because population density was higher?

Many contemporaries firmly adhered to the overpopulation thesis and as a result advocated various measures encouraging emigration to relieve the pressure. In a widely cited letter to Ricardo, Malthus wrote in 1817 that "the land in Ireland is infinitely more peopled than in England; and to give full effect to the natural resources of the country a great part of the population should be swept from the soil" (Ricardo, 1952, Vol. 7, p. 175). In his great *Essay on the Principle of Population* Malthus reiterated this position (Malthus, 1826, Vol. 1, p. 469). Later in his life Malthus seems to have had second-thoughts about Ireland. In his *Principles of Political Economy* (Malthus, 1836, pp. 345–56) he admitted that—given sufficient capital, demand, and security of property—Ireland could develop "prodigious" wealth and even become richer than England.

None the less, the earlier Malthusian view was widely adopted by British political economists. O'Brien (1921, p. 71) noted that the doctrines of Malthus were held by contemporary economists to be peculiarly applicable to Ireland and added that "the destiny of Ireland in the early nineteenth century was largely moulded by the ideas of two great economists, Adam Smith and Malthus, and of the two the latter was probably the more influential". The implication was, as Salaman (1949, p. 255) put it, that the attitude adopted by statesmen and men of affairs was one "of resignation to the inevitable . . . [a] policy [that] was dignified by a new philosophy and Malthus was its prophet. All economic evils were due to excess of population, and were not all authorities in agreement that Ireland was overpopulated?" A good example of such Malthusian influence can be found in the Railroad Commission Report, which stated that: "The proportion of the (product) reserved for the (labouring people) is too small to be consistent with a healthy state of society. The pressure of a superabundant and excessive population . . . is perpetually and powerfully acting to depress them" (Great Britain, 1837–8, Vol. XXXV, p. 483).

Modern historians concerned with prefamine Ireland have accepted the overpopulation theory with an uncharacteristic lack of criticism. K. H. Connell (1950a, p. 242) remarked that "Malthus was an accurate observer . . . it was topically platitudinous to point to food supply as the limit to population growth". A recent sociological history takes the Malthusian view as axiomatic: "Prefamine Ireland was a wretchedly poor country because there were simply far too many souls for the amount of good agricultural land" (Clark, 1979, p. 41).[5]

Criticism against the overpopulation hypothesis has come from a variety of sources. For Marx and writers in his tradition, any view derived from Malthus and his population theory was utterly anathema. George O'Brien, the most important of the nationalist economic historians writing in the 1920s, launched a penetrating attack against the hypothesis (O'Brien, 1921, pp. 71–86).[6] But the most vigorous attack against the Malthusian view was expounded by a large number of contemporary writers, pamphleteers, and Irish political economists. A few examples will suffice to illustrate this literature. M. T. Sadler (1829) conducted a spirited attack against Malthus, vehemently denying that "Ireland [was] overpopulated in reference to its potential produce" as well as "in reference to its actual produce". William Blacker, a land agent and agricultural expert, stated his opinion that "to whatever source . . . the evils of the day may be attributed, the mere increase in inhabitants can scarcely be considered a sufficient cause to account for them" and estimated that Ireland could actually support two and a half times its present population and that "all fears as to a surplus population are perfectly ideal" (Blacker, 1846, p. 4; see also Kane, 1845, pp.

295–315). In a number of pamphlets (1833; 1848), the able political economist George Poulett Scrope repeated his view that emigration was perfectly justified in overpopulated countries, but explicitly excluded Ireland from that definition. Rather, the sources of poverty were "the notorious paralysis of agricultural industry in Ireland and the sinful neglect and waste of its natural fertility" (Scrope, 1848, p. 4). The general consensus among all these writers was that Ireland possessed sufficient unreclaimed or improvable land to render any simple-minded statements about land–labor ratios suspect.

The lines of dispute are, thus, clearly drawn. And yet the overpopulation controversy has so far been conducted in what may best be termed an empirical vacuum. Neither side has made an attempt to utilize the 1841 Census or any other large quantitative source to buttress its position. In what follows below, an attempt to test the Malthusian hypothesis will be made. In principle three types of tests are conceivable. The first looks at the behavior of the Irish economy after the famine. If the decline in population was followed by a noticeable rise in income per head, it could be inferred that such a rise was consistent with the Malthusian hypothesis. The second test compares Ireland with other European countries and asks whether its labor–land ratio was truly exceptional. The third test utilizes the internal variation within Ireland to test the Malthusian model. The latter procedure forms the bulk of the tests performed here and will be presented in detail in the next section. Before that, I shall briefly discuss the former two.

Since the postfamine period lies outside the scope of this book, no possible justice can be done to the first test suggested above. But a few observations suffice to cast doubt on the simple Malthusian view. First, if prefamine Ireland was aptly described by a Malthusian–Ricardian model, one immediate prediction should be that a large decline in population should lead to a decline in the amount of land under cultivation by the abandonment of marginal soil. This did not occur. Although there are difficulties with the evaluation of the exact figures due to changing definitions, the total area under cultivation rose from 13·5 million acres in 1841 to 15·7 million acres in 1871. Secondly, the famine reduced both agricultural output in real terms and the agricultural labor force. Ó Gráda (1980c, p. 15) has estimated that during 1845–54 the value of output in constant prices dropped by about 17 percent and the male labor force in agriculture declined by 24 percent, which in his judgement seems "to disprove the so-called doctrine of labour of zero value". Zero marginal product of labor is a special and extreme variant of the overpopulation hypothesis. But the implied labor elasticity of 0·71 is inconsistent even with much more moderate versions.[7] It is true, of course, that these observations mask a more complex reality. The famine removed many of the constraints which prevented a shift from tillage to pasturage before the famine. None the less, they are hardly consistent with an economy whose surplus population has been "swept from the soil". Thirdly, there is not much evidence that the famine led to an appreciable increase in the standard of living of those who survived. While it is true that some rise in income occurred during 1850–75,

Ó Gráda attributes this largely to a shifting sectoral composition, not a rise in general incomes (Ó Gráda, 1973a, p. 147). In addition, before 1877 Ireland benefited from the rise in agricultural prices. Once these two effects have been taken into account, not much evidence remains to support the Malthusian view. Nevertheless, the issue can by no means be said to be closed, and more research on the postfamine period will be necessary.[8]

A comparison between Ireland and other European countries at about the middle of the nineteenth century risks ending up in a quagmire of incomparable statistics. In the case of looking at population density statistics, however, the numbers involved may be a bit less subject to such hazards than comparing, say, input or output figures. None the less, the definition of "cultivated land" is sufficiently ambiguous to make the data in Table 3.6 unsuitable for anything but simple rankings. Some of the data on land under cultivation are from later on in the nineteenth century, but since in most countries changes in the amount of land under cultivation were not very important after 1850, this probably does not distort the picture too much.

Table 3.6 shows that by no definition can Ireland be said to have been abnormally overpopulated. Column 1 shows that it was more densely populated than France and Prussia, and considerably more so than Scotland and Denmark. The Netherlands and England and Wales were about at par with Ireland, and Belgium was denser. Once we look at the population per cultivated acre, the picture is hardly changed except that Scotland and Sweden are about at par with Ireland, and France is considerably closer as well. Looking at the amount of cultivated acres per *agricultural* or *rural* population alters the picture considerably. However, the ratios in columns 3 and 4 do not really measure population pressure but rather what we may call backwardness or underdevelopment. The sole contention made here is that the latter cannot be explained by the former. Even if we confine our attention to the poorest province, Connaught, it is striking that the ratio of cultivated land per capita there is not lower than in many of the most prosperous economies of the time.

Table 3.6 is, however, not a very powerful test of the Malthusian hypothesis. First, the amount of land under cultivation is an ambiguous figure, since the quality of land varied with soil type, topography, and climate. Moreover, it might be argued that the quality of land itself was a function of population pressure. The more severe population pressure, the more poor lands would be brought into cultivation on the extensive margin, so that the *effective* land–labor ratios in countries with serious overpopulation problems would be biased upward. Secondly, even if we could correct for land quality, the absence of correlation between land–population ratios and income is inconsistent only with what may be termed the weak version of the overpopulation hypothesis. The weak version is a statement about raw ("zero-order") correlations, looking at two variables only: income (or any proxy for it), and natural resources per capita. It appears, however, that the strong version of the Malthusian hypothesis is really what has to be contended with. The strong version is a statement about partial correlations, which holds other factors constant. It asks, in effect, whether income would have been much higher if natural resources per capita were higher, keeping all other factors affecting income at a fixed level.

Table 3.6   *Measures of Population Density in Mid-Nineteenth-Century Europe*

Province or County	(1) Total acres/ Total population	(2) Cultivated acres/ Total population	(3) Cultivated acres/ Agricultural population	(4) Cultivated acres/ Rural population
Ulster	2·29	1·43	2·34	1·58
Leinster	2·47	2·01	3·39	2·59
Munster	2·53	1·62	2·29	1·93
Connaught	3·10	1·56	2·01	1·66
Total Ireland	2·55	1·65	2·49	1·91
Belgium (1846)	1·70	1·02	1·99	1·37
France (1856)	3·70	1·94	3·76	2·57
Prussia (1850)	4·58	2·80	n.a.	3·75
Netherlands (1849)	2·55	1·63	3·93	n.a.
England and Wales (1841)	2·35	1·50	6·82	2·71
Scotland (1841)	7·40	1·56	n.a.	n.a.
Denmark (1850)	6·55	4·82	9·77	n.a.
Sweden (1840)	31·85	1·54	n.a.	n.a.

Sources: Computed from figures in Great Britain, 1843, Vol. XXIV; Statistique Générale de la Belgique, 1852, p. 43. Mitchell, 1975; Mitchell and Deane, 1971; Mulhall, 1899; and McCulloch, 1866.

Both methodological and data problems render a test of the strong version of the overpopulation hypothesis at the international level impossible. In the next section, the test will be carried out on the national level, using the thirty-two counties of Ireland as observations. The underlying assumption behind that procedure is that if there was overpopulation in Ireland, it did not affect all regions equally. Casual glances at county-by-county statistics suffice to show that there is indeed sufficient variation in the four measures used in Table 3.6. The means and standard deviations of the four measures (32 observations) are: population per total area: 0·435 (0·262); population per cultivated acre: 0·630 (0·269); rural population per cultivated acre: 0·530 (0·131); and agricultural population per cultivated acre: 0·425 (0·135).

(3)   Testing the Malthusian Hypothesis

Any test of the Malthusian interpretation of the prefamine Irish economy requires a careful specification of the model actually being tested. A Malthusian system actually consists of two separate equations. The first of these relations captures the diminishing returns to irreproducible resources, as mentioned in Section 2. The second equation links the rate of change of population to economic variables. Specifically, the rate of population growth is *ex hypothesi* a function of differences between the actual level of income and some fixed level which could be termed "the minimum of subsistence" (although it need not have a biological interpretation). The model is closed by an identity relating the present size of population and, thus, the ratio of labor to natural resources to its past rate of growth. A similar model of Malthusian dynamics has been proposed by Lee (1978).

Only the first of the two Malthusian relations provides an actual explanation of the level of poverty in prefamine Ireland. The second equation is a description of the long-term dynamic relation between economic change and population growth. The two equations can be written formally as follows. Let L be the size of the population, Y total income, and R land or natural resources. The first equation can be written as:

$$\frac{Y}{L} = f\left(\frac{L}{R}\right) \qquad f' < 0. \qquad (3.1)$$

And the second equation is:

$$\frac{dL}{dt} = g\left(\frac{Y}{L}\right) \qquad g' > 0. \qquad (3.2)$$

The working of this version of the Malthusian model can best be illustrated by considering the four theoretically possible outcomes of the tests.

(1) *Both Malthusian equations are consistent with the evidence; this case is the classical Malthusian model.* If this hypothesis holds, it follows that in some sense the famine was not necessary to stop Irish population growth. Had the famine not occurred, population would have stabilized at a level not much higher than the 1845 level, or possibly declined after some point, though at a less cataclysmic rate. In this case the economy was poor because it was overpopulated, but as it was getting poorer, population growth would slow down until it eventually reached zero.

(2) *The first equation is satisfied but the second is not.* What this means is that Ireland was poor because it was overpopulated, but because population growth was independent of poverty, it kept growing until, possibly, some other disaster occurred. This unstable Malthusian model implies that the Great Famine was an inexorable punishment for Ireland's demographic profligacy. Population grew unrestrained, continuously exacerbating poverty, thus making the resolution of the problem by a catastrophe ultimately inevitable. Concerns about such a disaster were already expressed prior to the famine. Thomas Carlyle, for instance, wrote in 1839 that "This cannot last, Heaven disowns it, Earth is against it; Ireland will be burnt into a black unpeopled field of ashes that this should last. . . . The time has come when the Irish population must be improved a little or exterminated".

(3) *The evidence supports the second but not the first equation.* In this

economy, if income were such that population grew at a considerable rate, there would be no "feedback-effect" from the first equation, so that population growth would proceed unchecked unless exogenous shifts in the population growth function reduced the rate of population growth. Ultimately, of course, growth could not proceed forever. Sooner or later a time must set in when the first equation will be satisfied as well. While one might concede that Malthusian constraints were always present, it is clear that they were not always binding. The Netherlands had 3·1 million people in 1849 and 6·9 million in 1920. Had there been no famine and had other economic circumstances been more favorable, there seems to have been no reason why Ireland could not have sustained 17 million people or more by the end of the century (as Blacker, 1834, p. 31, predicted), although it might have had difficulty sustaining, say, double that number.

(4)   *Neither condition is satisfied.* This case is not essentially different from case 3 except that noneconomic forces controlled the rate of population growth. The European experience—excluding Ireland —could be interpreted as a transition from case 3 to case 4 in the second part of the nineteenth century, although some economies such as France may have entered that stage earlier. In these cases the relations between population and income break down and the two variables can be considered largely independent of each other. Modern-day Western Europe provides prime examples of such "non-Malthusian" economies.

The tests below regress measures of income per capita on a large number of exogenous variables, including measures of population pressure. These are followed by tests of the second equation which look at the determinants of population change. Such a procedure would seem problematic for at least two reasons. First, there is a problem of simultaneity in the model since demographic variables are really endogenous to the model. Secondly, there is considerable doubt whether the use of cross-sectional data in a model addressing dynamic issues is at all appropriate. The simultaneity issue seems the less serious of the two; in the first set of regressions, the land–labor ratio is exogenous to income. In the second set of regressions income is assumed to be an exogenous determinant of the *rate of change* of population. The model is subject to simultaneity biases only to the extent that the rate of change of population, the propensity to marry, the rate of fertility, and similar variables simultaneously determine the *level* of population. In a very long-run model this is so by definition: today's population is by definition equal to the sum of past increments. But in a model which looks at a cross section of the prefamine economy in the last decade prior to the famine, the assumption of independence between the *level* and the *rate of change* of population is certainly defensible.

The second objection stems from the fact that the procedure followed is tantamount to treating cross-sectional data "as if" they were observations over time. In other words, on the eve of the famine the several counties of Ireland were at different levels of development, which corresponded to different stages reached by the "average" economy over time. The primary objection to that view of cross-sectional data is that internal movements of workers would set into motion equilibrating mechanisms which tended to eliminate the differences between the counties. Such movements, of course, are impossible over time. To the extent, therefore, that internal migration in Ireland was of significant size, the use of cross-sectional data is hazardous. The 1841 Census reports (Great Britain, 1843, Vol. XXIV, pp. 446–7) that a total of 405,365 Irishmen (4·96 percent of the total population) lived in counties in which they were not born. Of these, however, 273,258 (3·34 percent) were living in counties adjoining the ones in which they were born, and some of these must have been visitors, as the 1841 Census was taken on a Sunday, the "great visiting day" in Ireland (Lee, 1981b, p. 54). It seems doubtful that internal migration of such dimensions would be sufficient to "level" counties at very different stages of advancement. External migration, if sufficiently selective, could have in principle achieved the same results, but was unlikely to have done so, as prefamine emigration did not emanate from the poorest counties.

Testing the first equation implies regressing measures of income against a set of explanatory variables one of which is the natural resources–labor ratio. The Malthusian explanation of Irish poverty falls and stands with the sign of this coefficient: if Irish poverty was in any sense determined by population pressure on the land, this coefficient should be positive; the higher the land–labor ratio, the higher income.

In Table 3.7 the results of both the weak and the strong tests of the first Malthusian equation are presented. The weak tests (panel (a)) examine the raw correlation between income and the land–labor ratio. The strong version (panel (b)) tests whether the expected positive relation exists, holding other things constant. The results indicate, surprisingly, that the data fail to support the Malthusian model as specified in the first equation. The weak test produces the expected sign on the land–labor ratio in some specifications but the significance levels are low and the entire regression equation has very little explanatory power. The strong tests, in which the land–labor ratio is one regressor among many, produce an unambiguous and striking result: the explanatory power of the equation is excellent, and all other regressors produce significant coefficients of the expected sign. The one glaring exception is the land–labor ratio. Regardless of specification and weighting procedure, the coefficients of LANLAB (area under cultivation divided by rural population) have the wrong sign or are not significant. Experiments replacing LANLAB by total population per acre or per cultivated acre (not reported) do not change this result.

One objection which could be made against the results presented in Table 3.7 is that the land–labor ratio is not correctly specified, since it is not adjusted for the quality of land. As was noted above, if the Malthusian hypothesis is correct we would expect more land of marginal quality to be brought into cultivation. Failing to account for this would bias the coefficient of the land–labor ratio downward. An

Table 3.7 *Regressions Testing the Weak and Strong Version of the Malthusian Hypothesis (t-Statistics in Parentheses; All Equations Employing Generalized Least-Squares)*

(a) Weak version

Dependent variable	Income per capita	Income per capita	Wage	Wage	Rent, p.c.
Constant	16·57	9·64	15·73	9·66	−0·13
	(16·23)	(5·59)	(8·51)	(6·09)	(−0·35)
Population pressure variable	Total area per inhabitant	Cultivated area per rural inhabitant	Cultivated area per inhabitant	Cultivated area per rural inhabitant	Cultivated area per inhabitant
PPV	−0·56	2·66	−1·46	1·60	0·89
	(−1·98)	(3·08)	(−1·35)	(2·01)	(4·70)
F-statistic	3·93	9·46	1·82	4·02	22·11
(d.f.)	(1,30)	(1,30)	(1,30)	(1,30)	(1,30)

(b) Strong version

Dependent variable	Income	Wage	Rent, p.c.	Income	Wage	Income
Constant	10·00	10·80	−1·22	14·10	9·78	14·87
	(3·06)	(3·68)	(−0·81)	(4·72)	(3·35)	(6·12)
PPV*	−1·70	−2·46	0·760	−2·89	−2·41	−3·10
	(−1·61)	(−2·60)	(1·56)	(−2·88)	(−2·84)	(−3·56)
CAPLAB	2·68	2·36	0·242	2·66	2·48	2·70
	(5·00)	(4·91)	(0·97)	(4·56)	(6·06)	(4·77)
Literacy rate	9·65	7·21	2·41	9·20	7·37	10·07
	(1·93)	(1·61)	(1·04)	(1·70)	(1·84)	(2·02)
Housing quality†	−11·57	−11·03	−0·39	−13·38	−9·97	−14·14
	(−3·39)	(−3·61)	(−0·25)	(−3·71)	(−3·30)	(−4·50)
Cottage industry‡	13·92	8·82	6·15		7·20	
	(2·33)	(1·65)	(2·22)		(2·18)	
Proportion urban	12·36	9·98	3·18	6·98	8·64	6·51
	(3·81)	(3·44)	(2·12)	(2·83)	(3·07)	(2·96)
Proportion manufacturing§	−7·94	−2·51	−5·93	1·78		
	(−1·44)	(−0·51)	(−2·31)	(0·45)		
F-statistic	38·22	37·36	5·08	37·12	31·01	45·91
(d.f.)	(7,24)	(7,24)	(7,24)	(6,25)	(6,25)	(5,26)

* Population pressure variable; in all versions the variable used was cultivated land divided by rural population, that is, the rural land–labor ratio.

† Measured as the proportion class 4 (worst) houses. Thus the higher this variable, the lower the quality of housing.

‡ Measured as the proportion rural men and women employed in "Occupations ministering to clothing" in the 1841 Census.

§ Measured as the proportion families employed in manufacturing.

easy way to see the reason for this bias is to envisage land in "efficiency" (that is, quality-corrected) units. In such a formulation "better" land is equivalent to "more" land, so that measuring land of uneven quality in natural units (for instance, acres) would fail to reveal population pressure on poor lands. One nineteenth-century source pointed out, for instance, that "countries consisting chiefly of mountainous and coarse tracts of lands are those which produce the greatest increase in population, whilst those that are fertile contain the fewest inhabitants" (Mason, 1814–19, Vol. 2, p. 360). This statement, if correct, implies that measuring population pressure in terms of agricultural workers per acre under cultivation could be misleading.

Adjusting for land quality is far from easy. Not only are adequate data lacking, but there are serious difficulties in specifying the proper adjustment. After all, the "quality" we most look for in land is its ability to produce "income". Adjusting the quantity of land by measuring it in efficiency units would involve using the same variable ("income"), as both the dependent and the independent variable. Moreover, with few exceptions, the quality of land unlike its quantity, is obviously not an irreproducible resource. Like genius, soil fertility was as much a result of perspiration as it was a gift from God. "Better land", therefore, was equivalent in part to "more land" and in part to "more capital".

Nonetheless, attempts to control for the quality of land can be carried out. A number of different proxies for land quality were used and tested in two specifications: land quality was entered as a separate independent variable and a standardized land quality variable was used to transform the land/labor ratio into "efficiency units". The proxies for land quality experimented with were:

(1)   The proportion of land under cultivation. The use of this proxy assumes that the quality of land within each county is distributed uniformly over the surface, and that the threshold level at which land is brought into cultivation is a function of the other independent variables in the regression. The proportion under cultivation is a function of the mean quality of the land and the threshold level. If we solve for the latter, the proportion of land under cultivation can be interpreted as a function of the average quality of the land.

(2)   A transformation of the proportion land under cultivation derived from the normal distribution. This variable is similar to the previous one except that the distribution of land quality is assumed normal. The precise assumptions underlying proxies 1 and 2 and the derivation of the estimated equations are presented in Appendix B to this chapter.

(3)   The mean elevation above sea-level, capturing the lower fertility of mountainous areas and highlands (Andrews, 1980, p. 47).

(4)   The variance of the elevation above sea-level. This variable captures altitude as well, but in addition captures the variability and unevenness of the terrain.

(5)   Rents per acre. This assumes a purely Ricardian model of rents, in which labor and other factors are assumed to be perfectly mobile and differences in rent reflect differences in land quality only.

(6)   The proportion uncultivated land which is "unimprovable for cultivation". The higher this proportion, the lower the quality of land not under cultivation, which should reflect—other things equal—the quality of the land presently under cultivation. Two versions of this measure were used, namely, the proportion

unimprovable land relative to the size of the county, and the proportion relative to total "Unimproved pasture and bog lands", as defined by the General Valuation Office in Dublin.

The results of the attempts to examine the Malthusian hypothesis while controlling for land quality are presented in Tables 3.8 and 3.9. In Table 3.8 the various measures of land quality are allowed to enter the regression equation unconstrained. In columns 1 and 2 the variables are purely physical. One of them has an insignificant coefficient, the other one has the wrong sign. In columns 3 and 4 the proportion under cultivation (or θ, which is a function of it) are used, without much more success. This is probably due to the assumption imposed on columns 3 and 4 that the standard deviation of the quality index is constant. Relaxing that assumption results in columns 5 and 6, in which the land-quality index is significant at the 1 percent level and has the expected sign. The other three measures of land quality, rents per acre and two variants of the proportion of unimprovable land all have the expected signs, but are not very strong statistically. In none of the nine columns does the inclusion of quality variables have the slightest effect on the seemingly perverse behavior of the population pressure variable (PPV), defined here as the land-labor ratio, or the number of acres under cultivation divided by the rural population. In Table 3.9 the quantity and quality of land are entered jointly by defining land "in efficiency units", which is accomplished by multiplying the land-labor ratio by indices of land quality if these indices measure quality directly, or dividing the land-labor ratio by the quality indices if they measure quality inversely. The result is that the perversely significant wrong sign on the land-labor ratio disappears in most cases, and its coefficients sink into statistical insignificance.

The conclusion suggested by these data is therefore that land appears to have been less of a binding constraint on the Irish economy than the "overpopulation" view would have us believe. In view of the assumptions we have had to make to carry out the tests described in Tables 3.7–3.9, this conclusion should be regarded with some caution. There appears to be no statistically significant relation between poverty (as measured by our estimated personal income series) and population pressure variables. The procedure followed was to assume that the land-labor ratio was exogenous and income endogenous, which produced a testable implication. The implication was tested and found inconsistent with the evidence. This, of course, is not the same as arguing that "land did not matter" which would be a rash inference from our data. Nor does it follow that a reduction of population size may not have meant more income per capita if such a reduction had somehow been carried out in a costless and frictionless way. The economy contains, after all, three factors of production. Reducing labor increases the capital-labor ratio and through that mechanism leads to higher incomes. The Malthusian hypothesis, as defined here, is concerned with the ratio of nonreproducible resources to labor, not total nonlabor inputs to labor. Low income caused by low capital-labor ratios is not an

Table 3.8 *Regression Testing for Malthusian Hypothesis (t-Statistics in Parentheses; all Equations Employing Generalized Least-Squares)*

	(1)	(2)	(3)	(4)	(5)	(6)	(7)	(8)	(9)
Dependent variable	Income per capita	Wage	Income per capita	Wage	Income per capita	Income per capita	Wage	Income per capita	Income per capita
Land-quality index used	Variance of altitude	Mean altitude	Proportion under cultivation§	Theta¶	Proportion under cultivation**	Theta**	Rents per acre	Proportion unimprovable, unimprovable, I*†	Proportion unimprovable, unimprovable, II*‡
Constant	14·20 (4·66)	7·53 (2·39)	11·55 (3·59)	11·85 (4·32)	1·29 (0·42)	1·07 (0·30)	10·68 (3·69)	15·01 (4·87)	14·92 (4·94)
PPV*	-3·20 (-2·57)	-1·40 (-1·36)	-2·78 (-2·46)	-2·95 (-3·14)	-1·46 (-2·20)	-1·61 (-2·00)	-2·24 (-2·27)	-3·40 (-3·10)	-4·21 (-2·96)
Land-quality index†	-0·25‡ (-0·44)	1·17‡ (1·61)	0·95‖ (0·86)	0·08‖ (0·33)	4·79‖ (2·43)	6·03‖ (2·14)	0·86‖ (1·76)	-0·85‡ (-1·13)	-0·63‡ (-1·30)
CAPLAB	2·84 (3·90)	2·08 (4·48)	2·79 (5·04)	2·38 (5·18)	3·10 (5·88)	2·93 (5·76)	2·05 (4·05)	2·88 (4·71)	3·47 (4·09)
Literacy rate	9·77 (1·73)	4·88 (1·17)	8·68 (1·70)	7·06 (1·61)	7·04 (1·56)	8·61 (1·89)	5·31 (1·17)	9·12 (1·70)	6·42 (1·12)
Housing quality	-13·25 (-3·60)	-8·89 (-2·96)	-10·90 (-2·81)	-10·48 (-3·18)	-7·09 (-2·16)	-8·03 (-2·39)	-9·37 (-2·79)	-12·79 (-3·53)	-12·09 (-3·27)
Cottage industry		9·36 (2·69)			11·09 (3·35)	9·93 (2·87)			
Proportion manufacturing	1·79 (0·45)		4·26 (0·99)	5·47 (1·48)			7·25 (1·90)	1·69 (0·43)	2·88 (0·73)
Percentage urban	7·08 (2·81)	10·14 (3·52)	4·55 (1·56)	4·85 (1·96)	9·36 (3·05)	9·06 (2·85)	2·79 (0·95)	8·54 (3·04)	8·10 (3·14)
F	30·82	28·65	23·40	23·45	30·29	29·06	37·97	32·35	32·93
(d.f.)	(7,24)	(7,24)	(7,24)	(7,24)	(7,24)	(7,24)	(7,24)	(7,24)	(7,24)

* In all specifications variable used is area under cultivation divided by rural population.

† Measured as deviations from the nationwide mean.

‡ Sign expected: negative.

§ Assumes quality uniformly distributed with constant standard deviation; see Appendix B (proxy 1).

‖ Sign expected: positive.

¶ Assumes quality normally distributed with constant standard deviation; for definition of θ, see Appendix B for precise specification.

** Assumes constant coefficient of variation; see Appendix B for precise specification.

*† Defined as unimprovable land divided by uncultivated land.

*‡ Defined as unimprovable land divided by total area.

Table 3.9 Regressions Testing for the Malthusian Hypothesis, Land–Labor Ratios, Expressed in Quality Adjusted Units

	(1)	(2)	(3)	(4)	(5)	(6)	(7)
Dependent variable	Wage	Income per capita	Income per capita	Wage	Wage	Income per capita	Wage
Land-quality index used in adjustment	Proportion cultivated	Theta*	Variance of altitude	Mean of altitude	Rents per acre	Proportion unimprovable, I	Proportion unimprovable, II
Constant	7·76	9·50	9·20	10·08	5·58	9·48	7·96
	(3·16)	(3·25)	(3·13)	(3·67)	(2·38)	(3·31)	(3·02)
PPV in "efficiency units"	-0·75	-0·07	0·0014	-0·58	0·29	0·02	-0·0013
	(-2·00)	(-0·41)	(0·017)	(-1·79)	(1·17)	(0·56)	(0·009)
CAPLAB	1·64	1·37	1·28	1·13	1·31	1·33	0·82
	(4·29)	(3·12)	(3·02)	(2·97)	(3·57)	(3·38)	(1·98)
Literacy rate	6·40	8·71	8·79	4·97	6·33	8·58	6·45
	(1·34)	(1·40)	(1·40)	(0·90)	(1·35)	(1·38)	(1·10)
Housing quality	-7·41	-8·32	-7·51	-8·24	-5·35	-8·04	-5·68
	(-2·18)	(-2·11)	(-2·03)	(-2·48)	(-2·01)	(-2·27)	(-1·71)
Proportion in manufacturing	9·97	6·67	7·10	7·45		6·76	9·56
	(2·82)	(1·62)	(1·73)	(2·02)		(1·68)	(2·58)
Cottage industry					12·54		
					(4·22)		
Percentage urban	5·89	8·49	8·56	8·10	10·10	8·32	8·32
	(2·22)	(3·07)	(3·03)	(3·36)	(2·83)	(2·99)	(3·24)
F	21·75	27·03	26·82	27·94	35·85	27·21	24·28
(d.f.)	(6,25)	(6,25)	(6,25)	(6,25)	(6,25)	(6,25)	(6,25)

* For definitions, see Appendix B.

indication of overpopulation in the classical sense, but indicates low levels of savings, underdeveloped capital markets, technological backwardness, or combinations of these factors.[9]

It is clear, however, that serious doubt has been cast on the simple and easy explanation which blames Irish poverty on excess population. The burden of the proof has now been shifted to those who still consider the history of Ireland in the nineteenth century to be a classical case of a Malthusian disaster. It also seems reasonable to conclude that any attempt to explain Ireland's poverty will have to start looking in other directions.

The other half of the Malthusian model is more complex. Historians have never been certain how the second equation of the Malthusian mechanism really operated if it did so at all. The classical model draws the link largely through nuptiality and birth rates, but alternative mechanisms (for instance, through infant mortality) are not less plausible. Even more intriguing is the possibility that emigration constituted one of the Malthusian checks. It is quite possible that some of these mechanisms were destabilizing: if emigration took place from the better-to-do regions, the Malthusian model would be operating in reverse.

Central to the issue of the effect of economic conditions on population growth is Connell's thesis with respect to the propensity to marry. Following many contemporary writers, Connell asserted that all other things equal, a negative relation existed between income and the propensity to marry: "The wretchedness of living conditions made marriage appear a welcome relief . . . [and] the utter hopelessness with which [the Irishman] had to survey the future inclined [him] towards early marriage" (Connell, 1950a, p. 59). If supported by the evidence, Connell's thesis has two interesting implications. First, it would indicate another element of instability in the Malthusian framework. Secondly, it suggests some behavior which at first glance appears surprising on the microeconomic level. Marriage was both desirable and costly, and should thus be regarded as an economic good. Connell's view seems to indicate that marriage was an inferior good. There are, of course, ways to rationalize this apparent paradox away. For instance, money income may be regarded as containing a price element as well as an income element, since wages were the price of leisure. If children were highly leisure-intensive, they would be less expensive to poor people, whose leisure had a lower opportunity cost. It is also possible that marriage age was a form of contraception and that the richer families wished to curtail in this fashion the number of their offspring in this equal-shares inheritance society.

Hypotheses on Irish demographic behavior, thus, abound. What do the data confirm and what do they reject? To start with, the view — closely held by Connell and not seriously challenged by anyone else — that the high birth rates in Ireland were determined first and foremost by the low marriage age and low celibacy rates in Ireland should be re-examined. We have already seen that, compared with other European countries, the Irish propensity to marry was not unusually high, and that its higher overall fertility rate was associated mainly with higher age-specific fertility rates. To test whether this is also the case for variations *within* Ireland, a simple test was carried out.[10] About 74 percent of the variance in the logarithm of the total fertility rate was explained by differences in the female propensity to marry; and 33 percent was explained by the variance in marital-fertility rates. In addition, –7 percent of the variance in the fertility index is due to the (slightly negative) covariance between the propensity to marry and marital-fertility indices. At the very least we may conclude that these results warrant an examination of both the propensities to marry and the marital-fertility rates as determinants of the overall fertility rate, the crude birth rate, and the growth of population.

A statistical analysis of demographic change in prefamine Ireland runs into both statistical and methodological problems. Ultimately, we are asking questions about the rate of population growth. Clearly, however, the rate of population growth consists of many components, and there is no reason to suppose that certain exogenous factors, such as dependency on potatoes, housing quality, income per capita, and so on, affect different variables in the same way. For instance, it is perfectly possible that cottage industry reduced the age at marriage on the one hand, but reduced marital fertility on the other, so that its net effect on the birth rate became ambiguous. If it, furthermore, increased infant mortality and enhanced outmigration, it becomes clear that a model which looks for simple relations between economic variables and the rate of population growth in preindustrial Europe cannot blindly be applied to the Irish case. In what follows four tables are presented, which examine the determinants of population growth, fertility and birth rates, the propensity to marry, and infant mortality.

Table 3.10 represents an attempt to analyze the determinants of population growth, both gross (columns 1 and 2) and net (columns 3–6) of emigration. The results are disappointing, to say the least. The majority of all exogenous variables have coefficients which are not significantly different from zero. Even those coefficients which are significant are sensitive to specification and cannot be considered clear rejections of the null-hypothesis that the rate of growth is independent of the exogenous variables. The only exception is the quality of housing variable, which indicates that low-quality and cheap housing led to (and possibly were also a result of) more rapid population growth. Dependency on potatoes also seems to have had some positive effect on gross population growth, and cottage industries seem to have had some positive effect on natural population growth but not on gross population growth. This finding is as expected, since while cottage industries are thought to have enhanced population growth, during the twenty years prior to the 1841 Census the crisis in cottage industry led to emigration from the regions in which it was concentrated. On the whole, however, the results are weak. The reason for the poor performance of this variant on the Malthusian equation linking the rate of population growth to economic and socioeconomic variables is simple: the dependent variable, population growth, is too aggregated and too crude. The total rate of population growth is the sum of birth, death, and migration rates.

Table 3.10 *The Determinants of Overall Population Change (t-Statistics in Parentheses)*

Independent variable	(1) Annual population growth, 1821–41	(2) Annual population growth, 1821–41	(3) Birth rate minus death rate*	(4) Birth rate minus death rate*	(5) Birth rate minus death rate†	(6) Birth rate minus death rate†
Constant	0·029 (1·69)	−0·0016 (−0·073)	−0·018 (−1·01)	0·032 (1·75)	−0·0046 (−0·24)	−0·0055 (−0·44)
Income per capita × 100	−0·088 (−1·49)	−0·016 (−0·46)	0·024 (0·66)	0·0035 (0·06)	−0·021 (−0·46)	0·012 (0·41)
Proportion Catholic	−0·0060 (−0·46)	0·0033 (0·24)	0·0097 (0·97)	−0·018 (−1·36)	−0·0095 (0·76)	0·0050 (0·71)
Potato dependency index	−0·0099‡ (−0·77)	−0·014§ (−0·74)	0·044§ (2·30)	0·048§ (2·61)	0·031§ (2·02)	0·060§ (0·39)
Percentage urban	0·015 (1·36)	0·0071 (0·78)	−0·0080 (−0·90)	−0·011 (−0·86)	−0·0033 (−0·31)	−0·012 (−2·17)
Cottage industry		0·050 (0·03)	0·033 (1·83)		0·041 (2·41)	0·019 (1·45)
Proportion manufacturing	0·0026 (0·001)	0·022 (0·90)		−0·037 (1·29)	−0·017 (−0·76)	
Capital/labor	0·0018 (1·09)			−0·0001 (−0·09)	0·0011 (0·84)	
Housing quality		0·024 (2·93)	0·014 (1·63)			0·022 (3·38)
Literacy rate	−0·020 (−1·52)	−0·0056 (−0·35)	0·021 (1·32)	0·0002 (0·012)	0·020 (1·43)	0·019 (1·54)
F	1·62	2·78	4·85	3·28	3·05	8·83
(d.f.)	(7,24)	(8,23)	(7,24)	(7,24)	(8,23)	(7,24)

* Death rate, version A (see Table 3.5).
† Death rate, version B (see Table 3.5).
‡ Potato acreage per capita.
§ Potato acreage per total cultivated land.

Each of these components is by itself a function of other variables: the birth rate, for instance, depends on the propensity to marry, on marital fertility, and on the age and sex composition of the population. The death rate depends on the adult death and infant-mortality rate, the latter again possibly a function of fertility. Even if these subcomponents all depend on the exogenous variables of the model, there is no reason to suppose that they all depend on it in the same way. As a result, the total derivatives of the measures of population growth with respect to the exogenous variables constitute the sum of many partial effects which offset each other. The crude Malthusian model which sets population change as a function of economic variables is wholly inappropriate, and in this sense the model is rejected. It is, however, of some interest to examine in some greater detail three separate determinants of population change: nuptiality, fertility, and infant mortality.

Table 3.11 The Determinants of the Propensity to Marry (t-Statistics in Parentheses)

(a) Rural males

Independent variable	(1) Singulate mean age*	(2) Singulate mean age*	(3) Median age*	(4) Median age*	(5) μ†	(6) μ†
Constant	33·24 (8·73)	31·60 (5·70)	18·84 (7·12)	28·28 (11·35)	0·67 (5·00)	0·52 (4·97)
Income per capita	-0·012 (-0·14)	0·0054 (0·06)	0·12 (1·34)	0·036 (0·71)	-0·0038 (-1·73)	-0·0029 (-1·38)
Proportion Catholic	0·010 (0·47)	0·016 (0·49)	0·042 (2·17)	0·017 (1·22)	-0·084 (-1·04)	-0·018 (-0·31)
Potato dependency index	-0·39§ (-0·08)	1·44‡ (0·44)	5·06‡ (2·23)	3·14§ (1·16)	-0·103‡ (-1·28)	-0·016§ (-0·14)
Percentage urban	-4·48 (-2·61)	-4·19 (-2·27)	-3·83 (-2·52)	-4·35 (-3·46)	0·125 (2·80)	0·115 (2·19)
Cottage industry	-5·70 (-1·42)	-4·19 (-0·83)		-4·85 (-1·93)	0·148 (1·20)	0·213 (2·02)
Proportion manufacturing		0·092 (0·016)	3·86 (0·92)		-0·123 (-0·91)	
Capital/labor			0·06 (0·27)			
Housing quality	-7·25 (-3·66)	-7·35 (-3·93)		-5·71 (-4·86)	0·135 (2·97)	0·174 (3·55)
Literacy rate	1·98 (0·53)	2·46 (0·65)	7·96 (3·49)	3·55 (1·57)	-0·101 (-1·11)	-0·054 (-0·57)
F	7·15	6·07	8·69	18·21	10·88	14·25
(d.f.)	(7,24)	(8,23)	(7,24)	(8,23)	(8,23)	(7,24)

(b) Rural females

Independent variable	(1) Singulate mean age*	(2) Singulate mean age*	(3) Median age*	(4) Median age*	(5) μ†	(6) μ†
Constant	13·29 (2·52)	22·77 (6·06)	23·75 (9·18)	24·36 (10·21)	0·80 (6·51)	0·60 (5·30)
Income per capita	0·44 (2·44)	0·21 (3·53)	0·076 (1·91)		-0·0040 (-2·09)	-0·0033 (-1·41)
Proportion Catholic	0·032 (0·81)	0·023 (1·00)	0·011 (0·74)	0·0076 (0·49)	-0·00069 (-0·94)	0·00013 (0·21)
Potato dependency index	7·84‡ (1·99)	8·01‡ (3·67)	4·96‡ (3·30)	4·15‡ (2·90)	-0·25‡ (-3·52)	-0·208 (-1·59)
Percentage urban	-7·02 (-2·06)	-2·23 (-1·52)	-1·60 (-1·57)	-0·17 (-0·17)	0·025 (0·53)	0·082 (1·44)
Cottage industry		4·75 (1·37)	1·05 (0·44)	2·12 (0·86)	-0·12 (-1·02)	0·079 (0·69)
Proportion manufacturing	9·97 (1·15)	2·23 (0·55)	0·021 (0·08)	-0·37 (-0·14)	-0·087 (-0·66)	
Capital/labor	-0·45 (-0·89)			0·32 (2·85)		
Housing quality		-11·30 (-9·13)	-6·81 (-7·99)		0·20 (4·93)	0·24 (4·56)
Literacy rate	5·74 (1·37)	-1·44 (-0·56)	1·27 (0·71)	0·95 (0·55)	-0·14 (-1·64)	-0·085 (-0·83)
F	6·99	36·48	26·67	23·57	20·58	15·65
(d.f.)	(7,24)	(8,23)	(8,23)	(8,23)	(8,23)	(7,24)

* Measures the propensity to marry inversely.

† Proportion persons aged 17–45 married, standardized for age distribution; measures propensity to marry directly.

‡ Potato acreage per capita.

Table 3.11 presents an attempt to identify the determinants of the propensity to marry. On the whole, these equations are much superior to the regressions in Table 3.10: the F-statistics are without exception significant at the 1 per cent level. None the less, the regressions still display some sensitivity to specification, and the results should be interpreted with caution. A few negative results are rather striking: religion seems to have no influence whatsoever on the propensity to marry. Holding other factors equal, the proportion Catholics in each county, which varied from 98·14 percent in Clare to 28·24 percent in Antrim, has no discernible effect on the various measures. Nor do the occupational structure (as measured by the proportion families employed predominantly in manufacturing) or the agricultural capital–labor ratio (as measured by the value of livestock per rural inhabitant). The literacy rate, too, has a rather ambiguous effect on the propensity to marry. While in most cases the coefficients of this variable have the right sign, their significance is too sensitive to specification to put much faith in.

Cottage industry, often claimed to be a central factor in the marriage behavior of society, does not appear very significant, but still seems to have the expected effect as far as males are concerned. The female propensity to marry appears unaffected by it. Insofar as birth rates were far more affected by the *female* propensity to marry, this result undermines the view that cottage industry greatly stimulated population growth by reducing the average age at marriage. For income, the reverse is true: the male propensity to marry seems independent of the level of income per capita, while the "Connell-effect", which links early marriage to poverty, seems to be operative for women. Even more surprising is the result that the dependency on potatoes does not seem to have a significant effect on the male propensity to marry, but apparently led to later and fewer marriages among women. This, indeed, is a perplexing result, until one recalls the increasing difficulty of securing potato land on the eve of the famine. High potato acreage could mean that most of the land which was appropriate for small-scale tillage farms was already in use and that landlords were reluctant to provide more. It is not clear, however, why that would affect women but not men.

The proximity of urban areas, with the perceived opportunities they provided to males, leads to significantly increased propensities to marry. The quality of housing variable strongly affects the propensity to marry: a large supply of cheap, fourth-class houses reduced the price of forming a family and thus enabled the average Irishman or Irishwoman to marry younger. Again, the possibility that causality runs in both directions cannot be ruled out here.

From a strictly Malthusian view nuptiality is interesting largely because of its effect on the birth rate. On a high level of abstraction this attitude is justified, but in practice the effect of the propensity to marry on the birth rate is not always straightforward. Regressing the crude birth rate on both female and male propensities to marry yields values of R-squared of about 0·50. In other words, 50 percent of the variation in the birth rate is unaccounted for by the marriage variables.[11] The effect of the male propensity to marry is negligible, that of women important

Table 3.12 *The Determinants of Birth and Fertility Rates (t-Statistics in Parentheses)*

Independent variable	(1) Crude birth rate (rural plus urban)	(2) Crude birth rate (rural plus urban)	(3) Crude birth rate (rural areas)	(4) Crude birth rate (rural areas)	(5) Total fertility, Coale index (rural areas)	(6) Total fertility, Coale index (rural areas)	(7) Total fertility standard def. (rural plus urban)	(8) Total fertility standard def. (rural areas)	(9) Marital fertility Coale index (rural areas)	(10) Marital fertility Coale index (rural areas)	(11) Marital fertility standard def. (rural plus urban)	(12) Marital fertility standard def. (rural areas)
Constant	0·023	0·010	0·019	0·0065	0·26	0·069	0·057	0·125	0·44	0·37	0·29	0·20
	(1·06)	(0·72)	(0·92)	(0·43)	(1·15)	(0·48)	(0·80)	(1·07)	(1·11)	(1·12)	(1·48)	(0·85)
Income per capita	-0·00010	0·000095	0·000001	0·000046	-0·0017	0·0012	0·0005	-0·0012		0·0043		0·0085
	(-0·20)	(0·28)	(-0·004)	(0·15)	(-0·33)	(0·36)	(0·33)	(-0·44)		(0·63)		(-1·53)
Proportion Catholic	0·0066	0·011	0·0046	0·014	0·036	0·12	0·05	0·024	0·094	0·24	0·0039	0·057
	(0·48)	(1·42)	(0·37)	(1·68)	(0·25)	(1·51)	(1·21)	(0·31)	(0·36)	(1·26)	(0·03)	(0·38)
Potato dependency index	0·036†	0·021†	0·015*	0·024†	0·44†	0·21†	0·062†	0·21†	0·55†	0·62†	0·20*	0·32†
	(2·19)	(1·15)	(1·25)	(1·46)	(2·49)	(1·16)	(0·70)	(2·30)	(2·28)	(1·70)	(1·68)	(1·72)
Percentage urban	0·021	0·015	0·014	0·0064	0·092	0·014	0·013	0·045	0·11	-0·16	0·053	0·047
	(1·79)	(2·35)	(2·09)	(0·84)	(0·75)	(0·22)	(0·40)	(0·70)	(0·65)	(-0·95)	(0·66)	(0·39)
Cottage industry	0·039	0·026	0·028	0·027	0·45	0·29	0·14	0·22	0·57	0·32	0·17	0·30
	(2·11)	(1·76)	(1·49)	(1·78)	(2·30)	(1·92)	(1·90)	(2·16)	(1·37)	(0·93)	(0·83)	(1·47)
Proportion manufacturing	-0·032				-0·44			-0·21	-0·32		-0·14	-0·17
	(-1·30)				(-1·72)			(-1·56)	(-0·72)		(-0·63)	(-0·62)
Capital/labor	0·0006				0·011				0·016		0·0054	0·026
	(0·44)				(0·72)				(0·84)		(0·59)	(1·65)
Housing quality		0·016	0·018	0·017		0·22	0·10		-0·012	-0·099	-0·0066	
		(2·15)	(2·56)	(2·34)		(2·87)	(2·77)		(-0·09)	(-0·62)	(-0·10)	
Literacy rate	0·011	0·011	0·0087	0·017	0·090	1·00	0·032	0·056	0·37	0·43	0·084	0·42
	(0·70)	(0·81)	(0·61)	(1·23)	(0·55)	(0·70)	(0·46)	(0·64)	(1·26)	(1·41)	(0·60)	(2·43)
F	2·78	3·95	3·85	5·55	4·83	7·96	6·46	4·34	0·98	0·52	0·45	1·22
(d.f.)	(8,23)	(7,24)	(8,23)	(7,24)	(8,23)	(7,24)	(7,24)	(8,23)	(8,23)	(7,24)	(8,23)	(8,23)

* Potato acreage per capita.

but by no means so strong as to exclude other variables from affecting the birth rate in a significant way. For one thing, a weak but suggestive negative correlation exists between the propensity to marry and marital fertility.[12]

The reason for this negative correlation is possibly the so-called "negative duration effect" (Page, 1978), which postulates that later-marrying women will tend to have higher age-specific fertility. The "negative duration effect" could be consistent with some degree of contraceptive behavior, but could also be due to the reduced fecundity resulting from earlier birth.[13] On the other hand, total fertility will, of course, be positively correlated with the propensity to marry. Consequently, the birth and fertility rates are connected to the exogenous economic variables by a combination of different links. The reduced form estimates presented in Table 3.12 do not allow the identification of some parameters, and indeed it is possible that some variables which appear to have insignificant coefficients conceal the mutually offsetting influences of counteracting effects.

Table 3.12 presents the regression results dealing with the birth and fertility rates in Ireland. On the whole, the table indicates that the attempt to find the causes of the high birth rate in Ireland is at best only partially successful. The F-statistics are low, and the vast majority of coefficients are insignificant or sensitive to changes in specification. It is possible that cross-sectional data are simply inadequate for the analysis of reproductive behavior in prefamine Ireland. It is also possible, however, that a population comparatively homogeneous with respect to diet, climate, cultural traditions, and social structure simply does not provide sufficient variation in the dependent variables. Still, a few tentative conclusions can be drawn from Table 3.12. First, neither income nor religion seems to have had a significant effect on reproductive behavior. The dependency on potatoes seems to have increased fertility, which is quite a surprising finding given our earlier finding that potatoes led to delayed marriages among women. Cottage industry, too, has the expected effect on total birth rates and total fertility rates, although it has no effect on marital-fertility rates. The housing-quality variable, too, has the expected effect. Literacy seems to have no clear-cut demographic importance, and the proximity of towns raises the crude birth rate but not the rate of fertility. The effect of urbanization is explained by the disproportionately large number of women living in urban areas and their surroundings. Finally, columns 9–12 show decisively that the exogenous variables of our model cannot account in any way for marital fertility, whether adjusted for age structure or not. In the majority of these regressions, the F-statistics are less than unity.

To summarize, the attempts to explain the components of demographic behavior in prefamine Ireland are quite disappointing. This is consistent with other work for Flanders and Prussia, in which the surmised relation between population growth and economic variables (especially cottage industry) could not be verified econometrically (Pollard, 1981, pp. 75–7). It would not be correct to conclude, however, that demographic behavior was not substantially affected by economic variables. Rather, the investigator is faced with the frustrating dilemma that the relation he seeks to investigate is rather delicate, and the crude nature of both the left-hand and the right-hand variables is such that standard techniques are barely adequate to isolate the causal connections postulated by economic analysis. It is clear, however, that whether the economic variables affected marriage propensities and birth rates or not, they did not have a dominant influence. The weakness of these effects is not surprising: despite a variety in economic experience in Western Europe, the demographic development shows a comparatively uniform pattern over 1750–1850 (with the notable exclusion of France). In econometric terms this means that there is perhaps too little variability in the dependent variables. Something similar is true for the various regions of Ireland, which explains the mediocre and ambiguous results reported in Tables 3.10–3.12.

We turn finally to the issue of infant mortality. Infant-mortality rates are more interesting than general mortality rates, because there is no reason to suppose *a priori* that the latter varied systematically among counties. The late 1830s and 1840 were not especially bad years, and it is only during disasters that the variance in cross-sectional death rates becomes interesting. The excess mortality rates during the Great Famine are thus of interest, and will be analyzed in a later chapter. Infant-mortality rates, however, were an important mechanism through which preindustrial society is supposed to have regulated its magnitude, so it is of some interest here.

The results of the regressions are presented in Table 3.13. The regressions are significant, with F-statistics considerably in excess of $3\cdot63$, which is the critical value of $F(6,25)$ at the 1 percent significance level. None the less, the interpretation of the results here, too, should be carried out with caution. Income per capita, for instance, has a consistently negative effect on infant-mortality rates—as is expected—but the statistical significance is low. The dependency on potatoes and proportion Catholic both seem to have had an effect on infant mortality: the potato index tends to be negatively associated with infant mortality, the proportion Catholic, positively. When *both* are included in the equation, the effect of religion tends to swamp the effect of potatoes, but *a priori* reasoning suggests that this may be a spurious result. When the proportion Catholic is omitted from the regressions, the effects of the potato index is significant at the 10 percent level or better. The percentage urban has the expected positive effect. Interestingly, this effect is sustained when the infant-mortality rate is calculated for rural areas as well. Cottage industry and literacy rates have no systematic and consistent effect on infant-mortality rates. Housing quality has the expected sign and is statistically significant. The plausible hypothesis that infant mortality tended to be high wherever birth or fertility rates were high is inconsistent with the data (columns 5, 6, 8, and 9). Including the crude death rate of the population as an independent variable as a proxy for the 'unhealthiness' of a county improves the overall performance of the equation as measured by the F-statistic but does not significantly reduce the explanatory power of the other included

Table 3.13 *The Determinants of Infant-Mortality Rates (t-Statistics in Parentheses)*

Independent variable	(1) Infant mortality rate A, rural areas*	(2) Infant mortality rate A, rural areas	(3) Infant mortality rate B, urban and rural areas†	(4) Infant mortality rate B, urban and rural areas*	(5) Infant mortality rate A, rural areas*	(6) Infant mortality rate A, rural areas*	(7) Infant mortality rate A, rural areas*	(8) Infant mortality rate B, urban and rural areas†	(9) Infant mortality rate B, urban and rural areas†	(10) Infant mortality rate B, urban and rural areas†
Constant	0·047 (0·50)	0·077 (0·58)	0·25 (3·92)	0·23 (1·57)	0·053 (0·54)	0·24 (2·97)	−0·078 (−0·57)	0·28 (3·26)	0·27 (3·53)	−0·029 (−0·40)
Income per capita	−0·0016 (−0·58)	−0·0039 (−1·52)	−0·0033 (−1·08)	−0·0044 (−1·56)	−0·0015 (−0·55)	−0·0036 (−1·14)	−0·0036 (−1·54)	−0·0042 (−1·59)	−0·0037 (−1·40)	−0·0022 (−1·22)
Proportion Catholic	0·0015 (2·72)	0·0018 (2·66)		0·00093 (1·23)	0·0015 (2·63)		0·0015 (2·35)			−0·00018 (−0·36)
Potato dependency index	−0·11¶ (−0·77)	−0·095‖ (−0·95)	−0·25¶ (−1·68)	−0·14‖ (−1·33)	−0·099¶ (−0·66)	−0·24¶ (−1·59)	−0·028¶ (−0·29)	−0·21‖ (−2·25)	−0·20¶ (−1·53)	
Percentage urban	0·13 (2·57)	0·088 (1·66)	0·29 (4·95)	0·24 (4·09)	0·13 (2·50)	0·12 (1·96)	−0·028 (−0·41)	0·18 (3·08)	0·25 (3·52)	0·025 (0·41)
Cottage industry	0·24 (2·16)	0·24 (1·57)	−0·33 (−0·64)	0·050 (0·30)	0·24 (2·11)	−0·033 (−0·60)	0·28 (2·00)	−0·14 (−2·34)	−0·049 (−0·86)	0·012 (0·13)
Housing quality	0·078 (1·27)		0·15 (2·31)		0·083 (1·25)	0·12 (1·51)		0·12 (1·83)	0·17 (2·19)	0·12 (3·07)
Literacy rate		0·73 (0·66)	−0·097 (−0·92)	−0·059 (−0·49)		−0·060 (−0·54)	0·090 (0·90)		−0·071 (−0·65)	
General death rate							6·89 (2·40)			10·56 (4·87)
Birth or fertility rate					−0·38‡ (−0·22)	0·14‡ (0·39)		0·31§ (0·18)	−0·14‡ (−0·37)	
F	6·24	6·28	9·37	9·46	5·15	3·31	7·23	10·15	5·73	16·82
(d.f.)	(6,25)	(6,25)	(6,25)	(6,25)	(7,24)	(7,24)	(7,24)	(6,25)	(7,24)	(6,25)

* Computed from data from 1840; see Table 3.10; version A is based on 1840 data, version B is an average for 1838–40 (see Table 3.5).
† Computed as an average for 1838–40.
‡ General fertility rate.
§ Crude birth rate.
‖ Potato acreage per capita.
¶ Potato acreage per total cultivated land.

regressors. This implies that omitted variables uncorrelated with the independent variables explain an important part of the variance of infant-mortality rates. Variations in climate, drinking-water quality, hygienic habits, and similar variables come to mind.

(4)   Some Further Reflections on Population in the Prefamine Economy

Irish population grew rapidly in the century preceding the famine. Its rate of growth was only slightly slower than that of Great Britain, and this difference vanishes and probably is reversed if we take into account emigration, including over 500,000 Irishmen who migrated to Great Britain. Traditionally the Irish were described as an early marrying, highly prolific people. Population growth slowed down on the eve of the famine in this view, but this deceleration was too late and too little. More recent scholarship has cast doubt on this interpretation. Cullen (1972, p. 118) has maintained that on the eve of the famine the birth rate and the propensity to marry in Ireland were not much different than in other European countries, which is confirmed by the data presented in Section 2. Irish marriage patterns, on the whole, were consistent with Hajnal's European pattern. The picture emerging from anecdotal and impressionistic evidence indicating a seemingly incredibly early age at which Irish women married simply does not apply to the bulk of the population.

But marriage ages do not tell the entire story. Birth rates in Ireland were high due to the high fertility of Irish women, and especially due to high marital fertility. As is well known, this feature of Ireland was preserved after the famine: Irish birth rates fell precipitously, but this fall was wholly due to a decline in the propensity to marry, not to a decline in marital fertility. Why were Irish marital fertility rates so high? In the absence of age-specific marital fertility data, it is not possible to decompose the high rates of fertility into a higher natural-fertility effect and a lack of fertility-control effect. It stands to reason, however, that both influences were at work. By the middle of the nineteenth century many Europeans were controlling their fertility in the sense that they were having fewer children than biologically possible given their ages at marriage. While we cannot be sure that this did not occur altogether in prefamine Ireland, it seems likely that the phenomenon was less widespread. Connell (1950a, p. 50) shows that the writings of contemporaries provide no hint about birth-control practices in Ireland. Arthur Young noted the affinity of the Irish for children: "children are not burthensome. In all enquiries I made into the state of the poor, I found their happiness and ease relative to the number of children" (Young, 1892, Vol. 1, p. 120). Townsend (1815, Vol. 1, p. 90) observed that the Irish derived their happiness from marrying early and living in "a group of smiling children". As modern economists such as Lebergott (1975, pp. 33–43) have argued, such preferences make comparisons of income per capita particularly hazardous, since in a society like Ireland a rise in population might increase economic welfare while at the same time in all likelihood reduce income per capita.

A high preference for children could stem from sources other than a high "utility" obtained from them directly. Children in all preindustrial societies worked and thus constituted a form of investment. Wakefield (1812, Vol. 1, p. 512) noted that children are thought "a valuable acquisition [*sic*], on account of the labour which they can perform when they grow up". There is some doubt, however, how much opportunity there was in Ireland for children to make important contributions to the household before puberty. In Ulster, where the linen industry was a major source of income, children were no doubt part of the domestic manufacturing sector. In areas where domestic industry was of less importance, children did not have much to do (Mason, 1814–19, Vol. 2, p. 73; Townsend, 1815, Vol. 1, pp. 209–10). With the decline of cottage industry in the late 1820s and 1830s, the economic importance of child labor declined, since the "jobs" destroyed by the collapse of the linen industry were not replaced by employment opportunities in factories and mines. The testimonies given before the Poor Law commissioners provide no support for the hypothesis that child labor was sufficiently important to be a factor in determining larger desired family sizes. The tables in appendix D to the report (utilized in the computation of the wage averages) do not separate women's and children's earnings, but the "baronial examinations" preceding them (Great Britain, 1836b, Vol. XXXIb, pp. 86–92) leave little doubt on the issue. Children were universally reported to have worked very little besides weeding the crops of their parents for a few days a year. Almost nowhere were children hired for money wages, and in the family farm and cottage the activities of children under the age of 14 years were minimal. A King's county witness asserted that there is "nothing to be earned by labourers' children until they grow 12 to 14 years old" (p. 80). For adolescents aged 14–17, the situation was only marginally better. One Co. Meath witness (p. 32) estimated that a young worker could count on only seventy days of work a year. The picture is complicated by the fact that employment opportunities for women were almost as rare as those for children. Low wages for women would tend to reduce the opportunity cost of children and, thus, to offset in part the absence of child labor.

A third possible cause of high marital fertility is the absence of a Poor Law in Ireland before 1838. As economists have long realized, people decide to have children not only for investment or consumption reasons, but also because children serve as insurance policies and pensions. An Irishman who became too ill or too feeble to feed himself did not have recourse to the outdoor relief provided by the parish, as his English counterpart did. Nor did the Irish Catholic Church have any resources with which to support him. Thus, unfortunate individuals had to rely on private and voluntary charity which, although quite substantial, was widely quoted to be irregular and insufficient (for example, Sadler, 1829, p. 60; OSM, box 27, file I; Nicholls, 1856, pp. 106, 140; Great Britain, 1835c, Vol. XXXI, pp. 310, 331, 336, 379, 482; Great Britain, 1836b, Vol. XXX, p. 25). Under these circumstances it can be understood that the "insurance motive" for having children was probably an important factor. The "pension motive" in Ireland may have been stronger than anywhere else in Europe due to the low level of monetization. After all, even in the absence of uncertainty and accidents, people have to save for their old age. Economists have pointed out (for example, Neher, 1971) that in the absence of a durable store of value, intergenerational transfers are the only way individuals can provide for their old age. The low level of commercialization, the lack of peasant ownership of land, the nondurability of the potato, and the high transaction costs associated with purchasing (rather than cultivating) potatoes imply that children in Ireland may have been an attractive form of old-age insurance. Neher (1971, pp. 386–7) argues that "share-alike" ethics are likely to evolve in societies in which the "pension motive" for children is important, since that ethic leads to automatic pensions in a world where interperiod storage of goods is impossible and financial markets are not developed. Prefamine Ireland seems a reasonable approximation to the type of peasant world assumed by Neher. None the less, the question of whether the "pension motive" was in fact a major source of high marital fertility cannot be answered except in the subjunctive mode, and a decomposition of the high fertility rates in Ireland must remain speculative at this stage of research.

In any event, it cannot be seriously doubted that part of the reason why the Irish before the famine had many children was that they wanted them. Furthermore, the regression results suggest that fecundity may also have been higher in Ireland. This higher fecundity was associated with the high-quality diet that the potato provided—the same diet which also seems to have reduced infant mortality.

What do the results of Section 4 imply for the Malthusian approach to preindustrial European societies? At least as far as prefamine Ireland is concerned, the models seem to have little explanatory power. Needless to say, this does not invalidate them as far as other countries are concerned. First, Ireland was not a typical preindustrial society. Even if the differences between Ireland and other countries may have been overstated in the past (for instance, with regard to the age at marriage), the differences remain of major importance. Secondly, the present conclusions are drawn from cross-sectional data and as a result may not constitute a fair test of hypotheses concerning the *longue durée* in other countries: the variation within one country at one point of time cannot be compared readily with the variation over centuries in larger regions. None the less, the results for the Irish case should stimulate tests of the Malthusian hypothesis in other time-periods. Malthusian models are plausible, and make economic sense, but they should not be accepted on those grounds alone. There is no reason why we should absolve them from the empirical tests to which we submit other, equally plausible, theories.

The results also indicate that more research is necessary before links can be drawn between economic developments in preindustrial society and demographic change. If such changes as the spread of cottage industry or the adoption of new crops affected female and male propensities to marry, marital fertility, and infant mortality in different and sometimes diametrically opposite ways, consequent demographic changes may have been more complex than the microstudies devoted to them seem to suppose (Fischer, 1973). To repeat: what is true for Ireland may not be necessarily valid for other areas. Malthusian or related theories will however, have to face more careful and complete testing before they can be fully accepted as a theory of population change in early modern Europe. One aspect which is especially important is to separate between *total* and *partial* effects. Discovering, for example, that agricultural areas experienced less rapid population growth than more industrialized rural regions does not allow one to conclude that there is any relation (let alone a causal one) between rural industry and demographic change. In order to draw that inference other things must be held constant. For that reason Almquist's (1977) conclusions in analyzing prefamine population change are difficult to interpret. The findings reported above are, on the whole, not inconsistent with his findings, but show that the actual relations were far more nuanced and complex than Almquist supposes, and that it is likely that he has overdrawn the role of cottage industry in determining the propensity to marry. The results also suggest that it is not possible to leap merrily from "marriage age" to "fertility" to "birth rates" to "population growth" (Fischer, 1973, among others, seems oblivious to such pitfalls in demographic modelbuilding).

Abstracting from the fact that the propensity to marry is by no means the only factor determining the birth rate (let alone the rate of population growth), we may ask ourselves to what extent our findings are consistent with a "neoclassical" theory of marriage. Such a theory would be distinguished by its assumption that aggregate data reflect the rationality of the majority of the population under examination. A first approximation to the problem would simply postulate that marriage is a desirable good for both participants (and their parents). Since marriage is costly (in the sense that housing and ultimately more food, clothing, and so on, are required) the propensity to marry is a function of income and the relative price of marriage to other consumer goods. While it may be difficult empirically to separate "income" from "price" variables, the conceptual framework is clear. Delayed marriage in order to reduce the number of children is, thus, tantamount to choosing a particular point on a budget constraint between "marriage" and "all other goods" which is *not* the corner-solution at which the number of children is maximized. Variations on this basic model could include an inheritance motive: if multiple-share bequests are the custom, there may be a tendency to have fewer children in order to avoid subdivision of the property. In that case the choice between "number of children" and "consumption of other goods" is generalized and extended to a multigenerational decision unit which we may call the family, which imposes restrictions on marriage age to protect future and yet-unborn members. Once we realize the appropriate constraints, however, the notion that marriage is a "good" can be accepted without too many qualifications.[14]

The data indicate that the propensity to marry is indeed sensitive to the "relative price" of marriage as provided by cottage industry, the cost of housing, and the proximity of cities. The income effect, however, has not been isolated. Theory predicts it should have a positive effect unless wholly offset by wealthier families attempting to protect the property of the family. Connell's view is that the effect was negative (although, as was stressed above, this is not necessarily equivalent to a negative income elasticity). The data show that income—at least as measured here—has only a small effect on either fertility, or nuptiality. Income seems to conform to its Malthusian role only in the infant-mortality equations, although even there the effect is not strong.

Why was Ireland poor? The answer does not seem to lie in the sphere of demographic change. Our attempts to find an association between population pressure and income per capita either *within* the country, or while comparing Ireland to other countries, have not been successful. In short, there is no evidence that prefamine Ireland was overpopulated in any useful sense of the word. If this conclusion is sustained by further research, it may be worthwhile to re-examine the view that the Great Famine was somehow "inevitable". Not all disasters should be regarded as "irrepressible" just because they actually occurred. It seems fair to speculate that had there been no famine, Ireland's population would have continued to grow like any other European country in the second half of the nineteenth century. Whether that in and by itself would have had any significant effect on the standard of living seems very much in doubt.

Appendix A: Estimating the Demographic Structure of Ireland on the Eve of the Famine

(1) *Birth Rates*
In order to compute the crude birth rate in prefamine Ireland, use was made of the age distribution of infants and toddlers as reported in the 1841 Census.[15] At first sight these data seem unusable, as indicated by Table 3.14, which presents the age distribution of children up to age 3 for Ireland as a whole (the county-by-county distributions have roughly the same shape).

Table 3.14   *Age Distribution of Children in Ireland, 1841*

Age	Number of children	Age	Number of children
1 month	26,892	8 months	8,926
2 months	21,699	9 months	24,729
3 months	27,334	10 months	10,051
4 months	17,374	11 months	7,798
5 months	12,164	12 months	158,958
6 months	35,221	2 years	230,804
7 months	10,278	3 years	218,149

Source: Great Britain, 1843, Vol. XXIV, p. 488.

In addition to considerable heaping around the ages of 6 months and 12 months, the table raises some rather serious questions as to the overall reliability of age statistics. Added up by years, the table seems to indicate that the number of children less than 1 year is 202,466, those aged 1–2 number 158,958, while those aged 2–3 number 230,804. Such an age distribution would appear absurd.

Consider, however, the possibility that a person whose age was given as X was not aged between X and $X + 1$, as we conventionally assume today, but actually aged between $X - 1$ and X. For instance, the 26,892 children aged "1 month" in Table 3.14 were actually born within the thirty days prior to Census day, and the 230,804 children designated as aged 2 years are actually 12–24 months old. If this assumption is correct, it would simultaneously solve two riddles which bedevil Table 3.14. First, it would return to existence all infants aged 30 days or less, a remarkable absence first noted by Tucker (1970) and recently reemphasized by Lee (1981b). Secondly, it would restore, to some extent at least, the shape of the age distribution.

Is the assumption correct? Incontrovertible evidence supporting it is supplied by the Census itself. If the assumption is true, the 158,958 children defined by the Census as aged "12 months" were actually aged 11–12 months. If so, the Census-takers must have thought that the total number of children aged up to 12 months was 202,466 plus 158,958 = 361,424. Plate 5 (opposite p. liv) in the Census quite unmistakably registers the number of children aged 1 year or less at about 360,000.

Unfortunately, the corrected procedure still does not produce a completely realistic picture. Clearly, the downward slope of the shape of the age distribution is overstated. Even with extremely high infant-mortality rates, it seems unreasonable that the number of children aged 1–2 years is only 64 percent of those under the age of 1. The reason for this anomaly is that some children reported by the Census to be "aged 12 months" were in actuality in the 1–2 years bracket. Since their number is unknown, it would be incorrect to use the number of children aged up to 1 year as an indication of the number of survivors of those born in the year before the Census.

To circumvent the problem of heaping, I shall use the number of children reported to be "aged 1 month" and thus in reality aged 30 days or less and multiply by twelve to convert it into an annual number of births. The biases and pitfalls associated with this procedure will be discussed below, but it is also important to emphasize the procedure's advantages. First, it does not rely on memory but on actually enumerated persons. Secondly, it reduces the biases caused by infant mortality. The number of children aged 1 month or less falls short of the number of children born during those thirty days by a factor equal to the probability of a child to die in its first 15 days of life. This is not by any means a negligible figure, but it is small compared to the probability of a child dying in its first 6 months. Moreover, the reported infant mortality of very young infants probably suffered somewhat less from under-reporting than that of all children.

The procedure used is subject to three sources of potential bias which require some further examination. The first is that there may have been heaping at the youngest age, that is, children actually aged older than 1 month may have been reported to be less that 1 month old. The chances of a major distortion in our estimate due to this factor are small. The total number of children aged 0–3 months is 75,925, which averages to 25,308 for each month. A plausible rate of infant mortality is consistent with a cohort aged less than 1 month of 26,892. Secondly, the probability of death in the first 15 days must be computed. The Census, in its appendix entitled "Tables of death" (Great Britain, 1843, Vol. XXIV, appendix, pp. 1–205), provides age-specific death rates for every year in the decade before 1841. There is reason to believe that these data contain serious undercounting.[16] The number of children reported to have died at age 1 month or less in 1840 was added to the estimated number of annual births, not corrected for underreporting, although these data, too, contain serious undercounting.

The most serious problem with the procedure is the fact that it uses the number of births during one month (the thirty days preceding Census day, 6 June 1841 to be exact) as a core which is to be blown up to an annual rate of birth typical of prefamine Ireland. Was this month an "average" month? There are two separate issues here: was the birth rate in May and early June typical of the monthly average for the entire year? And was the birth rate in 1841 representative of the decades before the famine? Some evidence can be put forward from other countries which strongly suggest that May 1841 was indeed a representative month.[17] But direct evidence from Ireland itself is necessary here, since the entire set of demographic estimates hinges on the birth-rate estimate.

Table 3.15   *Seasonality Index for Births, 1837–45 (Monthly Average = 100)*

	South	West	East	Center	North-west	North-east	Total *(weighted)*	Total *(unweighted)*
January	111·3	102·1	101·0	99·6	101·9	104·0	105·1	103·3
February	106·0	105·4	96·0	103·6	97·4	99·8	102·0	101·4
March	115·4	113·2	118·6	115·2	112·9	115·1	115·4	115·1
April	107·0	106·3	110·8	111·7	103·4	108·6	108·0	108·0
May	104·4	110·0	110·0	108·3	109·8	99·7	106·8	107·0
June	101·7	98·9	98·9	104·2	98·3	101·3	100·8	100·6
July	94·2	95·0	95·1	98·6	99·7	101·6	96·4	97·4
August	87·3	91·3	95·6	98·4	93·4	102·1	92·8	94·7
September	87·6	92·3	93·9	93·1	96·1	88·6	91·1	91·9
October	90·5	91·7	92·5	88·1	95·9	86·3	91·0	90·8
November	94·3	93·1	88·1	85·0	91·7	97·1	91·6	91·6
December	100·5	100·7	99·6	94·1	99·5	95·8	98·9	98·4
Census month	103·8	107·4	107·4	107·4	107·1	100·1	105·4	105·5

Source: Sample of Irish parish records; see text.

Parish records in the National Library in Dublin were used in order to evaluate the representativeness of the May 1841 birth rate in Ireland itself. Altogether there are 469 parishes for which birth records for the years 1835–45 are available. From these, seventy randomly selected parishes were chosen and the number of births for each of the 108 months over January 1837–December 1845 counted from the registers. Since the sample was not stratified, the parishes are not evenly divided over the country. The west, where few parish records survive, and the Ulster counties, where the proportion of Protestants (not included in the sample) was high, are relatively underrepresented, whereas the south and the midlands are heavily represented. For this reason, the computations were carried out on a regional basis, for which Ireland was divided into six regions. In Table 3.15 the seasonal indices are presented on a monthly basis, and in Table 3.16 the number of births in 1841 and the number of births in the Census month are given. As can be verified, the year 1841 was by and large a representative year, but the thirty days prior to 6 June (the "Census month") had about 5·5 percent more births than the average month. All in all, the bias resulting from the use of the births in the month prior to the Census is at most 8 percent. Correcting this bias on a county-by-county level is, however, not possible since in spite of the large size of the parish record baptism sample (a total of 117,474 births were counted) it would still suffer from small-sample bias: the average number of births for the month prior to the Census for each county is only thirty-four.

Table 3.16   *Births in Census Year and Census Month (Averages, 1837–45 =100)*

	South	*West*	*East*	*Center*	*North-west*	*North-east*	*Total (weighted)*	*Total (unweighted)*
1841	101·2	96·8	102·9	108·2	102·8	92·8	101·6	100·8
Census month, 1841	101·8	112·3	115·6	119·8	111·0	88·0	107·8	108·1

Source: Sample of Irish parish records; see text.

To see how the calculations were carried out for each county, consider the computation of the birth rate for Ireland as a whole. The total number of children aged 1 month or less was 26,892. Multiplying by twelve yields 322,704. To this number we add the total number of children reported to have died before the age of 1 month in 1840 and divide by two, yielding 322,704 + 6920/2 = 326,264.[18] This implies a birth rate of 39·9 per 1,000. As noted, this estimate is somewhat too high, since the number of births in the month before the Census was higher than average. There are, however, a number of downward biases which partially offset the upward bias. For one thing the estimate of infant mortality is definitely too low, as it is an annual number (and thus not subject to seasonality bias) and since 1840 was a year of unusually low births (5·5 percent below the average 1837–45). More serious is the assumption that the probability of infant mortality is uniformly distributed over the first thirty days of life. As this probability is clearly declining, the probability of a child dying in its first fifteen days is underestimated. In addition, the underreporting of infant mortality was rather severe, as will be shown below. The upper-bound estimates in Table 3.1 are uncorrected estimates, while the lower-bound estimates divide the county-by-county estimates by the bottom line of Table 3.15 prior to aggregation to the province level.

(2)   *Death and Migration Rates*

Once we have estimated the crude birth rate, it is easy enough to estimate the total crude death rate residually. It is far more complicated to arrive at county-by-county estimates of the annual death rate. The reason for this is that we have a total estimate of outmigration from Ireland during 1821–41 but the flow of emigrants is not broken down county-by-county. There are two alternative ways to solve the problem. One is to use the reported death figures for 1840. Since the correct aggregate death rate for the country as a whole was available, an under-reporting factor was computed, and each county's death rate was blown up by the correction factor. The accuracy of this estimate depends on the assumption that the variation in death and underreporting in the 1841 Census was relatively small and random. The underreporting stems primarily from deaths occurring in families which had no survivors in 1841 or deaths that were "forgotten". There is no particular reason to suppose that the proportion of such "forgotten deaths" would vary greatly from county to county.

The alternative version of the prefamine death rate was obtained by estimating the county-by-county breakdown of emigration for the period 1821-41, and then computing the death rates as a residual. The county-by-county breakdown of emigration is obtained by using a technique first suggested by Cousens (1965), but which cannot be used directly due to unacceptable inaccuracies in Cousens's original procedure.[19] The computation is carried out as follows: consider the cohort members who were in the age bracket 11–20 in 1821. It seems reasonable to assume that in the ensuing twenty years, mortality among persons in this cohort was comparatively low, while their propensity to emigrate was high. Total net outmigration of members of this cohort is by definition equal to:

$$T^i = Q^i_{21} - Q^i_{41} - H^i, i = 1, \ldots, 32 , \qquad (A1)$$

where Q^i_j ($j = 1821, 1841$) are the number of persons in this cohort in county i at time j, and H is the total number of cohort members who died in this period. To compute H^i, we have to assume that the age-specific death rates reported for the year 1840 in the 1841 Census are representative of the mean death rate for the period 1821–41 as a whole. Multiplying the reported death rates by the correction factor for under-reporting we can compute H simply from:

$$H^i = Q^i_{21} [1 - (1 - p^i)^{20}], i = 1, \ldots, 32 , \qquad (A2)$$

where p is the average probability of an average member of the cohort to die in any year in the period 1821–41, and is a weighted average of the annual age-specific death rates in 1840.[20] We then calculate the gross share of each county in total annual outmigration as:

$$\beta_i = \frac{T_i}{\sum\limits_{i=1}^{32} T_i} . \qquad (A3)$$

The interpretation of the βs is *total* net outmigration shares of each county. As such, they are not accurate estimators of a county's share in total *overseas* migration, since they include both overseas migration (which was always positive), and internal migration (which was negative if a county was a net recipient of internal immigrants). For the present purposes, it seems unwarranted to ignore internal migration. The 1841 Census provides a way of dealing with this problem, since it lists all persons who were not living in the counties in which they were born. Assume that all such persons aged 31–40 in 1841 did, in fact, migrate in the period 1821–41. If I_i is *net* outmigration to other counties, that is, the number of persons born in county i but living in another county minus those born in other counties and living in county i, let J_i be $\lambda_i I_i$, where λ_i is the ratio of those aged 31–40 to all adults over 16 in 1841 in county i. Since $\sum_i J_i = 0$, define:

$$\alpha_i = \frac{(T_i - J_i)}{\sum\limits_{i=1}^{32} T_i}, \qquad (A4)$$

which is the true share of county i in net overseas migration (immigration into Ireland was ignored).

Given estimates of α and β, they can be applied to the nationwide emigration figure and, thus, be used to estimate the number of people leaving each county every year in the period 1821–41 for Great Britain and North America. Since we assume that the birth rates calculated for 1840 obtained throughout the period 1821–41, an alternative set of death rates can be obtained by solving:

$$P_{ij} = P_{ij-1} e^{(b_i - d_i)} - \beta_i E_j, \qquad \begin{array}{l} i = 1, 2, \ldots, 32 \\ j = 1822, 1823, \ldots, 1841 \end{array} \qquad (A5)$$

for the unknown values of d_i, where P_{ij} is the population of county i in year j. The initial values of P_{21i} and the final values of P_{41i} are known, so that the death rates could be computed by an iteration procedure. This provides us with an alternative estimate of the death rates before the famine. The results of the two versions are presented in Table 3.2.

(3) Marriage Propensities

The propensity to marry reflects two separate variables, the marriage *rate* (that is, the proportion population who ever entered matrimony) and the marriage *age* (that is, the age at marriage of those who did marry). The measurement of the propensity to marry can be carried out in various ways. In the extreme case, in which almost all members of society get married at some age in their life, the marriage *age* is a sufficient proxy for the propensity to marry. In the other extreme case, in which all marriages, if they take place, occur at about the same age, the proportion ever-married is the best proxy. Both of these measures need to take account of the age distribution of the population, but that does not seem a major problem in the Irish case.

Ireland does not fit into either one of these extremes. Consequently, a number of different measures have been estimated. All measures were computed from the same data (the 1841 Census) but each involves somewhat different assumptions. The following notation will be employed: the subscript i denotes different cohorts ($i = 1, 2, \ldots, 5$), referring to cohorts 17–25, 26–35, . . . , 55 +. M_{ij} is the number of persons of cohort i in county j ever-married, and P_{ij} is total size of the corresponding cohort. The 1841 Census presents the number of persons in each of the age brackets broken down by status (total, married, or widowed), sex, county, and rural vs urban areas. Divorce was not a problem in Ireland, but it is not possible to separate first from second or later marriages.

Define:

$$b_{ij} = \frac{M_{ij}}{P_{ij}}.$$

(A6)

It is tempting to use as one index the weighted average of the b_is, the weights being the relative sizes of the cohorts in the total population aged 17 and above. This index would simply be:

$$\sum_{i=1}^{5} \frac{P_{ij}}{\sum_{i=1}^{5} P_{ij}} \, b_{ij} = \frac{\sum_{i=1}^{5} M_{ij}}{\sum_{i=1}^{5} P_{ij}},$$

(A7)

which is very easy to compute but misleading in so far as it reflects different age structures in different counties. A better index is:

$$\mu_j = \sum_{i=1}^{5} \frac{\sum_{j=1}^{32} P_{ij}}{\sum_{i=1}^{5} \sum_{j=1}^{32} P_{ij}} \, b_{ij}.$$

(A8)

The advantage of μ is that it imposes on each county the constraint to have the same age distribution as the country at large. Thus, differences in μs reflect differences in the b_is only. The dimension of μ_j is a proportion.[21]

Two other measures which can be used to approximate the propensity to marry have the dimension of an age. The first is the mean and median age at first marriage. The mean age at first marriage pertains, by definition, only to those who ever got married and is not sensitive to celibacy rates. The easiest way to calculate the mean at first marriage is to use Hajnal's (1953) formula, known as Hajnal's singulate mean (HSM). For the entire population, the HSM may be approximated by the formula:

$$HSM = \frac{17 + \sum_{i=1}^{5} V_i (1 - b_i) - (1 - b_5)\, \tilde{a}_5}{b_5}$$

where

$V_i = 9$ for $i = 1$ (A9)

    $= 10$ for $i = 1, 2, 3$

    $= \tilde{a}_5 - 55$ for $i = 5$

    $\tilde{a}_5$ is the median age of the cohort aged 55 +.

Alternatively, the median age at first marriage can be computed utilizing the nuptiality functions proposed by Coale (1971). Computing the median age at first marriage in this fashion involves estimating two parameters of the nuptiality function, and is only accurate to the extent that we have correctly estimated the median age at marriage within the age brackets. The procedure also assumes that the nuptiality function of males and females in prefamine Ireland is reasonably approximated by Coale's. The results of the various estimates of the propensity to marry are presented in Table 3.3.

In order to control for celibacy as well as for the age at marriage I propose a new measure, which can be termed the Highest Celibacy Age (HCA). The measure is defined as the mean age at which an adult "loses his celibacy status". This status can be lost either by marrying, or dying. The HCA is thus formally equivalent to the mean age at marriage for those ever-married, and the mean age at death for those who died celibate. If it is assumed that life expectancy is uncorrelated with marital status, the HCA is simply a weighted average of the mean age at marriage and the life expectancy at age 17, the weights being the proportions ever-married and celibate.

An alternative source to calculate marriage ages is provided by the "Tables of marriage" provided by the 1841 Census (Great Britain, 1843, Vol. XXIV, pp. 460–87). Unfortunately, these tables present the data on the level of the provinces and the three large towns only, and thus cannot be used for purposes requiring a higher level of disaggregation. The data are based on retrospective information (asking the persons when they were married) and are, thus, a bit more suspect than the information about marital status used in Table 3.3. None the less, the information is interesting as a check especially as it concerns only marriages in which neither partner was married before.

In Table 3.17 the estimated marriage ages are presented. The table is based on a few simplifying assumptions. Since the original data are presented on a year-to-year basis for the decade 1830–40, it was decided to compute the marriage age for the persons married in 1840 only, as these would be based on the most recent memories. For comparison purposes, the 1830 data are added. The measured rise in marriage ages during 1830–40 is too small to lend much support to Connell's hypothesis that marriage ages rose during the 1830s (Connell, 1950a, pp. 41–3; Drake, 1963, pp. 309–11; Lee, 1968a, pp. 288–91). Indeed, due to the deaths of persons married in 1830, the reported age at marriage for those married in 1830 should be a bit lower than for 1840. This is so because the probability that somebody who married very young in 1830 would live to tell the Census enumerator about it in 1841 was higher than for somebody who married in 1830 at a more advanced age. The estimated marriage ages for 1830 are thus somewhat biased downward, and the data in Table 3.17 do not confirm the hypothesis that marriage ages were rising in the 1830s. The calculations themselves were carried out assuming the following mean ages: for the bracket less than 17, 17; for 17–25, 22; for 26–35, 30; for 36–45, 40; for 46–55, 50; for 55 and over, 56.

Table 3.17   *Marriage Ages in Ireland, 1840*

	Rural areas		Urban areas		Total	
	Male	Female	Male	Female	Male	Female
Ulster, excluding Belfast	27·30	24·15	26·25	23·97	27·22	24·14
Belfast	–	–	25·94	23·57	–	–
Leinster, excluding Dublin	28·58	25·17	27·60	24·68	28·40	25·10
Dublin	–	–	27·15	24·02	–	–
Munster, excluding Cork	28·08	24·50	27·19	24·57	27·94	24·51
Cork city	–	–	27·22	24·26	–	–
Connaught	27·51	23·72	26·73	23·68	27·46	23·72
Ireland, 1840	27·86	24·40	27·02	24·24	27·72	24·36
Ireland, 1830	27·58	23·86	26·82	23·59	27·47	23·82

Source: Great Britain, 1843, Vol. XXIV, pp. 460–87.

(4)   *Coale's Indices*
In order to perform the computations, it was assumed that illegitimacy was small enough to be neglected.[22] It was also necessary to re-estimate the Hutterite schedules as presented by Coale (1967) and Henry (1961), since the Irish Census reports different age brackets. Rater than convert the Irish data into five-yearly brackets as required for the Coale formula, I have re-estimated the Hutterite fertility rates to fit the Irish data, using Eaton and Mayer (1953, p. 230). These rates are as follows: for the bracket 17–25, 0·555; for the bracket 26–35, 474; for the bracket 36–45, 0·336; for the bracket 46–55, 0·052.[23] The highest value of I_m in rural areas was in Kerry (0·537), the lowest in rural Queen's (0·371). The highest rural value of I_g was observed in Cavan (0·944), and the lowest in Roscommon (0·725). Total rural fertility (I_f) was between 0·459 (Kerry) and 0·306 (Carlow).

(5)   *Infant-Mortality Rates*
Infant-mortality rates, more than the crude death rate itself, contain interesting information on the population dynamics of any society. The 1841 Census contains a wealth of age-specific mortality data in its appendix entitled "Tables of death". The figures are given for each of the individual years 1830–40, and are broken down by sex, county, and rural vs urban. The conversion of these data into infant-mortality rates

is, however, far from immediate. To envisage the compounding of the age-heaping and underreporting problems, consider the number of deaths of infants and toddlers for the country as a whole by age (Table 3.18).

Table 3.18 *Deaths by Age, 1840*

Age	Male	Female	Age	Male	Female
1 month	4,008	2,918	9 months	1,202	1,177
2 months	1,219	1,059	10 months	403	360
3 months	1,556	1,458	11 months	419	350
4 months	733	609	12 months	5,020	4,743
5 months	413	395	2 years	4,164	4,155
6 months	1,424	1,363	3 years	2,288	2,240
7 months	404	296	4 years	1,538	1,524
8 months	373	340	5 years	1,156	1,164

Source: Great Britain, 1843, Vol. XXIV, appendix, p. 182.

The heaping and definition problems which confront us here are the same as those occurring in the process of estimating the birth rate: the ostensible "absence" of children under the age of 1 month, and the heaping at 6, 9, and 12 months. Unfortunately, a simple way to cut through the heaping problems similar to the procedure used above does not exist even if it is recognized that by a child aged i we mean a child between $i - 1$ and i. Three factors interacted to make the estimates hazardous and complex: underreporting; a variable rate of mortality among children less than 1 year old; and age-heaping.

The correction procedure used below, first, corrects for underreporting, then corrects the heaping of reported live children, and then tries to adjust for infant-mortality heaping. To facilitate the exposition, define K_i as the number of children aged i months reported to be alive, $\hat{K}_1$ the number of children alive corrected for heaping, T_i the theoretical number of children who would be around in the absence of infant mortality and heaping, M_i the number of children reported to have died at age i, and $\hat{M}_i$ the number of children died at age i corrected for both heaping and infant mortality. The true measure of infant mortality is:

$$IM = \frac{\sum_{i=1}^{12} \hat{M}_i}{\sum_{i=1}^{12} T_i}. \tag{A10}$$

Now consider Table 3.14. According to the raw data, $\sum_{i=1}^{11} K_i = 202{,}466$, while $K_{12} = 158{,}958$. Obviously, K_{12} contains children who are in $\hat{K}_{12}$ (aged 11–12 months), as well as younger children (aged 9–11 months) and an unknown but large number of children aged more than 12 months. We, therefore, have to know $\sum_{i=10}^{12} \hat{K}_i$, which is equal to K_{10} plus K_{11} plus a component of K_{12}. We, first, have to compute the infant-mortality underreporting factor B, where B is the underreporting factor:

$$\sum_i T_i = \sum_i \hat{K}_i + \sum_i \hat{M}_i = \Sigma \hat{K}_i + \frac{M_i}{B}. \tag{A11}$$

If for any cumulative age bracket i heaping is small in the sense that $\sum_i \hat{K}_i = \sum_i K_i$ and that $\frac{M_i}{B} = \hat{M}_i$, equation A11 could be solved for B. Of course, there will still be *internal* heaping in this group, but that would not be relevant to the calculation.

The difficulty in computing the underreporting factor B is compounded by the uneven degree of heaping of the ages of live children and the ages-at-death of the deceased infants. Both distributions show considerable heaping at 6 months, but the age-at-death curve is far more pronounced in its heaping. To solve equation A11 for B, we have to assume that the particular age bracket for which it is solved is not too heavily affected by heaping. Some illustrative results are produced in Table 3.19 in order to demonstrate the sensitivity of our estimates to the choice of bracket.

Table 3.19   *Alternative Values of the Infant-Mortality Underreporting Factor*

Age bracket	Cumulative no. of children ΣK_i	Cumulative no. of infant deaths ΣM_i	Implied value of B
7 months	150,962	17,854	0·526
8 months	159,888	18,568	0·373
9 months	184,617	20,947	0·407
10 months	194,668	21,710	0·322
3 years	810,377	45,089	0·362

Note: Computed from Tables 3.14 and 3.18. Values of B computed from equation A11 and the assumption of a birth rate of 38·5 per 1,000 spread evenly over the year.

The value of B used was computed from the 9-months bracket, that is, $B = 0·407$. At 9 months the effect of heaping was likely to have been small, since it fell between the two heaping centers of 6 months and 12 months. It also happens to be the case that 0·407 is precisely the mean value of B for the four brackets of 7–10 months. We now need to compute the values of $\sum_{i=10}^{12} \hat{K}_i$ and $\sum_{i=10}^{12} \hat{M}_i$. To do this, we use two equations. The first is the identity

$$\sum_{i=1}^{12} T_i = \sum_{i=1}^{9} T_i + \sum_{i=10}^{12} \hat{K}_i + \sum_{i=10}^{12} \hat{M}_i. \tag{A12}$$

The second equation is based on three assumptions. The first is that $\hat{K}_9 + \hat{K}_{10} = K_9 + K_{10}$, that is, the heaping into the ninth bracket and the heaping out of the tenth bracket approximately cancels out. The second is that $\hat{M}_9 + \hat{M}_{10} = (M_9 + M_{10})/B$, that is, the underreporting for the ninth and tenth brackets is approximately the same as the degree of underreporting for the first nine brackets. Finally, we have to assume that $\sum_{i=9}^{10} \hat{M}_i / \sum_{i=9}^{10} \hat{K}_i = \sum_{i=10}^{12} \hat{M}_i / \sum_{i=10}^{12} \hat{K}_i$, that is, that the average monthly death probability in the ninth and tenth months of life are not much different than the death probability in the tenth, eleventh, and twelfth months. These three assumptions jointly imply:

$$\frac{\sum_{i=10}^{12} \hat{M}_i}{\sum_{i=10}^{12} \hat{K}_i} = \frac{K_9 + K_{10}}{(M_9 + M_{10})/B} . \tag{A13}$$

Solving equations A12 and A13 yields

$$\sum_{i=10}^{12} \hat{M}_i = 19,006.$$

Adding this to

$$\sum_{i=1}^{9} \hat{M}_i = \frac{1}{B} \sum_{i=1}^{9} M_i = \frac{20,947}{0.407} = 51,530,$$

which implies an infant-mortality rate of 224 per 1,000. (All calculations are carried out on the assumption that the annual birth rate = 38·5 per 1,000.) The results are presented in Table 3.5.

Appendix B: An Econometric Solution to the Land Quality Problem

Let land quality in each county i be denoted by q_i. Assume that q is distributed in each county with mean μ and s.d. σ. Assume that there is some threshold level c which denotes which land will be cultivated at the extensive margin: all land better than c_i in county i is cultivated. Thus, the proportion land under cultivation in county i, P_i is equal to:

$$P_i = \text{prob } (q_i \geq c_i). \tag{B1}$$

Assume that the variable q_i is distributed symmetrically. Two convenient symmetrical distributions are the uniform distribution and the normal distribution. If the distribution is uniform, the p.d.f. can be written as:

$$f(q) = \frac{1}{b-a} \text{(subscripts suppressed)} \tag{B2}$$

where b and a are, respectively, the upper and lower bounds of the distribution. The mean and the s.d. for the uniform distribution are given by:

$$\mu = \frac{a+b}{2} \tag{B3}$$

and

$$\sigma=\frac{b-a}{\sqrt{12}}.$$
(B4)

In order to derive a relation between μ and P in each county, an assumption has to be made about the standard deviation. The simplest assumption is that it is the same in each county. Then, choosing our units appropriately, we set $b-a=1$ and obtain:

$$P=\frac{b-c}{b-a}=b-c.$$
(B5)

Solving equations B3 and B5, we obtain:

$$\mu=P+c-\frac{1}{2}$$
(B6)

which presents the desired variable, average land quality μ, in terms of P and c. The income equation estimated is (in simplified terms):

$$Y=a+b\mu+dZ$$
(B7)

where Y is income and Z is, say, the land–labor ratio. Now assume that the threshold level c is a linear function of Z:

$$c=m+nZ.$$
(B8)

The equation to be estimated is the reduced form:

$$Y=a'+b'P+d'Z$$
(B9)

in which $a'=-1/2+a+bm;\ b'=b;\ d'=d+bn$.

The assumption of constant intercounty standard deviation is simple but not very attractive. Assume, alternatively, that the standard deviation is proportional to the mean, that is, the coefficient of variation V is constant. This implies that:

$$\frac{b-a}{\sqrt{12}}=\frac{V(a+b)}{2}$$
(B10)

so that a and b are proportional, and therefore b and μ are proportional:

$$b=k\mu.$$
(B11)

The proportion under cultivation P is now given by:

$$P=\frac{b-c}{b-a}=\frac{2\,(k\mu-c)}{\sqrt{12}\,V\mu}$$
(B12)

which can be written as:

$$P=\frac{k\mu-c}{\mu}K$$
(B13)

so that the desired parameter μ is obtained from

$$\mu=\frac{cK}{Kk-P}.$$
(B14)

Substituting equation B14 into B7 and utilizing B8 yields the estimating equation:

$$Y = a' + \frac{b'}{k' - P} + \frac{d'Z}{k' - P}$$ (B15)

which has to be estimated using a nonlinear technique.

Now assume that q follows the normal distribution. From the normality assumption:

$$P = \psi \left[\frac{\mu - c}{\sigma} \right]$$ (B16)

where the function ψ should be interpreted as $1/2$ + the area under the standard normal probability distribution between the mean and the threshold level c.

Solving for μ we obtain:

$$\mu = \psi^{-1}(P) \cdot \sigma + c.$$ (B17)

Again, some assumptions have to be made about the variance of q. The assumption that the variance is constant among counties implies the estimating equation:

$$Y = a' + b'\theta + d'Z$$ (B18)

where $\theta = \psi^{-1}(P)$, and the coefficients have the same reduced form interpretation as in equation B9.

Now assume, as before, that the standard deviation is proportional to the mean. This yields:

$$\mu = \theta V \mu + c$$ (B19)

where V is the coefficient of variation. The desired parameter μ is equal to:

$$\mu = \frac{c}{1 - \theta V}.$$ (B20)

The estimated equation is once more nonlinear:

$$Y = a' + \frac{b'}{1 - \theta V} + \frac{d'Z}{1 - \theta V}.$$ (B21)

Equations B7, B15, B18, and B21 are reported in Tables 3.8 and 3.9.

Notes: Chapter 3

1 Emigration cannot account for this deceleration. For the province of Connaught, from which emigration was low relative to population growth, the implied average growth rate declines from 1·91 to 0·54 percent. A number of authors (Crotty, 1966, p. 39; Verrière, 1979, p. 67) have accepted the 1831 Census uncritically and concluded erroneously from it that emigration had a greater demographic impact than it in fact did, and that population growth was decelerating so rapidly that it would have reached the stagnation phase by 1851 even in the absence of the famine.

2 During 1821–41 an estimated 1,045,000 Irishmen emigrated from Ireland to North America or Great Britain. This amounts to an average outmigration of approximately 0·7 percent per annum. As average population growth was about 0·9 percent per annum, we calculate the death rate as $3·3 - 0·9 - 0·7 = 1·7$ percent.

3 Although these correlation coefficients are statistically significant, a formal F-test rejects the hypothesis that the two versions of the death and emigration rates are equal. The test is based on the idea that if two variables, say, X and Y, are identical except for random errors, the regressions $X = a_1 + b_1 Y$ and $Y = a_2 + b_2 X$ should *both* satisfy the simultaneous constraint of $a_i = 0, b_i = 1$ ($i = 1, 2$). The hypothesis of equality is rejected for both measures on the 1 percent level. The conclusion is that for econometric analyses on the county level, we have to use both sets of estimated death and emigration rates. This is so because there is no *a priori* reason to believe that either one of the two sets is preferable.

4 It may be added that smallpox, the great killer of small children, was anything but extinct in Ireland. The age-specific causes of death reported by the 1841 Census (Great Britain, 1843, Vol. XXIV, supplement, p. 182) shows that smallpox was the second largest single cause of death for the age brackets between 6 months and 10 years, accounting for 13·5 percent of all deaths at these ages. For the population as a whole, smallpox accounted for 5·1 percent of all deaths, more than twice as high as in England. Peter Razzell (1977, p. 157) has argued that smallpox mortality in Ireland was very low in the 1830s, which is true if it is compared to the seventeenth century, but not when it is compared to England. Razzell's own data show that in Maidstone, Kent, smallpox accounted only for 1·3 percent of all deaths, a quarter of the Irish proportion. See also Connell (1950a, p. 217), inexplicably not referred to by Razzell.

5 Other modern historians who subscribe to some version of the Malthusian hypothesis include Solow (1971, pp. 195–6), Grigg (1980, pp. 115–40), and Freeman (1957, p. 11).

6 Sadler (1829, pp. 30–3) and O'Brien (1921, p. 85) cited with glee writers from the seventeenth and early eighteenth century who attributed Irish poverty in their day on the scarcity of population. William Petty (1899, Vol. 1, p. 223) wrote in 1688 that "the greatest and most fundamental defect of this kingdom (is the want of people)". Dean Swift (1955, Vol. 12, p. 6) recommended to the Irish to increase their numbers "without which any country, however blessed by nature, must continue poor".

7 It should be added that the computation above is not a wholly fair test of the over-population hypothesis. As Ó Gráda emphasizes, the famine reduced not only the labor force, but also the land endowment because farmers could no longer rely on the potato crop. The realization of the risks associated with growing potatoes are equivalent to a decline in the supply of land in efficiency terms. On the other hand, the decline in the labor force used by Ó Gráda may be overstated. First, the fall in population and the shift in crops reduced seasonal unemployment, so that the actual number of days worked may have declined by less than 24 percent. Secondly, the famine struck most severely among those who were employed in agriculture only part-time, and who spent the rest of their time in cottage industry, peat-cutting, and ancillary activities. The death or emigration of these people implies that the effective labor force may not have declined *pari passu* with population.

8 It may be added here that writers observing the depopulated Ireland of the early twentieth century do not convey the impression that population decline had been to anyone's advantage. One of the most astute observers noted that "the thinner the population becomes, the lonelier will Ireland be; the emptier and stiller the life of this joyous people" (Bonn, 1906, p. 25).

9 In the simple neoclassical growth model in which no nonreproducible factors of production exist, the steady-state level of income per capita is independent of the *level* of population, although not of its *rate of growth*. In its original formulation the neo-classical model was allowed Malthusian features, which clearly change the model in a significant way (Swan, 1969).

10 The test is based on decomposing the variation in I_f. Since $I_f = I_m x I_g$, it follows that $\log I_f = \log I_m + \log I_g$. Taking variances on both sides: $VAR(\log I_f) = VAR(\log I_m) + VAR(\log I_g) + 2COVAR(\log I_m, \log I_g)$.

11 The equations were run both for total and for rural areas. The regressions in which the

median age at marriage was the independent variable yielded for rural areas only (*t*-statistics in parentheses):

Birth rate = $0.11 + 0.0006$ male age $- 0.0035$ female age $R^2 = 0.4838$ (adjusted).
$\quad\quad\quad\quad(7.43)\,(0.73)\quad\quad\quad\quad(-3.91)$

For rural and urban areas, using the HCA measure of the marriage propensity:

Birth rate = $0.10\quad -0.0005$ male age $- 0.0017$ female age $R^2 = 0.4252$ (adjusted).
$\quad\quad\quad(7.10)\,(-0.95)\quad\quad\quad(-3.34)$

These regressions imply that the gross effect of a rise in the median rural female age at marriage would be to reduce the birth rate by 0.35 percent; for instance, from 40 per 1,000 to 36.5 per 1,000. Using the HCA or the singulate mean as proxies for the propensity to marry the effect is somewhat smaller, which is to be expected, as the median age at marriage for women was about a year and a half lower than the mean age.

12 The raw correlation coefficient between rural marital fertility and median female age at marriage is -0.183.

13 J. B. Bryan wrote in 1831 that "early marriages are less conducive to a permanent increase in population than late ones, as in late marriages the term of female prolificness is lengthened (and) the intensity of the prolificness during what remains of its customary duration is increased" (cited by Connell, 1950a, p. 53 n.).

14 The opportunities for extramarital sex in prefamine Ireland were extremely limited. In 1851 there were a total of 1,368 prostitutes and brothel-keepers in Ireland, most of whom were located in Dublin. In Connaught there were only forty-two prostitutes. Connell (1950a, p. 48) produces evidence supporting his view that premarital sex and adultery were comparatively rare. While such evidence is always awkward to interpret, it is consistent with what we know about postfamine Ireland.

15 Using these age statistics was originally suggested by Tucker (1970). The conversion of the age statistics into crude birth rates, however, has to my knowledge not previously been attempted.

16 The Census compilers themselves admitted to serious undercounting (p. xlix). The aggregate crude death rate implied for 1840, the most recent completed year before the taking of the Census, is 17.4 per 1,000, which is unacceptably low.

17 The seasonal fluctuations of the birth rate in most European countries show that May falls between the abnormally high rates of February, March, and April, and the low rates of August and September. Belgium, France, the Netherlands, Germany, and Spain, all conform to this pattern, and only Scotland and central Sweden show slightly higher birth rates in May (Huntingdon, 1938, pp. 95–100). More recent work based on family reconstitutions in France shows precisely the same pattern (Smith, 1977, p. 41). Wrigley and Schofield (1981, pp. 286–9) report that before 1700 baptisms in May were below the annual average, in 1700–49 they were exactly at the annual mean, and after 1750 they exceeded the annual mean by 4 to 6 percent. As for the birth rate in the year 1841, in seven Western European countries for which data are available, these rates were all within 1 s.d. (standard deviation) from the annual average for the period 1835–44 (see, for all except the Netherlands, Mitchell, 1975, pp. 81–3; and for the Netherlands, Hofstee, 1978, p. 196):

Country	1835–44 mean birth rate	Standard deviation of birth rate	Birth rate, 1841
Belgium	33·5	1·0	34·0
Denmark	30·1	0·7	29·7
France	28·4	0·6	28·5
Germany	36·4	0·4	36·4
The Netherlands	37·1	1·0	37·9
Norway	29·4	1·6	29·8
Sweden	31·1	1·0	30·3

18 The reason for dividing by two is that the total number of deaths of children aged less than 1 month divided by the number of births represents the probability of a child dying in its first month. Yet the population of children used in the calculation is only about fifteen days old, so that some of them still died in the month after the Census.

19   Cousens ignored internal migration altogether, and heroically assumed uniform death rates throughout the country.

20   The weights used are the probabilities of a random member of the cohort to be in a given age group in a random year during 1821–41. Thus, the weights are: 11–15, 0·075; 16–20, 0·200; 21–25, 0·250; 26–30, 0·250; 31–35, 0·175; 36·40, 0·050.

21   In the absence of a procedure such as described by equation B8, one has to fall back on computing b_{ij} and analyzing each of the cohorts separately (see, for example, McKenna, 1978).

22   Connolly (1979) has shown on the basis of a sample of nine Roman Catholic parishes that illegitimacy in Ireland was around 2·5 percent of total births, less than half the proportion in England and Wales.

23   The Eaton and Mayer data stop at age 51. It was assumed that no conceptions occurred after age 51, and that the number of women in the sample continued to decline by two for the ages 52–5.

Chapter 4

Land, Leases, and Length of Tenure

(1) Introduction

Of all the explanations proposed in the nineteenth century for Ireland's economic woes, one of the most influential is the hypothesis which places the responsibility on the system of land tenancy. Throughout the nineteenth century complaints of this nature were put forward by administrators, political economists, agricultural reformers, and visiting travelers.[1] Many contemporaries viewed tenancy as the core of Ireland's difficulties. The government's response to this consensus on the cause of Ireland's ever-more pressing economic hardship was to establish (in 1844) the Commission of Inquiry into the State of the Law and Practice in Relation to the Occupation of Land in Ireland, generally referred to as the Devon Commission.

The Devon Commision's report is a true treasure of evidence in favor of the hypothesis that the form of land tenancy was the main source of Irish poverty, but also, unfortunately perhaps, of evidence against it. In its conclusion, this massive document pointed out that

> The uncertainty of tenure is constantly referred to as a pressing grievance by all classes of tenants. It is said to paralyse all exertion and to place fatal impediments in the way of improvement. We have no doubt that this is the case in many instances. In some, probably, the complaint is put forward as an excuse for indolence and neglect. (Great Britain, 1845a, Vol. XIX, pp. 15–16)

The *Digest of Evidence* of the Devon Commission (Kennedy, 1847, pp. 15–16) noted that the majority of witnesses attributed Irish agricultural backwardness to "the occupiers not having any certainty of receiving compensation if removed immediately after having effected valuable improvements; and to their not having leases or . . . security of tenure of their farms". While pointing out politely that this argument was, no doubt, "a most reasonable . . . substantial one", the Commissioners added that "there were not many cases on the evidence to prove that proprietors have taken such advantage of improving tenants". Nor did it appear that "the tenants who have the longest leases . . . have brought the lands that they hold to a more productive . . . state than others not possessing such security". The land system was blamed not only for creating a disincentive to investment in the land, but also for the failure of rural industry to develop in the south (Gill, 1925, pp. 22–9; Verrière, 1979, pp. 203–4; Black, 1960, pp.

156–7), and for the continuous agrarian violence which plagued the Irish countryside (Pim, 1848, pp. 50–4; Donnelly, 1973, p. 36; Maguire, 1972, p. 107). Clearly, however, the primary complaint against the land-tenure system in Ireland was that insecurity of holding land led to insufficient capital formation in agriculture. No doubt the investment aspect of the land tenure hypothesis (henceforth, LTH) was the chief concern of contemporaries. Even John Stuart Mill was tempted into uncharacteristic hyperbole (Mill, 1929, p. 323), asserting that the Irish tenant was "almost alone amongst mankind" in not being allowed to reap the fruits of his investment.

As is the case with the Malthusian hypothesis, there have always been some writers who dissented from the conventional wisdom of the LTH, or at least argued the case to be unproven. Beaumont (1839, Vol. 1, pp. 296–7) was one of many who argued that the length of the lease was not nearly as important as the spirit of the agreement between landlord and tenant. J. R. McCulloch (1854, Vol. 1, p. 514) agreed, adding that "a thousand" projects could be undertaken by tenants without any temptation to raise rents.

Modern historians of Ireland have recently become critical of the LTH (Solow, 1971; Crotty, 1966, p. 54; Donnelly, 1973, p. 20; 1975, pp. 63–4; O'Tuathaigh, 1972, p. 145). The notion that tenant security was a prerequisite for agricultural progress was not confined to Ireland, and can be found in England and Scotland as well. There, too, the hypothesis that security played a central role in agricultural development has fallen into disrepute (Chambers and Mingay, 1966, p. 46; Whyte, 1979).

The essence of the LTH can best be illustrated by way of a table describing all four possible arrangements in an agrarian economy in which the landlords do not farm themselves, but let the land to tenants:

	short leases	long leases
Landlord is responsible for improvements	I	II
Tenant is responsible for improvements	III	IV

This illustrates the difficulty encountered in an economic system in which there are two agents (landlords and tenants) but three factors of production (land, labor, and capital). Most agricultural capital took the form of soil maintenance, proper rotation and fertilization, drainage, irrigation, subsoiling, preservation of hedges, fences, trees, barns and other "offices", and similar activities. Capital was, therefore, "embodied" in the soil. Since the landlord owned the land, the capital invested remained in his possession when the tenant left.

Leases were documents which specified a fixed nominal rent over the holding period. If the leases contain no additional clauses, only possibilities I and IV are efficient. Situation I was characteristic of England and Scotland. It allowed the landlord to raise the rent whenever he introduced an improvement, reflecting the fact that rent payments contained a component which was a return to investment, in addition to pure rents. If the tenant was responsible for the improvements, he would have required some assurances that he would earn the appropriate return on his investment. A long lease which guarantees that the rent will not be raised in a manner that confiscates the return to his investment is one such assurance. Of course, a long lease is not a *necessary* condition for tenant-investment. Moreover, as we shall see momentarily, the entire matter is a bit more complicated than that.

Since in Ireland the vast majority of landlords did not carry out any improvements, the tenant being responsible for carrying out all investment activity on the land, only the bottom row of the table above is relevant. There is considerable evidence that after 1800 landlords began to offer shorter leases, and that many tenants lost their leases altogether and became tenants-at-will or yearly tenants; in other words, a movement from IV to III (Dubourdieu, 1812, p. 143; Coote, 1801a, p. 137; Thompson, 1802, p. 99; Kennedy, 1847, p. 1121).[2] The crux of the LTH is that the demise of long leases involved a movement from an efficient to an inefficient situation, and thwarted the process of capital accumulation necessary for the development and modernization of Irish agriculture.

Before turning to a more complete analysis of the relevance of the LTH in prefamine Ireland, it may be appropriate to wonder why the movement from long leases to short leases took place in the first place. This question has been analyzed in some detail by Maguire (1972, pp. 129–38) and what follows relies in part on his work. One explanation concerns the electoral reform of 1829. Until then, franchise was given to all freeholders holding land valued at 40s or more. Some landlords who were heavily involved in politics resorted to giving as many leases as possible in order to increase the number of voters on their estates and, thus, to maximize their political influence. With the disenfranchisement of the 40s freeholders in 1829, this motive for granting leases disappeared, and leases which fell in were not renewed. While it cannot be ruled out that this explanation was true for some individual cases, it cannot explain more than a small part of the disappearance of leases, which started well before 1829, and which encompassed all parts of Ireland, whether the landlords were politically active or not. Crawford (1975, pp. 18-19) also suggests the landlords' growing disillusionment with leases as an instrument of guaranteeing improvements and their exasperation with trying to enforce legally covenants stipulated in the leases.

The main cause for the increasing reluctance of landlords to renew leases and their inclination to replace leaseholders with tenants-at-will was related to the asymmetry of landlords and tenants with respect to changes in the price level. In a world in which the agents are symmetric, when contracts are signed in nominal terms and price movements are not fully anticipated, landlords gain from deflation and tenants from inflation. Differences in total wealth and the fact that labor was mobile whereas land was not, created an asymmetry which was only fully realized by landlords after the violent price movements during 1790-1820. When prices went up, landlords saw the real value of the rents decline without being able to raise the nominal rent to reflect the new price level, except when leases expired. When prices declined after 1814, however, many landlords discovered that the real value of the rents due did not rise in proportion. Tenants, claiming lower prices, demanded and often got reductions in rents. Others often fell into arrears, paying what they could, or simply abandoned their holdings. Evicting tenants for nonpayment of rent on this account made, of course, little sense, because the new tenants replacing the ejected farmers would pay a rent which reflected present rather than past prices. Long leases under rapidly changing prices thus involved a 'heads-you-win-tails-I-lose' situation for landlords, and it is therefore not surprising that long leases were becoming less frequent in the decades before the famine.[3]

A second reason for landlords' resistance to leases was their increasing desire to change the direction and the organization of Irish agriculture. On the whole, landlords had a strong interest in producing livestock on large grazing farms, while smallholders preferred to continue producing tillage products. The complications which resulted from that conflict of interest are discussed in Chapter 5. It is obvious, however, that if a landlord wished to consolidate small tenancies into larger units, he would have had to stop granting leases at some point, unless all leases happened to expire on the same date. A further reason—probably less important—was the tenants' refusal to sign leases. This could be explained by the cost of the lease itself (although these were not prohibitive) in conjunction with the belief of the tenant that his tenancy was secure anyway, or his trust that the landlord was decent and/or rational enough not to confiscate by means of higher rents the return to tenant-introduced improvements. Other tenants may have refused to sign leases simply because they had no intention to do much improving anyway.

The LTH, thus, maintains that insecurity of tenure on the part of the tenants led to "underinvestment" in agricultural improvements. The question immediately arises: *under*investment compared to what? There is no obvious candidate for the appropriate counterfactual situation. The actual situation could be compared to a hypothetical world in which tenants had long leases, or one in which landlords introduced the improvements, or even one in which society consisted of peasant-proprietors. In what follows, the comparison will be to a perfectly competitive world in which all agents are rational and markets work well, so that the socially optimal quantities of each input are used on the farm (that is, the social and private rates of return are equalized). This "neoclassical" model is not worse than any of the others and has the advantage that it is analytically easy to work with. A similar procedure is followed by Pigou (1932, pp. 174–83) in his famous discussion of the inefficiencies involved in landlord-tenant relations. Under some assumptions, the three other counterfactuals can be approximated by the "neoclassical" one.

How can the LTH be tested? The ideal test would be to collect data on individual farms, and then to test whether—all other things equal—there was a relation between agricultural investment and the length of lease. Such a sample is not available. From the testimonies of the Devon Commission witnesses and the reports of the Ordnance Survey memoirs, it is clear that there were important exceptions on both sides of the leases–improvement equation: some tenants at will introduced improvements, while some holders of long leases did not. Such exceptions, if they were sufficiently rare, do not necessarily refute the LTH, but we cannot judge whether they were 'sufficiently' rare without more quantitative information. A second difficulty is that the causality may have worked in both directions: there is some evidence to suggest that landlords preferred to give leases to improving tenants who raised or preserved the inherent fertility of the soil, while keeping doubtful tenants on yearly bases to keep the option of removing them open (OSM, box 27, file III). The tests of the LTH carried out below are, therefore, by necessity indirect.

(2)   The Theoretical Foundations of the LTH

The LTH is based on three presuppositions which must hold for the land tenancy system to have been a significant causal factor in Irish poverty. These assumptions are: (*a*) improvements were introduced predominantly by the tenants, not the landlords, (*b*) landlords maximized rents in the short run, or at least the tenants believed they did, and (*c*) most land in Ireland was held under very short leases or at will. These three assumptions are, as noted above, necessary conditions for the LTH to hold. If they do not hold, the hypothesis is false *a priori*. If they do hold, the hypothesis could be true, although we can still not be sure to what extent it explains Irish poverty.

Contemporary observers such as Foster (1847, pp. 405–6) and Pim (1848, p. 56) thought that the observation of the sequence in which a tenant invested followed by a landlord raising the rent was sufficient evidence for the LTH. That inference is false. In any theory of production, neoclassical or otherwise, the quantity of one input will affect the return on all inputs. As the factors of production in agriculture are complementary in the sense that increasing one factor raises the marginal product of the others, any increase in the amount of capital employed would raise the marginal product of land and thus raise the rent charged by landlords, if the market was as competitive as is claimed.

A simple model illustrating the interaction between investment and rent is presented in Appendix A to this chapter. The conclusions reached there can be summarized as follows. Land rents were, as Ricardo defined them, a payment for the natural and indestructible properties of the land. However, these properties were not independent of the quantities of reproducible factors (capital) utilized in the production process; the quantities of reproducible factors influenced the return on the irreproducible ones. Investment results in higher competitive rents even when the improvements are carried out by the tenant. Some increase in the rent following a tenant's improvement is therefore not rapacious and will not lead to underinvestment; it is perfectly consistent with competitive behavior. The question is, however, *by how much* the rent is raised. Underinvestment may indeed occur if the landlord raises the rent by the full amount of the increment in output resulting from the improvements made. It is this type of behavior which we will term "predatory" behavior. What makes predatory behavior possible at all is that the tenant cannot remove his investment from the land, so that when he leaves or is evicted, the entire value of the investment reverts to the landlord. It is the embodiment of agrarian improvements in the land which creates the imperfection in the assignment of property rights which is at the heart of the LTH.

Assume that all land in Ireland was held at will. In that case, it is clear that it was possible for the landlords to stifle all investment by leading their tenants to *expect* that they were predatory landlords. It is equally clear that such behavior would have been foolish on their part. The "neoclassical" landlord sees his rent increase steadily as the tenant accumulates capital. The predatory landlord earns a once-and-for-all windfall, but at the cost of a continuous flow of future rents. Note, however, that predatory landlordship is not *necessarily* irrational. A very high rate of time preference coupled to highly imperfect capital markets (for instance, to avert bankruptcy) could have led to occasional predatory behavior. The precarious liquidity of many Irish landlords makes this possibility quite likely. Nevertheless, predatory landlordship was not likely to persist among a large number of rational landlords, as it amounted to the willful sacrifice of future income on their part. Of course, it is still possible to defend the LTH using an *ad hoc* expectations theory. After all, the LTH only requires that the tenants *expect* predatory behavior. It could be maintained that the hostility, on political and religious grounds, between landlord and tenant in Ireland was such that the tenant expected predatory behavior even when there was no reason to suppose such behavior on the part of the landlord (see, for instance, Foster, 1847, pp. 324–8). Alternatively, it could be proposed that landlords resorted to predatory behavior on the (fallacious) assumption that the tenants would not translate such behavior into their expectations. The landlord may have believed that in spite of his predatory behavior, the tenants would time and again introduce improvements to the land, which he could continuously skim off. Such theories are not implausible but any systematic evidence here is lacking. In fact, as will be demonstrated below, the proportion of tenants who felt 'secure' may have exceeded those who had leases. It also remains to be demonstrated how divergences between perceptions and reality could persist over long periods.

Predatory behavior could, however, occur as a result of an entirely different set of circumstances. In this case it may be better to speak of quasi-predatory behavior, since it is not clear whether the landlord in this case is expropriating resources which ought to accrue to someone else. Quasi-predatory behavior could occur in an economy in which land is held under long-term leases, which specify a fixed rent until expiration. Using an argument similar to the one above, it can be shown that a fixed rent over a long period permits the tenant to "exploit" the landlord rather than vice versa. If the tenant carries out an investment but pays the landlord no increased rent, the landlord receives less than the marginal product of the land, while the tenant receives an income in excess of the marginal products of the two factors (labor and capital) he supplies. This situation will last until the lease expires, at which point the rent is renegotiated. If the landlord sets the new rent at the "competitive" level, his forgone earnings prior to the expiration of the lease will never be recaptured, so that if the income streams were capitalized to the starting-point, it would still be true that capital and labor together have "exploited" the landlord. If the landlord sets the new rent at the predatory level, the net result depends on which is larger: the tenant "exploiting" the landlord prior to the expiration of the lease, or the landlord "exploiting" the tenant after the new lease is signed (possibly with a different tenant).

It is, therefore, not possible to provide an unambiguous answer to the question whether quasi-predatory behavior actually constituted "exploitation" of the tenant by landlord or the reverse. In Appendix B to this chapter a simple numerical example is developed which explores a bit further what happens when there is a long-run contract between the landlord and the tenant. The conclusion reached from the example is that for a realistic range of assumptions about the length of the leases and the rate at which the future is discounted, the case for the LTH is not strong.

To summarize our conclusions so far: predatory behavior of land-lords, allegedly responsible for the underinvestment in and the underdevelopment of the Irish agrarian economy, could occur only when tenants held land "at will". Whether this practice was common enough even among tenants-at-will to cause retardation is hard to say: testimony abounds that such behavior *did* occur, but quantitative evidence that might determine the issue conclusively is slim, and contemporaries as well as historians differ in their overall assessment. The difficulty is that what may seem predatory behavior in the absence of a lease, could be tantamount to competitive behavior in the presence of a long- or medium-term lease.

The question which will have to be answered is: to what extent was Ireland *before the famine* a country in which land was predominantly held by persons who did not have any long-run commitment from their landlord? Solow (1971, p. 7) has asserted that by the middle of the nineteenth century perhaps 70–75 percent of all tenants held at will.[4] There is no evidence supporting this estimate, and it seems unlikely that the proportion was so high: in 1869, twenty years after the famine, the proportion of tenants holding at will was about 77 percent (Great Britain, 1870, Vol. LVI, pp. 737–57). As leases were renewed less and less both before and after the famine, Solow's estimate implies an unreasonably slow rate of increase in the proportions of tenants and land "at will". Moreover, while less than a quarter of all Irish tenants held leases, the proportion of land held under leases (in 1869) was considerably larger.[5]

(3)   Leaseholders and Tenants-at-Will: Some Evidence

The Devon Commission (Great Britain, 1845a, Vols XIX–XXII) is one of the most thorough and comprehensive investigations carried out by any nineteenth-century *ad hoc* agency. In addition to over 100 appendices and a long introduction, the report includes the "evidence", which consists of the testimonies of the 1,078 witnesses (actually there are 1,125 testimonies, but a number of witnesses testified more than once). The witnesses represented a broad sample of the Irish population, although the class of cottiers and smallholders was probably poorly represented. The largest occupational group among the witnesses defined themselves as farmers (41·8 percent), with land agents comprising 20·5 percent of the sample. Landed proprietors accounted for 15·5 percent, and parish priests for 7·7 percent. There were also lawyers (3·6 percent), surveyors (3·3 percent), civil servants (2·8 percent), merchants and manufacturers (3·2 percent together), Presbyterian ministers (1·0 percent), and doctors (0·6 percent). The minutes of the testimonies cover 2,960 pages containing about 3 million words in over 50,000 answers and questions, in addition to documents, tables, and other official depositions. While far from ideal, the Devon Commission witnesses provide a unique source from which to compose a picture of rural conditions not from the notes of a handful of travelers and diary-writers, but from many hundreds of intelligent and on the whole articulate and informed men.

The idea that this vast reservoir of information could be tapped systematically by treating the testimonies as independent "observations" seems to have occurred for the first time to Raymond Crotty in his attempt to re-estimate prefamine rentals and compare them to the official "valuations" (Crotty, 1966). For the present purposes, we focus on the issue of land tenure and leases. More specifically, what matters for our purpose are the answers to the questions: do tenants (in the witness's district) hold generally at will or by lease? What is the usual term of the lease? Has the mode of tenure an effect on the condition of the landholding and on the tenant's propensity to improve the land? Is there any anxiety among the tenants to obtain leases? While these questions were not posed in identical form to all witnesses, sufficient uniformity in the testimonies exists to quantify the evidence by simply counting witnesses. The results are tabulated in Tables 4.1 and 4.2.

The response of witnesses to three questions are summarized in Table 4.1. Question 1 pertains to all witnesses who were asked whether long leases were at all prevalent in their districts. Question 2 tabulates the response of all witnesses who were asked whether the tenancies in their district were "secure". The third question referred to whether tenants were anxious for leases in that district. The number of witnesses refers to the number of witnesses testifying on one point or more (so that the total of the first six columns does not add up to the seventh). Table 4.2 provides a breakdown of all witnesses who provided a subjective estimate of the frequency of long leases in their districts. About

500 of the more than 600 witnesses who responded to queries on whether long leases existed at all could be used for this purpose.

Table 4.1 *Evidence on Tenancy in Devon Testimonies*

Province	(1) Long leases?		(2) Tenants secure?		(3) Anxious for leases?		(4) No. of witnesses
	Yes	No	Yes	No	Yes	No	
Ulster	149	12	34	14	20	33	180
Leinster	142	3	17	11	27	23	158
Munster	200	12	20	29	63	28	234
Connaught	78	6	12	7	25	14	94
Total Ireland	569	33	83	61	135	98	666

Source: Devon Commission (Great Britain, 1845a, Vols XIX–XXI).

The evidence presented in Tables 4.1 and 4.2 underlines the complexities of the Irish land system on the eve of the famine. While in almost all of Ireland leases were in use to some extent, they seem comparatively rare in Connaught and dominant in Leinster, whereas in Ulster and in Munster they constituted a substantial minority. The fact that Ulster tenants were none the less more secure and at the same time anxious for leases seems to be consistent with the traditional account, according to which the Ulster tenants were secure on account of the "Ulster custom", which supposedly compensated Ulster tenants for investment carried out on their holdings. As Ulster and Leinster were the wealthiest provinces, it can easily be seen how the data contained in the testimonies given before the Devon Commission could be used to support the LTH and helped shape British land policies in the post-famine period.

Table 4.2 *Evidence on Long Leases in Devon Testimonies*

Province	Never	Rarely or seldom	Often or many	Always	No. of witnesses
Ulster	12	76	43	3	134
Leinster	3	49	63	2	117
Munster	12	100	69	2	183
Connaught	6	47	14	0	67
Total Ireland	33	272	189	7	501

Source: See Table 4.1.

Yet some doubt over whether Tables 4.1 and 4.2 support the LTH lingers on. First, in Connaught, the poorest and most backward province, the proportion of witnesses who reported the tenants as secure is higher (63 percent) than the nationwide average (58 percent). While the sample of Connaught witnesses who answered that question is of course small, it is none the less an indication that the simple link drawn from long leases via security to poverty and underdevelopment may not be accurate. Secondly, there can be little doubt that a "stocks and flows" problem existed in the answers provided by many witnesses in Table 4.2. When a witness reported that leases were rare in his district, it could be interpreted to mean that only a few tenants in the districts were holding under leases. But it seems that in many cases the witnesses meant: "leases are seldom given nowadays"—which did not exclude the possibility that most of the tenants *still held* under (old) leases. Thirdly, the LTH implies not only that most of the tenants should hold land "at will", but also that most of the *land* under cultivation should be held in that fashion. Otherwise, while the land cultivated by cottiers and small tenants might be in part suffering from underinvestment due to landlords' predatory behavior, most of the land (and thus of the economy) would not be affected. The total income of a county or a region would still be high, even though most of it would be generated by the larger farms who still held long leases and, thus, did not face an impediment to investment in land. In other words, if the LTH were true for cottiers and smallholders but not for medium-sized and larger farms which contained most of the cultivable land, the aggregate overall capital–labor ratio would only marginally be affected. It is that ratio which is crucial for the level of income per capita. As shown in Chapter 2, the smallholders and cottiers worked part-time for larger farms and graziers. Their productivity (and thus their wage) was determined by the improvements which the large farmers had introduced. Hence, the high-income farms would create positive pecuniary externalities for the cottiers holding at will through labor and other markets. If most land was held in large, secure farms, the insecurity of the cottiers as tenants-at-will probably was not a major factor in the distress of the economy as a whole. As the witnesses apparently referred in most cases to the number of tenants rather than the quantity of land when they expressed judgements about the frequency and relative importance of long leases in their district, information about the amount of land in question is necessary.

Moreover, the provincial aggregates in Tables 4.1 and 4.2 are to some extent misleading. In the destitute county of Mayo for example, only 54 percent of the witnesses said the tenants were anxious for leases, while in wealthy Antrim the figure was 60 percent. It is also true that differences *within* provinces are often more marked than those between provinces. All in all, the data in Tables 4.1 and 4.2 are less supportive of the LTH than appears at first sight: long leases were universally found over the country, the majority of witnesses reported that tenants were secure, and while it is also true that the majority were "anxious for leases", the latter is probably a reflection of excess demand rather than of the tenants holding at will being a preponderant majority. Not reflected in the tables but equally disquieting for the LTH is the fact that many tenants refused to take out leases when the landlords were willing to grant them. The traditional explanation that high stamp duties discouraged tenants from taking leases seems inconsistent with the low duties on leases involving small amounts of land.[6]

While the evidence presented by the witnesses of the Devon Commission is thus suggestive, it is not fully adequate to answer the question to what extent Irish land was let "at will". Nor is it very useful to employ individual estate records for this matter, as the problems of representativeness are insuperable. One source can, however, be employed for the purpose despite some serious shortcomings. After the famine had ruined many landlords, Parliament passed the Encumbered Estates Act of 1849, which removed many of the legal barriers impeding the orderly sale of land. From that time on, estates passed from hand to hand at an accelerating rate. Estates put up for sale were described in the so-called O'Brien Rentals, preserved in the Public Record Office of Dublin. It is from this series that a sample of over 2,000 rentals was chosen. Each rental contains information on the size of the estate or lot described, the annual rent paid by the tenants, and the annual head rent and tithe owned. If the tenant had a lease, that is, was not a "tenant-at-will", the details of the lease are provided, for instance, whether it was for years or for "lives" (or both), when signed, how long to expiration, and so on.

The sample chosen was not random, but rather was derived from the first volumes of the O'Brien Rentals. Since we are interested in the pre-famine structure of land tenure, the sample is useful only if it reflects pre-1845 conditions. Since the first volumes date from 1850, it seemed best to choose the earliest sets, in order to remain as close as possible to the prefamine era. None the less, the fact that a huge disaster separates the data from the reality they are supposed to reflect is rather disturbing. In part this could be remedied as large tracts of land, especially in the west, were "unoccupied", obviously due to the death and/or emigration of the occupiers during the famine years. These "unoccupied" farms are entered as a special class. On the whole, the use of a postfamine source to reflect prefamine conditions is likely to be biased in the direction of overstating the number of tenants at will. The famine, by killing more than 1·1 million people, was responsible for the termination of many leases that had "lives" written in them (and thus expired at the time the people expired). Not many of these leases were renewed. Emigrants, too, let their leases lapse when they concluded that their farms could no longer support them due to the repeated failure of the potato crop. Maguire (1972, p. 129) reports, for example, that in the Kilwarlin (Co. Down) estates, in 1816, 1,238 out of 1,383 holdings were held on lease. By 1855 that number had shrunk to 315. The decline in leaseholding is, however, not as severe as may seem, as many holdings had been consolidated during those forty years.

Even for 1850 the O'Brien Rentals sample may not be a representative sample of estates. It is not, after all, a survey of estates, but rather a description of land put up for sale. One may wonder whether it reflects the characteristics of the entire population. An objection could be raised against the use of the O'Brien sample on the grounds that tenants holding long-term leases were often paying rents which were below the current market rate. Therefore, assuming that the market rent had risen over time, there was a negative correlation between rent and length of lease, with tenants-at-will paying the highest rent.[7] It is, therefore, not inconceivable that the landlords whose estates ended up in the encumbered estates court gave relatively more leases and therefore had lower incomes. It is, of course, tautologically true that rent per acre was one of the determinants of landlord income. But it does not follow that the landlords who ended up in the court were the poorest by any definition. Some of the largest landowners in Ireland went bankrupt, such as Lord Donegal (Maguire, 1976) and the Earl of Kingston (de Tocqueville, 1958, pp. 152–4).

To be sure, the reasons *why* the estate was put up for sale typically involved insolvency of the owner. But financial difficulties could stem from a variety of reasons: mismanagement, family arrangements, high standards of living (especially gambling), political expenses, or debts incurred in the far past which reached the crisis-point during the famine. Many estates also reached the court precisely because the impediments to the sale of estates before 1850 made adjustments of landlords' port-folios impossible. While it may therefore seem that using the O'Brien Rentals for a description of the economy is not unlike using modern bankruptcy proceedings to analyze the business sector, the analogy is misleading. There is no strong reason to believe that the estates put up for sale were *systematically* different from those that were not.

The sample is described in Table 4.3. Its total size is about 1·5 percent of the land under cultivation and of the total rental income before the famine. The number of tenants exceeds the number of observations, as some rentals indicate that the lot is let out to more than one tenant. This happens often when the tenants are at will. The geographical coverage is far from perfect, and especially the northwest and some of the Ulster counties are poorly represented. The difficulties in taking a stratified sample with this type of data were, however, overriding.

Table 4.3   *Description of the O'Brien Rentals Sample*

Region	No. of observations	Total acreage (acres)	Total rental	No. of tenants
NE	429	38,115	14,164	1,207
NW	52	4,857	2,730	297
CENT.	322	35,701	22,882	689
EAST	356	24,746	17,484	654
S	612	76,686	42,599	1,177
W	418	54,471	13,865	1,091
Total	2,189	234,576	113,724	5,115

Notes: NE: counties Antrim, Armagh, Cavan, Down, Londonderry, Louth, and Monaghan. NW: counties Donegal, Fermanagh, Leitrim, Roscommon, Sligo, and Tyrone. CENT.: counties King's, Longford, Meath, Queen's, and Westmeath. EAST: counties Carlow, Dublin, Kildare, Kilkenny, Wexford, and Wicklow. S: counties Cork, Kerry, Limerick, Tipperary, and Waterford. W: counties Clare, Galway, and Mayo.
Source: O'Brien Rentals, Vols 1–4, 1850.

The data most crucial to the issue under discussion here are summarized in Tables 4.4–4.7. The conclusions are quite unmistakably at variance with the assessment of the Devon Commission that most of the land of Ireland was let at will: roughly speaking, only a quarter of the land under cultivation was let without lease, and only a third of the rental bill came from these lands. While it is true that the majority of tenants were tenants-at-will, this is but small consolation for would-be advocates of the LTH. The small tenants were partially employed on the larger farms, and their income was determined by the amount of capital employed on the land on which they worked.[8] If the poverty of the country as a whole is to be explained by insecurity of tenants, it is the amount of land that is insecure that counts, not the gross number of contracts "at will".

Table 4.4 *Land Tenure in Ireland, by Class (Percentages)*

Class	*Unweighted observations*	*Weighted by acreage*	*Weighted by rent*	*Weighted by number of tenants*
Class 1	8·1	10·4	8·6	4·87
Class 2	26·5	29·0	25·7	16·75
Class 3	12·5	10·7	13·1	11·99
Class 4	12·1	6·5	8·8	8·05
Class 5	7·1	7·7	9·5	4·85
Class 6	7·9	13·4	2·6	0·49
Class 7	25·6	22·2	31·6	52·94
Total	100	100	100	100
At will	28·3	26·5	32·7	53·6
Leases	71·7	73·5	67·3	46·4

Notes: Class 1: Extremely long leases (perpetuities, or leases longer than 3 lives *or* 41 years). Class 2: Very long leases (3 lives *or* 41 years, or a combination including at least one of them, or 2 lives *plus* at least 21 years). Class 3: Long leases (2 lives *or* 31 years, or a combination including at least one of them, or 1 life *plus* at least 21 years). Class 4: Medium leases (1 life *or* 21 years, or at least one of them). Class 5: Others (leases shorter than 21 years, in litigation, unclassifiable, and so on). Class 6: Unlet. Class 7: Yearly tenant (at will).
Source: See Table 4.3.

The O'Brien Rentals can also be used to measure the average ages of the leases extant in 1850, as an indication of the extent to which landlords refused to renew expired leases in the decades preceding the famine. In Table 4.8 the distribution of the ages of the leases in the O'Brien Rentals sample is provided. The interpretation of the table is as follows: if leases were rapidly disappearing so that the leases still held on the eve of the famine were largely holdovers of earlier periods, we should observe that the amount of land leased rises with the age of the lease. On the other hand, if the change in the landlord's propensity to give out leases is not yet of major importance, we would likely find the relation to be negative. The distribution of the ages of leases is thus a result of two opposing forces.[9]

Table 4.5   *Land Tenure in Ireland, by Class and Region (Percentages), Unweighted Observations*

Class	NE	NW	CENT.	E	S	W
Class 1	4·8	1·9	6·9	12·1	11·9	4·0
Class 2	28·2	5·8	34·9	31·7	25·5	18·4
Class 3	24·5	5·8	10·9	6·7	12·4	7·4
Class 4	18·4	21·2	10·9	11·2	9·8	9·3
Class 5	3·5	13·5	4·4	8·1	9·6	7·7
Class 6	0·1	9·6	7·2	3·7	7·4	19·9
Class 7	19·6	42·3	25·6	26·1	22·9	33·5
Total	100	100	100	100	100	100
At will	19·8	47·8	27·8	27·7	25·0	43·5
Leases	80·2	52·2	72·2	72·3	75·0	56·5

Source: See Tables 4.3 and 4.4.

Table 4.8 lends little support to the hypothesis that a landlord's unwillingness to give out leases after 1815 had such an effect that by 1845 most of Ireland's land was held at will. It is clear that the increased tendency to refuse to renew leases upon expiration was dominated by other forces. We can therefore not conclude that the phenomenon was absent or even that it was negligible. But we can conclude safely that the hypothesis relating Irish backwardness to the landlords' sudden aversion to long leases is not consistent with this evidence.

Table 4.6   *Land Tenure in Ireland, by Class and Region (Percentages), Weighted by Acreage*

Class	NE	NW	CENT.	E	S	W
Class 1	4·3	0·2	3·6	10·7	21·7	3·8
Class 2	31·4	2·5	46·6	31·7	31·3	13·8
Class 3	33·6	4·9	5·8	5·7	8·4	3·7
Class 4	16·3	7·0	4·2	7·8	4·5	3·2
Class 5	0·9	10·1	3·6	16·1	9·5	8·5
Class 6	0·6	11·0	9·6	4·3	4·8	41·5
Class 7	12·8	64·2	26·6	23·2	19·6	25·5
Total	100	100	100	100	100	100
At will	13·1	79·3	29·7	24·4	20·8	46·8
Leases	86·9	20·7	70·3	75·6	79·2	53·2

Source: See Tables 4.3 and 4.4.

The greatest difficulty in interpreting the O'Brien sample is that in focusing on the contractual arrangement between landlord and tenant we have abstracted from a crucial feature of Irish landholding in the eighteenth and nineteenth century, namely, the existence of a layer of middlemen who held long leases at low rents and then sublet them at higher rents. It is therefore possible that in some estates in which a long lease was reported, the tenants, that is, the people actually working on the land, were holding at will from a leaseholding middleman. The inference that the land was held at a long-term lease and that therefore the tenant was protected against predatory rent hikes would be incorrect. Middlemen have been blamed for a variety of real or imagined ills by contemporaries and historians alike (Young, 1892, Vol. 1, pp. 24–9; Tighe, 1802, p. 423; Weld, 1832, p. 695; Foster, 1847, pp. 360–3, 438; Donnelly, 1973, p. 16). At present we have to deal with one specific aspect of the middleman system, namely, to what extent does its existence invalidate the conclusions drawn above from the O'Brien sample?

Table 4.7 *Land Tenure in Ireland, by Region and Class (Percentages), Weighted by Annual Gross Rents*

Class	NE	NW	CENT.	E	S	W
Class 1	3·8	0·1	5·1	14·1	12·0	3·3
Class 2	19·3	3·3	37·5	21·8	27·5	16·8
Class 3	39·6	4·5	7·8	8·8	11·5	7·0
Class 4	15·6	8·3	7·3	9·3	7·1	8·6
Class 5	1·9	5·2	5·0	14·9	12·6	9·1
Class 6	0·6	0·0	5·3	0·2	1·3	7·4
Class 7	19·1	78·4	31·8	30·7	27·7	47·8
Total	100	100	100	100	100	100
At will	19·3	79·7	33·9	30·6	28·2	52·7
Leases	80·7	20·3	66·1	69·2	71·8	47·3

Source: See Tables 4.3 and 4.4.

A number of defenses are possible against the criticism that the O'Brien Rentals sample is distorted by the existence of middlemen. The first is that in many cases the "middleman" was for all practical purposes the owner of the land, even though he did not possess the fee simple. If he held land for very long periods, for instance, or held leases "renewable in perpetuity" paying some annual "head rent", his interest was hardly distinguishable from ownership and was indeed bought and sold as recorded in the O'Brien Rentals.[10] In some cases middlemen actually gave their tenants leases which expired a year or two before their own (Great Britain, 1836b, Vol. XXXIII, p. 189). A Galway witness testifying before the Poor Law Commission (Great Britain, 1836b, Vol. XXXIII, p. 143) pointed out that "all who have not the fee simple and have tenants under them are called middlemen". (For a useful survey of the types of middlemen and some details on their demise, see Dickson

(1979).) In other cases the existence of middlemen is irrelevant. Many middlemen held college or church lands, which naturally did not appear in the O'Brien Rentals. Secondly, the class of less substantial middlemen who held land for long or medium leases was decreasing rapidly in the nineteenth century. After 1815, the landlords failed to renew middlemen's leases and preferred to deal directly with the tenants, in some cases converting them to tenants-at-will, in others signing direct leases with the people actually farming the land. Furthermore, many middlemen backed out of their leases when the rent they had contracted to pay exceeded their income (as happened to those who had signed leases during the Napoleonic Wars). If it could be shown that by the eve of the famine middlemen had largely disappeared while leases were still prevalent, the existence of middlemen would not invalidate the use of the O'Brien Rentals for our purposes.

Table 4.8   *Analysis of Leases in O'Brien Sample*

(a) Average Ages of Leases, by Region

Region	Unweighted observations	Weighted by acreage	Weighted by rents
NE	25·41	24·72	17·80
NW	15·17	16·60	15·72
CENT.	28·87	25·06	25·65
E	20·40	18·99	17·88
S	21·76	30·18	22·94
W	20·49	20·78	19·05
Total	23·19	25·74	21·48

(b) Distribution of Sample by Age of Lease

Age of lease	No. of cases	in %	Acreage	in %	Gross rent (£)	in %	Rent per acre (£)
1–10	369	28·65	36,208	27·74	19,624	30·13	0·54
11–20	266	20·65	27,661	21·19	14,644	22·49	0·53
21–30	274	21·27	24,155	18·15	14,082	21·62	0·58
31–40	93	7·22	9,258	7·09	3,802	5·84	0·41
41–50	108	8·39	9,148	7·01	4,668	7·17	0·51
51–70	140	10·87	14,849	11·38	6,478	9·95	0·44
71–100	31	2·41	5,754	4·41	1,386	2·13	0·24
101 +	7	0·54	3,492	2·68	440	0·68	0·13
Total	1,288	100	130,525	100	65,124	100	0·50

Source: O'Brien Rentals, 1850.

How numerous were middlemen on the eve of the famine? One answer to that question can be obtained from the sample itself if we assume that no or very few new middlemen were created after 1815. Table 4.9 presents the O'Brien Rentals data, excluding all leases that were signed before 1815.

Table 4.9   *O'Brien Rentals Sample, Excluding Leases Signed before 1815 (Percentages)*

	Unweighted observations	Weighted by acreage	Weighted by rent
Class 1	6·8	7·5	6·4
Class 2	19·0	23·1	20·6
Class 3	13·8	11·2	14·0
Class 4	12·9	7·1	9·1
Class 5	8·2	9·0	10·8
Class 6	9·2	15·9	3·0
Class 7	30·1	26·5	36·6
Total	100·0	100·0	100·0
At will	33·7	32·1	37·8
Leases	66·3	67·9	62·2
Sample size	1,872	198,972	99,703
As percentage of total sample	85·5	84·8	87·7

Source: O'Brien Rentals sample.

Table 4.9 demonstrates that leases signed before 1815 (not all of which, of course, were actually sublet) comprise only about 15 percent of the total sample, and omitting them does not change the conclusion that most Irish agricultural land was let by lease on the eve of the famine. The unimportance of the middleman by the eve of the famine can also be verified using the Devon Commission testimonies. Hundreds of witnesses were asked point-blank whether in their districts tenants held directly from the proprietor or from middlemen. The answers are summarized in Table 4.10, which demonstrates the extent to which middlemen had become a rarity in prefamine Ireland. More than three-quarters of all witnesses whose replies to the question could be used said that middlemen either did not exist in their district, or held only a small fraction of the land, and that most land was held directly under the proprietor. While there were considerable regional differences in the responses, nowhere does the proportion of witnesses stating that middlemen held less than half of the land fall below two-thirds. The classification rules used to organize the results into Table 4.10 deliberately biased the procedure *against* the hypothesis that middlemen were insignificant. For instance, a witness estimating that "a good many middlemen" held land in his district was classified in class 4, although there is some reason to believe that this statement actually describes a situation in which middlemen were a distinct minority.[11] Other evidence corroborates this finding. In Co. Armagh, where leases were general, Greig reported in 1819 that middlemen were quite rare (Greig, 1976, p. 63). In short, the institution of middlemen vanished from the scene of Irish agriculture much earlier and much more quickly than long leases.

Table 4.10   *Holdings from Middlemen on the Eve of the Famine (Percentages)*

Region	Class 1	Class 2	Class 3	Class 4	Class 5	Total	No. of observations
NE	23·8	45·5	12·5	13·6	4·5	100	88
NW	11·1	48·6	15·3	18·1	6·9	100	72
CENT.	0	56·8	27·3	15·9	0	100	44
E	0	42·6	35·2	22·2	0	100	54
S	1·0	51·0	15·3	22·4	10·2	100	98
W	3·9	51·0	13·7	27·5	3·9	100	51
Total	7·9	48·9	18·4	19·7	5·2	100	407

Notes: Class 1: Middlemen absent.
Class 2: Very few middlemen, land generally held from proprietor.
Class 3: Some middlemen, but definitely fewer than half.
Class 4: Many middlemen, possibly as many as half.
Class 5: Most land held from middlemen.
For regions, see Table 4.3.
Source: Devon Commission, Great Britain, 1845a, Vols XIX–XXI.

We now come to the third line of defense. So far we have argued that (*a*) a large number of middlemen did not conform with the caricature of a *nouveau riche rentier*, a parasite who squeezed his fellow-peasants more than the landlord ever did, and (*b*) that the number of middlemen of any description in any event was not very substantial on the eve of the famine. It cannot be denied, however, that some specimens of the "ugly middleman" did persist in the 1840s, and that the O'Brien Rentals may not thus adequately reflect the degree of security of Irish tenants. In other words, a lease given to a middleman who kept his subtenants at will was equivalent for all practical purposes to a situation without a lease. Such equivalence assumes that middlemen behaved like land-lords, that is, they refused to invest in the land and help carry the burden of improvement. It has indeed been widely argued that most middlemen did little in the way of improving (Donnelly, 1975, pp. 62–3; Connell, 1950a, pp. 65–6), and one contemporary indignantly refers to them as "useless drones" (Foster, 1847, p. 435).[12] Yet it is not easy to see why middlemen would behave in this respect like landlords—they were, after all, mostly farmers themselves. Many middlemen, indeed, only received that title because as farmers employing nonfamily labor they paid their agricultural laborers in terms of the rent of a small potato plot, thus "promoting" them from landless laborers to cottiers (Maguire, 1972, p. 224). Why would such a middleman-farmer fail to improve the land? The worst that could happen to him is that his landlord would turn out to be a "quasi-predator" and raise the rent to the full amount of the marginal product of the improvement after the rent expired. Most of the alleged causes which explain why Irish landlords failed to invest in improvements, such as absenteeism, violence, indebtedness, the entail-ing of estates, and a social and political abyss between landlord and tenant, did not apply to the more substantial leaseholders even if they had sublet part of their holding. Most of them were Catholics, resided *in loco*, and were familiar with the conditions of soil, terrain, weather, availability of labor and fertilizer, and so on. They seemed, at first sight, to satisfy all the requirements of serious entrepreneurial activity in land improvement. Indeed, the middlemen were perhaps the only group which constituted anything like an agricultural middle class (Pim, 1848, p. 46; Inglis, 1835, Vol. 1, p. 82; Cullen, 1981a, pp. 99–100). Blaming them for Ireland's slow progress seems to be inconsistent with the frequent lament that Ireland lacked a middle class between the landlords and the tenants (Beaumont, 1839, Vol. 2, pp. 109–23). If these people failed to engage in such activity, the reasons must lie deeper than the form of land tenancy.

(4) Some Concluding Remarks on the Land Tenure Hypothesis

The land tenure hypothesis (LTH) attributed Irish economic backwardness to the insecurity of tenure of the tenants. Insecurity led to under-investment in agricultural improvements, and thus to overall lower incomes in agriculture. As Solow (1971) has emphasized, whether the hypothesis is correct or not, it had a profound influence on British policies toward Ireland in the postfamine years, and thus indirectly led to important economic consequences.

Was the hypothesis in fact correct for the prefamine years? Both the theoretical analysis and the data presented indicate that there is no unqualified answer to that question. Predatory landlordship could occur, even though it may not have been consistent with long-term rent maximization on the part of the landlords. Quasi-predatory landlordship, which occurred when leases were given, could under certain assumptions also lead to reduced investment. The main difficulty with the empirical testing of the LTH is that what in the final analysis mattered was what tenants *expected*, not what landlords did. The expectations of tenants on the length of their tenure and the return to their investment were likely to be correlated with the frequency and length of leases, but were by no means identical to it. A tenant holding a yet-unexpired lease might observe that landlords all around him were becoming increasingly reluctant to renew leases and thus might expect that he, too, could become a tenant-at-will, thus increasing the probability that the returns to the investment would be expropriated. But tenants knew more about their landlords than do historians. Many tenants who did not have leases, or whose leases were about to expire, had good reason to expect that the rent would not be raised at the renewal of the lease (or that the "fine" paid at the renewal of a perpetuity would not be of confiscatory magnitude). Many landlords were fully trusted by their tenants and encouraged them to introduce improvements by making it clear to them that rents would remain unchanged or raised by small amounts. In the long run this was plainly in their interest. The testimonies before the Devon Commission contain many examples of such progressive landlords (for example, Kennedy, 1847, pp. 262, 276, 278).

While tenants knew more about their landlords than we do, they still operated under uncertainty (Mokyr, 1981b). A magnanimous or timid landlord might die unexpectedly, and his heir might follow different policies. The estate might—as frequently happened—become the subject of a legal battle, in which case the tenants would typically not be granted long leases until the litigation was over, a process which could stretch out over decades. The only protection against predatory rent increases was a long lease, preferably for years rather than for lives, or for more than one life. A tenant holding a lease of known length (or at least a length expected with some reasonable certainty) was assured not only of his rate of return, but in many cases of a surplus in excess of the "competitive" rate of return. The above qualifications notwithstanding, the frequency of leases is therefore the most pertinent piece of information on the validity of the LTH.

The evidence presented demonstrates that for Ireland as a whole, the bulk of the land was let by long-term leases and was therefore protected from predatory behavior. Since this conclusion is based on evidence from 1850, it is *a fortiori* true of the three or four decades preceding the famine. Tenant insecurity was therefore probably a contributing factor to prefamine poverty, but it is simply inconceivable that it was the sole or even a primary factor. In some regions, however, the impact of insecurity could have been more than marginal. In the west and north-west, the poorest parts of the country, the amount of land held at will was considerably larger than in the rest of the country. This finding may seem consistent with the LTH, but the crude correlation between poverty and proportion land held at will could be misleading for two reasons. First, if landlords tended to refuse to renew leases in regions in which agriculture was backward in the hope of intervening directly or getting better tenants on somewhat larger farms, the causality would run the other way. Secondly, the west and northwest were particularly heavily affected by the famine and thus a larger proportion of leases fell in during the years 1845–50, which would create a larger downward bias in our estimates of the proportion of land held by lease for these areas than for the rest of the country.

The testing of the LTH is further complicated by the so-called "Ulster Custom" or tenant right. According to this custom, which was most widely practiced in Ulster although it occurred in most parts of Ireland, a change of tenants involved a cash payment from the incoming tenant to the outgoing tenant. Tenant right, as was recognized at the time, confused the rights of the landlords with the rights of the tenants, and introduced an element of vagueness into the definition of property rights (Kennedy, 1847, p. 290). If the landlord owned the land and received rent payments in exchange of his letting the tenant use it, what was the price of the tenant right or goodwill a payment for?

Contemporaries, such as Edward Senior, the brother of the economist, testifying before a House of Commons Select Committee (Great Britain, 1844, Vol. VII, pp. 556–63) distinguished among three different explanations for the existence of the tenant right custom. One possibility was that tenant right payment compensated the outgoing tenant for improvements he had introduced on the land but could not take with him. The second possible explanation was that the rent paid to the landlord was for some reason below the market clearing or "competitive" rent. If the incoming tenant expected to pay the landlord a rent which was lower than the maximum rent he would be willing to pay, the outgoing tenant could pocket the difference in exactly the same way as key money is charged for rent-controlled apartments (Solow, 1971, pp. 26–30). The third reason cited why incoming tenants paid for tenant right was the somewhat vague notion of "acquiring the good-will" of the outgoing tenant. The practice was, in fact, often referred to as the sale of good-will. An attempt to understand the historical significance of good-will is provided in Mokyr (1981b).

To the extent that the first two explanations of tenant right are correct, the practice is irreconcilable with the LTH. If the payment was indeed for improvements, the property rights of the tenant in the improvements introduced were assured, and no disincentive to investment existed. Some of the Devon witnesses indeed argued that the tenant right system superseded the need for a legal provision securing compensation to tenants for their improvements. The difficulty with that argument is that many witnesses maintained that tenant right was sold even if the outgoing tenant had effected no improvements or even caused the farm to deteriorate, and that the price of the tenant right exceeded the value of the unexhausted improvements on the land. The other explanation centers on the difference between the actual rent paid and the "equilibrium" rent. This theory requires the specification of a mechanism which kept the rents below the equilibrium level. One such mechanism was, of course, long-term leases, but the sale of tenant right was practiced even when the farms were held from year to year (Kennedy, 1847, p. 290). The Devon Commission witnesses were divided on the relation between tenure and the value of tenant right. Of the witnesses who made statements on the question, 49 percent answered in the affirmative, while 51 percent denied the connection. When asked whether the tenant right was sold even when no formal lease existed, 89 percent gave an affirmative answer. It is possible, of course, that even when there was no lease, the rents paid were much below the equilibrium level, which would indicate that landlords could not maximize their rents for one reason or another, and thus would in all likelihood not engage in predatory behavior. Thus, the "key money hypothesis" is not consistent with the LTH. How much support is there for this interpretation? That there were cases in which absentee, scared, kind-hearted, or incompetent landlords charged lower rents than the market would bear cannot be doubted. The evidence indicates, however, that the majority of landlords and their agents tried to maximize their rents and let the farms to the highest bidder (see Chapter 5).

If tenant right was widespread in Ulster, and if its primary *raison d'être* was a combination of compensation for improvements and key money, we should observe that in Ulster the LTH was less central a feature of contemporary discussions of the backwardness of agriculture than elsewhere. The Ordnance Survey memoirs, which contain the most detailed and voluminous evidence on agriculture of any prefamine region in Ireland, are largely confined to the Ulster counties and should therefore be able to shed light on the issue. Surprisingly enough, they contain very few references to the Ulster custom altogether. On the other hand, the reports contained in the OSM are replete with references to tenant insecurity and the absence of leases as a source of backwardness and underinvestment. For the parish of Dungiven, Co. Londonderry (OSM, box 39, file II), we read that "cultivation is but very slowly making advances . . . owing to the short terms by which the land is held and the idea which the farmers generally have that immediately (after) they have increased the value of their holding their rents will be raised in proportion". In Glenavy parish (Co. Antrim) leases for three lives were considered by some an uncertain tenure and tenants holding such leases "rarely ventured to improve" (OSM, box 11, file II). In Derryvullen, Co. Fermanagh (OSM, box 26, file VIII), the report states that "farms . . . such as have fallen out of lease or have lately been taken are for the most part held from year to year. And though few instances of the tenant having been turned out have occurred, yet the system is universally . . . most detrimental to improvement, as few are willing to expend their substance and labour from such uncertain demesnes." Devon Commission witnesses from Ulster made similar comments (Great Britain, 1845a, Vol. XIX, pp. 471, 570, 613, 624). One of them, from Armagh, explicitly denied that the sale of tenant right eliminated the danger of predatory landlordship (Great Britain, 1845a, Vol. XIX, p. 545). The Devon Commission witnesses were far from unanimous about the effect of leases and security of tenure, of course, but the fact that Ulster witnesses worried about the effects of security on agricultural investment as much as others, indicates that tenant right did not provide full security of property rights in investment. Whatever tenant right was a payment for, it is not likely that either the compensation for improvement explanation, or the key-money explanation, tells the complete story.

Demonstrating the predominance of long-term leases in Ireland does not necessarily imply that all was well on the land-tenure scene. A number of distortions resulted from the leases themselves. One distortion stemmed from the fact that not all investment took the form of discontinuous increments in the capital stock. Suppose a hypothetical tenant has a long-term lease in which the length of tenure is such that the two transfers examined in Section 2 precisely offset each other, and suppose that a distant expiration date does indeed lead to overinvestment (see note 14). At first it may be thought that on average the socially optimal amount of investment will be undertaken. In actuality, much agricultural gross investment took the form of proper maintenance of soil, drainage works, and fixtures, and thus could be looked on as a flow of comparatively small annual flows. Only radical overhauls of the entire cultivation system (such as enclosure, or adoption of a form of the New Husbandry) required large, lumpy outlays. Thus, a period of overinvestment will occur over the first half of the lease, followed by underinvestment, and possibly negative (net) investment, toward the end of the lease. By the time the lease expires, the land could be exhausted, farm buildings run down, and so on. Some evidence exists indicating that Irish tenants deliberately destroyed the improvements they had introduced during their tenancy when their leases expired (Tighe, 1802, p. 416; Wakefield, 1812, Vol. 1, p. 303 n.; Great Britain, 1836b, Vol. XXXIII, p. 155). Overinvestment and underinvestment do not offset each other precisely even if they are the same size. A "dead-weight" burden, that is, a loss in the efficiency of the economy, is incurred. In a society such as Ireland where property rights were not perfectly defined and where economic agents (peasants and landlords) distrusted each other, inefficient allocations of resources were inevitable to some extent. While we have seen that property rights may not have been as flawed as is often argued, some bias against capital formation in agriculture existed. Even though it was probably a second-order effect, the direction in which this bias operated is quite clear.

A second distortion was introduced by the curious habit of leases for lives, in which the lease "fell in" when the person named in it died. The expected length of tenure in a large number of leases thus depended on the health of those named, in many cases some public figure like the King of England. Consequently, the term of the lease was uncertain, and if the tenant was risk-averse, he would invest less than he would have if the lease had the same average length but its expiration date was known with certainty (Kennedy, 1847, p. 262). A third complication was associated with the amount of control the landlord had over the day-to-day operation of the farm. A tenant-at-will had, at least in theory, an incentive to please the proprietor by not exhausting the soil, whereas a tenant with a lease, according to one landlord, "considers that he cannot be put out . . . He immediately mismanages the farm" (Great Britain, 1845a, Vol. XX, p. 342).

Land tenure, therefore, was not quite neutral. While the absence of security was certainly not as important a factor as it appears from some of the opinions of witnesses before the Devon Commission, it was probably a contributing factor in some areas. Ultimately, however, it will be necessary to search for deeper roots. Not only because two-thirds of the land in Ireland on the eve of the famine was held on long leases, but primarily because in the long run land tenure itself was an endogenous variable. If it was so obvious that leases resulted in improving tenants while insecurity lead to neglect and poverty, why the great switch from leases to tenancy at will? In other economies the changes in tenurial arrangements seem to have responded to a "general attempt to increase the efficiency of agriculture" (Whyte, 1979, p. 3). Once more, we will have to ask ourselves: why was Ireland different?

Appendix A: Predatory Landlords: A Simple Model

One of the important clues to understanding the full implications of the LTH is to distinguish between a "neoclassical" and a "predatory" land-lord. To illustrate this point, let us assume for simplicity that there are only two factors of production, capital and land, and that initially the unit of production under consideration is in a competitive equilibrium. Now assume that an incentive for additional investment is created. There are two ways to represent this, namely, a decline in the (explicit or implicit) cost of capital, or a rise in its productivity. For the later computations I shall use the former, but the latter is a bit clearer for the purpose of a diagrammatic exposition (see Figure 4.1).

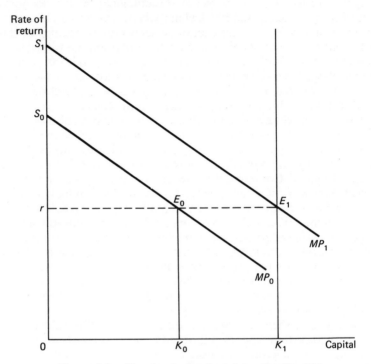

Figure 4.1   *Neoclassical and predatory landlordship*

Assume that capital is of the "putty-clay" variety with zero *ex post* malleability. Once an investment has been made, it is a "bygone" cost with zero scrap value. This means that once the investment has been made, the "capitalist" supplies it with zero elasticity. Capital is thus not only "embodied" in the land, it is "imprisoned" in it. In Figure 4.1 the original equilibrium is at point E_0, with capital receiving the rectangle $rE_0 0 K_0$, and the landlord, the residual claimant, receiving the triangle $rE_0 S_0$. The cost of capital is fixed at r. Now let the marginal product of capital shift to MP_1. If the tenant expects to receive a rate of return of r on the investment $K_0 K_1$, he will carry it out and he will receive the extra rectangle $K_0 K_1 E_0 E_1$ for his efforts. Rents will rise by the trapezoid $S_1 S_0 E_0 E_1$. There is nothing rapacious about the rise in rents: it is perfectly consistent with ordinary competitive behavior, and leads in no way to underinvestment. It is conceivable, however, that the landlord will try to raise the rent to the point at which he pockets the entire return of the investment. In terms of the diagram, that would be equivalent to a landlord raising his rent by the trapezoid $S_1S_0E_0E_1$ *plus* the rectangle $K_0K_1E_0E_1$. The tenant still receives his previous income $r_0E_0K_00$, and thus receives a rate of return of zero on his additional investment. The predatory landlord can completely expropriate the investment by including the rectangle $K_0K_1E_0E_1$ in the rent paid to him by the incoming tenant.

More formally, consider the production function:

$$Y = F(L, K, T) \qquad (A1)$$

where L is labor, K is the capital services used, and T is land. Let L and T be fixed in quantity. If the function exhibits constant returns to scale,

$$Y = F_L L + F_K K + F_T T. \qquad (A2)$$

Differencing equation A2 we get:

$$\Delta Y = \Delta K (LF_{LK} + TF_{TK} + F_{KK}K + F_K + F_{KK}\Delta K). \qquad (A3)$$

In equation A3 the right-hand side tells us what happens to each factor of production following an increase in K. $LF_{LK}\Delta K$ is the rise in the income of labor as a result of the increased capital, and $TF_{TK}\Delta K$ is the same for the landlord's rent. The term $(F_{KK}K + F_K + F_{KK}\Delta K)\Delta K$ is the change in capital income. The reason that the change in the income of capital is not just $F_K\Delta K$ is, of course, that investment reduces the rate of return on *all* capital, and not just on the new investment. The (negative) term $F_{KK}K$ subtracts the decline of the return on the intra-marginal capital stock from the marginal product of the new investment. The interaction term $F_{KK}\Delta K$ can be ignored for small changes in K. We now define the "neoclassical" or "competitive" landlord as the landlord who raised his rent by[13]

$$\Delta(RENT) = TF_{TK}\Delta K \qquad (A4)$$

while the predatory landlord is defined by

$$\Delta(RENT) = \Delta Y = \Delta K(LF_{LK} + TF_{TK} + F_{KK}K + F_K + F_{KK}\Delta K). \qquad (A5)$$

In the three-factor model the sin of the predatory landlord is double: he expropriates both the return on capital, and the increase in labor income due to the extra investment. In practice, as the worker and the man who provided the capital were typically the same person, this distinction is not observable.

Appendix B: Predatory Landlords: A Numerical Example

Suppose a lease contract determines a fixed rent for n years to be paid by the tenant. If the tenant introduces an improvement, the rent will stay the same although the land has become more productive. Suppose that by the expiration of the contract the landlord displays predatory behavior raising the rent by the full value of the improvement. Which of two deviations from competitive pricing will prevail? The issue is important because if the landlord "exploits" the tenant, this would imply underinvestment by the "neoclassical" criterion. If the tenant "exploits" the landlord, however, it is possible (though not certain) that it could lead to *over*investment.[14] A small numerical example can provide some idea on the numbers involved. Consider the Cobb–Douglas production function:

$$Y = L^{\alpha} T^{\beta} K^{1-\alpha-\beta}, \tag{B1}$$

in which we set experimentally $\alpha = 0.5$, $\beta = 0.2$. As K denotes the services supplied by capital, assume that the ratio between stock of capital and the flow of services is 3. This allows us to set the initial level of L, T, and K all to 100, with output equal to 100 as well. The marginal product of capital is 0.3, implying a rate of return on capital (stock) of 10 percent. Assume that the opportunity cost of capital declines from 10 to 6 percent. A brief calculation shows that a rate of return of 6 percent will be achieved when $K = 207.46$. Total investment is $322.38 (= 107.46 \times 3)$ and the total increment to output is 24.47 units, which in a perfectly competitive market will be divided up as follows: capital receives 7.34 more, labor receives an increase in income of 12.23, and land rents rise by 4.89.[15] The appropriate comparison is between the present discounted value of the flow of incremental rents from the completion of the investment until the expiration of the lease, and the present discounted value of the change in capital and labor income from the expiration of the lease forever. The results will depend, of course, on the remaining length of the lease and the rate of discount used. Tables 4.11 and 4.12 provide the results for a number of possible lengths and rates of discount.

Table 4.11   *Transfers from Landlord to Tenant after Improvement under Fixed Rent**

$r \backslash n$	10	15	20	40
0·04	39·66	54·37	66·44	96·78
0·06	35·99	47·50	56·09	73·57
0·10	30·05	37·19	41·63	47·82
0·20	20·50	22·85	23·81	24·44

*n is the number of years left to expiration.
r is the rate of discount used.

A brief examination of Tables 4.11 and 4.12 shows that for short leases and low rates of discount the tenant is, on balance, exploited by the landlord, while the reverse is true for high rates of discount and long leases. In the intermediate cases, in which the two amounts are in the same order of magnitude, quasi-predatory behavior on the part of the landlord is equivalent to competitive behavior: the landlord confiscates the tenant's returns at the expiration of the lease in order to compensate himself for the tenant having deprived him of his "share" prior to the expiration of the lease. In the latter case, if these flows are more or less anticipated in advance, over- and underinvestment could offset each other. As long as the sum of the present discounted values of the flows equal the marginal product, their precise pattern may not matter much. If the flows are not fully anticipated in advance, the net result is more likely to result in underinvestment than in overinvestment, because the tenant, when faced with a rate of return lower than the cost of capital, is certain to reduce his investment. On the other hand, a tenant faced with a rate of return higher than the cost of capital, may treat this as a lump-sum income increment and not increase his investment.

Table 4.12 *Transfers from Tenant to Quasi-Predatory Landlord after Expiration of Lease*

$r \backslash n$	10	15	20	40
0·04	330·50	271·65	223·28	101·90
0·06	182·13	136·10	101·69	31·70
0·10	75·45	46·84	29·08	4·32
0·20	15·89	6·36	2·55	0·06

Needless to say, this model is abstract, and its results depend on the values of the parameters assumed, which is an unattractive feature. As it happens, introducing more realistic features into the model weakens the LTH even more. First, consider the issue of depreciation of capital. Thus far we have implicitly assumed that the new capital (as well as the old) lasts forever. The result of allowing capital to depreciate will be to reduce the return of the quasi-predatory landlord relative to the return of the tenant-investor. In order to see this, assume that depreciation is of the "radioactive" form, that is, each year d percent of the capital stock evaporates. In that case d is simply added to the interest rate for all calculations, and as the tables show, the transfer from tenant to landlord is far more sensitive to the rate of return than the transfer from landlord to tenant. In fact, a simple calculation shows that the ratio of each entry in Table 4.11 to the corresponding entry in Table 4.12 rises monotonically with r (and with n). To illustrate the role of depreciation, consider an investment by a tenant whose lease still has ten years before expiration and who lives in a world in which "the" rate of interest is 10 percent. Clearly, if quasi-predatory behavior is expected, underinvestment will occur as the net transfer of the tenant to the landlord (from Tables 4.11 and 4.12) is $75·45 - 30·05 = 35·40$ units. A rate of depreciation of 7·5 percent on the contemplated investment is sufficient to eliminate the distortion.[16]

Recognizing the imperfection of the capital market and the consequent absurdity of the concept of "the" rate of interest also weakens the case of the LTH. As peasants had no access to capital markets other than the local usurers known as "gombeen men" and the "loan funds" which provided only small short-term loans, they faced a higher rate of discount than their landlords. The latter may not have been less impatient—indeed, there is evidence to the contrary—but they could borrow in comparatively well-organized capital markets and many of them were accordingly deeply in debt. If tenants and landlords faced different rates of discount, the appropriate rate of discount r to use the calculation such as performed in Tables 4.11 and 4.12 is the tenant's rate of discount, as it is he who makes the decision to make the investment. To the extent that the tenant rather than the landlord made the investment decision, the higher implicit interest rates faced by the peasants would make the lower rows of Tables 4.11 and 4.12 the appropriate ones, implying little or no underinvestment caused by the land system. While there is underinvestment in this economy because the rate of return on capital is higher than the rate of interest faced by landlords, it is not to be blamed on the land-tenure system but on the failure of capital markets, which prevents the landlords from lending to their tenants or investing directly in the land. Indeed, the land-tenure system tended, if anything, to mitigate the results of an ill-functioning capital market. The quasi-predatory landlord, in contrast to the predatory landlord, in effect lent money to his tenant. While such a loan may have been willy-nilly in many cases, that hardly changes the essence of the transaction. As long as the implicit rate of interest charged by the landlord to the tenant was between the two rates of discount, the "loan" made both sides better off. In equilibrium a fully rational tenant will choose his capital stock in such a way as to set the marginal product of capital equal to the implicit rate of interest. Underinvestment could still have occurred if the implicit rate were higher than the tenant's rate of discount, but it would be less severe.

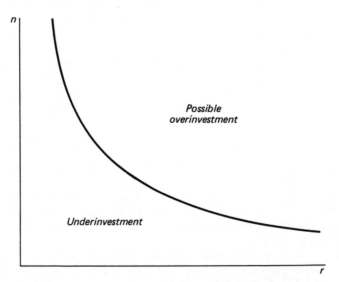

Figure 4.2   *Length of lease, investment and discount rates*

In any event, it will be clear that in the quasi-predatory case the underinvestment explanation of the LTH does not necessarily hold. Indeed, for every rate of discount there is a corresponding number of years before the expiration of the lease which will result in an investment which is just "right". In the Cobb–Douglas case the locus of optimal combinations or r and n is given by the formula[17]

$$n = \frac{\log(T/L) + \log(1+\alpha) - \log(1-\alpha-\beta)}{\log(1+r)}. \tag{B2}$$

The relation between n and r is depicted in Figure 4.2.

Notes: Chapter 4

1 For details, see for instance Mansergh (1975, p. 55); Solow (1971, pp. 1–14); Black (1960, pp. 24–8, 157–8); O'Brien (1921, pp. 98–108).

2 Solow (1971, p. 7) distinguishes between tenants-at-will and yearly tenants. While formally there is some difference between them, the distinction will be ignored here as it has no practical importance for the present purposes (cf. also Maguire, 1972, pp. 107–8).

3 A complete explanation along these lines was given by Daniel O'Connell in his testimony before the Devon Commission (Great Britain, 1845a, Vol. XXI, p. 933).

4 The Devon Commission was more cautious in its assessment and concluded that "the larger proportion" of the land was occupied by tenants-at-will (Great Britain, 1845a, Vol. XIX, p. 15). It is not clear precisely how that conclusion was reached.

5 The proportion of very large farms (valuation exceeding £100) let at will was only 24·4 percent, while among the farms valued at £50–£100, the proportion at will was 41·1 percent.

6 A lease specifying an annual rent of £10–£20 was levied a stamp duty of 10s, while a lease for a rent of £20–£50 paid 15s (Great Britain, 1845a, Vol. XXII, appendix 69, pp. 195–9). For a typical lease of £10–£20 per annum for twenty-one years, the stamp duty constituted between 0·6 of 1 percent and 0·3 of 1 percent of the present value of the rental flow (discounted to the date of signing at a rate of 10 percent).

7 To test the hypothesis of a relation between rents and leases, the following two regressions were run:

   (1) $RENT = b_0 + b_1 DCL1 + b_2 DCL2 + b_3 DCL3 + b_4 DCL4 + b_5 DCL7.$
   (2) $RENT = b_0 + b_1 AGLEAS.$

where the DCL variables in equation 1 are dummies for the various classes of land tenure, and AGLEAS is the age of the lease. The second equation was run excluding the tenants who held no leases. The results were as follows (t-statistics in parentheses):

   (1) $RENT = 0·508 + 0·668DCL1 + 0·252DCL2 + 0·950DCL3 + 0·391DCL4$
              (2·25)   (1·35)   (3·65)   (1·49)

         $+ 0·424DCL7$
            (1·93)

        $R^2 = 0·0072$
        $F = 3·175$
        $n = 2,189.$

   (2) $RENT = 1·046 - 0·0025AGLEAS$
                        (0·51)

        $R^2 = 0·0018$
        $F = 0·263$
        $n = 1,422.$

The interpretation of the findings is limited by the data. Since we have no data on land quality, equation 1 is mis-specified, and the resulting bias reduces b_5 below its true value. The fact that b_5 is higher than b_2 and b_4 but *lower* than b_1 and b_3 does not provide much evidence for "rental drag". The same holds for the coefficients of the long-lease variables. A further difficulty is that we do not fully understand why leases were short or long or absent. Some landlords rewarded tenants they considered to be "good" by giving them long leases. While "rental drag" thus remains a distinct possibility, there are other interpretations of the results.

8   In prefamine Ireland the majority of "laborers and cottiers" were unable to make ends meet without relying on some outside employment. While the small farm could usually feed the family, it could not provide sufficient income to pay rent, or to buy peat, fertilizer, tobacco, and similar goods. Many cottiers earned additional income in cottage industry and by joining the seasonal migration to Britain, but the majority worked on other Irish farms. Blacker (1846, p. 12) estimated that the occupier of 4–5 acres was "for half his time a competitor in the labour market for employment". Long after the famine, Bonn (1906, pp. 49–50) still observed the same phenomenon. In other words, the smallest tenants were only part-time employees on their own farms, so that the proportion of "tenants" who held at will is essentially meaningless.

9   In a hypothetical situation in which all leases were for a fixed term of m years and society was in a steady state, the distribution of leases by age should be uniform, as each year $1/m$ of all leases expire. However, since many leases were for lives rather than for fixed terms, and since the terms of the leases were definitively getting shorter after 1800, we would expect the number to be a declining function of their age.

10   Arthur Young (1892, Vol. 1, p. 26) referred to middlemen as "the class of country gentlemen". Many witnesses before the Devon Commission when asked whether the tenants in their district held from the proprietor or from middlemen pointed out that the man they regarded as the landlord was not the owner of the fee simple and thus ought to be regarded as a middleman.

11   One witness from Co. Wexford (Great Britain, 1845a, Vol. XXI, p. 512) explicitly defines "a good many middlemen" as "one-fifth". It should be added that the rise of the word "generally" also tends to bias the results: the question as formulated by the commissioners was "do tenants in your district generally hold from the proprietor or from middlemen?" If the reply was "generally from the proprietor", the witness was classified as class 2 rather than class 1, even though the word "generally" may not necessarily reflect the possibility of the existence of a few middlemen, but was used simply because the question was formulated in that way.

12   The numerous exceptions found to the rule that middlemen did not introduce improvements make one somewhat uncomfortable with Donnelly's (1973, p. 16) assertion that this was generally the case. One witness before the Devon Commission, a Mayo clergyman, heaped praise on the local middleman, who was active in the introduction of green crops and stone-clearing, and supported his subtenants in cases of need; cf. Great Britain (1845a, Vol. XX, p. 460). See also sources quoted by Connell (1950a, p. 66). Most explicit was Henry Inglis (1835, Vol. 1, p. 82), who pointed out that "many middlemen are excellent landlords ... I scarcely think the utter extinguishment of middlemen would be an advantage".

13   The term "competitive" is a bit misleading here, as there need not be competition in any real sense. What I mean is the change in rent which would have occurred if perfect competition had obtained. Some factor markets were competitive, especially the land market in which land typically was let out to the highest bidder. This does not ensure efficiency since the whole upshot of the LTH is that the capital market failed in a specific way. Hence, the term "competitive" here implies behavior "as if" *all* factor markets were competitive.

14   It is logically clear that predatory landlordship leads to underinvestment. It is less certain that if there is a net transfer from landlord to tenant, *over*investment will result. A profit-maximizing and perfectly rational tenant who can buy "investment goods" in infinitesimally small quantities will invest only up to the point at which the marginal product of capital equals its cost. The residual, which is positive by assumption, is pocketed by the tenant. Thus, in a sense, he is transformed into a part-time landlord. However, if the tenant follows the rule of thumb that he invests up to the point at which total costs equals total revenue (which is the rule the tenant would

follow if landlords kept the rent at the competitive level, so that none of the variable factors earns a return above its opportunity cost), overinvestment will occur. I am indebted to Professor Frank Lewis of Queen's University, Kingston, Ontario, for clarifying my thought on this issue.

15 Two clarifying observations on the simple model used here may prove helpful. The *average* social rate of return on the investment is dY/dK, which is equal to $24\cdot47/322\cdot38$ in our example, or approximately $7\cdot6$ percent. It would be a mistake to compute the private rate of return of the investor as $(F_K dK + F_{KK} (K + dK)/dK$, which is only $7\cdot34/322\cdot38$ or $2\cdot28$ percent. This calculation would be meaningless because the opportunity cost of the capital *already invested* has declined, too, from 10 to 6 percent. In fact, under constant returns to scale the increase in labor and rental income following an increase in capital precisely reflects the decline in the rate of return earned by intramarginal units, so that, in terms of equation A5, $LF_{LK} + TF_{TK} = F_{KK}(K + dK)$. In our example this sum equals $17\cdot12$ units, of which 12 units are the intramarginal losses on the original capital stock, and the remaining $5\cdot12$ units are losses on the "new" capital.

Secondly, the example can be used to see what happens when we relax our assumption that labor is fixed. Assume that labor, instead of being fixed, can be hired at a given wage rate w. Any situation between a perfectly inelastic and a perfectly elastic labor supply will yield intermediate results. An exogenous decline in the cost of capital or a rise in its marginal product will change our results quantitatively, since an increase in K will increase the marginal product of L, leading to more workers being hired, which will feed back into the productivity of capital, and so on. The solution is obtained by solving the following two equations simultaneously for K^* and L^*:

$$(1) F_L (K^*, L^*, T) = w.$$
$$(2) F_K(K^*, L^*, T) = r.$$

The Cobb–Douglas specification permits an explicit solution. An exogenous decline in the cost of capital from 10 to 6 percent will increase K from an initial level of 100 to $358\cdot7$ and L from 100 to $215\cdot2$. Total output rises from 100 to $215\cdot2$. The increment in output is distributed as follows: $34\cdot6$ units flow to the owners of capital $57\cdot6$ are spent in hiring more workers (at a fixed wage), and $23\cdot0$ units accrue to landlords.

16 A depreciation rate of $7\cdot5$ percent may seem high compared to Feinstein's work (1978, pp. 49 and 636, n. 58) which places the average life of improvements in agriculture at 100 years. Even for fixed capital alone, Feinstein's conjectures seem very high. It should be noted that for Ireland much of the investment took the form of proper fertilization, weeding, and crop rotation, which have a much shorter "life span".

17 Derived under the assumption that $r = F_K$.

Chapter 5

The Economics of Rural Conflict and Unrest

(1) Introduction

So far, we have examined two explanations of Irish poverty which were central to contemporary thought on the subject. Neither the Malthusian nor the land tenure hypothesis, seem to go a long way in explaining the economic failures of the Irish economy. In this chapter I take up another theme which figures prominently in nineteenth-century thought, namely, the violence and lawlessness which characterized much of nineteenth-century Irish rural life, both before and after the famine. The approach utilized in this chapter takes a somewhat roundabout way to the subject of rural unrest and conflict between classes. Before we can conclude anything about the impact of these phenomena on Irish economic development, we must first try to understand their economic background in a more abstract conceptual framework.

The causal factors which explain the relative poverty of nations can be classified from a theoretical point of view into two main categories. The first category is one in which the culprit is what is generally referred to as a "market failure". The second category is one in which poverty occurs because of the behavior of individuals and one cannot easily diagnose a failure of markets. This kind of poverty does not imply inefficiency, because it is an outcome which reflects the tastes and desires of the population.[1] The fundamental difference between the two categories is *ex ante*: in an economy in which the flaw is a market failure, there is ambition and potential for development, but the economic forces are led astray by institutional or entrepreneurial failure. A capital market failure, for instance, short-circuits the flow of loanable funds from savers to investors. The economy may generate sufficient savings, and there may well be numerous investment projects which produce high yields. But if the market fails to connect the two, the capital accumulation process is aborted. Whenever the social rate of return on capital exceeds the private rate of return for any reason, we can say that market failure is responsible in part for economic backwardness.

Poverty caused by factors which belong in the second category is quite different. It would be correct, though a bit harsh, to say that poverty of this type persists because people want it to.[2] That is not to say, of course, that people in such an economy do not prefer "more" to "less". Rather, they are unwilling to pay the price of economic development in terms of postponing present consumption, forgoing leisure, taking risks, uprooting their communities, and so on. An example of a theoretical model in which all markets could be efficient but the economy stays poor is given by Nelson (1956; 1960), who shows how a low-income equilibrium can persist even if all the "neoclassical" conditions are fulfilled.[3]

A few of the explanations proposed for Ireland's poverty fall clearly in the second category of "voluntary" or "efficient" poverty. Primary among those is the Malthusian hypothesis which maintains that Ireland was poor becuase it was overpopulated. Overpopulation—provided it stemmed from the birth of wanted children rather than a failure to control fertility—is a case in which we can hardly speak of a market failure in the ordinary sense of the word. The poverty of the nth generation is caused mainly by the desire of $n-1$ previous generations to enjoy large numbers of offspring. Other hypotheses of this kind focus on the alleged differences between Irish utility functions and other "national" preference functions (Hutchinson, 1970). Such differences could involve, for instance, a higher preference for leisure or a higher rate of time preference. We shall discuss some of these views in Chapter 7.

On the whole, however, Irish poverty has been explained mainly by hypotheses belonging to the "market failure" category. The most influential and *a priori* persuasive of these theories is the land tenure hypothesis (LTH) discussed in Chapter 4. A second "market failure" theory blames the union with Britain, which deprived Ireland from protective tariffs and, thus, thwarted Irish industrialization (Hechter, 1975, p. 92; O'Brien, 1921, pp. 419–35). Any model based on a variant of the "infant industry" argument requires some form of market failure (Baldwin, 1969).

One hypothesis which properly belongs to the "market failure" category and which provides a powerful explanation of Ireland's backwardness focuses on what contemporaries called the Irish peasants' "disposition to organized crime and disturbances" (Lewis, 1836b, p. iii). A modern social historian concludes that "prefamine Ireland was a remarkably violent country" (Clark, 1979, p. 66). There are a number of ways to approach the questions of the causes and consequences of agrarian violence, and the economic approach utilized here should be viewed as complementing more sociological approaches. Briefly stated, the hypothesis submits that Irish agricultural poverty can be explained in part by the conflict between the landlords and the large grazier farmers on one side, and the smallholders and cottiers on the other. The former wanted to expand grazing agriculture, while the latter clung to tillage farming by all means at their disposal, including violence, thus changing the "rules of the game" and causing a market failure. Much of the landlord–tenant relations in the decades before the famine can be characterized as a "noncooperative" game, in which both sides try to do as well as possible for themselves, but disregard the interests of the other side. Game theory demonstrates that such games result in situations in which both sides are worse off than they could have been had they co-operated. The net result is that the entire economy was much poorer, not only because the "game" was not efficient (that is, resources were misallocated), but more importantly because violence and lawlessness created serious negative externalities which impeded economic development. The hypothesis is close to the one offered by Ransom and

Sutch (1977), to explain the backwardness of the postbellum American south. Ransom and Sutch argued that the south was forced, due to a very specific market imperfection, to produce more cotton (relative to other crops) than the optimal level: the south was "locked" into cotton. Irrespective of whether Ransom and Sutch's view of the American south is correct or not, a similar approach will be adopted here.[4]

From a purely physical point of view, Ireland is a land ideally suited to pastoral agriculture, due to its natural grass coverage, humidity, and mild winters (Crotty, 1966, p. 4; O'Donovan, 1940, pp. 140–2). In mediaeval and early modern times Ireland had been predominantly pastoral. The wars of the seventeenth century led to a further reduction in land under tillage: soldiers robbed and burned field crops, whereas animals could be driven to the mountains and saved. When peace was restored, grazing agriculture was further stimulated by the opening of the British market, in spite of the 1698 Woolen Acts which damaged the exports of wool products to Europe. After 1750, however, a reversal occurred, and a trend to convert land from pasturage to arable farming began to emerge. The precise causes for this reversal cannot easily be established due to the paucity of eighteenth-century data. But it is often maintained that the terms of trade turned in favor of arable products when Great Britain became dependent to an ever-growing extent on grain imports. Acts providing government bounties to the exporters of grains in 1758 and 1784 reinforced this trend. The accelerating diffusion of the potato after 1750 must be regarded as a technological improvement in arable production as a whole. It is also possible that growing population reduced the price of labor and, thus, made a shift into more labor-intensive crops (that is, arable crops) more attractive.[5]

The relative profitability of arable production peaked during the Napoleonic Wars. After Waterloo, in spite of the Corn Laws, a tendency to try to return to pasturage can be observed (Connell, 1950a, pp. 114–20). Ó'Tuathaigh (1972, p. 135) and Crotty (1966, p. 36) have maintained that the terms of trade turned in favor of livestock after 1815. Is this view correct? Judgements of contemporaries on the behavior of prices are a poor substitute for price data. Because the relevant prices are export prices, and since most Irish agricultural exports went to Great Britain, British prices can be used to test the hypothesis that the relative price of tillage products fell after the Napoleonic Wars. The results, presented in the Appendix to this chapter, indicate that there is no evidence that relative prices changed in favor of pasturage products after 1814. This finding complicates the story but does not necessarily invalidate the hypothesis that pasturage products became more profitable relative to tillage products after the Napoleonic Wars. Rather, it redirects the search for the causes of the change. All we can say at this stage is that demand effects were probably not responsible for the widely reported enhanced attractiveness of pasturage crops after 1814. An increase in the relative profitability of two crops is, after all, consistent both with a rise and with a decline in the relative price of two crops. If technical changes favored pasturage more than arable crops, it would shift the supply curve of pasturage crops farther to the right than that of arable crops, implying, all other things equal, lower prices for pasturage crops relative to arable crops as well as pressure to expand the acreage devoted to pasturage. If there were changes on both the supply and the demand side simultaneously, the movement of relative prices could go either way, or could be trendless except for short-term fluctuations.

The introduction of steam transport across the Irish Sea and the considerable success attained with selective breeding in Ireland (O'Donovan, 1940, pp. 157–8, 178–90) suggests that changing supply conditions may cause the price-series to understate the increase in relative profitability of livestock production. In 1836 E. S. Shawe, a Kildare agent, noted that "according as they [the farmers] get wealthy, I consider that they give up tillage farming", and pointed out that farmers with capital devoted less land to tillage than before, while the "poor small tenants cannot do anything but till". The reason was that "during the [Napoleonic] war a great deal of land was turned up [converted to tillage], and since that we are getting it to grass as soon as we can" (Great Britain, 1836a, Vol. VIII, pp. 263–71). One witness testifying before the Poor Law Commission stated in 1836 that "tillage is not considered remunerating from the great decline in prices . . . give us Buonaparte again, and we'll soon till more" (Great Britain, 1836b, Vol. XXXIII, p. 206).

In spite of the increased desirability of livestock production, the attempts of landlords and large farmers to turn the clock back and return once more to a predominantly pastoral economy met with only limited success. Unfortunately, it is on this point that our evidence is the most unsatisfactory. It was therefore possible for Crotty (1966, pp. 42, 43, 46–8) to object to the conventional wisdom on this point, and maintain that the shift back from arable to pasturage—usually dated to the post-famine years—actually began before the famine. Crotty has been severely taken to task by Lee (1969b) and others on this point. In the absence of production or acreage statistics before the famine, scholars have had to fall back on sparse and scattered foreign trade statistics. The difficulty, as stressed by Goldstrom (1981, p. 162) who summarizes the debate, is that in a period of falling transport costs and rapid integration of Ireland into the British economic sphere, it is hard to conclude anything about what went on *within* Ireland from the export and import statistics.

For the present purpose, what matters is not only whether the landlords failed completely in their endeavor to "put the land to grass", but especially what effect the attempts had on landlord–tenant relations and on the general economic climate in the Irish countryside. It was not easy to convert arable land back to pasturage in the first half of the nineteenth century. Doing so involved, in the majority of cases, consolidation of holdings, clearing the tenants from the land, transforming smallholders and cottiers into landless agricultural laborers, and converting the agricultural sector from a partial subsistence economy into a market-oriented economy. Two major obstacles stood in the way of the landlord. First, as we have seen, most of the land in Ireland was held by lease. As long as leases were in force, there was little the landlord (or his agent) could do to influence the form of agriculture practiced on his estate. But even when leases expired, or when land was held at will, the landlords encountered resistance.

Rural unrest, or to use the term of the day "agrarian outrages", was nothing new in Ireland in the period 1815–45. Since 1760 the Irish countryside had witnessed repeated violence and acts of terror, perpetrated by "whiteboys", "steelboys", "rockites", and similar organizations (Lewis, 1836a, pp. 3–44). Many contemporaries believed that agrarian violence was related to poverty and unemployment (Foster, 1847, p. 11; Lewis, 1836a, pp. 78–87, 311–12; Kennedy, 1847, pp. 321–2). The result was a widespread feeling of insecurity and "turbulence" in the countryside, which discouraged capital investment, frustrated the efforts of well-meaning landlords to improve agriculture, and thus deepened poverty and unemployment. Relations between landlord and tenants in Ireland were, for obvious reasons, more likely to be spoiled by mutual suspicion, political and racial prejudice, religious differences, and the sediment of centuries of confrontation and violence than in other European countries. In the nineteenth century, an economic dimension was added to exacerbate and complicate an already-difficult situation. Consolidation and conversion of tillage lands to grazing was violently resisted by the tenancy, leading to persistent clashes, bordering at times on guerrilla warfare. Although of course not every part of the country was affected all the time, the inference drawn by contemporary writers, that such a climate was not conducive to the economic development of the Irish countryside, cannot seriously be doubted.

But why the *economic* conflict, on top of the existing sources of friction? On the highest level of abstraction, it might seem odd that landlords would willingly rid themselves of their tenants, thus reducing the labor–land ratio on their estates. The balance between arable and pasturage, without further elaboration, does not suffice to explain the conflict. In most economic models there is no conflict of interest between the capitalist or landlord and his worker or tenant as to *what* to produce. Unless there is some form of "market failure", landlord and tenant will always agree on the crop to be produced, although they may differ on the distribution of the revenue and even on *how* to produce it. It does not actually matter whether the decisions "what to produce" are made by landlord, capitalist, tenant, or a *deus ex machina* entrepreneur. What has to be investigated, therefore, is the source of the market failure.

(2)   The Sources of Conflict: a Theoretical Analysis

The precise cost of the conflict between arable and pasturage farming is shown in Figure 5.1. The cost consists of two components: the cost of preventing the economy from moving from points like A_1 to E_1 (the "cost of distortion"), and the cost in terms of loss of investment and entrepreneurship which shied away from Ireland as a result of the rural unrest, which is represented by a shift of the production possibility frontier from $F_1 F_1$ to $F_2 F_2$. The economy thus ends up at A_2. The net loss of income in terms of arable products is the distance $C_0 C_2$, of which $C_0 C_1$ is due to the first effect and $C_1 C_2$ is due to the second.

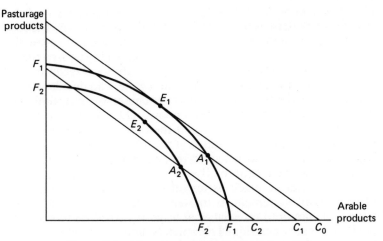

Figure 5.1   *The economic costs of rural conflict*

Assume, for exposition purposes only, that there are only two factors of production, land and labor. There are two crops, which are really "techniques to produce revenue". One crop is labor-intensive and will be called "arable", the other is land-intensive and will be referred to as "pasturage". Figure 5.2 describes the alternatives.

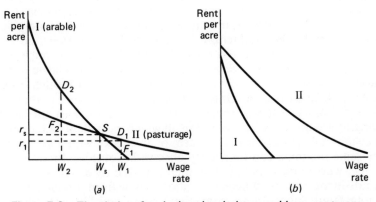

Figure 5.2   *The choice of agricultural technique: arable vs. pasturage*

The two factor-price frontiers I and II, determined by technological parameters and the relative price of husbandry to arable products, show the tradeoff between rents per acre and wages per worker. A landlord faced by a wage of W_1 would choose to produce at D_1, that is, devote the land entirely to pasturage. At a lower wage, say, W_2, he would switch to D_2 and specialize in arable products. Note that if the terms of trade improve sufficiently for pasturage, a situation such as depicted in panel (*b*) might prevail, in which pasturage dominates arable for any set of factor prices.

The important point illustrated in Figure 5.2 is that in a typical choice of crop problem there is harmony between the landlord and the tenant. For instance, if factor prices are such that technique II is preferred (wages higher than W_s or rents below r_s), it can readily be seen that both factors would be worse off due to an erroneous choice of technique. If the tenant rents the land at a given rent and it is he who decides what and how to produce, the techniques and crops chosen by him would be the same as those the landlord would choose. The "neoclassical" agents take their factor prices as given and then choose the best technique under that constraint. For instance, if the decision-making agent is the tenant who rents the land at a given rent r_1, he will maximize his (labor) income by choosing technique II at D_1. The landlord has no reason to resist, and he can be made better off by the tenant offering him an arbitrarily small increment in the rent. Precisely the same reasoning obtains if the landlord hires labor at wage W_1. Needless to say, if technique II dominates technique I completely, as in panel (*b*), the harmony in the choice of technique is trivial.[6]

If economic analysis suggests that harmony is the normal state of affairs between landlords and tenants, how can economists explain the conflict between them? Three separate effects should be distinguished: the "labor-demand effect", "the scale effect", and the "autarky effect". The first, which is the simplest, has been put forward in a different context by Ó Gráda (1973a, pp. 83–104). Assume that the amount of land is fixed, and that two crops can be produced, h (pasturage) and a (arable). Assume the arable crop is more labor-intensive, so that $l_a > l_h$, where the ls are the labor–land ratios. It can be seen immediately that if landlords make the production decisions and hire workers, no *single* worker has an interest to resist a shift from arable to pasturage. Competition guarantees that each worker faces a perfectly elastic demand curve for his services, so that he can costlessly shift to another occupation which pays the same. Only if a worker (or a family) earns more than its opportunity cost will there be an incentive to resist the change. Looking at a more realistic situation, in which individual tenants are the decision-makers operating on a farm of given size with a given rental, the same dilemma can be readily observed. Consider, first, the small farmer who employs only family members. If only a is produced, total family income is Lw_a, where w_a is labor income from producing a and L is total family labor. Now assume that a new crop h "becomes feasible", increasing the labor income of each family-member involved in it from w_a to w_h, but employing only l_h units of labor per acre. Will the new technique be adopted? The decision whether to adopt the new technique will depend on the difference between w_h and w_a, the difference between l_a and l_h, and the wage that can be earned outside the family w_0. In the absence of a nonagricultural sector, w_0 can be interpreted as the shadow price of leisure. It can be shown that the new technique will be adopted if[7]

$$\frac{l_h}{l_a} > \frac{w_a - w_0}{w_h - w_0}. \tag{5.1}$$

If inequality 5.1 is violated, the tenant will resist the switch, although his landlord will forgo rents by a failure to adopt the more efficient technique. A source of friction has emerged. The reason for the conflict of interest is that the tenant uses family labor: had the workers been hired in a competitive labor market, he would not have hesitated to lay them off and adopt a more efficient technique. The small, family-operated farms are thus at the root of the conflict, together with low values of w_0 (note that if $w_a = w_0$ the problem disappears).

Discussion of this "imperfection" or market failure requires some careful handling of the term "efficiency". In a typical competitive economic model higher rents are often equated with higher efficiency. This equivalence assumes $w_a = w_0$, so that the workers released by labor-saving changes can be costlessly shifted away from agriculture into alternative occupations. When $w_a > w_0$, it is possible that more efficient crops could imply a lower national product per capita. To visualize the difficulty involved, assume that crop a provides full employment, but crop h, being labor-saving, requires outside employment for part of the labor force. Define $R_h = Q_h - w_a L_h$, that is, the rents in pasturage are the difference between the value of output and the wage bill, and similarly $R_a = Q_a - w_a L_a$. Under arable national income equals $Y_a = Q_a = R_a + wL_a$, but under pasturage national income becomes $Y_h = R_h + w_a L_h + w_0 (L_a - L_h)$. Some simple rearrangement shows that a shift from arable to pasturage will be efficient for the economy as a whole only if

$$\frac{R_h - R_a}{w_a - w_0} > L_a - L_h. \tag{5.2}$$

If inequality 5.2 is violated, conflict seems almost inevitable since it is not possible for the landlords to compensate the workers for the latter's reduced income. If inequality 5.2 is satisfied, a shift to pasturage is pareto-optimal in that the landlords could compensate the workers to leave their incomes unchanged and still be better off themselves. As there is no indication that they actually would do so without being threatened, the satisfaction of 5.2 does not mean that outrages will not occur. It should also be noted that if 5.2 is violated, the income-reducing effect of economic conflict as depicted in Figure 5.1 is complicated. Point E_1 is no longer strictly preferable to A_1, since the diagram no longer represents the entire economy but only the agricultural sector.

The second mechanism leading to conflict will be termed the "scale effect". Assume that the "labour-demand effect" is not present, that is, $l_a = l_h$. Assume that technology and prices are such that we are on curve II on panel (*b*) in Figure 5.2, so that pasturage dominates arable completely. Suppose that there are scale economies in pasturage which are absent in arable, as represented in Figure 5.3. It is seen immediately that the dominance of pasturage is only well established at farms larger than A^* acres and the advantage of pasturage only fully realized on farms of size A_1 and larger. To see why friction can arise, assume that a tenant farming A_1 acres dies, bequeathing his lease to four heirs, each of whom receives A_2. Each son will produce arable products rather than pasturage products, forcing the farms to operate on frontier I in Figure 5.1, panel (*b*), even though that leads to global inefficiency.

It is not quite impossible for an equal-shares-inheritance society to avoid the losses involved in the forgone scale economies. Common ownership and joint tenancy were practiced to some extent in prefamine Ireland, but as contemporaries pointed out, the inefficiencies of that system were even worse than those of subdivision. We may also imagine that three brothers would sell their land to the fourth and work for him as common laborers (recall that we are assuming $l_a = l_h$). Bargaining costs would be high, of course, and highly imperfect capital markets would make it difficult for one to buy out his brothers. Moreover, as is typical in many peasant societies, working one's own land was deemed far more desirable than being employed as an agricultural laborer. Landlords who tried to convert smallholders into agricultural laborers discovered a tenacious resistance among their tenants (Lane, 1972, p. 57). The outcome that emerges from these contradictory forces is a mixed one: in the Irish countryside large grazing farms coexisted with small subsistence farms. The cottiers living on the latter also supplied much of the labor for the former. It is worth adding that the massive conversion of Irish agriculture from tillage to grazing after the famine was accompanied not only by a decline in population but also by a shift from partible to impartible inheritance at least as far as the land was concerned (Ó Gráda, 1980a).

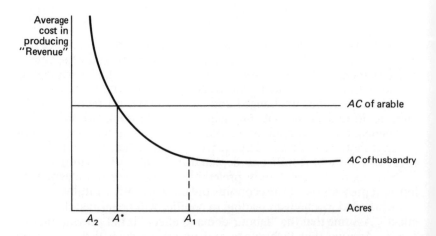

Figure 5.3   *Scale economies and the 'scale effect'*

Subletting was the second major source of the loss of scale economies. Landlords in the late eighteenth century let land at long leases to farmers at the market rate. Due to rising prices or other factors, the market rent rose so that many lessees found it profitable to sublet the land at higher rents than they paid themselves and live off the difference as rentiers. It might be thought that the "middleman" would find it profitable to preserve the farm as a whole so that the scale economies would be preserved, but from his point of view there could also have been advantages in dividing the land into smaller fragments, even at the cost of the loss of scale economies. One such advantage could have been diversification: the "quality" of the tenant may have been unknown to the middleman so that diversification made perfect sense. Moreover, as many aspects of the (usually informal) contract between middleman and tenant were subject to negotiation, the middleman might have felt that his bargaining position would have improved by a *divide et impera* policy. After 1815, the landlords gradually reduced the importance of middlemen by not renewing their leases and charged what they believed to be the market rent. In order to get the maximal rent and to realize the scale economies, it became necessary for them to consolidate holdings. It is clear now why the scale effect caused such efforts to be resisted by the tenants, even if consolidation did not involve a loss in labor demand.

Whether scale economies were of overwhelming importance in nineteenth-century Irish agriculture is difficult to say. That there were and are scale economies in grazing farms seems self-evident. The case for tillage farms is more complicated. There seems to be no evidence to support the existence of scale economies of a technical nature in tillage agriculture which produced potatoes, cereals, flax, and in some cases animal fodder. It is however quite clear that if information, entre-preneurial ability, and technical knowledge are not omnipresent and cost-free, a strong case can be made for managerial economies in scale. Many landlords made this argument when defending their attempts at consolidation. Another incentive for consolidation in tillage agriculture was created artificially by the imperfections of the capital markets. Landlords maintained that consolidation had to be resorted to in order to get more substantial tenants who had better access to capital.

The third source of economic friction between landlord and tenant may be termed the "autarky effect". To isolate it, assume that the labor-demand effect is inoperative and that there are no scale economies. Assume that all land is homogeneous and that the two crops are not used as inputs into each other. Under these assumptions, the production possibility frontier between arable and pasturage products is a straight line and a profit-maximizing decision-maker will normally specialize completely in one of two goods. In Figure 5.4, panel (*a*), it can be seen that the profit-maximizing farmer "plunges" into pasturage: at point P_0, faced by the relative price line P_0P_1, he cannot achieve a higher income given his production possibility frontier P_0F. Note that the procedure implies that this farmer does not consume any of the goods produced directly, or, if he does, he pays the market price for them. The prices are given, so that the slope of the price line is constant.

The thrust of the autarky effect is that the arable products grown by the tenants are not the same as the arable good contemplated by the landlord. While grain crops and flax largely found their way to markets, the potato was predominantly a subsistence crop, that is, grown by the same people who consumed it. Trade in potatoes was difficult and costly due to the high weight-value and volume-value ratios, and the tendency of potatoes to spoil when handled and loaded. The difficulties were compounded by the fact that potatoes could be stored at most for 9–10 months. While some trade in potatoes did exist, it was small relative to output. Once we realize this constraint, the tendency of the tenant to "plunge" disappears. He no longer maximizes money income, he maximizes utility. The choice is shown on panel (*b*) in Figure 5.4, where the indifference curve I is the indifference curve between "food" (that is, potatoes) and "income" (that is, the revenues received from selling tradeable goods). Point *E* in panel (*b*) is determined by the equality of the marginal rate of substitution between income and food to the price ratio. For the tenants, it is optimal to produce a "mix" of arable products and pasturage products, even though the landlord would like him to specialize completely in pasturage products.

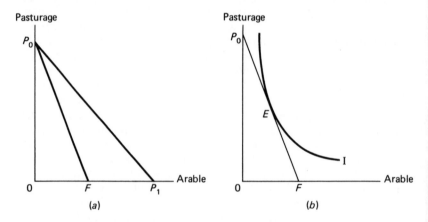

Figure 5.4   *The autarky effect*

Even if the production-possibility frontier is not a straight line so that complete specialization does not occur, the autarky effect is still operative. As potatoes and grain crops were produced jointly as part of a crop-rotation cycle in which grain crops typically followed a heavily manured potato crop, the adherence of Irish tenants to arable crops becomes easy to understand. Suppose, for instance, that the price of wheat declines due to, say, an increase in the supply of Baltic wheat to the British market. For a profit-maximizing, market-oriented farmer, this will be taken as a signal warranting a shift in the direction of more pasturage products. But for the potato-consuming subsistence peasant the shadow price of the unmarketed good, potatoes, matters too. The shadow price of subsistence of food products was subject to quite different forces than the market price of wheat. In other words, there was a wedge between the marketed tillage crop and the subsistence tillage crop, and the signals emitted by changes in relative prices meant different things to different people. The non-cooperative solution to the game played by landlords and tenants was probably closer to point E than to point P_0 in terms of Figure 5.4, that is, the tenants were more successful than the landlords. The point is, however, that precisely because this victory was achieved by means of threats and violence, it reduced the economic welfare of both players, in other words, of the entire economy.

The story above is, of course, heavily oversimplified. Potatoes were, to some extent, marketed; many Irish peasants did consume some food derived from grains, especially oats (Cullen, 1981a, 1981b). Livestock and arable crops were also inputs into each other, so that price movements were not independent. None the less, the story is consistent with the basic facts and in no way illogical in terms of simple economics. Standard "neoclassic" economic theory, unlike game theory, does not usually have much to say about conflicts between the economic agents. As in so many other cases, the fundamental fashion in which reality deviated from the frictionless, competitive model can be reduced ultimately to transactions costs. Each of our three "effects" requires some form of transactions costs. The labor demand effect has to assume that agricultural wages were above wages outside agriculture (inclusive of both nonpecuniary benefits and costs). The scale effect requires some mechanism which prevented farms from merging or splitting costlessly to attain the optimum scale. The autarky effect depends on transactions costs incurred in exchanging the subsistence crop and the cash crop. Historians may view this "search for transactions costs" as just so much sterile sophistry. However, for economists, trained in thinking of the world in the rosy terms of symbiotic cooperation and harmony, it may be useful to specify precisely where the standard model broke down, leading to a conflict—some may even think of it in terms of class struggle—which is otherwise not easily explained by economic logic.

How do the explanations proposed above square with other views of rural violence in prefamine Ireland? The most serious general hypothesis has been put forward by Clark (1979, pp. 69–70), according to whom the root of the phenomenon was the enforcement of a set of informal property rights regarding land tenure, grazing, turbaries, and similar areas. "In the first half of the nineteenth century", notes Clark, "the implicit terms of this traditional contract were more and more often broken". It should be pointed out, however, that it is not easy to explain without paying more attention to the economic background why this system of implicit contracts erupted suddenly in violence. After all, every legal contract or other definition of property rights is incomplete in some sense and there are almost always some contingencies which are left implicit or ambiguous. As long as no clear-cut conflict of interest emerges between the two sides, there is no reason to expect trouble. Similarly, as long as the formal contract precisely specifies each side's rights, and these clauses are mutually respected, economic conflicts can be settled without violence. When a conjunction of the two phenomena occurs, however, a breakdown of the accepted norms of conducting business becomes a real possibility.

The relations between landlord and tenant were not determined only by economic factors. Irish tenants viewed their Protestant landlords as conquerors and oppressors, while the landlords regarded their Catholic tenants with condescendence and scorn. Lack of communicaton and mutual trust led to the "noncooperativeness" of the economic game played between landowners and peasants. But this hostility does not explain the desire of Irish landlords to evict and eject their tenants, to encourage them to emigrate, and to perpetrate such atrocities as the "Gregory clause", which, in the middle of the famine, deprived from relief all tenants who held more than a quarter of an acre, leading to massive evictions. Only in terms of "what to produce" can we understand the *economic* roots of the conflict and see why the landlords were keen on getting rid of their tenants.

(3) Consolidation and Agrarian Outrage: Some Evidence

To recapitulate the hypothesis formulated above: in the decades before the famine, serious economic conflict arose between the Irish tenant farmers and their landlords. The landlords attempted to rid themselves of their tenants, to consolidate and rearrange the holdings, and to convert the land to pasturage. The resistance of tenants to these attempts led to increased turbulence and violence, which, whether successful or not, imposed a serious cost on the Irish rural economy.

Once we try to confront the hypothesis with evidence, however, it becomes clear that the reality was sufficiently complicated to make any simple tests quite impossible. First, economic conflict of the type described in Section 2 was by no means the only source of class conflict in rural Ireland. In his classic essay on Irish agrarian outrages Lewis (1836a, pp. 60–93) provided a long list of suspected causes for the phenomenon. Some of the items on Lewis's list should be viewed with caution. For example, the religious differences between landlords and tenants, and the fact that the Protestant ascendency was regarded as a class of usurpers may be crucial in explaining the background of the outrages, but are not very helpful in explaining why they erupted when and where they did. None the less, without the political, religious, and cultural abysses between the landowning and the tenant classes in Ireland, the more immediate economic causes may not have led to such dramatic events. The great tithe strike of the 1830s was not in and of itself an "economic" conflict of the type described above, but as Beckett (1966, p. 310) has pointed out, helped to make the local outrages possible by the general weakening of central authority, especially the British impotence to enforce the law in the face of local and well-determined resistance.[8] Some part of the violence can also be attributed to local feuds between neighbors, relatives, and "factions" and had no discernible profound economic causes.

Secondly, it has to be kept in mind that consolidation of farms and the ejectment of tenants or cottiers from the land were by no means two sides of the same coin. As the Digest of the Devon Commission points out (Kennedy, 1847, pp. 451–3), the consolidation of farms could take place either because the mean size of the holdings was increased by merging the plots of smallholders, or by the rearrangement of scattered holdings held under a system known as rundale, which in some respects resembled the scattered holdings of British open fields. Even if consolidation was of the first type, however, it did not necessarily reduce the demand for labor. In many cases consolidation of farms did not imply a major switch from tillage to pasturage, but a reorganization of tillage under a single farmer who was considered more competent or more reliable than the multitudes of poor cottiers among whom the land was subdivided. In a few cases the landlord himself took possession and increased his demesne.

Thirdly, consolidation did not invariably lead to the ruthless eviction of tenants from the land. Often tenants were compensated by the land-lord or bought out by neighboring tenants, sometimes with landlord encouragement. In other cases tenants emigrated and returned the farm voluntarily to the landlord. A landlord in prefamine Ireland could legally remove a tenant in several ways. A tenant holding an annual lease could, at least *de jure*, be terminated at the end of the year. A tenant who had a lease could be evicted by a landlord bringing a Civil Eject-ment Bill against him if he violated the terms of the lease. These violations typically were of two kinds: nonpayment of rent, or sub-division. Of course, a tenant holding a long-term lease could be got rid of when the lease expired. Furthermore, not all evictions were carried out for the purpose of consolidation. There were, as in any other country, many tenants who fell into arrears, who tilled the land poorly, and who were regarded for a variety of other reasons as undesirable tenants and replaced by others.

Fourthly, not all agrarian conflict necessarily pitted tenant against landlord (Clark, 1979, pp. 70–3). It has been maintained that many out-rages were concerned with the taking of land "in conacre". Conacre land was land which was let out by farmers to cottiers or landless laborers for the growing season only to raise potatoes, and thus constituted a special form of subletting (Beames, 1975). Joseph Lee (1973b) has argued that much agrarian unrest stemmed from the refusal of farmers to give land in conacre. Lee's hypothesis is a special case of the operation of the "autarky effect", in which the role of the landlord is played by someone who is actually a tenant. It is not surprising that in the complicated and often multilayered structure of land ownership in Ireland, the farmer was sometimes the victim of the cottier's wrath.

Before turning to examine the evidence, one digression. It has been argued that agrarian outrages served yet another function, which dwarfed in its importance all others, namely, the enforcement of a monstrous "cartel" by means of which the tenants prevented the landlords from raising rents to competitive levels. Solow (1971, p. 34) writes that "the landlord who exacted a competitive rent was the target of the blunderbuss; a farmer who outbid another was the subject of ostracism or worse; the history of the agrarian disturbances ... shows that an important aim of the secret societies was artificially to keep rents below the competitive level". Clark (1979, p. 167) makes a similar point.

The hypothesis that agrarian violence was aimed at keeping rents below their equilibrium level is important not only because, if true, it provides a powerful economic explanation of the conflicts between landlords and tenants in Ireland, but also because it would shed light on two other phenomena. First, it would provide a rationale for the sale of "tenant right", the value of the tenant right being equal to the present value of the difference between the market clearing rent and the actual rent to which the landlord was forced to agree. Secondly, it would provide an alternative explanation for the curious phenomenon of landlords actually trying to rid themselves of tenants. Simple economic theory would, of course, suggest the opposite: rents rise with the labor–land ratio, so that the landlord would be advised to get as many tenants as possible. If rents were, however, not being maximized for some reason, the tenants would be receiving more than the marginal product of labor. This implies that the landlord would actually increase his rental income by clearing them off his estate. The "cartel hypothesis" thus not only makes sense, it also fits neatly into our puzzle.

For the prefamine years, however, the evidence does not support the hypothesis. Qualitative statements of contemporaries indicate overwhelmingly that landlords and their representatives successfully maximized rental income. Witness after witness before the Poor Law Commission stated that severe competition among tenants permitted landlords to charge exorbitant rents. In fact, completion in Ireland was more severe than in England, so that nominal rents in the former were reduced less in the years after 1815 than in the latter, although presumably prices had declined approximately *pari passu* in both countries (Great Britain, 1836b, Vol. XXXIII, pp. 116, 144, 167, 174, 249, 287). In some cases there were large differences between rents charged by landlords on very similar and neighboring lots, but these differences were often absorbed by "exorbitant charges, fees, and charges on leases and other indirect modes of exaction ... underagents sometimes take a compliment (bribe) to give a tenant a preference" (ibid., pp. 163–4; Wiggins, 1844, pp. 44–6). The evidence given before the Devon Commission indicates that in the south and west "the rent [was] commonly determined by proposals made by those who wish[ed] to obtain a vacant farm. The highest solvent bidder [was] in most cases accepted" (Kennedy, 1847, p. 753). In other areas the landlord or agent carried out or commissioned a "valuation" and offered it to the tenant on a "take it or leave it" basis (for instance, Great Britain, 1845a, Vol. XIX, p. 549). Foster (1847, pp. 33, 234–5) noted that land was let to the highest bidder by "tender" or "proposal". The custom was sometimes referred to as "canting" (Wiggins, 1844, pp. 37–9; Donnelly, 1973, p. 33), and there is no evidence to support Clark's dismissal of canting as unusual (Clark, 1979, p. 167). Many other contemporary opinions expressing similar views can be cited (Beaumont, 1839, Vol. 1, p. 300; Coote, 1804, p. 118; Townsend, 1815, Vol. 2, p. 53; Rawson, 1807, p. 20). Connell (1950a, pp. 82–3) cites with approval O'Brien's exaggerated opinion that rents were such as to give the landlords "almost the whole produce of the land". The habit of letting the land to the highest bidder was also prevalent in Ulster, even in areas (such as Co. Antrim) where the Ulster custom was in force (OSM, box 9, file VI, relating to Drummaul parish, Randalstown near Lough Neagh). No evidence has been produced to support Solow's more recent claim that rent-maximization was a comparatively recent phenomenon in 1840, and that it was only a "significant but declining proportion of landlords who considered rent maximization not respectable" (Solow, 1981, p. 310).

It cannot be seriously denied, of course, that there were *some* cases in which the rent charged by landlords was below the market value, so that the property rights were, in some sense, shared by the landlord and the tenant. Old leases, reflecting past rather than present market conditions, were the primary source of this discrepancy. In other cases laziness, incompetence, and fear on the part of landlords or their agents could account for the phenomenon. The question is: how general was the phenomenon of rents being below their market value of the behavior of Irish landlords in general? Contemporary political economists believed it to be the exception. J. R. McCulloch—not exactly a radical social critic—thought that rents in Ireland were "enormously high" (McCulloch, 1854, Vol. 1, pp. 513, 571).

One source permits a more rigorous testing of the hypothesis that rents paid were consistently lower than the market-clearing "equilibrium" rate which would have prevailed under a regime of maximizing behavior and perfect competition. The Agricultural returns for Co. Tipperary, compiled in 1834 and published in 1941 (Simington, 1941), contain some data on actual rents paid compared to something called "real acreable value". The latter term seems to be as close as one can get to the equilibrium rent being "the sum an [Irish] acre is worth per annum based on the full productive capacity and deducting all outgoings and taking an average over a period of years, say five. The figure obtained . . . would include both the landlord's and tenant's interest" (Simington, 1941, pp. 249–50). "Interest" here should be taken to mean income above normal factor returns, so that the tenant's interest excludes his labor income, which was reckoned as an expense. The real acreable values were estimated by a commissioner appointed by the Lord Lieutenant, Ebenezer Radford, whose work was described by Simington as "painstaking and exceptional". Unfortunately, the rent data were available only for three of the six parishes, but the source is important none the less because it pertains to Co. Tipperary, the most violence-prone county in Ireland. If it were true anywhere that rents were forced below their equilibrium value by Professor Solow's blunderbusses, it should have been true there. Rents and real acreable values were available for a total of 117 farms, covering 1,967 Irish acres (which is 3,187 statute acres). The average rent paid per Irish acre on these farms was £1·657, which compares with a mean real acreable value of £1·503. The standard deviations were, respectively, 1·543 and 1·176, implying standard errors of 0·035 and 0·027. The hypothesis that rents were consistently below their market value is thus rejected at a level of significance better than 0·1 percent, the appropriate t-statistic being in excess of 10. It is, of course, possible to argue that for some reason Radford's estimates of the real acreable value were too high or that the three Tipperary parishes used here were an unrepresentative sample. It seems, however, that the evidence, qualitative or quantitative, does not provide much support for a systematic and widespread downward bias of rents paid for reasons other than "old leases". And yet, this is what is necessary to support Solow's contention that the contemporary notion of "fair rents" was equivalent to a rent below the equilibrium level, while "rackrents" were equal to competitive rents. Rackrents, like usury, seems more than anything a term symbolizing indignation at a phenomenon not quite understood by the participants in the market process.

Complaints about rackrents were rampant in prefamine Ireland and there are some—though not many—cases in which disagreement about rents led to agrarian conflict and violence. Once it is realized, however, that the landlords' intention often was not to raise rents within the given mode of production but to raise rents as a result of a radical change in the crops produced and the technology employed, disagreements about rent can be reconciled with the models in Section 2. My disagreement with the "cartel hypothesis" is thus in emphasis rather than essence: the "cartel" was primarily aimed against consolidation and eviction, lower rents were a byproduct of this process.[9]

Much evidence on consolidation and rural unrest in prefamine Ireland can be found in three remarkable documents published in the decade before the famine, namely, the Poor Law Commission (Great Britain, 1836b, Vols XXX–XXXIII), the Wharncliffe Committee (Great Britain, 1839a), and the Devon Commission (Great Britain, 1845a, Vols XIX–XXII).[10] Among them, these three bodies interviewed almost 3,000 witnesses from all social and economic classes. Agrarian unrest was very much on the mind of the British government and its relation with rural economic conditions was the subject of many detailed inquiries. The conclusion that the Devon Commission Digest drew from the massive evidence is worth quoting:

> There can be little doubt . . . that the real original source of agrarian outrage, as well as most other national disorders that exist in Ireland is the disproportion between the demand for and the supply of labour . . . The possession of land, however small its extent, has become the only security for a supply of food; and to lose that security is, in fact, to risk the very existence of the family from which it was taken. (Kennedy, 1847, p. 321)

Lewis, working with earlier parliamentary commissions published in the 1820s and 1830s, concluded that crime and disturbances were a result of forceful ejectment of tenants and cottiers for the purpose of consolidating farms (Lewis, 1836b, p. 36). The Deputy Inspector-General of the Irish Constabulary, Lieutenant Colonel William Miller, testified that outrages originated in the difficulties experienced by tenants in securing potato ground, especially in the best grazing grounds: "The owners and holders of lands are unwilling to break up ground [for tillage] which is profitable for pasture. The peasant, if unable to procure a potato garden, has no hope of feeding his family and is driven to desperation . . . [engaging] the sympathies of the surrounding population who lend a willing hand to redress such evils by violent means" (Great Britain, 1845a, Vol. XXI, p. 909).

These views, which are perfectly consistent with the features of the model proposed in Section 2, summarize hundreds of testimonies.

None the less, opinions and judgements of contemporaries alone, however well informed, are not a sufficient source to test our model. As was pointed out above, not all outrages, ejectments, and attempts to consolidate had the same character. Witnesses often disagreed with one another, sometimes contradicted themselves, and quite dramatic variations seem to have occurred between adjacent regions. A systematic investigation into the phenomenon is called for in order to establish what was typical and what exceptional. The tabulations below treat each witness as an "observation" when the question answered is similar or identical to those answered by others. This is more difficult for the 1,078 witnesses testifying for the Devon Commission than the 1,570 witnesses of the Poor Law Commission because the latter were asked a set of identical questions whereas the former were not, though similar questions did recur frequently. Needless to say, the technique of "content analysis" of these witnesses is far from being free of biases and distortions, but it is uniquely powerful in establishing *regional* differences in the phenomena observed and orders of magnitude of their frequency.

To start with, how prevalent was consolidation in the decades prior to the famine? Appendix 104 to the Devon Commission report (Great Britain, 1845a, Vol. XXII, pp. 303–19) presents a summary of all Civil Bill Ejectments, by far the most common way to remove occupants and tenants, for the years 1839–43. A total of 23,594 cases are listed, of which 7,588 or 32·2 percent are for "Non-payment of rent", 1,606 or 6·8 percent for "Overholding after expiration of lease", 14,320 or 60·7 percent for "Holding after notices to quit", and remaining 80 or 0·3 percent for "Absconding". Unfortunately, this breakdown does not provide information about how many of these ejectments were for the purpose of consolidation. It is, for instance, quite likely that arrears were used often as an excuse to evict when the real purpose was consolidation. Instances of such behavior can be documented (for example, Great Britain, 1845a, Vol. XX, pp. 439,548). One cause of mounting arrears among tenants after 1815 was the decline in agricultural prices, which made the high rents contracted during the Napoleonic Wars unrealistic. Clearly, turning out a tenant who failed to pay part of his rent for this reason does not help the landlord, since the incoming tenant will not pay the unnaturally high rent either. Turning out such tenants for nonpayment of rent, therefore, does not make sense unless the incoming tenant is expected to be a better tenant, or unless the ulterior motive leading to ejectment is to clear out the small tenants and consolidate their holdings.

An additional source of systematic information on the frequency and nature of consolidation of farms would, thus, be helpful. One source is the Devon Commission witnesses. By tracing all the witnesses who answered the question "Is the consolidation of farms prevalent in your district?" or some variant thereof, it is possible to get an indication of the dimension of the phenomenon. A total of 317 witnesses could be used for this purpose. The procedure has been to classify all questions into three categories: those who confirmed that consolidation was prevalent, those who acknowledged its existence but modified it by words like "few", "not much", and so on, and those who denied its existence altogether. The results, broken down by province, are presented in Table 5.1.

Table 5.1   *Devon Commission Witnesses on Prevalence of Consolidation*

Province	(1) Prevalent	(2) Somewhat prevalent	(3) Not prevalent	(4) Total	(5) Index*
Ulster	37	17	25	79	94·26
Leinster	34	17	24	75	88·52
Munster	69	20	35	124	104·10
Connaught	25	4	10	39	113·11
Ireland	165	58	94	317	100·00

* Calculated by scaling the first three columns by 2, 1, and 0, respectively, dividing by the total, and standardizing by the nationwide average.
Source: Great Britain, 1845a, Vols XIX–XXII.

The results show that consolidation was widespread throughout the country, although it was more widely practiced in the south and west than in Ulster and Leinster. Furthermore, there are only three counties in which there is not at least one testimony that the practice was prevalent. These counties are Leitrim and Fermanagh (for each of which there were only two usable witnesses) and Westmeath (for which there were five). Small-sample bias on the county level makes a higher level of aggregation thus unavoidable. We cannot infer from this type of evidence whether "prevalent" means that 1 or 40 percent of the land in the witness's parish was subject to consolidation, but even if 1 percent of the cultivable land was consolidated per annum, that would amount to a very significant proportion over the three decades between Waterloo and the famine.

The Poor Law Commission data on consolidation differ from the Devon Commission in three important respects. First, all Poor Law witnesses were asked an identical question, namely, "To what extent has the system of throwing small farms into large ones taken place in your parish and what has become of the dispossessed tenants?" The standardized question makes analysis of the data simpler and reduces the possibility of error due to lack of comparability in the testimonies, although many witnesses failed to respond to the point or said they did not know. Secondly, this question was the only one that dealt directly with consolidation as such; all other information about consolidation such as why it was resorted to, what mechanism was used to clear the lands, and what response was taken by the victims, was supplied only sporadically. From that point of view, the Devon Commission is a superior source. Thirdly, the sample is considerably larger (an average of forty-seven witnesses per county). The composition of the sample is, however, perhaps a bit less desirable: a majority of the witnesses were Anglican vicars or Roman Catholic parish priests, whereas among the Devon witnesses land agents and farmers—probably better informed about agricultural matters—were a majority. The results are presented in Table 5.2.

Table 5.2   *Poor Law Commission Witnesses on Prevalence of Consolidation*

Province	(1) Very wide- spread	(2) Prevalent	(3) Some occur- rences	(4) Few occur- rences	(5) None	(6) Total	(7) Index*
Ulster	0	7	20	184	310	521	73·87
Leinster	14	10	29	134	246	433	100·86
Munster	8	18	31	173	161	391	128·99
Connaught	3	8	16	48	83	157	112·22
Total	24	43	96	539	800	1502	100·00

* Computed by multiplying columns 1,2,3 and 4 by weights of 4,3,2, and 1, respectively, dividing by column 6, and standardizing by the nationwide average.
Source: Great Britain, 1836b, Vol. XXXIII.

Tables 5.1 and 5.2 both indicate that consolidation was more prevalent in Munster and Connaught than in the other two provinces, but the internal ranking of the provinces within each group is reversed. In part this may be attributed to the different natures of the two samples, but it seems plausible that in addition another factor was at work: in the ten years between the Poor Law Commission and the Devon Commission, Munster was especially subject to agrarian disturbances, and the violent reaction of the tenants may have slowed down the process of consolidation in these regions. Other elements may also have been responsible for a change in the geographical pattern of the consolidation movement: over forty witnesses in the Poor Law Commission (most of them in Ulster) who classify consolidation as absent or rare in 1835 added an ominous "not yet" to their statement. One reason why consolidation in some areas was slow in spite of the landlords' desire was the fact that rent-paying leaseholders could not be ejected prior to expiration unless they somehow could be shown to have violated the terms of their leases.

The evidence in the Devon Commission strongly supports the hypothesis that consolidation was slowed down considerably and in some places stopped altogether by violence, the landlords' fear of violence, or the landlords' compassion for the tenants who would be dispossessed. Eighty witnesses expressed their opinion on the profitability of consolidation or the landlords' anxiety to bring it about. Of those, only nine denied the profitability of consolidation and seventy-one confirmed it. Of those seventy-one, however, only twenty-eight witnesses testified that consolidation was prevalent in their districts. Among the others, the typical remark is that landlords would like to consolidate but are prevented by fear of outrages. A Tipperary landlord (Great Britain, 1845a, Vol. XXI, p. 651) expressed the feeling shared by many when he noted that "I have not the power to make farms as large as I could wish". Many landlords admitted utilizing every opportunity to consolidate, subject to the constraint of the preservation of the peace. Poulett Scrope, a noted political economist of the time, pointed out that "the Whiteboy System is the only check on the ejectment system" (cited by O'Brien, 1921, p. 55). On the whole, landlords and agents were more successful in preventing the further subdivision of farms that were still of workable size than in turning the clock back and consolidating farms that had already been fragmented into small plots. None the less, consolidation attempts were made throughout the period under discussion.

How was consolidation carried out? A large number of witnesses before the Devon Commission were asked questions to that effect and there is some interest in analyzing the returns. More than 150 witnesses provided usable answers, but the evidence is not very clear-cut because some of the information was provided after direct questioning, and some was volunteered. The results are summarized in Table 5.3.

Table 5.3   *Devon Commission Testimonies on the Mechanisms of Consolidation*

	(1)	(2)	(3)	(4)	(5)
			Non-renewal of lease upon expiration		
	Ejectment of tenants				By purchase
Province	Yes	No	Yes	No	
Ulster	8	10	6	2	27
Leinster	20	4	14	0	7
Munster	48	7	25	3	3
Connaught	17	7	12	1	1
Ireland	93	28	57	6	38

Source: Great Britain, 1845a, Vols XIX–XXII.

As Table 5.3 indicates, there were three ways in which undesired tenants could be removed. First, Bills of Ejectment could be brought against tenants with leases who violated their leases or against tenants-at-will who were denied renewal of tenure but refused to leave. Secondly, tenants with long leases could be refused renewal of the lease upon expiration. In many cases expiration of the middleman's lease led to the expulsion of his subtenants. At times the line between the two methods is not sharp, but most of the witnesses made a clear-cut distinction between the ejectment of direct tenant and the removal of subtenants. A third method was to entice some of the tenants to buy out their neighbors, and thus to create large and contiguous farms. As can be seen, this custom was largely confined to Ulster. Among the other patterns that can be discerned is a strong propensity of Munster landlords to use ejectment for the purpose of consolidation, while in Connaught and to a lesser extent in Leinster, landlords appear to have been more cautious in using ejectment bills for this purpose.

What happened to the dispossessed tenants after consolidation? The answer to this question determined to some extent the response the landlord could expect to his attempts to consolidate his estate, although there were cases in which resistance to the clearing of lands was inevitable irrespective of the landlord's attempts to pacify the tenantry (for instance, in Co. Kilkenny, Great Britain, 1845a, Vol. XXI, p. 381). First, not all tenants who were dispossessed were forced to leave the region. In many areas the Irish consolidation, like the English enclosures half a century earlier, did not reduce the total demand for labor. Consolidation involved a change of management and of production techniques, but did not always mean a shift to a less labor-intensive technique. Of the thirty-eight Devon Commission witnesses who expressed their opinion on the effect of consolidation on the demand for labor, eighteen maintained that it increased the demand for labor, while twenty said that it reduced it. Witnesses before the Poor Law Commission estimated the reduction in labor requirement per acre after consolidation and conversion to pasturage at a factor of ten. But others took exception to these estimates, and pointed out that the demand on pasturage farms was steadier and spread out over the entire year rather than concentrated in a few peak seasons (Great Britain, 1836b, Vol. XXXIII, pp. 82,119, 256). While the evidence is thus contradictory and difficult to interpret, it seems that on the whole, consolidation did reduce the demand for labor, although probably by much less than a factor of ten. In any case, as was shown above, the economic conflict between landlord and tenant does not require a decline in the labor–land ratio in order to arise, and even when consolidation was not for pasturage purposes, it could lead to disturbances.

One way in which the landlord could, at least in theory, avert disturbance was by compensating the dispossessed tenants. Compensation was practiced in all parts of Ireland, although it probably was seldom sufficient to prevent large-scale resistance. Liquidity problems prevented landlords from mortgaging part of the expected future profits of a consolidation project to buy out his present tenants. In many cases the compensation took the form of forgiving arrears, which may not have helped the former tenants in the relocation process. More often, however, compensation to the outgoing tenant implied the purchasing of his tenant right or simply a payment to avert outrages, as a

Tipperary witness candidly admitted (Great Britain, 1845a, Vol. XX, p. 560). While the "tenant-right" custom was largely confined to Ulster, blackmail was a nationwide phenomenon. An index measuring the frequency of compensation could be constructed from the ninety-one witnesses who made usable comments on it before the Devon Commission. These testimonies indicate that the highest frequency of compensations occurred in Munster, with an index value of 117·74 Ireland = 100), followed by Ulster (109·68) and Leinster (108·06). In Connaught, where the tenants had the least bargaining power, the index equals 45·16.

Using the Poor Law Commission data to examine what happened to the dispossessed tenants is not less hazardous than using the Devon Commission witnesses. Although the Poor Law witnesses were asked explicitly what had become of the dispossessed tenants, the majority of them ignored that part of the question. Those who answered it (a total of 326) often gave multiple answers such as "Some emigrated to America and some remained in the parish as landless labourers" without indicating what the proportions were. In analyzing the data, we ignore all witnesses who failed to respond to this part of the question, and assume that in cases of multiple answers, each has equal weight. In cases in which the answers were not mutually exclusive (for example, "were compensated" and "went to nearby town"), the answers were not weighted. In spite of the crude nature of the evidence, Table 5.4 shows that emigration was most prevalent in Ulster, while in Connaught the availability of uncultivated land made it possible to settle dispossessed tenants in the neighborhood. Urban areas were clearly not able to absorb many of the dispossessed tenants, although some of the entries under "Emigrated or moved" could be rural-urban migrants.

Table 5.4   *Fate of Dispossessed Tenants (Percentages)*

Province	Dispossessed and reduced to poverty	Became landless laborers	Moved to nearby towns	Received other holdings in bogs	Emigrated or moved	Total
Ulster	14·79	12·68	7·04	3·52	61·97	100
Leinster	27·93	18·99	11·73	3·35	37·99	100
Munster	15·19	30·38	10·97	9·28	34·18	100
Connaught	32·98	15·96	7·45	24·47	19·15	100
Ireland	21·27	21·32	9·82	8·59	39·11	100

Source: Great Britain, 1836b, Vol. XXXIII.

We turn now to agrarian disturbances. The contemporary conventional wisdom is summarized by the Devon Commission Digest: the great majority of outrages arose from "the endeavors of the peasantry to convert the possession of land into an indefeasible title", but the real original sources of agrarian outrage were the oversupply of labor and the inefficiency of agriculture, ignorance, and the want of unemployment (Kennedy, 1847, pp. 319–22). How widespread and frequent were these outrages? Criminal statistics, even much more recent ones, are notoriously unreliable. Still, some idea of the orders of magnitude involved can be obtained from a table submitted by the Constabulary Office (Great Britain, 1845a, Vol. XXI, appendix, pp. 118–19, reprinted in Kennedy, 1847, pp. 326–7). The table lists all crimes reported to the Constabulary Office in 1844, distinguishing between those that were "of an agrarian character"and those that were not. How this distinction was actually carried out is not made clear and it seems that the proportion of agrarian crime (that is, crime stemming from an economic conflict concerning land) is understated. For instance, of the fifty-eight cases of "levelling" (pulling down of fences), only twenty-eight are classified as "agrarian". Of the forty-seven "illegal meetings or processions", only two were classified as "agrarian".

None the less, the data are useful in establishing regional differences in rural disturbances. The nationwide average for the proportion of "agrarian" to all crime was 16·1 percent. Compared with that figure, the highest rates of agrarian crime were in Leitrim (31·6 percent), Roscommon (35·2 percent), King's (29·6 percent), and Tipperary (27·9 percent). Low agrarian crime rates were recorded in Armagh (3·9 percent), Wicklow (3·7 percent), Londonderry (3·7 percent), and Kildare (2·6 percent). A second index of agrarian crime is the number of agrarian crimes committed per capita (rural population only). Tipperary has the highest rate by this measure, with 6·9 crimes per 10,000 people, followed by King's (5·2), Leitrim (4·6), and Roscommon (3·8). Very low rates of agrarian crime by this measure were found in Londonderry (0·15), Mayo (0·19), and Down (0·19). On the surface, then, it is far from easy to establish a pattern and no obvious correlation between the incidence of agrarian crime and location or economic conditions appears to emerge. Even the observation that Ulster was spared the frequent occurrence of agrarian crimes is not without exceptions: Monaghan and Cavan are above the national average, Donegal at about the national level.

Once more, supplementary information on agrarian crime can be obtained from the testimonies given before the Devon Commission and the Poor Law Commission. A large number of the Devon Commission witnesses were asked whether agrarian outrages were prevalent in their district. A total of 202 witnesses provided usable answers. Of those, seventy-seven gave affirmative answers, 104 qualified affirmative (for instance, "some", "a few", "from time to time", and so on) and only twenty-one defined their districts as perfectly peaceful. Unfortunately, this sample is clearly unrepresentative, since the commissioners tended to ask about agrarian outrages when they suspected that outrages were prevalent in the witnesses' district. Thus the sample contains thirty-three witnesses from Tipperary but only two from Antrim, two from Galway and none from Fermanagh, Louth, and Mayo. Because of the small size of the sample, a county-by-county index of agrarian outrage would not be meaningful, but a provincial index is contained in Table 5.5 and should be read subject to the caveats mentioned.

Every Poor Law Commission witness was asked the standard question: "Has your parish been disturbed or peaceful during that period (i.e., 1815–35)?" Although the sample is much larger than the Devon Commission (a total of 1,527 usable responses), some caution is required here as well. A number of witnesses clearly did not realize that the question referred to agrarian outrages and complained about disturbances such as burglary, drunken brawls, and at times even blasphemy. Others emphasized that the parish was briefly disturbed in the past (especially referring to the tithe war of the early 1830s) but had since then returned to tranquillity. The various indices of agrarian outrages are summarized in Table 5.5.

Table 5.5   *Indices of Agrarian Unrest Before the Famine (Ireland = 100)*

Province	(1) Constabulary Office data relative index (1844)	(2) Constabulary Office data per capita index (1844)	(3) Devon Commission witnesses index (1845)	(4) Poor Law Commission, index 1 (1835)	(5) Poor Law Commission, index 2 (1835)
Ulster	67·70	40·37	85·94	56·67	50·00
Leinster	81·99	102·88	95·31	150·00	131·42
Munster	119·25	152·25	106·25	103·33	127·14
Connaught	119·88	114·56	108·59	105·00	111·43
Ireland	100·00	100·00	100·00	100·00	100·00

Notes:
Column 1: Computed from Great Britain, 1845a, Vol. XXI, appendix, pp. 118–19, by dividing total number of "agrarian crimes" into the total number of crimes reported.
Column 2: Computed from the same source by dividing the total number of agrarian crimes into the rural population.
Column 3: Computed from Great Britain, 1845a, Vols XIX–XXII, by assigning a weight of 2 to "prevalent," a weight of 1 to "some" or a similarly qualified response, and a weight of 0 to negative responses, and dividing the total score into the number of witnesses.
Column 4: Computed from Great Britain, 1836b, Vol. XXXII by assigning a weight of 0 to "perfectly peaceful", a weight of 1 to "few' or "little" disturbances, a weight of 2 to "some" or "at times", and a weight of 3 to "frequently" or similarly affirmative responses. All responses indicating "formerly disturbed but presently quiet" assigned weight of 0; total score divided into the number of witnesses.
Column 5: Same as column 4, except that witnesses indicating "former" disturbances are weighted by the severity of these outrages.

The interesting feature of Table 5.5 is the rather remarkable shift in the regional pattern of agrarian outrages over 1835–44. According to all three measures in columns 1, 2, and 3, Leinster was not more disturbed than average, and probably less. The Poor Law Commission data show that in the 1830s Leinster was far more disturbed than any other. Some of the individual counties in Leinster have startlingly high indices: Co. Queen's has a relative index of 388 (index 1); and county Kilkenny, 243. The most perturbed county in the 1840s, Tipperary, was only slightly more disturbed than the country as a whole in 1835 (index 1 =116). The only area to be relatively quiet was Ulster, where the frequency of disturbance was consistently below the national average.

General crime statistics not distinguishing between agrarian and nonagrarian crimes were reported by Thomas Drummond, undersecretary to the Lord Lieutenant of Ireland, to the Wharncliffe Committee (Great Britain, 1839a, Vol. XI, pp. 1081–1100). Of particular interest are the tables which provide the number of persons committed to prisons in each county (rural areas) from each year over 1826–38. Needless to say, the data are a very imprecise approximation of the levels of agrarian crime. While the prison data are the only source that allows comparisons over time and across counties simultaneously, variation in the data can be due to differences in the intensity of enforcement and the efficiency of reporting, as well as changes in the level of nonagrarian crime. The data are useful, however, to obtain some rough notion about the regional differences in the trends in rural criminality, especially since they are obtained from committal to prison rather than conviction data.[11]

Table 5.6   *Committals to Prison in Ireland, 1826–38*

Province	*(1)* Total committals to prisons	*(2)* Annual committals per capita (rural only) × 10,000	*(3)* Logarithmic trend coefficient	*(4)* Standard error of trend coefficient
Ulster	45,409	16·17	0·0101	0·0086
Leinster	57,916	29·10	0·0607	0·0123
Munster	50,635	19·39	0·0249	0·0111
Connaught	36,552	21·00	0·0507	0·0084
Ireland	190,512	20·82	0·0368	0·0081

Source: Great Britain, 1839a, Vol. XI, pp. 1096–7.

Table 5.6 shows that law and order were deteriorating at a rate of almost 3·7 percent per year, which is more than twice as fast as population was growing. In part this could reflect higher crime registration rates, but other evidence confirms that the country was getting more disturbed and unruly. Regional differences were quite marked: the proportional rate of growth in Leinster was six times larger than in Ulster. The standard errors reflect the sporadic nature of crime: in Ulster and Munster the crime rate fluctuated more violently around the trend than in Leinster and Connaught. Individual county data show the same thing: the crime rate in Clare grew at a (statistically insignificant) rate of 0·5 percent a year, while in neighboring Limerick and Tipperary it grew at 6·4 and 10·2 percent per annum, respectively. The Irish county constabulary were generally ineffective in controlling rural crime and often exacerbated local conflicts by police brutality, although they were, on paper at least, the most advanced police system in the British Isles (Broeker, 1970, pp. 235–6).

A comparison with England can also be illuminating here, although differences in law enforcement and criminal justice systems make such comparisons tenuous. During 1831–45 the number of convictions per 100,000 in England increased from 100 to 109. During the same period the corresponding figure in Ireland declined from 123 to 89 (with a short-lived peak in 1836 of 229 convictions per 100,000). However, the conviction rate (convictions per committals to prisons) was declining in Ireland (from about 65 percent in the early 1830s to 42·5 percent in 1845), while in England the rate was stable at slightly over 70 percent. The average number of committals per annum per 100,000 for the fifteen years 1831–45 was about 250 in Ireland, while in England and Wales the number was about 150 (*Thom's Directory*, 1848, p. 158). Moreover, it seems likely that the ratio of committals to crimes was considerably lower in Ireland, though evidence on the number of crimes reported is not available.

Of the various sources used, only the Devon Commission lends itself to an analysis of the causes and targets of agrarian outrage. As far as causes are concerned, 153 witnesses presented some background to their affirmative or qualified-affirmative answers to the question whether agrarian outrages were prevalent in their district. The small-sample biases are quite evident here, but the overall orders of magnitude are instructive.

Table 5.7   *Causes of Agrarian Outrages (Percentages)*

	(1) Ejectment for consolidation only	*(2)* Ejectment for non-payment of rent	*(3)* Ejectment for both or not specified	*(4)* Conflicts relating to conacre	*(5)* Rents too high	*(6)* Other	*(7)* Total
Ulster	39	17	26	0	17	0	100
Leinster	19	22	31	0	3	3	100
Munster	26	26	31	12	5	1	100
Connaught	5	5	10	40	30	10	100
Ireland	24	21	32	11	10	3	100

Source: Great Britain, 1845a, Vols XIX–XXII.

Ejectment was clearly the main source of agrarian unrest in 1845. For the country as a whole, 77 percent of all outrages were attributed to ejectment. If we had a similar source for the 1830s, it is likely that refusal to pay tithes would have figured more prominently as a cause, but otherwise the results would have been comparable. The data do not permit a precise assessment of the role of consolidation in generating disturbances, but in view of the fact that many witnesses emphasized that agrarian outrages were far more likely to occur when a rent-paying tenant was ejected than when the tenant had fallen in arrears of a rent which was not considered exorbitant, we may conclude that the bulk of cases in columns 2 and 3 were either cases involving ejectment for consolidation, or reorganization of agriculture or cases in which arrears were used as an excuse to attain the same goals.

Who were the victims of agrarian crimes? Beames (1978) has investigated this issue, but his sample is confined to twenty-seven murder cases in Tipperary alone. The Devon Commission witnesses confirm Beames's conclusion that most outrages were aimed against landlords, landlord agents, or the incoming tenants replacing those ejected. Out of a total of ninety-three witnesses whose responses could be used, 35 percent identified the incoming tenant as the target, 31 percent identified the landlord as the target, and 17 percent pointed to landlord's agents as victims. Farmers (in most cases involved in conacre disputes with subtenants) were victims in 11 percent, and government officials, judges, and policemen in 5 percent. Munster accounts for more than half of the sample, but looking at the other provinces alone does not reverse the basic findings: in Ireland without Munster, incoming tenants were identified as victims of agrarian disturbances by 49 percent of the witnesses, landlords by 23 percent, and landlord representatives by 16 percent.

Lee (1973a, 1980) has emphasized the conflict between landless laborers and tenant farmers, mostly concerning conacre land. As Table 5.7 shows, this view has considerable merit as far as Connaught is concerned, but does not hold as strongly for the rest of Ireland. Lee's main source is Great Britain, 1846b, Vol. XXXV. The problem with that report is that it pertains to the first months of 1846, during which the partial potato failure of 1845 was already felt. Clearly, the failure of potato crops must have placed a strain on the relations between farmer and conacre-taker. In Co. Roscommon, in which Lee observes a particularly high rate of conacre-related offenses, twenty-nine out of fifty-two electoral divisions reported a potato failure rate of 40 percent or more, as opposed to 834 electoral divisions out of 1,957 nationwide (Great Britain, 1846c, Vol. XXXVII, p. 36). Payment for conacre was seldom made in advance (although some farmers started to insist on that before the famine). When the potato harvest failed and many laborers defaulted on their payments, the farmers could not even try to seize the crop (which was illegal anyway). It should, therefore, not be a surprise that they were more reluctant than usual to give conacre land in the spring of 1846. Conacre, while a contributing factor to agrarian unrest, was not the primary cause, and the conflict between large tenant farmer and laborer was just another special case of the conflict between those with some property rights in land and those who provided the labor for that land.

(4)   Consolidation and Agrarian Outrage: a Model and Some Tests

What was the connection between agrarian violence and the consolidation-cum-ejectment movement? A brief glance at the evidence presented above suffices to demonstrate that there is no *simple* correlation between the intensity of agrarian disturbances and the frequency of consolidation.[12] Yet the evidence also suggests a strong causal connection between them. The solution to this seeming contradiction is that the two phenomena were connected by a network of multiple causal connections. Once these connections are identified by means of a simple model, an attempt can be made to interpret the data.

Consolidation was desired by landlords because it increased rents, reduced uncertainty, eased the management of the estate and the rent collection, reduced poor rates, or any combination of these factors. Had consolidation been "a free good", it is likely that it would have occurred all over Ireland, in a manner comparable to the enclosures in England which, while not totally gratis, were cheap enough compared to the benefits (McCloskey, 1975). But Ireland's landlords had to pay a high price to achieve consolidation: the Irish tenants resisted, threatening the landlords with violence, and by threatening the incoming tenants they could nullify the benefits. The landlords' behavior can be analyzed in terms analogous to a demand curve for consolidation: the higher the intensity of outrages, the less will the landlord be inclined to risk ejecting his tenants. The *location* of the demand curve is determined by the returns to consolidation, which are a function of many factors such as the relative price of livestock products, the adaptability of the land to livestock raising or the introduction of better tillage techniques requiring consolidation. The tenant's behavior can be described by a supply function, reflecting the rising resistance with increasing ejectments. The location of the supply curve is determined by the costs which the tenants incur when consolidation is effected. The more difficult it is for tenants to relocate, or the higher $w_a - w_0$ in inequality 5.1, above, the higher the supply curve will be. The demand and supply model of consolidation is conceptually analogous to any other supply and demand analysis, although the notion of a "market" here is merely metaphorical. The "quantity" sold and bought is measured by the extent of consolidation. The "price" paid is the frequency of rural disturbances per "unit" of consolidation.

In the simplest terms the logical insights that the demand and supply model provides in the causal relations underlying the issues of rural violence and consolidation are as follows. First, consolidation was a cause of agrarian unrest. The higher the desire for consolidation of holdings, the more resistance was forthcoming. Note that the model does not imply that consolidation was necessarily the only cause of disturbances: the shape of the supply curve could be such that even if there was no attempted consolidation, there could still be unrest. Secondly, violence was usually a partially successful check on consolidation. The outrages prevented some consolidation which would have taken place in their absence, but it is not likely that the tenants were able to stop consolidation altogether. Thirdly, the degree of success that the tenants had is determined by the parameters of the model. If, for example, the profitability of consolidation was immense, the demand curve for consolidation would be so high that resistance would have been largely ineffectual. Or if the losses suffered by tenants on accounts of eviction were very large, we could expect a lower supply curve, that is, a more determined resistance. Depending on the location of the curves, *any* combination of consolidation and unrest is conceivable.

In practice, of course, there was no market for consolidation, and as a result the analogy has to be qualified in at least two respects. First, in many instances the landlord *did* pay the price for consolidation in money rather than in terms of disturbance. Bribing the outgoing tenants or buying them out was an alternative widely pursued. It would be interesting to speculate theoretically under which circumstances the landlord would resort to compensation rather than risk violence, but in the absence of information such speculation may not prove very fruitful. More serious, perhaps, is the complication that the demand curve is a description of the relation between an *ex ante* price and the amount of consolidation desired, but the price on the vertical axis of the supply curve is *ex post*. Translating this into the terms of the present problem, we could say that the landlords were scared away from consolidation by *expected* riots, but consolidation resulted in *actual* disturbances. Consequently, any attempt that combines them in a single two-equation demand and supply model has to make an explicit assumption about *actual* disturbances leading to *expected* disturbances, and expected disturbances stemming from actual occurrences. The cross-sectional approach adopted here is thus quite clearly flawed, although even if time-series were available, it would not be clear how to capture fears and expectations.

The two-equation demand and supply model proposed to explain the relation between agricultural reorganization and rural unrest is logically acceptable, and is empirically refutable. Confronting it with actual data is, however, rather involved. Some of the assumptions which must be made to carry out the tests below should be made explicit. First, as already noted, we have to make an assumption relating *ex post* (actual) outrages to *ex ante* (feared) outrages. Secondly, in order to identify the supply and demand curves, we have to assume that these curves are stable in the sense that their shifts over time or different locations in cross section are a result of variation of known and observed shift factors. These shift factors can then be used as instruments in order to estimate the slopes of the demand and supply curves. Statistically, of course, the estimation procedure which will perform this task is precisely the same as the one used in estimating a demand and supply model. The difficulty is that economic theory does not provide us with good *a priori* instruments to be used in this model, unlike the standard demand and supply one. Some discussion of the instrumental variables chosen is, therefore, necessary.

To be more specific, let *OUTR* stand for various indices of the intensity of agrarian outrages and *CONS* for the degree of consolidation or ejectment. Testing the model requires the estimation of the following two equations:

$$OUTR = a_0 + a_1 CONS + \sum_{i=2}^{k+1} a_i X_{i-1} \text{ (supply)} \tag{5.3}$$

$$CONS = b_0 + b_1 OUTR + \sum_{i=2}^{m+1} b_i Y_{i-1} \text{ (demand)} \tag{5.4}$$

where the k X-variables are instrumental variables necessary to identify the supply equation, and the m Y-variables identify the demand equation. Some of the Y- and X-variables could be the same variable, but there has to be at least one X-variable which does not appear as a Y-variable and vice versa to obtain identification. As it happens, there are more than one X- and Y-variables which satisfy this condition, so that the system is overidentified and a two-stage least-squares technique is required. The acid test of the supply and demand model proposed is whether the coefficients a_1 and b_1 have the expected signs: a_1, the slope of the supply curve, is expected to be positive, whereas b_1 is the slope of the demand curve and thus should be negative.

The instrumental variables in the demand curve should reflect the profitability of consolidation. The three instruments used are the capital–labor ratio as approximated by the value of total livestock to rural population, to reflect the suitability of a county to raising livestock relative to tillage; the quality of the land as approximated by the variance of the elevation of the land;[13] and the ratio of Civil Bills of Ejectment decreed to total Civil Bills, to measure the degree of support landlords could expect from the courts. The instrumental variables used in the supply equation should reflect the costs imposed on the tenants by their removal from the land, but also their general inclination to rebel rather than to consent. The instrumental variables thus include income per capita; the overall level of crime per capita (including nonagrarian crime); the proportion of nonagricultural labor; the percentage Catholics in the population; and the average annual emigration rate (included to reflect the alternatives open to dispossessed tenants to relocate in the region).

The two dependent variables in the model are indices of eviction and of agrarian outrage. As emphasized above, these variables are only approximations of the "true" but unobserved variables. As the index of evictions, we have used the number of Civil Bill ejectments per cultivated acre. The index of agrarian outrages is computed from the 1844 Constabulary Office data. The details of the estimations are presented in the notes to Table 5.8. The setup of Table 5.8 is such that the first three columns and the last three columns are estimated consistently, so that columns 1 and 4, for example, form a pair of consistently specified demand and supply equations in the sense that they employ the same definitions and weights, and use each other's independent variables as instruments. County Kerry had to be omitted from the estimation, since no data for the acreage subject to eviction was reported. Table 5.8 should be regarded as an illustration rather than as definitive confirmation of the model. Some alternative specifications of the model did not work, and the variable capturing outrages was decided upon after some experimentation, not all of which yielded satisfactory results. There are no clear-cut *a priori* rules how to set up this test, and some experimentation was inevitable. The results should therefore be interpreted with caution, and excessive claims for a rigorous confirmation of the model cannot be made. In this sense, perhaps, the "accuracy" of the econometrics may mislead the unwary reader: no such accuracy can be claimed here.

Table 5.8 *Estimates of "Demand" and "Supply" Functions, Asymptotic t-Ratios in Parentheses*

	(1)	(2)	(3)	(4)	(5)	(6)
Nature of equation	Demand	Demand	Demand	Supply	Supply	Supply
Dependent Variable	EVICL*‡	EVICO*§	EVICT*||	OUT-RAGE	OUT-RAGE	OUT-RAGE
Constant	48·14	23·12	43·45	−19·94	8·22	−17·63
	(2·95)	(1·82)	(2·78)	(−0·68)	(0·32)	(−0·66)
OUTRAGE*	−0·62	−0·62	−0·64			
	(−1·40)	(−1·69)	(−1·51)			
CAPLAB	−9.46	−5·36	−9·13			
	(−3.56)	(−2.59)	(−3.58)			
VAREL†	−0·17	−0·0047	0·027			
	(−0·38)	(−0·01)	(0·06)			
SUCRAT‡	3·83	13·95	11·44			
	(0·22)	(1·03)	(0·68)			
EVIC				0·33*¶	0·46**†	0·39**‡
				(1·33)	(1·30)	(1·53)
CATHOL§				0·087	−0·024	0·067
				(0·43)	(−0·13)	(0·36)
INCOME				0·79		0·83
				(1·39)		(1·49)
CRIME||				7·42	8·35	7·15
				(2·80)	(3·70)	(2·68)
IND¶				−22·34	−32·67	−37·34
				(−0·53)	(−0·88)	(−0·90)
EMIG**					−783·43	
					(−1·75)	
Estimated Elasticity*†	−0·21	−0·29	−0·39	1·03	1·01	1·56
	31	31	31	31	31	31

* Defined as total agrarian outrages in 1844 divided by the number of acres subject to ejectment. The reason for this definition is that total outrages has the dimension of a "price" (outrages per unit of eviction) times "quantity" (units of eviction).
† Variance of elevation above sea-level, in feet; coefficients multiplied by 1,000.
‡ Ratio of petitions decreed to total petitions.
§ Percentage Catholics in population, 1834.
\|\| Total number of crimes committed, per capita ($\times 1,000$).
¶ Proportion labor in "manufacture".
** Average net outmigration per annum, 1821–41.
*† Computed from the formula $\dfrac{\partial(\text{EVIC})}{\partial(\text{OUTR})} \times \dfrac{\text{mean of OUTR}}{\text{mean of EVIC}}$.
*‡ Ejectments for land only (excluding ejectments from houses alone), per acre under cultivation.
*§ Ejectments excluding those brought for nonpayment of rent, per acre under cultivation.
*\|\| Total ejectments, per acre under cultivation.
*¶ Variable used: EVICL.
**† Variable used: EVICO.
**‡ Variable used: EVICT.

Table 5.8 shows that the cross-sectional data used in Section 3 are consistent with the two-equation model proposed above. The regression results are not overwhelmingly strong, to be sure, which is to be expected in view of the difficulties in measuring the appropriate variables and capturing "expected" consolidations (which triggered more outrages) as well as "feared" outrages (which prevented further evictions). None the less, the coefficients of the demand and supply curves, which are given by the coefficients on OUTRAGE in columns 1–3 and the coefficients on EVIC in columns 4–6 all have the expected signs and have t-statistics which are at or above the value of $1·314$, which is the 10 percent critical value of t (one-tailed test). Note also that demand is highly "price-inelastic", which implies that small changes in the location of the supply curve could lead to large differences in prices. In our model agrarian outrages play the role of a "price", and it is therefore possible to explain in this fashion the large differences in the levels of agrarian disturbance experienced by different counties which often amazed contemporaries.[14]

(5)   Conclusions

A recent sociological study of nineteenth-century Ireland emphasizes the unusually high incidence of rural conflict. "Nothing could have been further from the peaceful society of some anthropological folk-lore" (Clark, 1979, p. 66). It is quite correct, as Clark points out (p.67), that Irish violence seldom took the form of food riots. The struggle, as Clark adds, was not motivated by a desperate attempt to "preserve the means of existence" (p. 70). Rather, it was a struggle between the working tenants and those who controlled the land, whether they were landlords, middlemen, or farmers with long leases. The economic source of the conflict was a difference of interests between landowners and tenants. In some sense such a difference always exists: tenants want high wages and low rents, landlords the reverse. Yet, the depth and persistence of agrarian conflict and its violent nature are uniquely Irish in nineteenth-century Europe, and one is led to ask what it was that was different in the Irish economy leading to this state of affairs.

I have argued here that changes in the relative profitability of pasturage and tillage products and in agricultural technology led to conflict between landlord and tenant in prefamine Ireland. Attempts of landlords, their agents, or even well-to-do farmers to reorganize agriculture into larger and better-managed units, and to devote more resources to husbandry, ran into resistance from smallholders, cottiers, and landless or quasi-landless laborers. The background of the difficulties in Ireland was the changes taking place on both the supply and the demand side in the market for agricultural products. During 1750–1814, tillage products were more profitable and land was converted from pasturage to arable. At the end of the Napoleonic Wars this trend was reversed. As economists would predict, the economy responded to changes in the relative profitability by trying to change the allocation of its resources. Adaptation to changing market conditions was, however, neither costless nor readily reversible, a fact well known by historians but often ignored by economists. In Ireland, the movements toward and then away from tillage were a primary—though not the sole—cause of violence and lawlessness, and thus imposed vast negative externalities on the rest of the economy. As one contemporary sighed in 1836, "It would [have been] better for the Irish farmer if Buonaparte never lived or never died" (Great Britain, 1836b, Vol. XXXIII, p. 317). Not all of the victims of economic fluctuations resorted to "voice" as opposed to "exit", to utilize Hirshman's popular framework. Increasing waves of emigration left Ireland for Britain and North America after 1815. None the less, sufficient turbulence occurred to cause great concern among Irish landlords and the British government. As a fortunate result of unfortunate events, considerable information on Irish rural conditions was collected by the British government which can be utilized to analyze the connections among consolidation, economic conflict, and economic backwardness.

Why did the Irish tenant resist consolidation, while his British counterpart, generally speaking, showed little or no organized resistance against the enclosure movement half a century earlier? Without belittling the traditional hostility between landlord and tenant in Ireland and such specifically Irish problems as the tithe, it seems likely that the general economic conditions in Ireland contributed to the wave of rural unrest which engulfed more or less the entire country at some stage or another in the three decades prior to the famine. Four economic elements can be identified: the absence of adequate nonagricultural employment which paid wages comparable to the income earned in agriculture; the desire of Irish peasants to hold land even at the cost of forgoing higher income elsewhere; the bargaining costs involved in combining or merging small units into larger ones which could be managed better and permit the realization of scale economies; and the presence of a nontraded subsistence crop. In a perfectly competitive "neoclassical" world none of these elements can occur, hence we have referred to them as "market imperfections".

Comparing the Irish experience with that of England, illustrates the unique circumstances in the Irish countryside. Before 1830, including periods of intensive parliamentary enclosures, the English countryside was remarkably quiet (Hobsbawm and Rudé, 1968, pp. 81–3). The "Captain Swing" riots of 1830–1 can be compared to the Irish agrarian outrages but clearly the differences between the two cases are as instructive as the similarities. First, the riots in England were far more localized than those in Ireland. Four counties (Berkshire, Kent, Hampshire, and Wiltshire) account for half of all the disturbances (Hobsbawm and Rudé, 1968, pp. 304–5). None of the industrialized regions was seriously affected. Secondly, the Swing riots were closely related to the wrath of the agrarian laborers against a specific labor-saving innovation, mechanical threshers. The conflict in England was about "how" rather than "what" to produce. Although the thresher spread more slowly in southern England than elsewhere, it was there that it led to rebellions.

Hobsbawm and Rudé (1968, p. 74) point out that threshing was largely carried out in the late autumn and winter. The relative absence of alternative employment opportunities in that season corresponds to our condition $w_0 < w_a$ and, thus, makes a conflict more likely. The "scale effect" was also present, since the cost-saving effects of the thresher were only important on large farms, although one wonders to what extent renting and sharing of threshing machines were practiced. Thirdly, the riots in the south and east of England were ephemeral in nature, an aberration from a generally placid course. As Rudé (1967, p. 89) points out, the rebellious movements in England at the time were completely eclipsed by events in Ireland. In short, in England agrarian violence was the exception, in Ireland it was the rule. In addition to the political differences, two economic factors were responsible for the different experiences of the two countries: England's higher degree of economic development, which provided more employment opportunities outside agriculture, and the existence of a Poor Law in England, an institution absent in Ireland until 1838. As a result, a permanent conflict between economic groups in rural England did not occur. While there are thus certain similarities in the origins and causes of English and Irish agrarian unrest, quantitatively the two movements were of entirely different orders of magnitude.

The model used here serves to formalize a more complex system of causality in which consolidation caused outrages and was simultaneously prevented by them. The results of the econometric tests indicate that the economist's tools of supply and demand have wider applicability than the explanation of short-term price fluctuation. Markets do not have to be perfect in order to function; indeed, the "market" for consolidation did not exist in any formal sense. And yet we have been able to identify supply and demand curves reflecting the behavior of tenants and landlords.

One link is missing in our chain of evidence. In Figure 5.1 the loss inflicted on the economy due to resistance to consolidation was illustrated and shown to consist of two parts: one part reflects the inability of the economy to reach the optimal combination of outputs, while the other effect reduces the production-possibility frontier of the economy as a whole. Evidence for the effect of agrarian outrages on the location of the production-possibility frontier is not easy to come by. It is likely that the *perceived* absence of security and the ineffective enforcement of property rights were worse than the *actual* situation, and it was the former that mattered for the economic development of the country. A few large riots and spectacular crimes, colorfully reported in the press, might be amplified in people's perceptions of what went on in rural Ireland. Moreover, county boundaries may not have meant much to potential foreign investors or entrepreneurs, so that disturbances in King's or in Tipperary could also have been responsible for the economic backwardness of Waterford or Wexford, compared to what these areas would have achieved in the absence of outrages anywhere. The only firm evidence that the insecurity and violence led to a flight of capital and entrepreneurship from Ireland consists of the beliefs held by contemporaries. Since we are, after all, dealing here with expectations as much as with actual events, citing contemporary opinions rather than facts is suggestive.[15] Rather than quoting the many opinions of individuals, however well-informed, I shall confine myself to the conclusions reached by the three most thorough and scholarly parliamentary commissions to investigate Ireland before the famine, namely, the Drummond or Railroad Commission (Great Britain, 1837–8, Vol. XXXV), and the two commissions on whose work this chapter has relied heavily, the Poor Law Commission and the Devon Commission.

The Railroad Commission was the most cautious in its assessment of the sources of poverty, largely because it took a generally optimistic view of Ireland's economic potential in order to persuade Parliament to support the construction of a railroad network in Ireland. None the less the report concedes (p. 563) that "In a district [Munster and Leinster] which has been long represented as the focus of unreclaimed violence and barbarism, where neither life nor property can be deemed secure . . . many persons . . . have been so misled or inconsiderate as to repel, by exaggerated statements, British capital from their doors". While the tenor of the report was to try to assure the reader that in spite of this "barbarism", investment and enterprise in Ireland could be profitable (Bianconi's carriage company was cited as an example), the commissioners apparently were convinced that venture capital was scared away by disturbances. The Poor Law Commission was far more explicit. In its report (Great Britain, 1836b, Vol. XXX, pp. 24–5), it rejected the absence of natural resources as playing a role in inhibiting the industrialization process in Ireland. Instead it asserted that "what they [manufactures] are prevented by is want of order, or peace, of obedience to the laws, and that security of property which never can exist until the general habits and condition of the people are thoroughly improved".

The most resounding statement linking rural unrest to underdevelopment was made by the Devon Commission. In discussing the effects of agrarian outrages the commissioners exclaimed:

We wish it were possible to make the peasantry in these unhappy districts [in which agrarian outrages occur] aware, that all measures for improvement presuppose the security of life and property; that the districts in which both are rendered insecure must be regarded as beyond the reach of such plans of amelioration as we can suggest; and that while crimes of so fearful a character prevail, it is hopeless to expect, in reference to those districts, much practical improvement in the relation of landlord and tenant, or any security for the permanent happiness of the people. (Great Britain, 1845a, Vol. XIX, p. 43)

Appendix: A Note on Relative Prices, 1812–50

The data used to construct the relative price index were obtained from the unpublished data appendix of Gayer, Rostow, and Schwartz's magisterial work (1953). Seven price-series were used, four for livestock products (beef, butter, pork, and mutton), and three for tillage crops (oats, wheat, and flax). The weights used are the proportions of these seven series in the value of agricultural output in Ireland as computed from Ó Gráda (1980c). The seven series cover about two-thirds of total Irish agricultural output, most of the rest being potatoes, of which small quantities (relative to output) were exported. Gayer *et al.* (1953) provide monthly data over 1790–1850 of which the January and July figures for each year were selected (122 observations).[16]

The relevant index measuring the relative price of tillage products in terms of animal products is constructed by dividing the tillage-price index by the animal-products index. Of course, both indices turn sharply down after their unnatural high during the last days of the Napoleonic Empire. The question is, what happened to the relative price? There is no doubt that in the short run the index behaved in the way contemporaries said it did: in 1810–13 the index averaged 113·4 (1821–5 = 100), while in 1814–15 it averaged 77·1. Once we start looking at the longer run, however, the picture becomes more complex. The downward trend between the end of the Napoleonic period and 1850 is weakly significant but it seems more of a once-and-for-all decline after 1813 than a continuous decline.[17] If we choose 1814 or 1815 as our first observation, the significance of the trendline (logarithmic or linear) disappears. The trend coefficient is, however, not necessarily relevant: if the relative price was at a permanently high plateau over 1790–1813, and at a permanent but lower plateau over 1814–50, it could well be the case that a trendline could produce a poor, possibly insignificant fit, while the signal emitted by the price mechanism to shift from grazing to tillage before 1814 and back into animals after was unambiguous. To test whether the average relative price declined significantly in the years after 1813, we can carry out a simple test on the difference in means in subperiods. Since the choice of the periods to be compared is somewhat arbitrary, various breakdowns have been experimented with. The results are presented in Table 5.9.

Table 5.9   *Tests of Changes in Relative Prices, 1790–1850*

Period 1	Period 2	$\mu_1 - \mu_2$	$S\mu_1 - \mu_2$	$Z = \dfrac{\mu_1 - \mu_2}{S\mu_1 - \mu_2}$
1790–1812	1813–45	3·81	3·67	1·04
1790–1812	1813–45	2·57	3·74	0·69
1790–1813	1814–50	5·06	3·60	1·41
1790–1813	1814–45	3·87	3·70	1·05
1790–1814	1815–50	2·92	3·59	0·81
1790–1814	1815–45	1·56	3·65	0·43
1790–1815	1816–50	1·60	3·54	0·45
1790–1815	1816–45	0·11	3·60	0·03

Table 5.9 supports Connell's warning that "it would be tempting and wrong to single out corn prices when examining the impact on agriculture of marketing conditions" (Connell, 1950a, p. 116). Column 3

shows that the mean price ratio of tillage and pasturage products was higher in the years before 1813–14 than in the years after. But it is clear that the difference is small, and that it cannot be distinguished from the annual fluctuations in prices. This does not necessarily mean that relative prices did not decline after Napoleon. What it does mean is that the data at hand are consistent with the hypothesis of no price decline at a high level of probability, although it is possible that a decline is concealed by the severe annual fluctuations in the observed prices.[18]

Notes: Chapter 5

1   There is, as always, a grey area which defies easy classification. Inability to adopt a more efficient technique due to ignorance could be termed a failure of the market for information, but that may be stretching the definition of market failure a bit.

2   We abstract here from poverty caused by natural disaster or war, which do not involve a market failure even though they are not "decided" upon by the victims.

3   For empirical examples in which efficiency and poverty are shown to coexist, see Schultz (1964, pp. 41–8).

4   The market failure approach of Ransom and Sutch has been criticised by proponents of the poverty-cum-efficiency hypothesis; see especially Decanio (1979a; 1979b) and Temin (1979).

5   Cullen (1968b) has tried to stretch this argument further into a theory of the adoption of the potato in Ireland. The alternative approach, which views the introduction of the potato as an exogenous technological improvement leading both to the expansion of tillage, and to population growth, is equally plausible. For an attempt to distinguish between the two empirically, see Mokyr (1981a).

6   Note that Figure 5.1 is more realistic than Figure 5.2 in one aspect: no complete specialization in one crop or the other is implied. Even under extreme conditions, it is not likely that either landlords or tenants will "plunge" into complete specialization. For one thing, land is not homogeneous, and by necessity some land will be better suited to tillage than other land. If the suitability of land to tillage compared to husbandry is a continuous variable, a concave frontier like F_2F_2 is implied. Secondly, arable and livestock products are inputs into each other, and in the absence of well-working markets for intermediate goods such as manure, fodder, and draft animals, it would pay to diversify quite independently of any risk considerations.

7   The technique will be adopted if:

$$w_a L < w_h L_h + w_a L_a + w_0 (L - L_h - L_a)$$

where L_h, L_a are the total quantities of labor allocated to h and a after the adoption of h, and $(L - L_h - L_a)$ is the unemployment created by the adoption of the less labor-intensive technique. Rearranging provides:

$$\frac{w_a - w_0}{w_h - w_0} < \frac{L_h}{L - L_a}.$$

But note that the right-hand side of the last inequality is simply $1_h/1_a$, since $L_h = kT1_h$, $L_a = (1 - k)T1_a$, $L = T1_a$, where T is total land and k is the proportion of that land devoted to husbandry.

8   The resistance of Irish Catholics to paying tithes provided the background of much of the turbulence of the eighteenth century. The Rightboy movement in the 1780s, for instance, originated as a movement against tithes (Wall, 1973). Interestingly enough, this movement extended its protests to Catholic targets (such as marriage dues).

9   Complaints and resentment against high rents continued into the postfamine period, leading ultimately to the 1870 land legislation. Yet the years 1850–70 are a period in which agrarian violence subsided (Vaughan, 1978). Vaughan adds (p. 218) that "rents,

although controversial, were not the most emotive aspects of the landlord–tenant relations. More public attention was probably devoted to evictions and agrarian outrages than to rents". This view seems an accurate description of prefamine Ireland as well.

10   The information provided by the Poor Law Commission data in appendix F to its report (Great Britain, 1836b, Vol. XXXIII) and the Devon Commission testimonies (Great Britain, 1845a, Vols XIX–XXII) was first used by Connell (1950a, ch. 6).

11   Convictions on agrarian crimes were notoriously hard to obtain due to the reluctance of the populace to testify against the culprits, resulting in part from a genuine solidarity among the tenants, and in part from intimidation. Total conviction-committal ratios (average 1826–38) were 68 percent for crimes against persons and 62 percent for crimes against property and public peace. The conviction rates for typical agrarian crimes were far lower: for killing and maiming cattle, it was less than 16 percent; for "the administration of unlawful oaths", the rate is 32 percent; and for "assembling and appearing armed at night", the conviction–committal ratio is 44 percent. It should be emphasized that the actual conviction to crime ratios were far lower than that, since it was as difficult to identify the persons responsible for agrarian crime as it was to convict them once they had been arrested. (All data from Great Britain, House of Lords, 1839a, Vols XVIII–XXI, pp. 1082–7.)

12   The absence of simple correlation between consolidation and outrage was verified on the county level. Simple correlations were run between the two agrarian-outrage indices presented in Table 5.5, columns 1 and 2, and six measures of Civil Bill ejectments per capita, computed from the data on Civil Bills presented in the Devon Commission. The mean value of R^2 from these twelve regressions is 0·0075.

13   The variance captures both the absolute level of the terrain, *and* the variability of altitude. Other measures of land quality tried were the proportion of land under cultivation and the proportion of total area defined as bogland.

14   One Devon Commission witness from Waterford, for instance, was at a loss to explain the tranquillity of his district in comparison with the heavy disturbances in neighboring Tipperary (Great Britain, 1845a, Vol. XXI, p. 428).

15   Modern historians have joined the consensus of contemporaries that imperfect security of property and disturbances were a factor—though not the only one—in Ireland's backwardness. See, for example, Black (1960, pp. 136, 157); Crotty (1966, p. 45).

16   The series for mutton prices are unavailable for 1790–5 and were interpolated using the predicted values of a regression equation of the price of mutton on the price of pork and beef for the period 1796–1850 (110 observations).

17   For example, for 1813–50 the line estimated is:

$$P = 112·87 \quad -0·288t \quad R^2 = 0·041, \quad DW = 1·055$$
$$(15·81) \quad (-1·78)$$

while for 1812–50 the line estimated is:

$$P = 118·4 \quad -0·401t \quad R^2 = 0·074, \quad DW = 1·11.$$
$$(16·19) \quad (-2·40)$$

18   It may be added that the Dublin market prices during 1812–40 cited by Crotty (1966, p. 35) do not confirm his own conclusion that animal products declined less in price than cereals. Grantham (1978, pp. 316–17) shows that in France the relative price of livestock products did not rise before the late 1830s.

Chapter 6

The Problem of Wealth

(1) Poverty and Wealth

Why are some economies poorer than others? To some it may seem to suggest that capital or wealth lay at the root of the problem of poverty. If being poor is defined as being "not wealthy", poverty and the lack of capital are identical and one cannot "explain" the other. But if the criterion for being poor is the size of the annual flow of income rather than the stock of assets, the identity disappears. If the criterion is generalized, moreover, to include some variables other than income (as was suggested in Chapter 2), the correspondence between the lack of wealth and poverty is further complicated. In societies which have not yet fully entered the era of sustained economic growth, it makes more sense to define poverty as the probability of starvation. The chances of perishing in a famine depend, however, to a great extent on real income and specifically on labor income. Since wealth, by definition, consists of assets that are either instrumental in production, or are consumed directly, wealth is a primary determinant of income. This truism holds regardless of whether one utilizes a neoclassical, Marxian, or any other paradigm. The productivity of labor, both average and marginal, is positively associated with the amount of nonlabor inputs per unit of labor.

What are these nonlabor inputs? Roughly speaking, they can be classified into three groups. First, there are natural resources which are not reproducible such as land, minerals, and climate. The supply of these inputs available to the economy is determined by geography. Secondly, there is reproducible nonhuman wealth generally referred to as capital or as the stock of capital goods. Thirdly, there is human wealth or human capital which takes such forms as technical skill and knowledge, training, dexterity, organizational ability, resourcefulness, and physical health. Given the size of the population, the labor force participation ratio, and the "state of the art" technology, a complete and accurate specification of all nonlabor inputs should contain all the elements on which both total income per capita and labor income per worker depend.[1]

Moreover, wealth improved the resilience of preindustrial economies to disasters in other respects. The most important consideration here is that once a very rainy day arrived, some forms of stored-up wealth could be used either by consuming the assets directly (for example, livestock), or by selling them abroad and purchasing food with the proceeds. It is true that the distribution of wealth is traditionally more unequal than that of income, and therefore the usefulness of accumulated wealth in times of famine to the vast majority of the poor may be doubted. If a wealthy few own the vast bulk of the physical resources in an economy, why should one expect that they will liquidate these assets to prevent the masses from starving? The answer to that question is complex. The economic value of assets is determined after all by their future profitability, which itself is a function of the amount of labor available to work with these assets. A rich landlord who kept a well-filled granary closed in times of famine and let his tenants starve, clearly would pay a high price in terms of future rents that he could expect to collect. In addition, greater wealth reduced the vulnerability of preindustrial economies directly. Certain forms of capital, such as better transportation and communication facilities, were an input into the reduction of the impact of disasters by spreading local scarcities more thinly and over a wider area.

The subject of this chapter is the role played by natural resources and capital in Irish poverty. The distinction between the two is not always immediately obvious. In principle, the criterion is reproducibility. In practice, however, certain assets were partially reproducible and partially God-given. Land, for instance, is often thought to have certain "indestructible" properties, but it is far from easy to distinguish them from manmade improvements in fertility. The same holds for minerals: while man cannot create mineral wealth, the exploitation of certain minerals is complementary with investment, and a clear-cut distinction between the two is difficult to make.

(2) Natural Resources

Was geography to blame for Irish poverty? The argument is tempting. Ireland has very little iron ore of quality and few usable coalfields. It is often argued — erroneously, I believe — that economies which lacked these resources could not undergo an industrial revolution except under unusual circumstances. It is also sometimes maintained that the overall quality of Irish soil may have been inferior, at least in comparison with that of Britain (Ó Gráda, 1980c, pp. 8–9). As the difference in soil quality does not appear very important, I shall focus here on the question of whether Ireland failed to industrialize because of its poor mineral endowments.[2]

The idea that Ireland failed to undergo an industrial revolution because of its poor natural endowments and not because of some more fundamental problems with the Irish economy was most forcefully expressed recently by O' Tuathaigh:

> Ireland's economic problems in those decades [the first half of the nineteenth century] were similar to those being encountered in certain areas within Britain and throughout Western Europe ... Regions hitherto prosperous began to decay and new centres of industry, wealth and population arose ... This dramatic change in the balance of regional economic activity owed its origins to the supply and use of the natural resources of industrial expansion; it was

a function of the location of the sources of industrial power and energy. (O' Tuathaigh, 1972, p. 119)

Once again, we encounter a hypothesis which is reasonable, even plausible. But is it actually supported by evidence? The logic of the natural resources hypothesis (NRH) as we may term it is compelling, but the actual importance of the geographical location of resources depends on several assumptions, few of which are ever made explicit. How decisive was the lack of natural resources to Ireland's economic development in the nineteenth century? In the last two decades economic historians have searched for various indispensable factors in economic development, the two best known of which are Fogel's celebrated study on American railroads and Von Tunzelmann's work on the steam-engine in the English Industrial Revolution. In most cases the net effect of the factor in question was small enough to fail the test for indispensability, although one could argue about how such a test ought to be set up in the first place.

Ireland had few of the minerals which played a significant role in the Industrial Revolution. It did not undergo an industrial revolution to speak of. Were these two facts causally connected? For this relation to hold, three things have to be true. First, importing these resources should impose additional expenses that would strongly affect the cost differential. Secondly, there should be no economically feasible substitutes to replace the absent coal and iron. Thirdly, in order for the NRH to hold, it has also to be true that an economy could not industrialize by concentrating on producing commodities which used little or no iron and coal. If any of these conditions does not hold, the power of the NRH in explaining the absence of an industrial revolution in Ireland is severely impaired.

Debates concerning the importance of natural resources in economic development have been conducted in many contexts. In the case of the Low Countries, the NRH seems particularly plausible. However, although Belgium was much better endowed with natural resources than the Netherlands, this difference was at most a marginal factor in the divergent economic development of the two countries in the nineteenth century (Mokyr, 1976a, pp. 204–8). One could also cite the examples of Switzerland and Japan to underline that coal and iron were not indispensable in the Industrial Revolution, both in its early and its later stages. While such comparisons are suggestive, it may be misleading to argue solely from analogy and the experience of other economies.

The most devastating criticism of the NRH for the case of Ireland was made not by a modern economic historian, but by a contemporary scientist, Robert Kane.[3] In an influential book (Kane, 1845) he set out to refute the view that Ireland was poor due to natural and geographical causes. After dealing with the problems of energy supply, geology, agriculture, and internal transportation, Kane concluded (p. 412): "The fault is not in the country, but in ourselves; the absence of successful enterprise is owing to the fact, that we do not know how to succeed . . . we want special industrial knowledge." In some cases Kane's enthusiasm has led him to overstate his case.[4] None the less, the basic arguments he makes are logically sound, and keeping in mind the limits of scientific knowledge of the time, I have found no reason to doubt seriously his facts or his analysis in most cases.

The absence of coal is the central feature of the NRH. In fact, there was a fair amount of coal in Ireland (Great Britain, 1837–8, Vol. XXXV, pp. 505–8), but neither in the quantity nor of the quality to fuel manufacturing on a large scale. Ireland's options were to import coal from England, or to use alternative sources of energy wherever possible. Neither of these two alternatives was as cheap as using the cheapest coal, but their total effect on production costs depended on two crucial parameters, namely, the additional cost incurred due to having to import coal and the proportion of fuel costs in total costs. The product of these two numbers is the upper-bound estimate of the increment in total costs which can be attributed to the absence of coal. The reason why it is an upper bound is that the ratio of fuel costs to total costs is itself a declining function of the price of fuel. In Britain, where coal was cheap, the techniques were likely to be more energy-intensive than in Ireland. The computation of the "social cost" of scarce natural resources, which simply multiplies the British share of fuel costs in total costs by the British-Irish price differential, assumes that the Irish had no choice but to adopt the coal-intensive technique used in Britain.

What was the difference in coal prices between the two countries? The price of coal in the coal districts in Britain in the 1830s and 1840s hovered around 6s per ton (Von Tunzelmann, 1978, p. 96). The price of both local and imported coal in the 1840s in Ireland was 11s–12s, although it may have been somewhat higher in remote regions (Kane, 1845, pp. 53, 65–6). Kane himself seems in this case to have overstated the cost differential between Irish coal and the cost of coal in British industrial districts. He cites a price of 3s per ton in Leeds (p. 64) but this price seems too low compared to von Tunzelmann's figures, which never fall below 5s for Leeds (and indeed for any place in Britain). For earlier years the price differential was similar. In the early years of the nineteenth century the price of coal in Ireland was about 20s per ton (Tighe, 1802, pp. 76–7; Kane, 1845, p. 49). Von Tunzelmann's estimates for 1800 for the industrial counties of Britain vary between 9s and 11s (Von Tunzelmann, 1978, p. 148). Although these comparisons are easily confounded by the substantial quality variations of coal, it seems that the estimate of a cost differential of a factor of four assumed by Kane and which I have used elsewhere (Mokyr, 1980a, p. 440) is too high, and that a differential of two to two and a half seems more accurate.

The proportion of fuel costs in total industrial production costs is far more difficult to ascertain. Ideally, one would need a complete input-output table of the economy to establish this figure. Looking at the proportion of fuel costs in some fuel-using industries could be misleading, because the intermediate goods used by these industries could embody a large amount of indirect fuel used in the industry. All the same, the shares estimated from firm records show that without exception the share of fuel costs was much less than 5 percent. Kane computed that for the British cotton industry as a whole, coal accounted for only 1·08 percent of total costs in 1833. A Leeds woolen manufacturer spent only 0·4 percent of the value of output on coal, so that if the firm were to be transplanted to Ireland, fuel costs would have risen according to Kane to at most 2 percent. At a Mulholland flax mill in Belfast coal cost 13s per ton in the mid-1830s, so that fuel amounted to £3,042 a year, or about 3·8 percent of total value of output. In the cotton industry fuel costs typically amounted to 2·7 percent (Kane, 1845, pp. 63–8). If we let the cost of fuel in Britain be responsible for 4 percent of total costs in the nonmetallurgical industries (definitely an upper-bound estimate), and we do not allow any fuel-saving differences in technique between Ireland and Britain, it follows that Nature was responsible for at most a 10 percent total cost differential between Ireland and Britain.

A few observations on this estimate are in order. We may ask whether a 10 percent cost differential is important enough to explain the absence of industrialization in Ireland. Some powerful arguments can be raised to support the contention that a 10 percent cost differential, or even half that much, could indeed have made a large difference. What matters for our purposes is not differences in fuel costs but differences in profitability. A 10 percent difference in fuel cost could make a much larger difference in profits. If the share of profits in total product is 0·25, a difference of total costs of 10 percent could give to the owner of cheap fuel a profit rate which was 40 percent higher (for instance, 14 percent instead of 10 percent, assuming a capital–output ratio of 2·5:1). In competitive markets, therefore, in which all firms are selling at the same prices and in which no other excess profits are earned, the access to cheap fuel could imply an economic rent which was likely to be of major importance. Within England, the evidence is surely consistent with that hypothesis. The location of the textile industry in Britain was strongly and negatively associated with the price of coal. Von Tunzelmann (1978, pp. 65–6) demonstrates decisively that the vast majority of all textile industry in Britain was located in that 15–20 percent of the land area of Britain where coal was cheap, that is, below 10s per ton.

The problem with these arguments is, however, that they hold only *ceteris paribus*. The difference in fuel costs is crucial only if all other costs are the same. If, however, there were additional differences in input prices, fuel costs become only one factor among many. While the direction of its effect remains of course unchanged, it can no longer be regarded as decisive. Kane insisted that the lower wages in Ireland more than offset any cost advantages that Britain might have had due to cheaper coal. His figures indicate that wages in England were approximately 55 percent higher than in Ireland, while the share of wages in total costs varied at 20–35 percent (Kane, 1845, pp. 64, 65, 68). Since we have once more to take into account the effect of higher wages on intermediary inputs, a lower bound on the proportion labor cost in either country is 25 percent. Clearly, then, the lowest possible cost differential in Ireland's favor due to its cheaper labor was larger than the highest possible cost differential in Britain's favor resulting from fuel prices. Kane carried out a hypothetical transference of a Belfast flax mill to England, and concluded that £22·5 would be saved in fuel cost and £60 per year lost in labor costs. The fuel-price differential used by Kane in this computation is much lower than is implied by other figures he provides, since he uses the average (rather than the lowest) price of coal in England. However, this is more than offset by the lower-bound wage he uses for England, which is only 6s 6d. Using more realistic wage-rate differentials, Kane concluded that "a difference of one fortieth in the average rate of wages compensates for whatever difference can arise in the cost of fuel from the prices in Ireland and in Lancashire" (Kane, 1845, pp. 65–6). The concentration of textile industry in cheap-coal regions in Britain is, thus, not inconsistent with the conclusion that the lack of resources was probably a minor factor in Ireland's failure to industrialize. If the variation in all other costs within Britain was small, so that the only consideration for location was energy cost, we would precisely expect such a pattern. Moreover, as Von Tunzelmann remarks, correlation is no proof of causality in this case. It could well be argued that the correlation tended to be spurious in large measure, since the regions in which fuel was cheap tended to coincide with those regions in which there was much cottage industry prior to the Industrial Revolution. The regions which had cheap coal also tended to be the regions in which labor was cheap and widely available.

The negative effect of expensive coal in Ireland could be and was reduced further in three ways: the Irish could use less fuel-intensive processes, they could specialize in the production of commodities which used less fuel, and most importantly, they could substitute other forms of energy for coal. Very detailed evidence on this adaptation of Irish manufacturing to high coal prices is hard to find, because industry in Ireland was so much less developed than in Britain. Kane noted (1845, pp. 50–6, 62) that the cheapness of fuel in England led to excessive waste of it. He pointed to Cornwall as an example of a district in which coal was expensive, and where, by a few simple improvements in the boiler, considerable fuel savings were achieved. As far as the composition of output was concerned, there was perhaps less choice in the first half of the nineteenth century than in later years. Ironsmelting and chemical industries never developed in Ireland, and the shipbuilding industry, which developed after 1850 in Belfast, provides an example of a low energy-intensity industry. By far the most important adaptation to the lack of coal, however, was the use of other energy sources, mainly water power and peat.

Economic historians have long been aware of the role of water power in the Industrial Revolution as a second-best source of power wherever coal was expensive. The New England textile industry before the Civil War was almost exclusively powered by water power. Even in Britain water played an important role. Total water power in textile industries in Britain in 1838 was about 26,000 h.p., declining to 21,000 h.p. in 1856 after considerable improvements in the design and efficiency of steam-engines (Von Tunzelmann, 1978, p. 139). In the United Kingdom as a whole, water supplied 37 percent of total power supplied in the three main textile industries (cotton, wool, and flax) in 1838. Removing Ireland from that computation barely affects the result. Von Tunzelmann has insisted that water power was a feasible alternative for steam power in Britain as well. Regardless of whether this view is correct for England, it certainly seems to hold for Ireland. The implication for the interpretation of Irish backwardness in the first half of the nineteenth century is of central significance: if other factors had been more conducive to economic development, the lack of coal would not have impeded an industrial revolution in Ireland, although it may have been an industrial revolution which, as in Switzerland or in Massachusetts, was largely based on water power.

Water power has played an important role in Irish economy from the sixth century AD. By the eve of the famine, water mills were used not only in their traditional role of grist-milling, but were an indispensable part of the linen industry, the only industry in Ireland which showed any signs of modernization. The scutching of flax was largely carried out in water-powered scutch mills, of which there were about 1,000 in Ireland in 1830, and maybe as many as 1,500 in 1845 (McCutcheon, 1977, p. 51). There were 130–40 bleach greens in Ulster on the eve of the famine. The majority of these depended on water power, although a few had switched to steam power (Gribbon, 1969, p. 88). As late as 1907, water power accounted for 38 percent of the energy supply in the linen-finishing industry. Water power was also used by spade mills, which produced agricultural implements (Gribbon, 1969, pp. 77–8), and in smaller industries, such as distilleries, breweries, candlewick-making, and paper mills.

Actual use of water power in Ireland is, however, of little use for answering the question of whether Ireland *could* have developed more than it did. What we are really interested in for the purpose of testing the NRH is potential use. Ireland is well suited to the use of water power due to its considerable rainfall, mild temperatures, and large differences in elevation. Using somewhat heroic assumptions Kane estimated from data on rainfall, evaporation, and elevation that water power provided a maximum potential of 3 million h.p., of which about 1·25 million was usable (Kane, 1845, p. 78). These estimates are about 20 percent lower than the estimates Kane presented just one year earlier in the first edition of his book, but as Von Tunzelmann points out, even if his figures are overstated by several hundred percent, they indicate none the less that Ireland could have had all the energy it needed.

Water power supplied, of course, kinetic energy but not thermal energy. Coal supplied both. The supply of fuel for space heating and cooking in Ireland was based almost exclusively on peat. In Britain the quantity of coal consumed in steam-engines was estimated in 1856 to be 8–10 million tons, or roughly 13–16 percent of total coal output. Not all of the rest was used for space heating: about 7 percent was exported, 5 percent used in mines, and between a quarter and a third was used in the iron industry. A cautious estimate of the proportion of coal used for space heating, lighting, and cooking would be 45 percent.[5] For all these purposes, peat was an excellent substitute, and it is likely that for the average Irish family the cost of energy was considerably less than for the average British family. Lower prices of necessities could imply lower wages, and for that reason could have constituted a further encouragement of manufacturing.

Peat could, moreover, also be used as a direct input into manufacturing. Steam-engines could be run on peat, as well as on culm, a coaldust of low quality. Peat was used in coal-poor regions in Britain, such as Cornwall and Devon (Von Tunzelmann, 1978, p. 62) as well as in the Netherlands (Mokyr, 1976a, p. 205). In Ireland, too, there is some evidence of the use of peat in steam-engines. Kane reported that a lead-mine in Derrynoos (Co. Armagh) used inferior black mountain turf to fire its engines. The Inland Navigation Co., which ran steamers on the River Shannon, converted around 1840 from coal to turf and saved a third on its fuel bill by doing so. On the whole, turf provided less than half the calories of an equal weight of coal (depending on quality and water content), but at 3s 6d per ton (Kane, 1845, p. 57), turf provided more calories per unit of cost. Moreover, in Ireland peat was all but ubiquitous, so that in most regions transportation costs were low.[6]

Peat had other industrial uses as well. It could be turned into coke using processes quite similar to charcoalmaking. Turf coke was used in ironsmelting and puddling in Bohemia, Bavaria, Prussia, and France (Kane, 1845, pp. 158–63; Leavitt, 1867, pp. 69–72). In Ireland, and especially in Ulster, peat was used by local blacksmiths and small iron-works (OSM, box 31, file II; box 44, file I; box 21, file IV). The larger ironworks at the Arigna mines (Co. Leitrim) used coal for smelting, and the use of peat for large-scale blast furnaces seems to have been inefficient (Coe, 1969, p. 166). But peat was used for other energy intensive industrial uses, including distilleries, brickmaking and lime-burning (see, for example, OSM, box 26, files I, VI, pertaining to Co. Fermanagh). It was perhaps not as good a substitute for coal as Kane's wishful thinking led him to believe. But it was close enough to coal for many uses and cheap enough for Ireland to have developed a peat-based industrial sector if other factors had permitted it. The decline in the price of coal after 1840 due to ever-falling transportation costs and the rise in labor costs (turf-digging was highly labor-intensive) ultimately determined that turf was not to play a central role in providing energy for the Industrial Revolution. It would be wholly fallacious, however, to conclude from the fact that peat did not *actually* play a crucial role in the Industrial Revolution that under no circumstances *could* it have done so.

It is on factors other than natural endowments that we must concentrate for our purposes of unearthing the roots of Irish poverty. As Townsend (1815, Vol. 1, p. 32) remarked, "Ever provident to the wants of man, nature compensates in one way what she denies in another". While poor in coal and iron, Ireland cannot be considered sufficiently deprived by nature for it to be eternally condemned to poverty.[7] Its economic hardships were largely manmade, and should be analyzed as such.

(3) Capital

Was there a scarcity of capital in prefamine Ireland? The answer, in brief, is affirmative, provided the terms are well defined and we avoid certain conceptual pitfalls which have caused some confusion in the past. In what follows below I shall first discuss some theoretical issues in the problem of capital formation in the prefamine economy, showing what is meant by a scarcity of capital. We then turn to the evidence, showing how slow investment affected Irish agriculture, including such areas such as tree-planting, fisheries, and land reclamation. This is followed by a discussion of the impact of capital scarcity on the manufacturing sector, and we end the section with a discussion of investment in social-overhead capital.

The hypothesis that capital scarcity was indeed an important element in Irish poverty seems on the surface inconsistent with the evidence that some groups saved considerable amounts. Lee (1969a), pointing to cases in which Irish investors bought out the English shareholders of a railroad after 1850, and to Irish investors investing in Britain, has even maintained that there was an oversupply of capital in Ireland. Lee concludes (pp. 54–5) that "Ireland saved far more capital than she invested at home but this capital was rarely risk capital . . . it was not capital, but confidence that Irish investors lacked". The same position is expressed by Cullen (1972, p. 129).

Evidence on savings propensities is not available. Lee's conclusions are based on suggestive but fragmentary shreds of information. Applying information taken from postfamine experience to answer prefamine questions could be particularly hazardous here. Moreover, on the aggregate level, in a society like prefamine Ireland in which population was growing at about 1 percent a year, the savings rate had to equal the rate of population growth times the capital–output ratio in order to keep the capital–labor ratio constant and to avoid declining income per capita. In this simple model a sudden decline in population (as occurred during the famine) creates an oversupply of capital. Post-famine information can, therefore, be rather misleading. Furthermore, prefamine information indicating considerable saving among one social class (urban bourgeoisie) cannot be fully evaluated until we know to what extent these savings were offset by the dissavings of the land-owning class. The mechanism by which these flows offset each other was land purchase, cumbersome and difficult before the encumbered estates Acts of 1849 and 1850, but none the less a significant factor.

My disagreement with those who proclaim with Professor Lee that capital was not a binding constraint on the Irish economy is, therefore, more apparent than real. Few would disagree that the country lacked producer durables and an ability to generate certain intermediary inputs in the two crucial sectors of agriculture and modern manufacturing. I will document these assertions in detail below, but it is useful to keep certain conceptual points in mind when discussing capital formation in premodern economies. In the absence of capital markets most accumulation took the form of self-finance. In other words, investment was seldom "financed" in the literal sense of the word. In agriculture land was improved by "investing" in soil fertility through drainage, weeding, crop rotation, the judicious application of manure, and the raising of more farm animals. Since farmers were forgoing present consumption and/or leisure for the sake of greater output in the future, such actions were an investment, although capital markets had little or nothing to do with them. In the Industrial Revolution, both in England and on the continent, self-finance in the form of plowed-back profits was doubtless the main source of fixed and circulating capital, although under exceptional circumstances outside sources could be tapped.[8]

Consider, first, the problem of the individual entrepreneur. A "neo-classical" approach would be misleading here, since any kind of analysis of that type would have to assume the existence of capital markets. Rather, it may prove useful to follow the approach outlined by McKinnon (1973), which is based on an explicit realization that highly imperfect or nonexistent capital markets lead to a failure of rates of return to converge. In the presence of such discrepancies, McKinnon argues, it is erroneous to consider capital formation as simply the accumulation of homogeneous capital of uniform productivity. In McKinnon's world the economic decisions are made by households or firms which are largely isolated from each other. It is hence possible to have "entrepreneurs" with excellent investment opportunities who fail to realize these rates of return because they lack resources of their own and have no access to external finance. At the same time, there may be others who own considerable resources but lack high-return investment projects. When endowments do not coincide with investment opportunities, the real rates of return are dispersed, reducing the overall social rate of return and repressing new accumulation (McKinnon, 1973, pp. 8–11). In such circumstances it is perfectly possible and indeed inevitable that we observe simultaneous "excess supply" and "excess demand" of capital. Focusing on one of the two to deny the other (for example, Cullen, 1972, p. 129) is, thus, both meaningless and misleading. None the less, an economy which is characterized by this "McKinnon syndrome" can be said to suffer, in some sense, from a lack of capital.

Next, consider the problem of agricultural saving and investment. In peasant economies capital formation is impeded by indivisibilities. As McKinnon points out, in the absence of indivisibilities self-finance will ultimately achieve the same goal as "neoclassical" growth, albeit at a much slower pace. The lumpiness of many investment projects and the absence of capital markets create a synergistic effect. Each of them separately can be overcome; jointly they imply that the peasant may be caught in a low-income trap, an equilibrium of poverty. To illustrate how such a trap occurs, consider Figure 6.1. Panel (a) demonstrates the case of self-finance with perfectly divisible capital. In the absence of investment the individual consumes the same quantities in periods 1 and 2 (Q_1 and Q_2, respectively). The slope of the line $C_1^*C_2^*$ reflects the rate of return on investment (assumed constant). At point E^*, the individual invests D_1Q_1 and consequently increases his income in period 2 by D_2Q_2. This analysis can be generalized to many periods. As long as the rate of return stays above the subjective rate of time preference, capital accumulation will occur.[9]

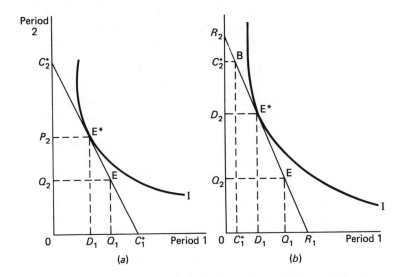

Figure 6.1 *Lumpy investment and imperfect capital markets*

Now consider panel (*b*) and assume that investment is "lumpy" of nature. For simplicity of exposition, let the feasible project be indivisible to the point where the entire project is summarized by point B. An investment of $Q_1C_1^*$ will lead to a return of $Q_2C_2^*$ but anything less will bear a zero rate of return. "Neoclassical" theory predicts that if the peasant can borrow or lend freely (that is, move along the line R_1R_2), he will borrow the quantity $D_1C_1^*$, produce at B, and ultimately end up at a point like E*, which is preferable to E, his initial position.

The crux of McKinnon's argument is that without the capital market a point like B may be unattainable. If the distance $0C_1^*$, which measures what is left over to consume in period 1 after the investment has been made, is less than the biological minimum of subsistence, or if it is zero, so that the peasant has to forgo consumption altogether in period 1 in order to reach B, the entire project will become unachievable. The peasant will be trapped at E, without ever being able to reach E*. There may be plenty of capital in this economy; unless our peasant can get to this capital, he will be grasping like Tantalus for a seemingly feasible project which is just beyond his reach.

In manufacturing, the problem of accumulation is somewhat different. Indivisibilities were less of an obstacle here not because there were no lumpy investment projects in the industrial sector, but because the subsistence constraints were less binding on the entrepreneurs. Nevertheless, the imperfection of capital markets still implies that some individuals were "saturated" with capital, and lent it to governments or foreign investors while at the same time local entrepreneurs were severely constrained by the lack of long-term funds. In such an economy the rate of accumulation is the product of the proportion of profits plowed back into the firms and the rate of profit. The rate of capital accumulation is, thus, a function of the determinants of these two parameters (Mokyr, 1976b). True, the imperfections in capital markets serving industry were in general less severe than in agriculture. The cost of evaluating potential investment projects was smaller, because the information on agricultural projects was always site-specific. None the less, self-finance remained the primary mechanism of capital accumulation in European manufacturing until late in the nineteenth century and in many places beyond that time.

What evidence exists to demonstrate that the lack of capital was in fact a major constraint on prefamine Irish agriculture? It may not be very useful to cite contemporaries professing their opinion about "capital" since the term among nineteenth-century political economists had different connotations from our present concepts, and not all contemporary writers used the term in the same way. What matters here is what contemporaries were saying about the reasons why agriculture was not producing more. Among the complaints most frequently heard was the lack of fertilizer. Townsend (1815, Vol. 1, p. 196) pointed out that in Cork the lack of fertilizer was most acutely felt among smaller farmers who did not own enough cattle. One Co. Mayo witness pointed out to the Poor Law Commissioners that "want of manure is the cause always assigned by the poor man for the portion of his land which is annually allowed to remain untilled . . . the tenant of ten acres gets more value from his holding than the tenant of one acre because he is more likely to have manure or the money to purchase it" (Great Britain, 1836b, Vol. XXXIII, p. 84). The main source of demand for manure was the potato crop. The potato consumed most of the available manure, leaving little for other crops which followed it in the crop rotation (Weld, 1832, p. 315; Tighe, 1802, p. 216). The acreage of potatoes was limited by the supply of manure, and there were strong indivisibilities in manure production because the capital good which produced manure, livestock, was subject to strong scale economies. Small farmers were unable to invest enough in soil fertilization because they could neither raise enough cattle nor borrow to buy sufficient quantities of fertilizer. Weld (1832, p. 662) noted that potato crops in Connaught were smaller due to the fact that small farms produced proportionally less manure. Witnesses from counties as different as Leitrim and Kilkenny affirmed before the Poor Law Commissioners that smallholders were usually unable to secure enough manure (Great Britain, 1836b, Vol. XXXIII, pp. 214, 240).[10]

Agricultural experts agreed that the lack of manure was one of the main stumbling-blocks on the path toward modernization of agriculture. William Blacker, an Armagh land agent and a widely respected author on agricultural matters, emphasized that small farms in Ireland suffered from the effects of a constant succession of grain crops which were continued until the land was completely depleted, at which point it was let out to rest. The cause of this inefficient setup was the want of manure. Twenty-five barrels of lime per statute acre, Blacker estimated, should be enough to break the vicious circle in which smallholders found themselves. Furthermore, as Blacker realized, in order to change the agricultural technique to a more capital-intensive one based on green crops, the tenant needed a loan to permit him to survive the year in which he sowed clover or another green crop which was then used to feed cattle. Blacker thought that the most likely candidate to advance the peasant the sum needed was the landlord, but he realized that the landlord may reasonably ask "how can I be secured in the repayment of the sum I may thus be called to advance in lime in order to make this plan practicable?" (Blacker, 1834, pp. 8–11). Blacker's optimism that the Irish landlords would see the light and lend money to their tenants was largely misplaced, but his view that one could measure the degree of improvement in agriculture by the size of the manure heaps (Blacker, 1845, p. ix) summarizes an important truth about prefamine Irish agriculture.

Fertilizer was a capital good which took many forms. In coastal regions seaweed or kelp and seasand were widely used. Lime, turf ash, and farm dung were used in other regions. Markets for most of these fertilizers existed, but because they were needed in large quantities, transportation costs made haulage across long distances impracticable. Most tenants therefore had to rely on their own sources of manure either by procuring their own seaweed or lime, or by using the farm manure produced by their animals (Great Britain, 1835d, Vol. XXXIII, p. 311; OSM, box 31, file II, pertaining to the parish of Balteagh, Co. Londonderry). But the costs of all forms of manure were high, and in some cases the rent reflected the proximity to and permission to use seaweed (Great Britain, 1835d, Vol. XXXIII, p. 218). In some cases the ownership rights on the sources of seaweed were actively disputed between landlord and tenant (Kennedy, 1847, p. 63). Seaweed was widely regarded as the best fertilizer for potato crops, but in many areas lime was also sold at high prices. Farm manure, the best fertilizer of all, was enormously valuable (Trimmer, 1809, p. 10). Even around towns animal manure could not be procured, said a Kilkenny witness, because the townspeople often rented pieces of land around the city on which they grew their own potatoes, which used up all the manure (Great Britain, 1836b, Vol. XXXIII, p. 240).

The one option available to Irish agriculture to produce the fertilizer it needed was to switch to a mixed farming system in which "green crops", such as clover, turnips, and mangel-wurzel were intermixed with the "white crops" (cereals) and potatoes. The "green crops" fulfilled two basic functions. One was to provide fodder for animals and thus to produce not only a more efficient way of generating cash directly, but also to increase the local supply of manure and in that way to increase the output of cereals and potatoes. A second function was to restore the fertility of the soil. In this function not all crops were similar. Turnips, like potatoes, rested and cleaned the soil by breaking the lifecycles of pests and diseases. Artificial grasses, clover, and vetches restored the nitrogen content of the soil. At the beginning of the nineteenth century few of these crops had become widespread in Ireland, but by the time of the famine there were no counties unfamiliar with them. The problem is that the first statistics of agricultural crops become available in 1847, and were heavily affected by the potato blight (Great Britain, 1849a, Vol. XLIX, p.10). For what they are worth, the 1848 data show a total of 25,000 acres under beans and about the same acreage under peas. Of the root crops, aside from potatoes, which were abnormally low in 1849, 235,000 acres were under turnips, and another 20,000 acres under other root crops. There is some reason to believe that the acreage under turnips in 1847 was higher than the normal acreage in the immediate prefamine years. The Constabulary Survey of 1846 explicitly asked the farmers which crops they had substituted for the diseased potatoes. The majority pointed to turnips, which is to be expected in view of the similar roles that potatoes and turnips played in the rotation. Prefamine turnip acreage, thus, was probably less than 150,000 acres. (For details on the Constabulary Survey, see Mokyr, 1981a.) The amount under grasses and clover amounted to 1·154 million acres, or 22·5 percent of total land under crops. This proportion may again be somewhat unrepresentative of prefamine crops due to the reduced potato tillage, but it is clear that artificial grasses and clover were being adopted as part of the rotation in many parts of Ireland in the decades before the famine. But diffusion was slow, and errors in the usage of the new tillage were widespread.

Examples of specialists exhorting the adoption of this type of farming and pointing to inefficiencies in its use are numerous. An early and very elaborate example is provided by Tighe (1802, pp. 280–1) in his massive and learned essay on Kilkenny. Tighe compared a twenty-year course of crops under the old system to one that involved green crops. The advantage of fertility-restoring crops was not so much that they did away with the fallow but that they prevented the land from being taken out of use after its exhaustion, which under the "old system" occurred after the twelfth year. The total value of output over twenty years was doubled in this fashion, but most of the gains were concentrated in the last seven of the twenty years.

The exact nature of the "old" and the "new" system of rotation varied from place to place, but significant gains were made possible by switching to the new rotation. By keeping "house-fed" cattle, two or three acres planted with turnips or clover could feed three cows all year round rather than provide a meager summer pasture for a single cow (Blacker, 1845, pp. 38–9). The increased output of fertilizer, combined with the beneficial effect on soil quality, permitted an increase of potato crops as well as larger cereal crops and more livestock products. The order of magnitude of gains from switching to green crops is indicated by a comparison between potatoes and turnips as "preparation crops" before cereals or flax. As a part of the crop rotation they fulfilled very similar functions, and the potato was often referred to as "Ireland's answer to the turnip" (see, for example, Lewis, 1840, Vol. 1, p. 33). As human food, of course, the turnip was unacceptable. But a third of the total potato crop was eaten by animals and not by human beings. What advantages did the turnip offer as a cattle fodder relative to the potato? William Blacker, the great advocate of turnips, admitted that it was a "disputed point, whether turnips or potatoes are the most beneficial crop", but left no doubt where his own views lay (Blacker, 1845, pp. 82–3). Some of Blacker's supporting facts are, however, exaggerated. For instance, he claimed that "a stone of turnips will yield as much manure and milk as a stone of potatoes and the same land will yield five stones of the former . . . for one of the latter". Contemporary accounts indicate that potatoes fed to cattle were about three times as nutritious pound for pound as turnips (Kane, 1845, p.276; Bourke, 1968, p. 85). Modern nutritional analysis indicates a somewhat lower gap: a pound of potatoes has slightly less than twice the calorific content of a pound of turnips, 60 percent more protein, but only a third of the fat (Adams, 1975, pp. 129, 168). The yield statistics cited by Blacker are also distorted. Turnip yields were higher than potato yields, ton for ton: post-famine statistics show that average output of turnips in the 1850s was about 14 tons per statute acre (Mitchell and Deane, 1971, pp. 80, 92), whereas prefamine potato crops were about 6 tons per acre (Bourke, 1969). It is likely, however, that the lumper potato so widely grown in prefamine Ireland contained more water than the modern potato, and that the actual yield differences were larger (see, for example, Great Britain, 1845a, Vol. XX, p. 821, where a Co. Limerick witness estimated the yield of turnips to be four times that of potatoes). We can conclude that turnips were superior to potatoes as a fodder for livestock, though by a much smaller margin than Blacker claimed. The other argument made by Blacker, that potatoes had to be fed to livestock half-boiled, whereas turnips could be given raw (so that a shift from potatoes to turnips would imply a saving in fuel) is also incorrect. Arthur Young reported that horses, cattle, and sheep did well when fed raw potatoes, although horses would fatten more on boiled potatoes (Young, 1892, Vol. 1, p. 331). Pigs, on the other hand, had to be fed boiled potatoes, which may have been the cause of Blacker's confusion (Burton, 1968, p. 302).

On the whole, it seems that the relative profitability of the turnips compared to the potato was considerably less marked in Ireland than in Britain. The enthusiasm of many contemporaries notwithstanding, it is quite likely that the predominant role of the potato at the expense of the turnip was not wholly a consequence of backwardness. Crotty (1966, pp. 29–30) points out that the value of fodder crops eaten *in situ* was much smaller in Ireland than in Britain in the eighteenth century, because of the lack of local demand for livestock products. With the increasing integration of Ireland into a large British agricultural free-trade area, that problem vanished. It should also be recalled that in parts of Ireland poor drainage made turnip cultivation unprofitable.

Nevertheless, the slowness with which green crops were diffused in Ireland made too deep an impression on agricultural experts of the time to be totally dismissed by the modern historian. It seems likely that a form of husbandry in which the potato, the turnip, and artificial grasses shared the role of the principal alternate crop to cereals was admirably suited to conditions in most parts of Ireland. Such a system required, however, considerable expenditure in deep field draining, and marling and liming to reduce soil acidity. In addition, some funds would be needed for the purchase of fertilizer, until the farm started to produce sufficient quantities by itself.

The revolutionary advantage of the new husbandry was that under "convertible" farming, arable and pasturage were no longer competing usages of the land, but complemented each other, effectively increasing the total supply of land available for farming. The introduction of some form of the new farming, modified to suit the particular conditions of Ireland, would have relieved to a large extent the cruel dilemmas of the choice between arable and pasturage and consequently reduced — though not eliminated — the tensions between landlord and tenant described in Chapter 5. Ireland's inability to generate enough capital formation to make the transition to the new husbandry helped to perpetuate the rural conflicts; the latter fed back into the inhibition of the process of capital formation. It is of such "closed feed-back loops" that the stuff of Irish poverty was made. A Co. Louth witness told the Poor Láw Commissioners that "the quantity of land now devoted to grass, if used in producing green and root crops for (stall) feeding would rear or fatten probably four times as much stock as at present and would furnish employment to ten or perhaps twenty times as many persons in cultivating the crops and attending to the stock, besides so amazingly increasing the manure as to cause progressive improvement in the fertility . . . of the land" (Great Britain, 1836b, Vol. XXXIII, p. 247). Timmer (1969) confirms that turnip cultivation was a form of labor-using technological change. While Timmer doubts that Norfolk rotation increased the product of labor at all, there can be little doubt about the effect of the turnip in Ireland, where tillage was much more labor-intensive than in premodern England. Green crops thus increased the productivity of both land and labor, but it is likely that they increased the productivity of land by a larger factor.

The crucial question was however: did it pay? Exact rates of return on the investment in green crops are not easy to compute because of the difficulties in estimating the costs. One Co. Wicklow witness testifying before the Devon Commission estimated the cost of converting 20 acres at £200. The net profits realized by this mode of farming over a five-year period were £7·63 per acre, as opposed to £1·93 net profit on unimproved grazing land. The rate of return implied by these figures is 57 percent annually (actually a bit higher, since most of the increased profits were concentrated in the first years) (Great Britain, 1845a, Vol. XXI, pp. 712–13). Compared to interest plus depreciation estimated at 7·5 percent annually, these rates seem incredibly high. They are confirmed, however, by the estimates of the rate of return on livestock produced in Tables 3.7, 3.8, and 3.9. The coefficient of the *CAPLAB* variable in these regressions represents the amount of increase in annual income per capita resulting from an increase of £1 in the value of livestock. These coefficients vary between 2·50 and 1·30 in most of the regressions. Mis-specification of the equation tends to bias the coefficients of *CAPLAB* upward. The lowest estimates, however, still imply rates of return on investment in livestock of 30–50 percent annually. Arthur Young remarked of the investment of land improvement in Ireland that while capital invested in English trade and manufacture yielded a return of 5–10 percent, Irish agriculture promised rates of return of 15–20 percent, in addition to a variety of other advantages (that is, external economies) that would be brought about by such investment (Young, 1892, Vol. 2, p. 18). Seven decades after Young, the Devon Commission Digest estimated the rate of return on the investment in drainage and subsoiling of present productive lands in Ireland at 15 percent. Since this estimate presumably reflects an *average*, there must have been many feasible projects ensuring rates of return of double that figure or higher (Kennedy, 1847, p. 569). Even if they are somewhat overstated, the estimates indicate that it is likely that the McKinnon syndrome characterized Irish agriculture in the prefamine years.

Why did Irish peasants not switch sooner and in much larger numbers to the New Husbandry? Ireland is not the only economy for which this question has been posed. George Grantham, writing about French agriculture, has maintained that the intensive mixed husbandry system was the principal means of raising agricultural productivity in Western Europe before 1840 and estimated that improved tillage was capable of increasing crops by 20–50 percent (Grantham, 1978, p. 333; 1975, p. 303). Why did these techniques spread so slowly? The main cause according to Grantham was the insufficient level of demand for animal products in France. This argument is not applicable to Ireland, which sold most of its animal products on the British market. Other explanations mentioned by Grantham are small-scale farming, a high degree of self-sufficiency, and a lack of agricultural capital. Capital scarcity in the sense defined above was certainly not the only impediment. One reason for the tardy improvement in agriculture was knowledge. There was no simple "green-crop technology". Soil conditions, climate, elevation, and other factors, required local adaptation and many variations in practice. Some soils did not take well to mangel-wurzel, others were not appropriate for turnips or vetches. In many parts of Ireland climate and soil conditions were unfavorable to an unmodified adoption of the new husbandry, compared to Denmark or east England. Artificial drainage was essential, fertilizer tended to be more important because the heavy rainfall washed the nutrients out of the soil, and weed growth was a serious problem because of the wet summer. These difficulties varied considerably within Ireland, however, where average annual rainfall rises from east to west, and where topographical variation is more striking than almost anywhere else in Europe. Reading the booklets published by William Blacker and others — which were very popular — did not, then, suffice.[11] Expert advice from professional agriculturalists familiar with local conditions was needed for successful implementation of the new husbandry. Furthermore, there was considerable resistance against the "new system", because the vanguard of the new technology consisted of local gentry and their agents, who were mistrusted and·sometimes hated by the tenants. One consequence thereof was that turnips tended to be stolen from the fields. The result of this habit was, of course, to quell the incentive to shift to the new system (Great Britain, 1836b, Vol. XXXII, pp. 39–67; Coote, 1801b, pp. 95, 123). Complaints about potatoes being stolen were rare. Turnips, however, were unsafe. Perhaps turnips were associated with landlords and therefore deemed fair game, but a general resistance against something new and threatening provided the background to this curious phenomenon. As pointed out in Chapter 5, tenants also resisted consolidation even when it did not imply a reduction in labor demand, because they refused to be reduced to the state of landless laborers. The Pollock estates in Co. Galway provide a good example of the difficulties a landlord set on improvements could encounter (Lane, 1972). The irony of the resistance to the new tillage was that it was the only system which was capable of resolving or at least attenuating the landlord–tenant conflict.

One particular aspect of Irish agriculture which struck contemporaries as indicative of its backward nature was the primitive nature, and often the complete absence, of "farm offices". Barns, stables, and pigsties were described repeatedly as miserable hovels. Tools, implements, and carts were often left on the fields, carts left in gaps in ditches. Tighe (1802, pp. 411–12) provided a vivid description of the apparent neglect of farm buildings. Decades later, McCulloch (1854, Vol. 1, p. 519) wrote that Tighe's description was "still generally applicable" (see also Pim, 1848, p. 56; Foster, 1847, pp. 56–7; Kennedy, 1847, pp. 127–30; Townsend, 1815, Vol. 1, pp. 212–16). Although it is impossible at this stage to conclude anything about the rate of return on the investment in farm buildings in Ireland, it seems likely that their absence in comparison with Britain, Belgium, and other countries with which Ireland was compared was part of the general low capital intensity from which Ireland was suffering.

While other factors were at work, the major stumbling-block in Irish agricultural progress was thus the lack of capital required for adoption of the new husbandry. As was pointed out above, indivisibilities can explain how such a "low-income trap" can come about. The existence of indivisibilities can be amply illustrated. Blacker pointed out the need for cooperation and coordination among small farms: "as long as small enclosures remain, no regular rotation can be introduced over *the entire* farm — and until this is done, very little improvement in the general appearance of any district will be visible" (Blacker, 1845, p. ix; italics in original). Because the new tillage system involved the overhaul of the *entire* rotation system of the farm, a farmer could not switch to it gradually. It was often an "all or nothing" decision. As William Marshall wrote in 1795, "The whole system of the Norfolk management hinges on . . . the quantity of dung. No dung—no turneps—no bullocks —no barley—no clover—no teathe [manure] upon the second year's ley for wheat" (cited by Timmer, 1969, p. 385).

Another key to successful maintenance of soil fertility, as Blacker emphatically pointed out, was the "fourth maxim" of the new farming: never take two crops of the same kind in succession from the same land (Blacker, 1845, p. 59). Moreover, successful adoption of the new farming required other changes which required capital. All green-crop substitutes for potatoes in the "new agriculture" needed better implements and, thus, more capital input, since the land had to be more perfectly pulverized than for potatoes (Kennedy, 1847, p. 79). More cattle was, of course, a rather obvious complementary input. Furthermore, as noted above, in most cases drainage and green crops went together (Freeman, 1957, p. 62). A Co. Limerick witness testifying before the Devon Commission (Great Britain, 1845a, Vol. XX, p. 821) estimated that a *combination* of green crops and subsoiling trebled total output.

A second form of investment in agriculture was drainage. Blacker made thorough drainage the first of his "ten maxims of good farming". In Ireland, drainage is crucial. The country has one of the highest levels of rainfall in Europe and its cloud cover prevents rapid evaporation. Topographically it resembles a saucer, with mountains around much of the coastline, slow-running and tortuous rivers, and poor overall natural drainage (Crotty, 1966, pp. 69–70). The rainfall tends to leach out the humus and minerals and encourages weeds. Two classes of drainage should be distinguished. One was the problem of general drainage or flood control, and which was basically a public-sector problem (Wakefield, 1812, Vol. 1, pp. 471–3). The second class of drainage projects consisted of relieving individual farms and fields of "superfluous moisture", as the Devon Commission Digest put it (Kennedy, 1847, p. 80). Drainage was widely regarded as one of the most valuable forms of agricultural investment. The Devon Commission Digest summarized the many hundreds of witnesses who testified before it as follows:

> It has been stated almost universally throughout the evidence, that the lands in nearly every district of Ireland require drainage; that the drainage and deep moving or subsoiling have proved most remunerative operations wherever they have been applied; that these operations have so far been introduced but to a very limited extent . . . the enormous ratio of improvement that the operations themselves produce upon the land, insures a remunerative return where a costly method [of drainage] is adopted . . . it is impossible to imagine any other legitimate investment that could be expected to make so large a return. (Kennedy, 1847, pp. 14–15, 84, 85)

Rates of return are difficult to estimate. The Devon Commission Digest provides data on twenty-four projects reported by witnesses, from which some order of magnitude can be estimated. The figures report the number of years after which the cost of drainage was reimbursed by the consequent increased produce of the land. If the term "reimbursement" meant the equality between the undiscounted flow of net profits and the original investment, the rate of return is simply the reciprocal of the number of years stated. Since the average number of years needed for "reimbursement" was four, the implicit rate of return was 25 percent. If the implicit rate of discount used in discounting future incomes is 10 percent, the rate of return rises to 31·5 percent.[12] Foster (1847, p. 327) provides some figures for the costs and profits of a land drainage and subsoiling project proposed in Co. Limerick. Over the first four years, total costs were estimated at £23·65, while total income added up to £40·23. On the most unfavorable assumption about the exact time-pattern of these flows (about which Foster is ambiguous), the internal rate of return implicit in these figures is 37 percent.

Drainage costs varied enormously with the location of the site drained and the materials and techniques used. The costs of draining a statute acre reported by competitors for the Agricultural Society's prize in 1843–4 varied between £1 12s 2d in Mayo to £5 8s 3d in Meath. With such dispersion in costs, it is certain that there were considerable differences in the rates of return. The rates of return on flood-control projects, where the social rate of return was certain to exceed the private rate, were definitely lower than the ones realized on individual drainage and subsoiling projects. Nevertheless, even as far as "general drainage" was concerned, the rates of return that could be realized were respectable. More detailed information on the rate of return on public drainage projects can be obtained from the annual reports on drainage in Ireland presented to Parliament by the Office of Public Works in Dublin (Great Britain, 1845b, Vol. XXVI; Great Britain, 1846a, Vol. XXII). These reports present estimates concerning projects in process or in planning stages. The data provided contain estimates both of the costs of the projects and the anticipated increase in the letting value of the land resulting from the works. Thus, they present lower bounds of the social rate of return, since it is likely that some of the returns were not captured in the rents (for example, benefits captured by consumers of the final products). On the other hand, some of the expenses of the projects could be charged to the counties, so that the rate of return that landlords could expect on *their* investment was higher. The tables presented in Great Britain, 1845b, Vol. XXVI (pp. 50–3) yield a mean rate of return of 12·38 percent on the landlords' investment, and 13·87 percent on the total investment. These rates are similar to the 13 percent return figure provided by Kane (1845, p. 273). It is hard to know to what extent these figures reflected the actual returns, since Irish conditions changed dramatically in the late 1840s, and the many projects initiated in the 1840s were not completed due to the financial difficulties of Irish landlords in the 1845–50 crisis. One source that could give us some indication of the accuracy of the estimates is the summary of "cost over-runs" provided in Great Britain, 1849b. Vol. XLIX (pp. 225–9). According to that source, the estimated costs of 138 projects in progress were £1,406,000. Of those funds, £602,000 had been spent, and another £1,027,000 was anticipated. Even if the latter sum is not totally accurate, a cost over-run of 15·9 percent does not seem large enough to invalidate the calculation of the rate of return. Moreover, the number of acres expected to be affected by the drainage projects was also revised upward by 13 percent (from 302,000 to 342,000 acres), so that it seems likely that the rent increase subsequent on drainage works used for the rate of return computations is probably somewhat too low as well.

Why were these seemingly profitable projects not undertaken in view of the claimed capital abundance in Ireland? In part, the answer is that the abundance of capital is overstated in that the "capital" accumulated by some individuals failed to find its way to profitable projects. Institutions, such as investment banks, which were supposed to channel funds from savers to investors to spread risk over many projects, and to convert technical information on production and innovation into pounds, shillings, and rates of return, either failed in these tasks or did not exist. Land tenure was blamed in some instances, but it was widely realized that the impediments to drainage projects were "in some cases the absence of leases and in many more cases the want of capital in the tenant and of assistance and encouragement from the landlord" (Great Britain, 1835d, Vol. XXXIII, pp. 231, 236). The net result was that the economy was capital-starved, in spite of some groups which saved substantial amounts.

Perhaps no better example of the low capital–labor ratio can be provided than the lack of trees in Ireland. The example of trees is often used in capital theory as a classic case of a project in which investment consists of postponement and waiting. The tree should be cut down when the implicit or explicit rate of interest equals the rate of growth of the tree.[13] Trees were an important input in construction and some industries, and in some parts of the country were an effective protection against westerly winds, but it can hardly be maintained that Ireland was poor because it had no trees. What can and should be argued is that Ireland was poor because not enough was saved in productive forms, and that the absence of trees was another manifestation of this tendency. In the sixteenth century Ireland was still a wooded country. Spenser, writing in the 1590s, spoke of "goodly woods even fit for building of houses and shippes so commodiously as that, if some princes of the world had them, they would soon hope to be lords of all the seas". In the seventeenth and eighteenth centuries a large amount of deforestation took place (Hall, 1825–40, Vol. 3, p. 407; O'Brien, 1918, pp. 153–6). By 1800 Ireland was notorious for its lack of trees. "The whole island is remarkably bare of trees and exhibits a naked appearance", wrote Wakefield (1812, Vol. 1, p. 9). Similar observations by contemporaries are numerous (Foster, 1847, p. 373; Mason, 1814–19, Vol. 1, pp. 13, 175; Vol. 3, p. 405; Townsend, 1815, Vol. 1, p. 14). Of the total surface area of 20·8 million statute acres, only 1·80 percent were forested in 1841, and another 0·54 percent were covered with detached trees, making a total of 2·34 percent of the surface of the country (Great Britain, 1843, Vol. XXIV, pp. 452–3). Various causes for the deforestation of Ireland were cited by Kane (1845, p. 3): the increase in the arable surface, the exports of oak timber, the consumption of charcoal for iron manufacturing, even the defoliation for purposes of warfare against bands of outlaws. The main cause of the lack of trees, contemporaries agreed, was that "no one planted; all sought their immediate profit and cared not for the future".

Since trees were almost invariably the property of the landholding class, it was that class which was blamed for the lack of trees. One nineteenth-century writer (Rawson, 1807, pp. 72–3) provided a quantitative analysis of a project to plant 1 acre with trees. According to his data, the total cost of planting plus the present value of rent would amount to £60. Three harvests of trees, one of £50 after three years, one of £100 after twelve years, and one of £1,000 after twenty-five years, assured profitability. Actually, the internal rate of return implied in Rawson's figures is about 18 percent per annum.

Another manifestation of capital scarcity in the prefamine Irish economy was the backwardness of the fishing industry. The absence of extensive fishing astonished many contemporaries. Ireland is favorably located on the Continental Shelf of Europe, richly endowed with natural harbors. None the less, the number of fishermen, as reported in the 1841 Census, was only 9,211 or about 0·3 percent of the employed population. Dubourdieu (1812, p. 569) spoke for many observers when he noted that "in respect to fish, no country can be better situated than Ireland . . . but certainly these natural and obvious benefits have never been turned to the best advantage". Apart from the coastal regions, fish played a minor role in the Irish diet. Freeman (1957, p. 94) remarks that the Irish never became a maritime people like the Norwegians or the Dutch, and at no time has Ireland ever acquired the position in European fisheries that its location would suggest.

Capital in the fishery industry consisted of private capital (boats and nets) and public goods (harbors, piers, light-towers, and curing stations). The hazardous waters along the western coast required a high degree of seaworthiness. The Earl of Glengall noted in an appendix to the Devon Report that "there is scarcely a portion of the coast of Ireland off which there are not the most superior fishing banks; but the fact is, the people have not the means of fitting out proper boats for going out to sea twenty or twenty-five miles where the [fishing] banks lay: it costs above £300 to fit out a boat of the proper class. At present fishing is carried out in very small wretched boats, which dare not venture beyond two or three miles from the shore" (Kennedy, 1847, p. 938). In Liscannon, Co. Clare, people fished with canoes, although it was obvious that the further they ventured into the sea, the better were their catches (Mason, 1814–19, Vol. 1, p. 485). The indivisibilities in fisheries were much larger and more prohibitive than in agriculture, and there were some hesitant attempts of the government to aid in overcoming such potential "market failures".[14] Conflict between different villages, often accompanied by violence and sabotage, thwarted attempts to pool individual resources into fishing companies (Foster, 1847, pp. 598–600; Kennedy, 1847, p. 939). Many contemporaries and historians have tended to place the blame for the failure of the Irish fisheries on the British government, in some cases complaining that the Irish fisheries were deliberately discriminated against to protect Scottish and English fishermen. This accusation amounts to an implicit concession that the industry could never have pulled itself up by its bootstraps.

To be sure, other factors for the failure of Irish fisheries have been proposed. Wakefield (1812, Vol. 1, p. 129) asserted that the minute division of land was a principal impediment to the development of fisheries, although it is never made clear precisely how. It stands to reason that fishing was not likely to develop as long as it remained a part-time employment of peasants. The seasonal peaks of agriculture and fishing all but coincided (Mason, 1814–19, Vol. 1, p. 233). What was necessary was a class of specialized fishermen trading with other classes. The root of the problem was, however, an inability to direct resources to the formation of capital. Once more: the failure of the Irish economy to generate a fishing industry was not in and of itself a cause of poverty. But the flaws which thwarted the development of fisheries characterized most other sectors of the prefamine economy.

One frequently discussed failure of the Irish rural economy was the reclamation of land. According to the 1841 Census, on the eve of the famine 6·3 million acres, or 30 percent of the total surface area, were uncultivated. It was generally agreed that much of that land was reclaimable. Richard Griffith presented data to the Devon Commission which suggested that of the 6·3 million acres of unimproved land, 3·75 million could be improved, of which 38 percent were suitable for tillage (Great Britain, 1845a, Vol. XXII, p. 290). O'Brien (1921, p. 127) maintained that, a few exceptions notwithstanding, land was not reclaimed in prefamine Ireland, and blamed the usual scapegoats of prefamine rural society. Contemporaries expressed similar views. Foster (1847, pp. 374–5) was astounded by the inexplicable coexistence of a land-hungry peasantry with hundreds of thousands of reclaimable acres lying waste in peat bogs and mountains. A Westmeath witness testifying before the Public Works Select Committee (Great Britain, 1835b, Vol. XX, p. 401) estimated the upper bound of the cost of draining red bog at £13 per acre, which was subsequent to reclamation let at £1 per year, implying a rate of return of 7·7 percent. On other land the cost and value of a reclaimed acre of black bog were £6 and £2, respectively, impying a rate of return of 33 percent. Blacker, testifying before the same committee, estimated the increase in annual value of a 4·5 acre lot to be about £1 16s on an investment of £4 10s, implying a return of 40 percent (Great Britain, 1835b, Vol. XX, p. 481).

The conventional wisdom on this subject was challenged in a remarkable paper by Connell (1950b), who showed that much land reclamation actually took place during 1780–1845. The principal mode of reclamation was draining and fertilizing boglands. Most of it was initiated and carried out by peasants, not by landlords. Still, landlords often took the initiative, encouraging and sometimes financing reclamation projects. A frequent occurrence was the settlement of evicted tenants on bog and mountain lands, on the condition that they bring the land under cultivation.

Is Connell's finding that land reclamation was far from negligible in prefamine Ireland inconsistent with our view that scarcity of capital severely constrained the development of the Irish economy? First, it has to be pointed out that Connell overstated his case (see also Bourke, 1965b, for a similar argument). Most of the evidence he produced is of the "for example" variety. Such a methodology is inevitable in the absence of systematic data, but it is noteworthy that Connell tended to dismiss or ignore evidence damaging to his conclusion that land reclamation at a feverish rate was taking place in the prefamine economy. A Committee on Public Works (Great Britain, 1835b, Vol. XX, p. 191) found that land reclamation was confined to a few cases. Some contemporaries doubted that drainage of bogs was profitable at all, and claimed as their support that not a single extensive bog had been drained by speculators and brought into a state of profitable cultivation (McCulloch, 1854, Vol. 1, p. 348; *Parliamentary Gazetteer*, Vol. I, p. XXXVII). Connell responded to this evidence (p.47) by asking "whether the absence of evidence is anything like proof that there was no reclamation". Such uncharacteristic slighting of contrary evidence confirms the suspicion that Connell's enthusiasm may have led him too far in this case. The data he cited from the 1841 and 1851 Censuses show that land under cultivation increased by 10 percent in the famine decade. Connell attributed this increase wholly to reclamation, and then admitted, a trifle puzzled, that the literary evidence scarcely confirmed the very rapid rate of reclamation indicated by the statistics (Connell, 1950b, p. 50). It is unthinkable, however, that much land was reclaimed during the decade of famine. According to the Census data, land under cultivation in Connaught increased at a rate faster than the national average (10·8 percent). Table 4.6 shows , however, that in the west of Ireland, 41·5 percent of the land was unoccupied due to the ravages of the famine. The increase of reported land under cultivation in the famine decade raises some questions about changes in crops induced by changes in factor prices, or about the consistency of the definitions of land under cultivation and the techniques used by enumerators (Bourke, 1965b, pp. 388–91). They certainly do not provide an answer to the question of how much land was being reclaimed in the fifty years before the famine.

Land reclamation in Ireland was very different from the capital-intensive methods by which the Dutch have wrung land from the North Sea or the Israelis from the desert. Fuel and cultivable land were sometimes joint products when peatbogs were entirely cut away. Potatoes played a crucial role in the process. The first two crops grown on a reclaimed lot were usually potatoes and served as preparations for subsequent cereal crops. Land reclamation needed large quantities of something Ireland was very short of: fertilizer. By making demands on the limited supply of fertilizer, land reclamation thus may have caused a reduction in the productivity of land already under cultivation.

All the same, most would agree that some land reclamation was taking place in prefamine Ireland. The problem, as Bourke (1965b, pp. 389–91) points out, is to convert Connell's notions of "a fair amount" into a numerical estimate of land brought into cultivation. Bourke's own crude estimates for the prefamine years show a slow but far from negligible rate (about 0·7 percent per annum which is somewhat slower than the net rate of population growth of 0·9 percent per annum in the period 1821–41). It is possible that it was land reclamation which was one of the factors which removed land scarcity as an effective constraint on income and prevented a Malthusian crisis. If that view of Irish history is correct, it follows that land reclamation—in stark contrast with capital accumulation and technological progress—did little to raise incomes and was largely a passive side-effect of population growth.

To put it another way, what kept most of the Irish poor was not the amount of land available to each farmer, but the way the land was farmed and the quantity of other inputs which were available apart from labor and land. Small farms, as Blacker, Crawford, and others have pointed out, could have been viable in Ireland. The minimum farm size estimated by Devon Commission witnesses to be necessary for the maintenance of a family of five varied between 6·25 and 10·50 acres, depending on the level of sophistication of the farmers and the amount of capital available (appendix 15b to the Devon Commission, Great Britain, 1845a, Vol. XXII, p. 77; see also Kennedy, 1847, pp. 398, 741). The average farm in Ireland was considerably larger than that: the Census data presented in Table 2.4 imply a ratio of 13·8 acres per family employed in agriculture and 19·6 acres per farm. The Devon Commission data imply an average farm size of 14·7 statute acres. Of course, many farms in these distributions would still find themselves below the "minimum" farm size, but that fact is largely irrelevant to the argument presented here, because what mattered for income determination is the amount of land a worker had to work on, not who formally controlled it.[15] Furthermore, the results presented in Tables 3.7–3.9 support the hypothesis that land in and of itself was not a binding constraint on income for the country as a whole. This should not be taken to deny that Irish peasants coveted and desired land, as many contemporaries pointed out (for example, Beaumont, 1839, Vol. II, p. 237, in a much-cited paragraph). All the same, as one witness employed in the Government Valuation pointed out, capital would be better employed in improving land already under cultivation than in bringing new land into cultivation (Great Britain, 1845a, Vol. XIX, p. 288). The same view is expressed by Andrews (1980, p. 50). In short, a simple two-factor model of land and labor, in which a gradual increase in population leads to the immiseration of the population, is not applicable in its crude form to prefamine Ireland. What was missing in Irish agriculture, more than anything else, was nonhuman resources that *could* have been produced in the system but were not.

One brief digression: some recent work by new economic historians such as Ó Gráda (1980c) and Solar (1982) attempts to compute the total factor productivity (TFP) of prefamine agriculture in Ireland and compare it to British agriculture. Their conclusions are quite similar: while Ireland does display a somewhat lower productivity than England and Scotland, the difference is smaller than what they think is implied by the accepted view of Irish agriculture. Solar, for example, places his "best-guess" estimate of Irish TFP at between 77 and 91 (Scotland = 100). This finding warrants in his view a "more optimistic view of Irish agricultural performance" and he suggests that "contemporary judgments of Irish agriculture may have been unduly harsh" (Solar, 1982, p.

18). Even if we ignore the severe data problems and methodological pitfalls marring this exercise, TFP estimates by themselves could be misleading here. In principle, it is perfectly possible for a country to be "efficient" and yet poor at the same time. It is also possible for a country to be "inefficient" and rich. What matters is not only the efficiency of the production process but also the amount of nonlabor inputs that are at the disposal of the workers and determine output per capita. Solar's data show that agricultural output per unit of labor was 50 percent lower in Ireland than in Scotland, but it stands to reason that some part of that gap was due to the Scottish advantage of 172 percent in the capital–labor ratio that he computed. How much of the difference in output per worker can be attributed to different factor endowments as opposed to differences in "efficiency"? The answer to this question depends on the values of the input coefficients or elasticities. If, for example, we set coefficients of labor and land equal to 0.8 and 0.2, respectively, Irish TFP is, according to Solar's figures, 77 percent of Scottish. But a different set of elasticities, not necessarily less realistic, would be 0.5, 0.3, and 0.2 for labor, land, and capital, respectively. Under this set of parameters, the gap in TFP vanishes; the two economies are equally "efficient" though by no means equally prosperous. In the latter case the difference in output per worker is wholly due to differences in factor endowment. Thus, TFP analysis does not and cannot explain poverty by itself. Only in economies with very similar relative endowments is the technique capable of addressing the issue of poverty directly.

Outside agriculture and fisheries, the "scarcity" of capital is far more difficult to trace. There were some notable exceptions to Ireland's industrial failure. In the first quarter of the nineteenth century there was considerable development of the cotton industry, especially in Ulster. By 1811 there were fifteen steam-driven spinning mills in Belfast, one of which employed 200 workers within the factory and contained 14,000 spindles (Green, 1949, p. 97). Smaller cotton mills sprang up all around Belfast Lough, and for a while it seemed that the Industrial Revolution had arrived in this part of Ireland. Monaghan (1942, p. 4) reported that by 1812 the cotton industry employed about 52,000 people, but that figure is in error. The number of spinners was not 22,000 but 2,000, and the 30,000 weavers were largely part-time workers in rural areas (Dubourdieu, 1812, pp. 404–6; see also Geary, 1981, for the same criticism). It is clear, however, that Ulster as a whole remained an industrial backwater. In 1816 the cotton industry in Belfast started a decline from which it never recovered, and by 1836 it had largely vanished.

The weakness of the Irish cotton industry resulted from two causes. One was the slow adoption of power looms, which resulted in the exclusion of Ireland from export markets. Hand-woven Irish cotton goods could not compete with the higher-quality cheaper goods woven mechanically. The Belfast cotton industry remained firmly anchored in the cottages of the surrounding rural areas. By 1838 there were still 12,000–15,000 muslin weavers within a ten-mile radius of Belfast (Green, 1949, p. 105). The second cause was the rise of the linen industry, which competed directly with cotton for buildings, sites, and equipment. When the Mulholland cotton mill burned down in 1828, it was rebuilt as a linen mill. The Railroad Commission stated that several of the mills originally designed for the spinning of cotton were employed in spinning flax (Great Britain, 1837–8, Vol. XXXV, p. 481). Inglis (1835, Vol. 2, pp. 254–5) pointed out that "in several of the new spinning mills of Belfast, we see, not the investment of new capital, but the transfer of capital from the cotton trade, for which flax spinning has been substituted ... the change from the cotton to the linen trade appears to be a very natural transfer of capital".

Many aspects of Ireland's stunted industrialization can be traced in one way or another to inadequate capital formation. Consider the failure of the Ulster cotton industry. What it meant was that entrepreneurs were unable or unwilling to plow back profits made in spinning, printing, or the domestic handloom weaving sector to purchase the equipment necessary to switch to mechanized weaving. Continued reliance on cheap handloom weavers was not a viable solution, and this fact was well understood by entrepreneurs in the 1820s when large-scale adoption of power looms took place not only in England and Scotland, but in Belgium and in France as well. The plight of the Irish hand-loom weaver in the 1830s and 1840s fully matched that of his English counterparts. The difference was that in Ireland there was very little poor relief or alternative employment that could absorb these workers who were becoming increasingly redundant.

The story does not end here, however. It starts here. Why did Ireland not build more factories which could have employed the labor which was rapidly being released by a rapidly declining cottage industry? Part of the answer is that to some extent it did. The linen industry provides the primary example of a successful sector. The story of its growth is well known and needs no repetition here. Power spinning grew at a rapid rate from adoption in 1825 of the wet spinning process. In 1839 the thirty-five linen spinning mills of Ulster employed 7,758 workers (Great Britain, 1839b, Vol. XLII, p. 336). About half of these mills were in Belfast, the others were located in towns in the vicinity of Belfast, such as Ballyclare, Banbridge, Larne, Gilford, and Carrickfergus. During the late 1820s and 1830s the industry slowly moved from water power to steam power as its main driving force. In 1829 the first steam-driven flax-spinning mill started to operate. Ten years later steam accounted for 48 percent of all horsepower in flax spinning in Ulster. The advantage of steam was not all that clear-cut, however. As late as 1862, the flax-spinning mills derived 20 percent of their power from water (Gribbon, 1969, p. 97). The linen industry in Ulster continued to grow right through the catastrophe of the 1840s, its employment rising by 147 percent during 1839–50, and another 54 percent during 1850–62.

Nevertheless, the success of the Ulster linen industry serves in some sense to underline the failure of Ireland to become more of a diversified economy. For one thing, the industrial revolution in the linen industry was largely confined to Ulster, and to a small part of Ulster at that. A brief examination of the data confirms that conclusion. The 1841

Table 6.1 *The Textile Industries in Ireland,* circa *1839*

Region	Employment	Power in h.p. steam	Power in h.p. water	Percentage of power capacity utilized	Number of mills total	Number of mills in operation
(a) Cotton						
Belfast*	2,587	332	195	84	13	13
Dublin	342	41	51	83	3	3
Cork	55	—	36	83	1	1
Others	1,638	144	290	94	8	7
Total	4,622	517	572	88	25	24
(b) Linen and flax						
Belfast	6,671	788	598	76	26	26
Dublin	297	—	60	100	1	1
Cork	—	—	—	—	—	—
Others	2,049	140	394	88	17	13
Total	9,017	928	1,052	80	44	40
(c) Wool						
Belfast	—	—	—	—	—	—
Dublin	544	30	234	80	12	12
Cork	178	14	62	93	5	5
Others	509	14	227	76	29	14
Total	1,231	58	523	80	46	31
(d) All textiles						
Belfast	9,258	1,120	793	78	39	39
Dublin	1,183	71	345	84	16	16
Cork	233	14	98	89	6	6
Others	4,196	298	911	87	54	34
Total	14,870	1,503	2,147	82	115	95

* Defined as counties Antrim and Down for this purpose.
Source: Great Britain, 1839b, Vol. XLII, pp. 334–51.

Census does not distinguish between those employed in flax-spinning mills and domestic spinsters (many of whom clearly were no longer spinning much but still chose to classify themselves as "spinsters"). Linen spinning was the most important industry which had adopted the factory system. Its employees were most likely to classify themselves as "factory workers". Thus, we can take that occupational class as an approximation for those employed in the linen mills, although some workers employed by these mills could conceivably have classified themselves as "flax spinners" or "spinners, unclassified". The total number of "factory workers" in 1841 was 8,193, of which 81 percent were in Ulster alone, with 76 percent in Belfast and its environs. Somewhat more detailed data are provided by Mr James Steuart, in his report accompanying a return to the British Factory Inspectors (Great Britain, 1839b, Vol. XLII, pp. 334–51). A summary of Steuart's data is presented in Table 6.1. The data confirm that about three-quarters of all steam power in the textile industry and the same proportion of the employment in the linen industry were concentrated in the Belfast region, whereas Cork and the rest of Ireland dominated the moribund woolen industry.

The transformation of the Ulster cottage industry was not followed by other parts of Ireland. Most of Ulster itself—the counties of Donegal, Tyrone, Cavan and Monaghan especially—was also little affected by it. It is also worth remembering that for a variety of reasons, linen may have been a poor choice upon which to base the industrial sector. While linen in Ulster did become the main textile-manufacturing sector in Ireland, the history of linen in the nineteenth century was largely one of an uphill battle with cotton. The rapid technological advances in the various stages of cotton production made it more and more difficult for linen to hold its own, since in most production stages technological change in linen was slower and later than in cotton. The two products were not perfect substitutes, and the linen industry survived and grew throughout the century in Ireland and in other countries. Still, there was an important truth in what one witness told R. M. Muggeridge, the Assistant Handloom Commissioner (Great Britain, 1840, Vol. XXIII, p. 569): "I remember when [linen] was the best occupation in Ireland; now it has gone to nothing. The cotton trade has ruined the linen; formerly everybody wore linen, and now everybody wears cotton." Muggeridge added that "fabrics so little dissimilar in their nature and their uses, and capable of being so frequently substituted one for the other, must necessarily partake of something like rivalry; but when the cost of the one is reduced to less than one fourth of the other . . . it needs no philosopher to foretell which would ultimately gain the preference" (ibid., p. 568).

Furthermore, one might ask why the Ulster linen industry had to be built upon the ashes of the decaying cotton industry. The relation and interaction between the two industries over 1770–1835 is a fascinating and intricate story to which no justice can be done here. For our purposes, it is sufficient to say that cotton grew at first at the expense of linen, and had injected a competitive and capitalist element in the entire textile industry when it began to retreat in the 1820s (Gill, 1925, chs 7–9; Dickson, 1978; Green, 1949, chs 4 and 5). The notion that in the long run the two industries were somehow incompatible and that the stronger of the two ultimately won out is untenable. Elsewhere in Europe, in Ghent and in Scotland, for example, cotton and linen co-existed. It was not inevitable that the plant and equipment of cotton manufacturers had to be converted to linen production. In Belgium profits accumulated in cotton manufactures were utilized in developing linen industries (Mokyr, 1976a, p. 40). Ulster had sufficient water power, cheap labor, and good sites for *both* the linen and cotton industries to prosper. Why, then, did the linen industry have to take over the assets of cotton manufacturers rather than accumulate its own? There is no strong evidence that the cotton-spinning industry was intrinsically unprofitable (Geary, 1981). The repeated complaint among contemporaries was that the cotton industries in Belfast could not compete with Lancashire industry, to which they were fully exposed after the elimination of all tariffs between Ireland and Great Britain in 1825. C. G. Otway noted in 1840, that after 1826 the Irish cotton trade had "greater difficulties and more powerful competition to contend against . . . it has had to compete with the extensive and long established cotton manufactures of England" (Great Britain, 1840, Vol. XXIII, pp. 443–4). Historians have accepted these conclusions (O'Brien, 1921, p. 311; Monaghan, 1942, p. 9; Hechter, 1975, p. 92). Ultimately we will, however, have to face the question of *why* the Irish cotton industry could not compete.[16]

As we have seen, the higher cost of fuel and raw material had probably only a small effect on the production cost of manufactured goods, and this negative effect was more than offset by cheaper labor cost. Contemporary specialists had few hesitations as to where the answer lay. Robert Roe, director of the Bank of Ireland, testified in 1830 that "the superiority of the English manufacturer in machinery and capital renders it scarcely possible for the Dublin manufacturer to compete with him" (Great Britain, 1830, Vol. VII, p. 533). Otway, too, spoke of England's power looms and spinning factories, her direct market for raw materials, and "all her capital and skills" (Great Britain, 1840, Vol. XXIII, p. 444). Direct access to raw materials was, of course, a result, not a cause of England's industrial advantage. But the lack of capital seems to have been widely recognized as the fatal weakness in the Irish cotton industry. One symptom of this weakness was the industry's vulnerability to the inevitable fluctuations in demand for the final product. British and Belgian cotton manufacturers were equally subject to the crises of 1816, 1825, and 1837, but while some firms changed ownership, the industry recovered rapidly with the upturn of business and resumed its expansion. In Ireland temporary gluts meant blows from which the industry could not recover. The cotton industry collapsed during the first two downturns. "The Dublin manufacturers having little capital . . . any occasional surplus of stock is productive of considerable distress", explained Roe (Great Britain, 1830, Vol. VII, p. 533; see also Green, 1949, p. 109, for a similar statement regarding Ulster). The lack of fixed capital was responsible for a more expensive and inferior product; the lack of circulating or working capital deprived the firm of resilience during business downturns. Ireland's cotton, and to a lesser extent its other textile industries, suffered from both.

The cotton industry before its crisis in the late 1820s was not, perhaps, as severely undercapitalized as contemporaries claimed. Nor are there signs of acute capital shortages in the modern linen industry. But somehow there was not enough capital around for *both* industries to grow side by side. It can hardly be any other factor which constrained the growth of the modern textile industry: labor was plentiful, good industrial sites widely available, and raw materials and fuel could be purchased at constant cost in the world market. Given the limitations on capital accumulation, however, the resources were allocated to the sector where the rate of return was higher. Hence, the growth of linen at the expense of cotton which, as Geary (1981) points out, does not necessarily imply that the cotton industry was somehow defective and moribund from its inception.

The above does not mean that a lack of capital *caused* the failure of Ireland to undergo an industrial revolution. It would be more accurate to say that the failure to accumulate capital and the industrial failure of Ireland were by and large the same thing. Capital goods, such as buildings, plant equipment, machinery, inventories, and trained personnel, carried the new technology, which made better and cheaper goods and provided jobs for displaced workers from rural areas. Capital accumulation was not a *cause* of the Industrial Revolution, and its absence was not a cause of its failure. Rather, investment was a mechanism through which deeper factors in the economy transmitted signals resulting either in successful industrialization as in Britain, Belgium, or Switzerland, or in late and slow industrialization as in the Netherlands or Ireland. Similar results do not imply that the underlying factors were necessarily the same. Many elements were needed to accomplish a successful transition to industrial capitalism and the process could be short-circuited by a variety of factors at different levels.

Outside industry and agriculture, other forms of capital were of major importance, although the roles they played in the economic development process were less direct. One major component of the fixed capital stock of any economy is the stock of houses for dwelling. As we have seen in Chapter 3, the quality of housing is an important variable in explaining income. The reason for this relation is, in part, that housing quality was endogenous and to some extent determined by income. In addition, the quality of houses is correlated with other variables on which there is no information, such as land improvement, farm buildings, and other forms of capital. According to the 1841 Census, there were 1,328,839 houses in Ireland. These houses were classified by the Census into four classes: first-class houses, which were the best type of houses, down to fourth-class houses, which were "mud cabins having only one room". The value of the capital stock in housing in Ireland cannot easily be assessed, since the Census does not provide money values of average units of housing in each class. Some indirect information on the value of housing can be derived from the Poor Law Report (Great Britain, 1836b, Vol. XXXII, pp. 39–67), which provides many contemporary estimates on the cost of erecting cottages. The cheapest cottages cost £3–£5 to build, the better ones £6–£10. Assuming that these types correspond more or less to the lower-quality Census classes and taking the upper values in each, the total value of third- and fourth-class houses comes to about £7.8 million. A second-class house was a good farmhouse, or in urban areas, "a house in a small street". Since the number of these houses was half the number of third-class houses, their average value cannot have exceeded £40. Setting, finally, the price of an average first-class house equal to £200, we obtain an estimate of the total value of housing for dwelling purposes in Ireland of about £26·4 million, which, with reasonable margins of error, comes to about £3–£4 per capita. Even the most approximate comparisons with Great Britain show this figure to be extremely small. Colquhoun's figure for privately owned buildings in Great Britain in 1812 is £330 million, or about £27 per capita, while for Ireland his estimate is £70 million, or about £11 per capita (Colquhoun, 1815, p. 55). Since residential dwellings were only part of Colquhoun's estimate, the comparison may not be entirely fair to Ireland, although the absence of warehouses, factories, and other non-residential buildings in Ireland are part of the problem which we are trying to explain. Michael Mulhall (1899, pp. 314–16) provides figures which imply that in the United Kingdom, including Ireland, the value of houses per capita was £18 in 1831 and £28 in 1841. For Great Britain, excluding Ireland, the figures were, respectively, £23·8 and £36·5. It is not quite clear where Mulhall's data came from, but if we use the separate data on Great Britain and the United Kingdom as even approximately consistent, they imply values of housing in Ireland of £6·3 per capita in 1831 and £8 per capita in 1841.[17]

There appears to have been one exception to the general slowness with which capital accumulated in Ireland: social overhead capital. On the eve of the famine Ireland was widely reported to have one of the best networks of roads in Europe. The testimonies of contemporaries on Irish roads are virtually unanimous. Johann Georg Kohl, a widely traveled German writer, noted that Ireland's fine roads were evidently not the work of the wretched Celtic inhabitants, but constituted some of the benefits which the Irish reaped from the British rule (Kohl, 1844, p. 38). The condition of the Irish roads was widely felt to be incongruous with the overall poverty of the rest of the economy. Wakefield (1812, Vol. 1, p. 659) wrote that "there are few things in Ireland, which astonish the stranger more than the magnificence of its excellent roads". J. E. Bicheno (1830, pp. 40–1) expressed his amazement at the fact that "the traveller witnesses on every side the appearances of beggary and filth, he feels he is rolling over roads as well-formed and made as he may have passed over in more fortunate countries". Long before that, Arthur Young noted that for a country so far behind England, the quality of Irish roads was "a spectacle that cannot fail to strike the English traveller exceedingly" (Young, 1892, Vol. 2, p. 76). Young explicitly excluded the privately run turnpikes from this statement which were as poor as the byroads were admirable. Clearly, however, the main roads were much improved in the half-century before the famine (Great Britain, 1835d, Vol. XXXIII, pp. 344–56). The consensus among the witnesses before the Poor Law Commission was that in the twenty years after the Napoleonic Wars, the roads had improved to such an extent as to triple the average load a horse could draw, from 7–10 cwt per load to 20–30 cwt. The net benefits which the Irish economy derived from its roads may have been more limited than the enthusiasm of travelers suggests. The carriage of heavy loads was more difficult on these roads than the movement of travelers (Lee, 1969c, p. 78). Moreover, Ireland lacked the draught animals and the cars to move its agricultural products over long distances. The main beneficiaries of the expensive road system were graziers and landlords, who needed it to have consumer goods transported to them, and who stood to benefit from higher livestock prices and higher rents that better roads produced (Connell, 1950b, pp. 58–9).

The grand jury system of local government played into the hands of these segments of the population who stood to gain from roads, and it seems likely that from the point of view of the entire economy, there may have been an overinvestment in roads in the sense that some of the capital which was used to build these roads would have been more productive had it been applied elsewhere in the economy.

The same may have been true *mutatis mutandis* for the canals built in Ireland during 1759–1817. The Royal Canal, between Dublin and Termonbarry on the Shannon (Co. Longford), was viewed as unnecessary and built only because of a dispute among the directors of the Grand Canal (Freeman, 1957, p. 119). The Grand Canal itself served as the main route by which wheat, flour, butter, and other agricultural goods were transported to Dublin, but freight rates were high due to the high costs of construction and maintenance. Modern historians have concluded that most of the canals built in the late eighteenth and early nineteenth centuries were a disappointment to those who built them (O'Tuathaigh, 1972, p. 122; Aalen, 1978, p.195), although this says nothing about the *social* rate of return.

A second feature of Irish society which can be regarded as a large investment in overhead capital was its schooling system. Connell (1950a, pp. 248–50) has argued on the basis of the Census data that "throughout the country there was little enough schooling". This view rests on an unreasonable interpretation of the Census data. It is true, as Connell notes, that in Ireland as a whole there were five times as many children aged 6–15 than there were children attending primary schools (the proportions vary from 23·61 percent in Leinster to 11·08 percent in Connaught). But as the census-takers emphatically point out (Great Britain, 1843, Vol. XXIV p. xxxix), most children did not attend school for ten years, so that the proportion of children who attended some school was much higher. There was also under-reporting due to refusal of some schools to show returns, so that "any error must be in defect, not excess". The comparatively strong effort to provide Irish children with schooling was a fairly recent phenomenon in 1841. Before 1831, education was a privately financed business, and the poverty of the country reflected on the education provided to children. The teachers were poorly paid and generally regarded as of low quality, and classes were conducted in small damp cabins or in chapels. None the less, contemporaries repeatedly mentioned the desire of the Irish to educate their children (Mason, 1814–19, *passim*; Wakefield, 1812, Vol. 2, pp. 395–400). In 1831 the government established a National Board of Education, in charge of the formation of a centralized and non-denominational uniform education system. By the time of the famine the Board's budget was approaching £100,000, and it employed the majority of Ireland's 12,000 teachers. In 1849 the Board controlled 4,321 schools with close to half a million pupils.

Comparing Irish educational data with other countries is difficult and possibly meaningless. School enrollment and attendance data are notoriously ambiguous. In Ireland, for instance, the number of children on the rolls of National Schools jumped from 560,000 to 776,000 in

1856–57 due only to a change in the method of computation (Akenson, 1970, pp. 275–6). In 1824 a parliamentary committee estimated the number of children in schools at 560,000–568,000 (Balfour, 1898, p. 98). These enrollments imply a primary school enrollment of about 800 pupils per 10,000 population, which would place Ireland at the forefront of Europe as far as education is concerned. The 1841 Census data, however, imply a ratio of only 582 per 10,000 of population. After the famine, the ratio picks up again and reaches 800 per 10,000 in 1851, but the strong decline in the denominator in 1845–50 suggests that the prefamine figure may have been lower than that. Even the lower estimates place Ireland well ahead of countries such as Spain and Italy which were at comparable levels of development and at a level more comparable to France (Easterlin, 1981, table A1).

Table 6.2 *Literacy in Ireland in 1841 and 1851 (Percentages)*

	1841 11–15	1841 16–25	1841 26–35	1841 36–45	1841 46–55	1841 Total	1851 Total
Ages:							
Males							
Read and write	35	47	46	46	44	37	41
Read only	23	18	16	15	13	17	17
Neither read nor write	42	35	38	39	43	46	42
Total	100	100	100	100	100	100	100
Females							
Read and write	22	27	21	19	17	18	25
Read only	28	28	24	22	19	23	24
Neither read nor write	50	45	55	59	64	59	51
Total	100	100	100	100	100	100	100

Source: 1841: Great Britain, 1843, Vol. XXIV, pp. 438–9.
1851: Great Britain, 1856c, Vol. XXXI, p. xlii.

The net effect of these schools on Irish society is hard to assess. The 1841 Census provides data on literacy by age, from which it can be inferred that there was a secular rise in literacy long before 1831. Table 6.2 presents some summary statistics on the long-run trends in literacy. The 1841 Census does not adequately reflect the impact of the National Board, because it had not been in operation long enough by the time the Census was taken. It is clear, however, that it merely reinforced an already-rising trend in literacy in Ireland. While the overall level of literacy was still low, the trend upward (especially among females) is marked. Comparison between the 1841 and 1851 figures is complicated by the famine, which affected the lower classes more than the wealthier and more educated groups. Still, the rise in literacy over 1841–51 extended to counties like Wicklow and Down, where the effects of the famine were comparatively limited. One historian summarizes the role of the National Board of Education not unfairly as follows: "in a country where so much was futile and faulty the national board accomplished an enduring piece of work" (McDowell, 1957a, p. 60). Whether the new schooling system had any immediate economic effects, however, is doubtful. The schools did at best a mediocre job in teaching the three Rs: 20 percent of the population were taught to read but could not write. The schools taught, as one historian puts it, "large chunks of platitudes on polite behaviour (modesty; deference to one's betters) which represented a turgid amalgam of social ethics and political docility. In this way it was hoped to inculcate a loyalty to the State and to the status quo" (O'Tuathaigh, 1972, p. 106).

The overhead capital which was invested in Ireland between the Union and the famine was thus not insubstantial, but it did very little to help the economy. Much of this effort was made by the government for political or security reasons. All the same, it was better for the Irish economy to have better roads, more canals, and an improved education system than not to have them. It cannot be doubted, however, that public efforts did not and could not replace the failure of the private economy to increase and improve its capital stock. It is to the explanation of the latter that we now turn.

(4)   Investment and Accumulation in Prefamine Ireland

Why was there such a scarcity of capital in prefamine Ireland? The conceptual framework developed in the previous section indicates that the search for the cause of an *aggregate* low savings rate may not prove very fruitful. To paraphrase Postan's famous metaphor, the supply of capital consisted of a multiplicity of small, disjointed puddles of savings. A "capital market", which could channel these savings to deserving investors, equalizing rates of return in the process, did not exist. The failure of financial institutions to provide long-term loanable funds to Irish industry cannot be attributed to any failure specific to Ireland. The type of financial institution which specialized in large-scale intermediation did not exist anywhere in Europe save, perhaps, in Belgium. Almost nowhere did banks and similar organizations play a central role in the process of capital formation before 1850.

There were, of course, banks in Ireland. In fact, the twenty years before the famine witnessed a spectacular growth in Irish banking. In 1824 there was one joint-stock bank in Ireland, the Bank of Ireland. During 1821–4 this monopoly was lifted, and for twenty years Ireland was the scene of a rapid spreading of branches of ten banks, which increased the number of branches during 1824–30 from one to thirty-one, reaching 173 by 1844 (Barrow, 1975, p. 220). Even some rather insignificant towns such as Carrick on Shannon (Co. Leitrim) and Moate (Co. Westmeath) had bank branches. These banks were important in the monetization of Ireland, and doubtlessly were useful to local merchants, importers, and possibly to landlords and other notables. Banks also played some role in agriculture. John Reynolds, secretary of the large National Bank (and later Lord Mayor of Dublin), testified before the Devon Commission that banks often discounted farmers' bills for small amounts (of £8–£20). The effective interest on these bills was at 10–12 percent. In the vast majority of cases, however, these loans were not made for improvements, the purchase of livestock, or other investment projects. People borrowed from banks primarily in order to pay rents on time (Great Britain, 1845a, Vol. XIX, p. 1066). Pierce Mahony, a Dublin solicitor specializing in banking matters, testified in 1837 that rents were due on 29 September, while pork (an important source of cash income and essential to the payment of rents) was often not marketed until two months later. Other sources of short-term credit were hard to come by and expensive. Mahony noted that butter merchants often charged up to 60-percent interest (Great Britain, 1837, Vol. XIV, p. 260).

It is unlikely, therefore, that the banks were instrumental in producing major increments to the productive resources of the country. Banks were fragile structures in this period, and committing funds in large quantities to anything less certain than government securities was always hazardous. One Irish bank, the Agricultural and Commercial Bank, which ventured into more hazardous projects promptly failed in the crisis of 1836. Moreover, the Devon Commission Digest noted that "the tenant willingly expends any capital he may possess in obtaining possession of the land and thus leaves himself without the means of tilling it effectually afterwards" (Kennedy, 1847, p. 194). This statement seems to suggest that working capital "used up" in paying for rent came at the expense of long-term investment. At least as far as circulating capital is concerned, banks possibly helped to reduce the crunch, but even in that their contribution was marginal.

The second reason tenants resorted to borrowing had even less to do with capital accumulation. Potatoes lasted no more than nine or ten months after harvesting, and food supplies often ran out by midsummer. To bridge that gap, peasants had to purchase oatmeal and other food for a month or two. The money-lenders who catered to that demand charged very high interest rates and at times tried to institute some form of "debt peonage". These "gombeen men" as they were called were often "meal mongers", that is, merchants in oatmeal. Like all rural usurers, they were universally despised but quite indispensable for the survival of the unfortunate peasants who needed their services. The only alternative to these lenders was the so-called Loan Fund, a publicly operated lending institution which lent small sums to farmers at reasonable rates and at longer terms than local usurers or banks. Loan fund credit, too, often was used to pay rent, but there is evidence that in some cases these loans were used to finance drainage and to purchase fertilizer, implements, and livestock (Great Britain, 1845a, Vol. XIX, p. 1048; Vol. XXI, p. 350). The regulations of the loan funds required borrowers to pay back in weekly installments, which created some difficulty among the borrowing peasants (Great Britain, 1845a, Vol. XIX, p. 1069). There were also widespread reports on inefficiency, mismanagement, and corruption. The Devon Commission Digest remarks wryly that "as loan funds are usually constituted, the highest praise which can with truth be allowed to them is, that they are less ruinous than private usurers" (Kennedy, 1847, p. 196).

Outside agriculture, the operation of capital markets was even less important as a determinant of the rate of capital accumulation. Lee (1968b) has estimated that in 1847 about half of Irish railroad shares were owned by Irish investors. But as Lee shows, the Irish investors displayed a very high degree of risk aversion. With a few exceptions, Irish investors subscribed to railroad capital only after somebody else had borne the risk. As Lee succinctly put it, "companies come and companies go, but the rentier goes on forever" (Lee, 1968b, p. 50). The parallel between Ireland and the Netherlands is striking here, in spite of the enormous differences between the two countries in other respects. Both simultaneously "had" capital and lacked it. The wealth of rentiers did not find its way into investment projects that could have helped the economy to modernize. As far as economic development is concerned, this capital is then irrelevant, it might as well not have existed (Mokyr, 1975).

The modern industrial sector in Ireland depended, as it did elsewhere, on its own resources for capital accumulation. The reinvestment of profits in the firm was the primary if not the sole mechanism through which capital accumulated and industry grew. The practice to retain profits was not a strictly nineteenth-century custom. Modern Irish industry still relies on retained profits for most of its fixed capital. Heelan and Henry (1962–3, pp. 155–6) have pointed out the difficulties Irish industry experienced in the 1950s in mobilizing funds from financial institutions and the advantages of self-financing. They cite figures which imply that in the three-year period 1951–3 net undistributed profits after tax constituted 62 percent of gross fixed-asset formation. What holds for the 1950s surely holds *a fortiori* for the decades before the famine. Robert Kane stated it most eloquently:

England has capital, Ireland has not; therefore England is rich and industrious, and Ireland is poor and idle. But where was the capital when England began to grow rich? It was the industry that made the capital, not the capital the industry ... when money is made in England it is re-invested in the same or in a similar branch ... until the amount of capital attains the vast dimensions which we now see. (Kane, 1845, p. 408)

Historians seem to agree (Lee, 1969a, p. 55; Coe, 1969, p. 187).

The explanation of the low rate of accumulation in the Irish economy thus cannot be readily explained in terms of low aggregate saving. What has to be done is to examine the individual decision-making units, that is, the tens of thousands of farms and hundreds of industrial enterprises, and try to determine the behavioral reasons for low investment and the physical and social constraints on self-financed capital accumulation. The savings behavior of three separate classes should be examined. First, why did peasants not invest more in their farms? Secondly, why did their landlords not spend more to improve Irish agriculture? Thirdly, why did the Irish manufacturing sector not expand faster, that is, why did Irish industrial entrepreneurs not plow back more profits into their firms?

As far as the tenants are concerned, the main reason they invested so little was simply because they were so poor. As was demonstrated above in Section 3, the statement that somebody did not invest because he could not afford to do so, makes sense only in the simultaneous absence of capital markets and presence of indivisibilities. This condition seems to have held for large segments of the Irish peasantry. While not tantamount to a proof of the actual existence of the low-income equilibrium ("poverty trap"), the argument seems plausible. It is not quite clear how it would be possible ever to prove the hypothesis that Irish agriculture was aptly described by McKinnon's model in a definitive way. In any event, other factors clearly contributed to the slow pace of capital formation in Irish agriculture. One factor, discussed at length in Chapter 4, is the absence of well-defined property rights in agricultural capital. To the extent that the tenants feared that landlords would expropriate the returns to investment by raising rents, we have seen that most—though not all—land was protected from that by leases. But the property-rights issue does not end here. Lawlessness and violence, which were common in many rural areas, made agricultural investment unattractive. The stealing of turnips, maiming of cattle, and pulling down of fences and hedges, were all used as tools in a war which may have had its roots in a conflict between landlords and tenants but dragged in so many innocent bystanders that it often appeared a *bellum omnium contra omnes*. Little wonder, therefore, that wealthy farmers and graziers often accumulated money in savings banks rather than using it to improve their own farms. Finally, as is shown in Chapter 8, emigration tended to reduce capital formation among those members of the emigrating classes who remained behind.

It is perhaps more surprising that so little agricultural investment was carried out by Irish landlords. Contemporaries declared almost without exception that the custom in Ireland prescribed that all improvements on the farm were carried out by the tenant, and that the landlord was not responsible for fences, farm buildings, drainage, and so on. The investment behavior of Irish landlords was contrasted unfavorably to that in Britain, where the converse usually held. It is this custom which is the empirical foundation of the LTH discussed in Chapter 4. The custom can be traced to the seventeenth and eighteenth centuries when leases in the newly occupied Irish landed estates were very long. Consequently landlords had very little incentive to invest in improvements, since rents were fixed for the duration of the leases (Roebuck, 1981, p. 153).

Resorting to "custom" does not dispose of the difficulty, however. First, the habit was not enshrined in any law, and it reflects an outcome of the game, not an initial constraint imposed on it. Secondly, even if we assume that landlords could not for some reason invest directly in their estates, there was no reason why they could not have financed in one way or another such projects undertaken by their tenants. Thirdly, the absence of capital markets which often presented an insuperable obstacle to farmers and smallholders did not apply to landlords, at least not in the same way. Rich landowners were constantly faced with opportunities—and sometimes temptations—to borrow large amounts.

Less wealthy or more encumbered landowners who were considered worse risks paid higher interest rates, 5–5·5 percent instead of the 4 percent charged of the best customers (Curtis, 1980, p. 339). The contradiction between our argument of nonoperating capital markets and the ease with which landowners could obtain mortgages is more apparent than real. The market for loans looked at *actual* current income as a measure of what the estate could afford to borrow. What was needed for sustained capital accumulation was a group of potential financiers who were willing to provide loans on the basis of *expected* sources of income which did not exist at the time of the loan and which would be created by the very project for which the loan was obtained. The latter kind of loan was far more difficult to obtain. Landlords could, or course, circumvent this obstacle by mortgaging *existing* income to generate new sources. But the vast majority of mortgages taken out by Irish landlords, both before and after the famine, were clearly not of this nature.

Some landlords, in fact, did invest in their estates, either directly or indirectly, which underlines the feasibility of the option and the need to explain why it was so rarely chosen. To understand the role played by Irish landlords, it is imperative to realize that Irish landlords felt and behaved like English landlords, although Irish agriculture, from which they drew their income, was very different from English agriculture and becoming increasingly so. Large (1966, p. 29) has pointed to the interesting phenomenon of Irish landlords during the Napoleonic Wars who tried to raise rents *pari passu* with their English colleagues, without realizing that a large proportion of the higher rents in England derived not from higher prices, but from improved farming. Irish landlords, whether they lived in Ireland or not, adopted the life-style and consumption patterns of English gentlemen, but this "demonstration effect" was not backed up by equivalent rises in Irish agricultural income (de Tocqueville, 1958, p. 159; Pim, 1848, p. 242; Curtis, 1980, p. 336). As a result, little of the rents found their way back into the estate. Even the enlightened landlord Earl Fitzwilliam spent 90 percent of his income in England (Large, 1966, p. 29). Contemporaries tended to think that the source of Irish troubles was that the absentee landlords spent income abroad. The real problem was that they spent their income at all, and that even those who saved some portion of it did not invest it in their (or anybody else's) estates. Not only did Irish landlords save little and invest even less: many of them actually saved negative amounts for decades prior to the famine. Landed proprietors in Ireland seem to have been impatient or, to use the economists' term, exhibited a high rate of time preference. One observer, who had acquired considerable familiarity with Irish conditions as an estate agent, wrote that "some [Irish landlords] make the early discovery that improving the land . . . is expensive without *immediate* return, and discontinue at once" (Wiggins, 1844, p. 204; emphasis in original).

A second drain on the rental income of Irish landlords were family settlements. Younger sons, unmarried sisters, and surviving widows were all provided for by settlement, which meant that their income came directly out of the proceeds of the estate and thus was totally outside the discretion of the landlords. Wakefield, among others, noted the existence of estates from which the net income was essentially nil after settlements and jointures had been taken care of (Wakefield, 1812, Vol. 1, p. 245). It could be objected that these settlements were irrelevant, since they did not directly affect the rental, only the identity, of the beneficiary. What these settlements represented was an attempt to keep consumption per member of the landlord class growing faster than rental income. In the eighteenth and nineteenth centuries the landlord class grew numerically, and since primogeniture and entail restricted the subdivision and alienation of estates, settlements for widows, younger sons, and other "landlords without land" were inevitable. Roebuck (1981, p. 136) has maintained that this form of indebtedness should not be viewed as extravagance but constitutes an exogenous factor for which individual landlords cannot be blamed. In effect, however, the responsibility of the landed gentry and aristocracy stands undiminished: the class as a whole still were rightly accused as profligate spendthrifts, though we must include *all* members of the landlord class.

In any case, settlements to the landlords' relatives reduced the net resources available for investment in the estate, since if the landlords were reluctant to invest in land improvement, their aunts living in England or younger brothers serving in the British Army were even less likely to do so. Moreover, the deflation which followed the Napoleonic Wars redistributed income in favor of those who had claims which were specified in money terms (including family members). Family arrangements also earmarked the income of the estate in other fashions: families often borrowed large amounts to provide for future dowries and younger sons. Although theoretically this money would not be spent until the person in question came of age or married, the money was earmarked and could not be invested, while the interest on it came directly out of the proceeds of the estate (Large, 1966, p. 42).

Landlord consumption patterns contributed to their financial distress. During 1780–1815 a residential building boom occurred which must have drained a large amount of current income in interest payments and maintenance in later years. The comparatively well-managed estates of Lord Gosford in Co. Armagh—which employed such excellent agents as William Greig and William Blacker—spent over £80,000 in the 1820s and 1830s on the construction and decoration of a lavish new residence, a "crenellated extravaganza" which drained the resources of the estate (Greig, 1976, pp. 5–6). But other, more efficient, ways to squander away large amounts of money played an equally important role. Gambling, hunting, and foreign travel used up vast sums. So did politics. Lord Downshire spent, by his own admission, over £30,000 on one election alone (Maguire, 1972, p. 91). Expensive litigation further drained the resources of the Irish landowning class. One Co. Cork gentleman spent over £20,000 to obtain a verdict worth perhaps £500, thus essentially ruining himself (Donnelly, 1975, p. 69).[18] The net result was that on the eve of the famine large segments of the Irish landowning class found themselves deeply in debt. For our purposes, this is important because it implies that landlords as a class saved very small and possibly negative amounts. There were, of course, exceptions. The Devon Commission and other sources contain many references to solvent and improving landlords, or landlords who lent money to their tenants for investment purposes. But the rule was more like the situation described by one Poor Law Inquiry witness from Co. Meath: "The embarrassed state of so many of the [proprietors] is one great cause, if not the chief, of the bad state of agriculture, by creating the necessity for keeping up exorbitant rents, and not assisting in making improvements" (Great Britain, 1836b, Vol. XXXIII, p. 164). Even the landlords who generated positive savings were often reluctant to invest them in their estates. Investment invariably implied some radical changes in agriculture, and thus was likely to cause some dissatisfaction among some of the peasants at least. The violence and lawlessness characterizing the Irish countryside, thus, produced a major disincentive to landlord investment.

The failure to modernize Irish agriculture was a failure of capital formation but it was much more than that. Capital formation and technological change were highly complementary. It was not possible to have much technological change without acquiring the capital goods which embodied the new techniques. Conversely, investment was not very productive unless it was accompanied by expert advice, guiding the tenant in the adoption of new and unfamiliar farming techniques. The failure of the Irish landlord, thus, goes much further than improvidence and risk-aversion. Far more than their English counterparts whom they tried so often to emulate, they were alienated from their tenants, from the land, and from agriculture in all its technical and economic aspects. The root of the failure of the Irish landlords was a failure of entrepreneurship as well as one of savings behavior. These aspects will be discussed in Chapter 7.

What about manufacturing? The question of why there was so little capital formation in Irish industry is more or less equivalent to the question of why there was no industrial revolution in Ireland. Ireland's resource position, as we have seen, was far from disastrous, and in any event the higher cost of fuel and materials was more than offset by the low wages and vast supplies of labor available in Ireland. It was favorably located in the Northern Atlantic region and part of the most advanced political and economic empire in the world. And yet by 1845 a gap had opened between Ireland and other economies in the Northern Atlantic region which has never quite been closed. Some historians and contemporaries have tried to explain Ireland's disadvantages in terms of "critical mass" or "economies of agglomeration" type of arguments. Otway cited an entrepreneur complaining that while Ireland provided cheap water power and labor, it lacked the mechanical infrastructure that could repair and maintain sophisticated equipment (Great Britain, 1840, Vol. XXIII, pp. 435–6). Other regions outside Britain, however, overcame such problems without too much difficulty, and within Belfast, at least, the linen industry after 1830 seemed to have had no trouble in this respect. The complaint made by the entrepreneur cited by Otway was made at the end of the eighteenth century, when Ireland's engineering industry was just started. Coe (1969) points out that Irish engineering followed a similar pattern to the British, maintaining and later producing machines and equipment used in textile and other industries. For a few highly specialized industries, it may have been true, as Coe claims, that the chief advantage of English manufacturers was that they produced on a much larger scale than in Ireland, so that Irish industries seldom were able to reach the optimal scale which minimized the costs of production (Coe, 1969, p. 134). On the whole, however, the statement is contradicted by the simple fact that within Britain itself the vast majority of firms in all but a very few industries, remained small, seldom employing more than a few hundred workers. There may have been interfirm external economies—though their existence has never been demonstrated—but then the question arises why these economies could not have spilled over to Ireland. Coe's argument may be somewhat more relevant for the postfamine period, but it certainly does not hold for those industries in which Ireland specialized: linen, brewing, and shipbuilding. For a more detailed criticism of the "critical mass" type of theories, see Mokyr (1977).

A second explanation sometimes proposed for Ireland's lack of industrialization centers on the backwardness of its agricultural sector (Goldstrom, 1969). Before an industrial revolution could take place, it is argued, agriculture had to be modernized and made more productive. While it is true that in England the Industrial Revolution was preceded by a sustained increase in agricultural output, there were also cases in which there was little agricultural progress prior to a spurt in industrial capital formation (for example, Switzerland and New England). One could point, in addition, to cases in which a highly productive agriculture did not assist and possibly prevented industrialization (for example, the Netherlands). Ireland's poor and semi-commercial peasants probably did not provide a very strong market for manufactured goods, but Irish industry had access to the same markets open to British manufacturers, and it is hard to see why the backwardness of Irish agriculture put it at a disadvantage.

Economic reasoning, while it cannot fully explain why countries failed to undergo industrialization, can assist us by indicating where we should search. In a simple model of accumulation without capital markets, in which all capital originates in the profits made in previous years, the rate of accumulation equals the rate of profit on capital multiplied by the reinvestment coefficient, that is, the average propensity of capitalists to plow back their profits into their firms (Mokyr, 1976a; 1976b). The search for the determinants of the rate of capital accumulation thus is reduced to a search for the determinants of the rate of profit, which is largely exogenous to the behavior of the class of industrialists, and for the determinants of the saving behavior of industrial entrepreneurs (note that the distinction between capitalists and entrepreneurs is meaningless in this type of model).

The primary cost of production was labor, both directly and indirectly. Irish wages were considerably lower than British wages. Kane (1845, p. 397) said flatly that "human labour can be obtained in this country on lower terms than almost any other in Europe [which is] too well known to require example". It is, however, arguable that at least in the case of Ireland the cost of labor and the level of wages diverged considerably. Capital accumulation is driven by the engine of profits. If workers, entrepreneurs, and technology are more or less comparable (at least *ex ante*), low wages mean high profits which could lead to more capital formation. This difference helps us understand the difference between the rates of industrialization of Belgium and the Netherlands (Mokyr, 1976a). If all other things were not equal, however, low profits could exist in spite of low wages. The various differences between Ireland and other economies will be discussed in some detail in Chapter 7.

A low rate of profit would, thus, be an acceptable explanation of Irish industrial failure if it could be adequately documented. As a practical matter, it is very hard to say much about the rates of profit earned in nineteenth-century manufacturing. It is for that precise reason that an indirect approach, focusing on costs of production, has to be taken. Furthermore, profits do not tell the entire story. The importance of profits is that they make accumulation possible, but they do not make it inevitable. The behavior of entrepreneurs was also crucial. If profits were used for the expensive imitation of an aristocratic life-style, or to purchase civil service careers for the next generation, or invested largely in government securities, they were withdrawn from the modern sector and, in view of the bias of capital markets against the modern sector, unlikely ever to return there. The process at work is described with precision by Kane (1845, pp. 408–9): "If some money (profits) be made in trade in Ireland it is not so treated (reinvested), it is withdrawn from trade and stock is bought, or land is bought, yielding only a small return, but one with the advantage of not requiring intense exertion or intelligence, and free from serious risk." Lee (1969a, p. 56) cites examples of brewers who bled their businesses dry to buy landed estates or government stock, and concludes that families retired from business not because they lacked capital, but because they had acquired capital. Even the highly successful Italian entrepreneur, Charles Bianconi, who single-handedly built a stagecoach empire in prefamine Ireland was infected by this tendency. A recent study of Bianconi points out that "he had built up his business by ploughing his profits back into it. In 1846 he was able to become a landed proprietor, the aim of many a businessman of the period" (O'Neill, 1973, p. 95). On that occasion alone, Bianconi spent £22,000 for the purchase of an estate in Co. Tipperary. Another successful business whose expansion was checked by investment in other assets was the Guinness brewery. In 1829 Arthur Guinness wrote to his niece trying to convince her to sell the government securities she owned since the firm was in great need of capital. Lynch and Vaisey pointed out that "the urge for security" led the Guinness brothers to starve the business of capital after the Napoleonic Wars (Lynch and Vaisey, 1960, p. 125). The Guinnesses also owned large estates in Wexford and Wicklow, and there can hardly be any doubt that these and similar transactions reduced the rate of expansion of the entire industrial sector.

Very complete evidence on this behavioral pattern of Irish capitalists does not exist. But if true, what it implies is that much of the savings of Irish merchants and manufacturers were withdrawn from the modern sector. From a purely macroeconomic point of view, these transactions do not necessarily imply that the economy had "lost" these savings. But in so far as they were used to buy out bankrupt landlords who had lived beyond their means in the past, what it meant was that the negative savings of some landlords offset the positive savings of the bourgeoisie.[19] The picture is compounded by the fact that the positive savings of other landlords did not, typically, offset this flow. To be sure, manufacturers who spent profits on "unproductive" purposes could be found everywhere. But differences in degree mean everything here. We thus have to face the question why an Irish bourgeois entrepreneur would tend to reinvest a smaller proportion into his (or somebody else's) business than his English, Scottish, or Belgian counterpart.

Once more, the data on "outrages" in Chapter 5 may be relevant. Ireland was a country in which the political situation was uncertain, in which property rights were insecure. Although most of the friction between the classes occurred in agriculture and not in manufacturing, and attacks on industrial property were rare, spillover effects may have been considerable. The "bad name" Ireland received because of rural outrages imposed externalities on the rest of the economy. One obvious effect was that foreign capital was scared away and could not replace the deficient rate of domestic saving. G. C. Lewis wrote in 1836 that "the insecurity of property in Ireland, whether real or supposed . . . prevents the English or Scotch capitalist from transmitting materials to be manufactured in Ireland, and makes it necessary to bring the operative to the work, instead of the work to the operative" (Great Britain, 1836b, Vol. XXXIV, p. 454). Moreover, even if we assume that the willingness of the Irish entrepreneur to bear risk was no less than his counterpart elsewhere, inherently risky investments in industry were made even riskier if the site of the planned project was in Ireland. If the supply of risk-bearing is normally shaped, that is, the lower the risk, the more investment would be forthcoming, a more risky environment implied a smaller investment in risky assets. Furthermore, if the rate of profit was lower in Ireland, it stands to reason that the reinvestment coefficient would be lower too. A lower return on investment plowed back into the firm would cause an entrepreneur to divert more of his savings into alternative assets (land and government bonds), and possibly to save less altogether. This synergistic effect would therefore produce a rate of accumulation that would be lower than what the lower profit rate and lower reinvestment coefficient would separately imply.

Notes: Chapter 6

1   Strictly speaking, one has to make two more assumptions for this conclusion to follow. One is that there are no differences between the supply curves of labor. In some sense this distinction is spurious, however, since a nation with high leisure preference and thus a lower supply curve of labor would have lower income as traditionally

defined, but not lower income once the value of leisure is allowed to enter the calculation. Secondly, the conclusion requires the standard assumption of constant returns to scale in the production function.

2 Ó Gráda bases his conclusion on modern soil maps, and is therefore unable to distinguish between truly geographical factors and the effects of population decline in Ireland since 1850 on soil maintenance and improvement. In any event, Ó Gráda's soil-quality differential explains only 2·2–3 percent of the difference in agricultural output per man between the two countries. It should be added that Arthur Young (1892, Vol. 2, p. 17), writing in the late eighteenth century, maintained that Irish soil was inherently more fertile. A similar point was made by the correspondent of the *Parliamentary Gazetteer*, writing on the eve of the famine (*Parliamentary Gazetteer*, Vol. I, p. lx).

3 Some of the points made below were originally present in Mokyr (1980a). After this chapter was completed, I learned that a number of the arguments were developed independently by Frank Geary; see Geary (1981).

4 A modern geographer (Freeman, 1957, p. 94) points out that Sir Robert wrote before the detailed investigations of the Geological Survey made clear that his considerable optimism with respect to Ireland's coal resources was unfounded.

5 Computed from Deane and Cole (1969, p. 219), assuming all domestic use and half the usage by "general manufacturing" were for space heating and light.

6 In the middle of the nineteenth century about 2·8 million acres, or one-seventh of Ireland's total surface, was covered by peatbogs. As late as 1920 there were still 4 billion tons of turf (250 times the annual fuel requirement of Ireland). Peat was dug at the surface by hand, so that its price was determined by the level of wages—which was very low in prefamine Ireland. The main difficulty after cutting was drying, which had to be done under some kind of cover. Although some peat was available in practically every county of Ireland, the richest deposits were concentrated in relatively remote areas. In some of the more developed regions earlier usage had in many places depleted the best turbaries. As a result, large quantities of turf were shipped within Ireland, although the average distances were not large.

7 Ireland had operating lead and copper mines in the years around 1840, although the resources were not very large, and ultimately succumbed to foreign competition (Kane, 1845, pp. 118–248; Great Britain, 1837–8, Vol. XXXV, p. 505; Freeman, 1957, pp. 98–106).

8 For some evidence for the importance of self-finance in the Low Countries, see Mokyr (1976a), pp. 39-40, 50, 64. For references to other countries, see the sources cited in ibid., p. 134, n.3.

9 A positive subjective rate of time preference means that faced with the option to consume equal quantities Q_1 and Q_2 in periods 1 and 2, the consumer would prefer to consume more in the earlier period at the expense of later consumption. This rate is measured by the slope of the indifference curves at the point where they intersect with a 45° line emanating from the origin.

10 The scarcity of manure led hard-pressed peasants to experiment with almost any material which could be added to the soil. An extreme, and possibly apocryphal example, is the attempt to use salt as a fertilizer (Great Britain, 1835d, Vol. XXXIII, p. 284).

11 Blacker's *Essay on the Improvements . . . of Small Farms by the Introduction of Green Crops and House-Feeding* went through six editions in 1834–45.

12 The "reimbursement" statement is equivalent to

$$V = \sum_{j=1}^{4} \frac{R}{(1+i)^j}$$

where V is the cost of drainage, R the marginal productivity of the capital, and i the rate of discount. Solving for R/V yields

$$R/V = \frac{1}{\left[\sum_{j=1}^{4} \frac{1}{(1+i)^j} \right]}$$

13 Some contemporaries fully realized the value of trees. One advocate of tree planting cited a Scottish saying, "Be aye sticking in a tree, Jock: it will be growing while you are sleeping" (cited by Freeman, 1957, p. 60). Enthusiastic recommendations for more timber cultivation were made by Trimmer (1809, pp. 34–6, 60–2; 1812, pp. 21–8).

14 These vacillating policies are summarized by O'Brien (1921, pp. 289–92).

15 The Devon Commissioners, in appendix 95 to the report (Great Britain, 1845a, Vol. XXII, p. 289), performed an interesting calculation. They asked how much land would have to be reclaimed in order to provide every farming family in Ireland with farms not less than a certain minimum size. The number of families holding less than 8 acres was 326,084. In order to bring these holdings up to 8 acres, the commissioners estimated, 1,538,944 acres would be needed, which was only 110,000 acres more than the land classified as improvable for tillage, and about 41 percent of total improvable land.

16 Dickson (1978) has attributed the decline of the Irish cotton industry to the decline of Ireland's extra-English trade links, the absence of coal, and the external economies enjoyed by British manufacturers as a consequence of industrial concentration and an early start. The loss of markets outside the British Isles was surely a result, not a cause, of Ireland's industrial backwardness. The lack of coal was of secondary importance, and in any event should have applied to linen as well. The external economies explanation is more difficult to deal with, and it has been made the center of an argument put forward recently by O'Malley (1981). O'Malley's viewpoint is closely related to "critical mass" theories of economic growth inspired by the work of François Perroux. Whether or not these models have any general validity, their applicability to prefamine Ireland is dubious for three reasons. First, neither Dickson nor O'Malley provide any evidence that such external economies and "advantages of the early starter" really existed. Such evidence would have to include the existence of "learning by doing" effects, scale economies, and interfirm externalities. Secondly, even if interfirm spillover effects existed, one would have to show that these advantages could not be obtained from other regions; in other words, why could externalities not "spill over" directly from Scotland and England? Thirdly, the argument cannot explain how other relatively late industrializing regions overcame their infancy diseases, while the Ulster cotton industry did not.

17 A possible reason why Mulhall's data are comparatively high, is Mulhall's procedure of using a factor of 18 to compute the value of the housing stock from rental flows, a conversion coefficient which seems rather high. Mulhall's figures, however, are supported by Feinstein (1978, pp. 38, 42), who has estimated the value of residential dwellings in Britain in 1830 at £390 million in 1851–60 prices, which comes to about £370 in 1841 prices, or about £22·7 per capita. While these calculations are crude, the difference between Ireland and Britain is of such a large order of magnitude that the conclusion is likely to survive any conceivable modifications.

18 Sir Murtagh Rackrent, in Maria Edgeworth's novel *Castle Rackrent*, boasted that he had a lawsuit for every letter in the alphabet: "Out of forty-nine suits that he had he never lost one but seventeen; the rest he gained with costs, double costs, treble costs sometimes—but even that did not pay" (Edgeworth, 1964, pp. 15–16).

19 It is reasonable that the streamlining of the Irish land market after 1849 had a negative effect on postfamine industrialization, because it made it easier for the bourgeois classes to purchase rural estates. It is doubtful, however, whether much of the money which was spent on estates would have been used to buy fixed capital and equipment in commerce and industry.

Chapter 7

The Human Factor: Entrepreneurship and Labor

(1) The Irish Landlord

Superficially, the Irish landlord resembled his English counterpart. Lifestyle, customs, language, religion, even ideology were in certain ways adapted from England's aristocracy. Yet, while the praises of the British landed gentleman as an agent of economic progress and technical innovation have been sung by contemporaries and historians alike, the Irish landlords have come in for nothing but contempt and scorn. Beaumont wrote in 1839 that "all the evils of Ireland, and all its difficulties arise from the same principal and permanent cause—a bad aristocracy . . . whatever may be the fortunes of the Irish aristocracy, no tears will be shed over its fate . . . it is nothing better than a scourge and a nuisance which should be removed as soon as possible" (Beaumont, 1839, Vol. 2, pp. 193, 204). These are strong words indeed, and their spirit is echoed in the writings of other contemporaries. The dilemma with which nineteenth-century political economy was increasingly faced was that in Ireland the sanctity of property rights seemed to collide with the well-being of the nation. Landlords holding title to land were not making the best use of that land, or so it seemed. This dilemma is the focus of economic thought on what became known as the Irish Question in the postfamine years, but it clearly occupies an important place in discussions of the prefamine Irish economy as well.

Of the many complaints launched against the Irish landlord, none was more widespread and popular than absenteeism. Almost every tract and book dealing with Ireland's economic and social difficulties engaged in harsh criticism of the absentee landlord. One contemporary summed up the conventional wisdom on the subject by the phrase "les absents ont toujours tort" (cited by Black, 1960, p. 72). The *Statistical Accounts* edited by Mason contains condemnations of absentee landlords from areas as diverse as Donegal, Westmeath, and Cork (Mason, 1814–19, Vol. 1, p. 436; Vol. 3, pp. 125, 309). Other contemporary writers such as Hall and Hall (1825–40), Foster (1847), Pim (1848), and Bicheno (1830), all agreed that landlord absenteeism was the bane of Ireland's economy.

Matters were, however, more complex than some of these simplistic accounts imply. Arthur Young (1892, Vol. 2, p. 114) pointed out that there were few countries in the world that did not experience "the disadvantage of remitting a part of their rents to landlords who reside elsewhere . . . In Ireland the amount proportional to the territory is greater probably than in most other instances" Wakefield (1812, Vol. 1, p. 289) argued sensibly that the term "absentee" was ambiguous and misleading, since many landlords spent summers on their estates, or lived nearby if not on the estate itself. Others maintained that absenteeism was not a cause of problems but a symptom of a far more profound affliction of Irish society. Beaumont (1839, Vol. 1, p. 282) summed up this view: "The aristocracy of Ireland is not bad because it is absentee; it is absentee because it is bad." Some modern historians, such as Cullen (1981a, pp. 45–7), have even argued that the absentee problem has been overblown and that landlords were "in the main" resident.

Absenteeism had two aspects to it, a macroeconomic and a microeconomic. The distinction is not necessarily anachronistic. One persistent accusation made against landlords was that they drained resources out of Ireland, thus creating employment in their areas of residence, while unemployment in Ireland was rampant. The quantitative dimensions of this drain are uncertain: Young estimated that the rental going to absentee landlords amounted to £732,000. Adding pensions, interest, and other payments, he reached an annual figure of £1 million for the total drainage of funds from Ireland, which amounted to at most 20 percent of the annual rental (Young, 1892, Vol. 2, pp. 15, 116). A parliamentary committee in 1804 estimated the remittances to absentees at about £2 million, but Wakefield (1812, Vol. 1, p. 290 n.) thought the actual figure was higher. Estimates for later periods are unavailable. The exact numbers are, however, of secondary interest. To a Leitrim peasant it was immaterial whether his landlord lived in London, in Paris, or in Dublin. Moreover, even if the proprietor lived on the estate, his consumption bundle would probably have included a very large imported component.

Furthermore, from a purely macroeconomic point of view, residency is of no relevance to the economy. J. R. McCulloch pointed out in a celebrated (or notorious, depending on one's point of view) testimony before a Select Committee (Great Britain, 1825b, Vol. VIII, pp. 815–16) that it made no difference to the Irish economy where the landlord spent his rental income. The economic foundation of this opinion does not depend, as Black (1960, p. 75) maintained, on the accepted classical doctrine that "industry is limited by capital". It was based purely on an argument concerning the balance of payments. In the long-run (or even the medium run) no economy could have a consistent deficit in its current account. The price-specie-flow mechanism, or some other regulator of international trade, would lead to exports which matched the imports implied by the spending of Irish landlords abroad. The attack launched on McCulloch's position by Black (1960, pp. 75–81), therefore, seems to miss the point. McCulloch's "justification" of absenteeism was not invalid, it simply barked up the wrong tree. The costs of absenteeism were not macroeconomic but microeconomic in nature. The debate between McCulloch and other political economists on the macroeconomic implications of absenteeism does not deal with the real cost of absenteeism. Black implies that in an economy suffering from Keynesian underemployment, absentee landlords reduced aggregate demand. Quite apart from the problem of whether indeed Irish unemployment can and should be regarded as "Keynesian" in nature (discussed below), it is quite clear that the logic used in holding absentee landlords responsible for unemployment suffers from the same fallacies implied by "beggar thy neighbor" policies: the erroneous idea that imports provide employment to foreigners and import substitution provides employment to workers at home.

The microeconomic effect of landlord absenteeism is more persuasive and more compelling than the macroeconomic effect. The cost of absenteeism to society was not so much that it caused consumption of the wrong goods in the wrong places, but that it led to a monumental case of entrepreneurial failure.[1] This can be made clear by considering again the simple production models we have considered in Chapters 4 and 6. In these models agricultural output was assumed to be a function of three inputs: land, labor, and capital. Simple comparative statics can highlight the role of the variable factor (capital), but such an analysis assumes that everyone has access to the best techniques and is fully aware of the opportunities available to him. It, thus, glosses over a crucial role of the entrepreneur in economic development: to collect, absorb, process, and transmit information concerning better production methods. Capital and the knowledge of how to use it most effectively were highly complementary inputs. Informed contemporaries like Blacker and Kane frequently mentioned the lack of capital and the lack of knowledge in one breath. In the absence of technical knowhow, the opportunities described in Chapter 6 were meaningless. While people may have known, however vaguely, that some opportunities existed, the actual utilization of these opportunities required specific knowledge of farming techniques, and even more specific knowledge of the techniques suitable to the peculiar topographic, climatic, and geological conditions in a particular region and on a specific site. It is the slow diffusion of this type of knowledge which stood in the way of rapid agricultural development.

Although agriculture was a highly competitive industry in some respects, the actual speed at which informed, progressive, and energetic entrepreneurs could make the economy adopt new techniques was usually much slower than in industry or in transportation. After all, agriculture differs from industry and transportation in the crucial respect that no technological information is truly general. To highlight this point, consider what happens in manufacturing. Suppose that one or two industrial entrepreneurs start using a new technology. If others fail to follow suit, the successful entrepreneurs will expand at their expense, and ultimately take over the industry. It is, therefore, to be expected that arguments relying on entrepreneurial failure outside agriculture are not likely to be accepted without challenge. Each time the argument is raised, one has to be prepared to answer the inevitable question of why others did not replace the local entrepreneurs, if they proved too inept to adopt the new technology (see, for instance, Kindleberger, 1964, p. 134). Technology was not location-specific. If a technician could build a mule-jenny in Manchester, he could build one in Ghent or in Pawtucket. A steamship that could steam up the Hudson could steam up the Elbe or the Shannon. By contrast, in agriculture the costs of information were much higher because, being site-specific, they had to be paid over and over again. The information necessary to adopt the new technique could not as a rule be introduced or imposed by outsiders. Local entrepreneurs had to be able and willing to learn the new technique and subsequently take the risk of trying it. Moreover, the mechanism by which successful entrepreneurs could drive out bad entrepreneurs was far less efficient and was possibly short-circuited by the existence of a fixed factor, land.

Consider, first, for comparative purposes, the nonagricultural sector. The entrepreneur purchased labor, capital, and intermediary inputs in competitive markets. If one entrepreneur was more efficient than others, he earned a rent, which allowed him to accumulate capital faster than his less efficient competitors. If capital markets had functioned well, the process by which the efficient drove out the inefficient producers would have been even faster, since the successful entrepreneur could have borrowed on the collateral of his higher future profits. In any event, lower product prices and/or higher wages would ultimately drive his competitors out of business if they failed to adopt the superior technology. In agriculture the process could, in theory, work in a similar fashion by way of the more efficient landlords buying out the less efficient ones. If land was held purely for profit (and not for reasons of social prestige) and land markets were free of transactions costs, this is indeed what we would expect. Land markets in Ireland were, however, notoriously inefficient. Entail, family settlements, jointures, and other incumbrances made it very difficult for landlords to liquidate their estates. Moreover, the land market was complicated vastly by the almost impossibly cumbersome legal system, which did not require a centralized registration system of charges against an estate. Registers were spread out over different courts, so that it was an enormously costly and time-consuming process to estimate the net value of an estate. Title searches were reported to take fifteen years or longer. It seems that with regard to the Irish rural economy, the notion held by some economists that property rights will ultimately revert to those who can use them most efficiently does not hold much water. Some landlords were improving their estates, while others were not; but the mechanism by which improving landlords would "inherit the earth" was gravely impaired.

It is the entrepreneurial failure of the Irish landlord which is the main implication of absenteeism, not the presumed effects on aggregate demand. One contemporary writer, George Lewis Smyth (1844–9, Vol. 3, pp. 81–3), summarized the situation as follows:

> In Ireland we have to cultivate not the soil only, but the peasant; and that ascending still higher in the social scale we have also to reform the character of the landlord. The latter will not prove a light labour. He has to be taught and untaught much of what he has hitherto learned and acted on ... too many of them betray palpable ignorance of the

relations by which they stand connected with the rest of the community ... This evil is sensibly aggravated by the number of those, who, though possessed of only small estates of land will make no effort to better their condition ... nine out of ten ... will look upon themselves as independent country gentlemen and disdain the pursuits of commerce ... such men are not to be saved from insolvency or ruin.

Absenteeism was very relevant to the ability of the landlord to carry out these entrepreneurial responsibilities. It is, of course, true that residency was neither a sufficient, nor a necessary, condition for a progressive and improving landlord. There are examples of resident landlords who were utterly ineffectual in implementing improvements as well as absentees who employed energetic and well-informed agents. Such counterexamples do not refute the general association between absentee landlordship and the backwardness of Irish agriculture, and the implication that the structure of landownership and the nature of landlord–tenant relations were important factors in Irish poverty. What we have to do first, therefore, is to try to describe in some greater detail the nature of the absentee-ownership phenomenon. Once more, the Poor Law Inquiry commissioners supply us with the necessary quantitative information. Question 33 in the supplement to appendix F, asked specifically whether the landlord in the respondent's district was typically absentee or resident, and if absentee, where he lived. A total of 1,546 responses to the absenteeism question could be used, but the interpretation of the data is not straightforward, because it is not clear to what extent, if at all, the responses were weighted by land actually owned. For instance, in a situation in which one large absentee landlord owned three-quarters of a certain district and the rest was divided up among a dozen resident gentlemen, the response might very well have been "most of the landed proprietors are resident". It is not impossible that the witnesses used some form of implicit weighting of their answers, but this possibility has to remain speculative. Even an unweighted index of absenteeism is of some use, since to the extent that the improving resident proprietor provided an example for his neighbors, their absolute number mattered as well as the amount of land they controlled.

Table 7.1   *Index of Residency in Ireland, 1835*

Province	Number of witnesses	Mean Score
Ulster	540	1·24
Leinster	444	1·45
Munster	404	1·29
Connaught	158	1·25
Ireland	1,546	1·32

Source: Computed from Great Britain, 1835d, Vol. XXXIII, supplement, pp. 2–393.

The responses of the witnesses were scaled between 0 (no resident landlord) and 3 (most or all resident). Thus, the lower the score, the more severe the absenteeism problem. In three counties the problem of absenteeism appeared far worse than in the country as a whole: Londonderry (0·62), and Leitrim and Longford (0·65). The highest rates of residency were in Westmeath and Kildare (1·77). A summary of the data province by province is presented in Table 7.1. The table shows that the country as a whole was rather evenly affected with absenteeism, with Leinster being somewhat less affected than the other provinces. The standard deviation of the Residency Index is 0·33, which is rather low (25 percent) relative to the mean.

One reason why absenteeism was so widespread is that there were many kinds of absenteeism. The kind of absentee proprietor depicted by Cecil Woodham-Smith in her *The Reason Why* (1958) was one form which the phenomenon took: peers, Members of Parliament, and officers in the British Army constituted an important proportion of the landlords, and most of them looked at their estates in Ireland the way a rentier looks at his assets, rather than the way an entrepreneur looks at his firm. But other kinds of absentees may have been more important quantitatively. The London Companies, for instance held immense estates in Ulster, especially in Counties Londonderry and Donegal. In Londonderry alone, the Fishmongers, Grocers, and Drapers owned about 79,000 acres, constituting 15 percent of the total surface area of the county (Robinson, 1962, p. 104). Technically, the companies should be considered absentees. Quite a lot of land was owned by Trinity College, Dublin: in 1843 Trinity owned 195,000 statute acres, which was about 1 percent of the total surface of Ireland. Its holdings included 7·0 percent of Co. Armagh, 6·4 percent of Co. Kerry, and 5·3 percent of Co. Donegal. The provost of the college owned another 35,000 acres *ex officio*, almost all of them in Co. Galway (Carney, 1975, pp. 38–9). Perhaps the most pervasive of all causes for absenteeism was the fact that many landowners residing in Ireland had their estates scattered over wide regions, so that they could not possibly be resident at all of their property. Many Irish landlords also happened to own large estates in Britain, and it is possible, as Malcomson (1974, p. 21) points out, that many of them tended to pay their non-Irish estates disproportionate attention. In any event, the most important group of absentees were what Malcomson has called "internal absentees". A long list of such absentees is provided by Malcomson (1974, pp. 23–5). Co. Leitrim serves as a good example: while it was one of the most deserted counties in Ireland, all but one of the principal landowners in the county (Lord Bessborough) seem to have lived elsewhere in Ireland.

Malcomson's persuasive article is fully corroborated by the Poor Law Commission witnesses. The question as originally phrased asked the respondents where the proprietor lived if he was not resident in the district. The responses designate three basic locations: Ireland, England, and "all others". Some witnesses responded by naming two or three locations (for instance, "some in England, some in Ireland"). If we denote the residency index presented in Table 7.1 as R, let the index i ($i = I, E, C$) denote whether the proprietor lived respectively in Ireland, England, or elsewhere, and set W_i equal to 1 if the residents were reported to live in i and equal to $1/n$ if residents lived in n locations, we can define the index:

$$A_i = W_i(3 - R) \qquad (7.1)$$

For example, if a witness reported that very few landlords were resident (receiving a score of 1 on the residency index), and that the landlords lived in Ireland, then $A_I = 2$, $A_E = 0$, and $A_C = 0$ for this witness. If a witness stated that "some landlords were resident, others absentee", thus receiving a score of $R = 2$ on the residency index, and that the landlords lived in England and France, the score for the As is $A_I = 0$, $A_E = 0\cdot5$, $A_C = 0\cdot5$. The data in Table 7.2 are presented in percentage form and should be interpreted as an indication of where the landlords tended to reside (according to the Poor Law Inquiry witnesses, of course) *given that they were absentee.*

Table 7.2   *Weighted Observations on Residence Places of Absentee Landlords (Percentages)*

Province	In Ireland	In England	Elsewhere	Total
Ulster	62·6	35·2	2·3	100
Leinster	67·6	27·2	5·3	100
Munster	63·4	33·9	2·8	100
Connaught	73·4	22·8	3·9	100
Ireland	65·3	31·3	3·4	100

Source: Computed from Great Britain, 1835d, Vol. XXXIII, supplement, pp. 2–393.

The aggregated data in Table 7.2 indicate that the majority of Irish absentee landlords resided within Ireland. Only about a third of them lived abroad. It is likely, however, that the latter represented more than a third of the total rental. In some counties the proportions were quite different from the provincial averages. In Londonderry only 38·6 percent of the reported landlords lived in Ireland, while 58·7 lived in England. Similar figures hold for Antrim (44·1 and 55·0 percent, respectively). In Kerry, Monaghan, and Longford almost half the testimonies indicate landlords living abroad. In Leitrim, on the other hand, 83 percent of the absentees lived in Ireland, while the figures for Fermanagh, Queen's and Dublin were 89 percent, 70 percent, and 84 percent respectively.

Absenteeism was costly because it made a cooperative effort between landlord and tenant, so vital for efficient and progressive agricultural production, impossible. Tenancy arrangements often reflected the need to adjust and renegotiate contracts when circumstances changed unexpectedly (see, for example, Reid, 1976, pp. 570–6). Sharecropping is one such arrangement, but there is no evidence of its existence in Ireland. The reason for the lack of sharecropping is in part that such an arrangement requires a resident landlord (or a good agent). Moreover, the particular crop mix in Ireland, where the potato crop constituted most of the small tenant's income and the cash crop went to the landlord and other residual claimants, may also have been a factor (Mokyr, 1981b). In fact, one of the most marked advantages of residency was the increased flexibility of contractual arrrangements. A Co. Clare witness (Great Britain, 1836b, Vol. XXXIII, p. 176) noted that resident landlords were more inclined to forgive rents in bad years. Being present *in loco* was important for landlords to identify such years, and thus to absorb some of the risk.

Moreover, the resident landlord—provided he took an active interest in agriculture—fulfilled an important function in the diffusion of agricultural information. When a new technique became available, there were costs associated with receiving and evaluating the information. There was the further cost of experimenting, choosing, and demonstrating the variant of the new technique best adapted to the specific location. This information was transmitted largely through emulation. Tenants on absentee proprietors' estates were less efficient because nobody "set a good example". The frequency with which this complaint was sounded suggests that it was acutely felt by those who realized the opportunities available (OSM, box 9, file VI; box 15, file VI; Great Britain, 1836b, Vol. XXXI, p. 35; Vol. XXXIII, pp. 172, 176, 201; Great Britain, 1845a, Vol. XX, pp. 518, 899). Landlords further were expected to encourage improvements financially: either to finance the project, or help the tenants do so. In view of the poverty of most of the tenants, wherever financing was necessary, the project would stand or fall depending on the landlord's encouragement. In addition, someone had to supervise and coordinate the actual implementation of the new technique, continuously updating the information and supplying the tenants with technical advice on short notice. It was also important to make sure that no negative externalities were imposed by improving tenants upon others, and to mediate conflicts which were almost inevitable when old and trusted cultivation techniques were overthrown.

The failure of the Irish landlord class can only be made meaningful in a comparative context. A precise evaluation of the relative merits of Irish and English landlords cannot be attempted here. It is clear, however, that most authorities on British agricultural history in the eighteenth and nineteenth centuries still agree about the important role played by the landlord, though some of the admiration shown to the great landlord-improvers by Lord Ernle and similar writers may have been exaggerated. Jones (1974, pp. 73–4), for example, emphasizes the role of the landlord in stimulating his tenants in making productive investments. Mingay (1963, pp. 163–88) has pointed out that the actual innovations may have been the work of a few maverick pioneers, and that the landlord class was rather conservative. In the eighteenth century the main function of the landlord class was "to establish conditions under which improved farms could develop ... the provision of fixed capital and the creation of a favourable environment for the adoption of better farming" (ibid., p. 171). In the last third of the eighteenth century and the first half of the nineteenth the role of the landlords and their agents in the establishment of a highly productive agriculture became more active. Chambers and Mingay (1966, p. 168) conclude that "despite many errors and shortcomings, the justification of the landed interest is that in their hands English farming responded successfully to the swelling demands of a new urbanized economy". Agents, managers, and stewards played a major role in this transformation, but the landed aristocracy did not rely passively on their agents and tenants and often took the initiative in encouraging technical and economic efficiency (Thompson, 1963, pp. 151–5).

Jones (1981b, p. 76) points out that entrepreneurial, innovating landlords who were concerned with methods of husbandry and management were the agents of economic progress. By their ability to solve problems in a systematic manner and their access to information at a national level, they were "well placed to seek better combinations of factors of production" which meant the best-practice technique given the topographical and ecological parameters of a site. On the continent, to the extent that agriculture was improving at all in the first half of the nineteenth century, the role of the landlords was equally important. For example, the continuing development of Czech agriculture, was sustained by the entrepreneurial activities of innovative Bohemian landlords (Milward and Saul, 1977, p. 285).

In Ireland, some exceptions notwithstanding, the performance of the landlords was disappointing. Whether it was because of absenteeism alone, or whether other factors were at work as well, the Irish landlords did not take active part in the process of agricultural production. As the Devon Commission Report put it, "It is admitted on all hands, that according to the general practice in Ireland, the landlord builds neither dwelling houses nor farm offices, nor puts fences, gates, &c., into good order", (Kennedy, 1847, p. 1123). The same was true for "various agricultural operations, such as draining, deep trenching, and even manuring".

It is not likely that a *single* answer to the riddle of the un-economic behavior of the Irish landlord will ever be provided. Even when landlords were interested in agriculture, they often seemed insulated from the Irish environment and hence created few positive spillover effects. One contemporary wrote that "Our great farming landlords and agents are lost in admiration of their own calves and the wonderful effects of their abilities upon 100 acres ... altogether neglecting the ten, fifty or hundred thousand acres which they possess beyond the little boundary enclosing themselves" (Kennedy, 1835, p. 81; see also Wiggins, 1844, p. 203). The *Parliamentary Gazetteer* (1846, Vol. I, p. xxv) cited with approval J. R. McCulloch's correspondent who noted the stark contrast between the well-cultivated gardens and parks around gentlemen's residences, and the desolate and neglected view of the rest of the estate (McCulloch, 1854, Vol. 1, p. 320). The *Gazetteer* added that nowhere else in Britain could such sharp differences be seen.

Nevertheless, landlord residency—however delinquent and incompetent the proprietor—was of importance. One further way residency mattered was that—given that improvements were typically introduced by tenants—residency and familiarity with local conditions allowed the landlords to favor and encourage improving tenants and discriminate against bad ones (Thompson, 1802, pp. 56–8). In a few cases resident landlords also helped set up the infrastructure for activities ancillary to agriculture, thereby creating important positive externalities for agriculture. Lord Caledon, an Armagh resident country gentleman, erected two flour mills at a cost of £20,000 and purchased grain from his tenants at the Armagh market price (Inglis, 1835, Vol. 2, p. 278). Landlords also took the initiative in eliminating the hopelessly inefficient open-field systems known as "rundale". A famous example is the reallocation of about 50 scattered holdings to form six contiguous lots carried out by Lord George Hill in Co. Donegal in 1838. This reshuffling was, according to Hill, "effected with much difficulty, the people themselves having the greatest antipathy to any change . . . each man's case was attentively considered so that no injury or loss was incurred by any" (Great Britain, 1845a, Vol. XXI, p. 799). The opportunities for direct landlord intervention were, by all accounts, both large and varied. Most witnesses and contemporary writers expressed views agreeing with the Irish proverb "the master's eye fastens the steed" (Great Britain, 1836b, Vol. XXXIII, p. 200).

The debate concerning the problem of estate management relates to the question of economies of scale. The agricultural history of pre-famine Ireland reveals a paradox: on the one hand there were the persistent attempts of some progressive landlords and their agents to consolidate farms into larger units, on the other hand there are no clear indications of economies of scale in tillage farming. Blacker (1834) and Crawford (1850), among others, argued strongly for the viability and efficiency of small farms. The Poor Law Inquiry, in its investigation of consolidation, was repeatedly told that there was no difference between the yields of small and large farmers (Great Britain, 1836b, Vol. XXXIII, pp. 92, 105, 107). If there was any difference in productivity between smallholders and larger farmers in favor of the latter, it was attributed to the better ability of the latter to procure adequate quantities of manure, which basically is a statement about capital markets of the type discussed in Chapter 6.

How can these two phenomena be reconciled? In part, the reconciliation has to do with the indisputable scale economies in pasturage. In so far as the reorganization of farms was attempted in order to put the land to grass, consolidation was a natural consequence. But consolidation also occurred when land remained under tillage, as must have been the case in the districts of those eighteen Devon witnesses who maintained that employment actually went up as a consequence of consolidation (see also Great Britain, 1845a, Vol. XX, p. 158). The answer must be that there were some forms of economies of scale in tillage agriculture, but that these were not so much technical in nature as managerial. One Devon Commission witness from Co. King's stated that in small farms, with numerous tenants, the estate required a management that neither landlord nor agent could provide (Great Britain, 1845a, Vol. XXI, p. 664). Certainly, there were scale economies in rent collecting and in the enforcement of contract clauses. The managerial function of spreading information contained a fixed cost component, which, too, implied scale effects. Foster (1847, p. 371) pointed out that what the land needed more than anything was farms which raised tillage crops using the technologies incorporating green crops in the course rotation. But he added that these farms had to be large: the tenants needed to be guided, led, governed, and disciplined, which could only be done if they were regularly employed on large units.

The inability of Irish landlords to supply the managerial and entrepreneurial inputs was well realized even by the most enthusiastic supporters of small-scale agriculture. Blacker, in his proposal for a rural economy based on small farms utilizing green crops and stall-fed animals, recognized that a necessary condition for the successful implementation of his plan was "to establish upon each estate an experienced Agriculturalist, to instruct the tenantry, whose duty should be to go from farm to farm, day after day, and point out to the occupier wherein his practice was erroneous and how it might be improved and . . . he should be authorized to lend, wherever necessary, lime, guano, or other manure, seeds, and in some cases money" (Blacker, 1846, p. 11). It hardly needs to be said that the creation of such an army of agricultural experts was beyond the resources of any economy in the 1840s, let alone the Irish economy. The Devon Commission Digest agreed with Blacker that resident agricultural experts were of great value and that they were able to "overcome prejudices against the introduction of new systems" (Kennedy, 1847, p. 31). The supply of such agricultural experts was woefully inadequate. There were thirteen agricultural schools associated with the National Board of Education, with a total of 360 "day scholars" and another twenty-nine boarders. Not all of these schools, however, taught much agriculture: the one in Larne (Co. Antrim) taught only four hours a week, and only about half of all students were instructed for more than twenty hours a week. The agricultural seminary at Templemoyle had seventy students enrolled in 1843 (Kennedy, 1847, pp. 35, 57). Inevitably, perhaps, these schools recruited their students from the wealthy farmers and gentry, neglecting the educational needs of the small peasantry (Kennedy, 1835, pp. 77–81). The Poor Law witnesses agreed unanimously that the establishment of agricultural schools and model farms would be "of the greatest advantage to every class", adding that, at present, no resident proprietor encouraged the tenants to improve their tillage techniques or attended to this improvement himself (Great Britain, 1836b, Vol. XXXIII, pp. 344–56). Dutton (1824, p. 71) wrote that the landlords in Galway were responsible for the backwardness of agriculture because they did not establish farming societies. It seems that "improving landlords" and agricultural experts were regarded as close substitutes for each other and the low supply of the former manifested itself in the desirability of the latter. The contemporary view held landlords responsible for agricultural improvement, and if they could not or would not carry out this function, they should at least provide a substitute.

In the absence of Blacker's army of agricultural experts, landlords could stretch out the available expertise by the consolidation of farms. Consolidation meant that landlords could realize some of the scale economies resulting from imperfect and costly information and not pay the costs of instruction, guidance, and supervision many times over. In addition, it allowed them to weed out bad and incompetent farmers and to concentrate the land in the hands of those who were best able to implement better farming techniques. Clearly, such considerations were a major motive of consolidation, but, as we have seen in Chapter 5, consolidation led to resistance. The tragedy of Irish rural life was that improving landlords who persisted in overhauling their estates often paid a price for consolidation in terms of a polarization of their relations with their tenants.

Absenteeism was thus a factor in the entrepreneurial failure of Irish landlords, but it was by no means the whole story. One way in which the absentee landlords—whether they were absentee by necessity, or by choice—could undo the consequences of their absenteeism was by hiring competent resident agents and stewards who would allow the landlords to fulfill their entrepreneurial roles vicariously. The practice in Ireland varied considerably, and there is no doubt that there were many competent agents, the most striking example of whom was William Blacker. Other examples can be cited, such as the agents in Co. Limerick mentioned by Lieutenant-General Bourke (Great Britain, 1845a, Vol. XX, p. 726, W. H. H. Beecher, ibid., Vol. XXII, pp. 135–6, appendix 32) or some of the agents employed by Lord Downshire (Maguire, 1972, ch. 6). Wiggins (1844, p. 46) assessed that agents generally managed estates far better than proprietors ever could. But on the whole, agents could not fill the entrepreneurial vacuum created by the Irish landlord. More often than not, the agent was an absentee himself, frequently a Dublin solicitor or a professional rent collector going from estate to estate to carry out his function.[2] Absentee agents were widely denounced, and the Devon Commission witnesses emphasized the gap between the perceived duties of agents and their actual role. The Digest summarized the evidence as follows: "nearly all the witnesses concur in considering the duties of an agent to be extensive and most important in their nature; but a large majority state that the collection of rent is the chief duty, and many, that it is the only duty generally fulfilled" (Kennedy, 1847, p. 1026). A similar statement was made thirty years earlier by Wakefield (1812, Vol. 1, p. 244). It is likely that the situation was somewhat improving in the first half of the nineteenth century. Maguire (1972, p. 190), for instance, speaks of "a growing professionalism among agents". But the overall situation leaves little doubt that the 5,000 persons who designated themselves as "land stewards" or "land agents" in 1841 could not replace the landlords in the latter's natural function as entrepreneurs in the rural economy. Even when the agents were on the whole of high quality, ultimate control had to stay with the landlord and initiative for change had to come from him, as was the case in Britain. Maguire (1972, p. 216) concludes that the landlord was an irreplaceable element in the development and improvement of the estate. The landlords studied by Maguire were unusually careful in the selection of their agents. For many of the absentee landlords in Ireland, Blacker's stern criticism applied:

The embarrassments under which gentlemen of landed property in Ireland labour may, in most cases, be traced to the improper selection of their agents . . . too fond of pleasure and amusements to attend to the details of business, it might at least be expected that men of fortune would have been at some pains to select proper persons to attend to those matters . . . But the very contrary seems to have been the fact; and until of recent years . . . men have been too often chosen [who were] as little capable of attending to its details as their employers. (Blacker, 1834, pp. 1–2)

Later in the century, when the quality of Irish agents had improved considerably, British land agents were still much superior to their Irish colleagues, especially with regard to "a real understanding of the ordinary farmer's problems" (Donnelly, 1975, pp. 183–7; see also F. M. L. Thompson's introduction to Greig 1976, pp. 5–6).

If English estates were managed on the whole more efficiently than Irish estates by a close cooperative effort of owners and agents, why did more trained and experienced British agents not offer their services to Irish landlords? One can only conjecture that on the supply side, the conflict-ridden and often violent nature of landlord–tenant relations made Ireland into an unattractive environment for Britons to operate in. On the demand side, it is likely that many landlords were so remote and detached from the actual management of their estates that they did not even realize the gains realizable by hiring more effective agents. There were, of course, some British agents such as William Greig (Greig, 1976, p. 35) who *did* operate in Ireland. The Englishman John Wiggins traveled annually to Ireland for thirty years to manage the estates he was in charge of. It is telling, however, that Wiggins was an absentee land agent and did not actually live on the estates. Wiggins's impressions of his Irish experience led him to place the blame for Irish agricultural backwardness squarely on inept estate management by Irish landlords (Wiggins, 1844, pp. 39 ff.).

A fascinating and instructive case study of the economics of absentee landlordship is provided by Robinson (1962) in her study of the London Companies estate in Co. Londonderry. The London Companies, like so many other Irish landlords, eliminated their middlemen in the late 1810s, and from then on attempted to manage their estates directly. Relative to other Irish absentee landlords, the London Companies were clearly among the best. Special Irish estate committees were established which were responsible for the administration of the estate, and members of these committees often traveled to Ireland. The daily management was none the less in the hands of estate agents who were required by the company to reside on the property and to supervise personally all improvements and inspect every holding on the estate (Robinson, 1962, p. 106). Contemporaries such as Inglis (1835, Vol. 2, p. 222) and Foster (1847, p. 151), agreed that the London Companies were on the whole good landlords and served as examples to other local landlords.

In spite of their good intentions, the Companies' attempts to implement a more advanced agriculture on their Londonderry estates were not very successful. Robinson insists that their failure was not due to their absenteeism, thanks to the efficiency of their resident agents. But her evidence here is basically negative: that is, there was no evidence that the Companies suffered from absenteeism. This conclusion flies in the face of Robinson's own statement that the Companies depended largely on their agents for all information concerning their estates, and that the absence of the landlords deprived their tenants from direct contact with them. It seems at least open to question that the lack of success of the London Companies in their endeavors and their absenteeism were unrelated, which is the basis for Robinson's conclusion that "the advent of a better quality of landlordism then was prevalent in nineteenth century Ireland would not have assured the prosperity of the occupying tenantry and their agriculture" (Robinson, 1962, p. 118). Robinson points out, for instance, (ibid, p. 118, n. 1) that the improvements needed to increase the productivity of small farms required considerable investment—presumably more than the 1s 2d per acre which the companies spent annually per acre in the fifty years 1820–70. The Companies themselves thought that their disappointing results were largely due to one factor: the smallness of the farms and their inability to consolidate them. As we have seen, the scale economies implied in this complaint were themselves a result of absenteeism. An additional reason for the lack of success of the Companies in improving their estates was their inability to realize that agricultural improvement required large outlays rather than piecemeal and gradual investment in small projects. There is also evidence that the Companies invested in low-priority projects. They spent large sums on streets, churches, schools, and agent-mansions but "did little for the *lands*" (Wiggins, 1844, p. 204; emphasis in original). Their failure as entrepreneurs led to a situation in which the rates of return seemed lower than they would have been in the presence of active, aggressive, resident landlords.

To summarize: the problem which plagued Irish agriculture was not that there were too many landlords who should have been eliminated somehow as Beaumont suggested, but rather (as Pim and others maintained) that there were too few of them (Pim, 1848, pp. 44, 236). It was widely recognized that landlords had a managerial responsibility, in which most of them failed miserably. The void created thereby was never adequately filled. The Irish landlord had earned a reputation among his contemporaries as an indolent, reckless spendthrift of unbusinesslike habits, to many of whom the idea of capital accumulation and technical progress never even occurred (Scrope, 1848, pp. 17–18). Absenteeism was without question an important element, but absenteeism in Ireland was not preordained either. To be sure, to some extent absenteeism was inevitable due to the fragmentation of landed estates. But this cannot explain the phenomenon entirely. For example, the Earls of Ely owned two widely separated estates in counties Wexford and Fermanagh and from the 1760s, in Malcomson's words, "compromised between them by residing on neither" (Malcomson,

1974, p. 24). Apparently, rural Ireland was simply an unpleasant or undesirable place to live in for members of its landowning class. Some of these reasons had little to do with the quality of life in Ireland *per se* (for instance, the fact that Parliament met in Westminster) but the insecurity which dominated life in many parts of Ireland at some time or another in the late eighteenth and nineteenth centuries played a role here as well (Great Britain, 1825c, Vol. IX, p. 129). The same insecurity also dampened the enthusiasm of improving residents and increased the riskiness of investment. Many—though by no means all—landlords in Ireland remained utterly alien to their Irish tenants, separated from them by an abyss of cultural, political, and religious differences. They were regarded by the non-landed classes as usurpers, and many landlords must have thought of themselves in similar terms. Beaumont's eloquent if somewhat overly melodramatic description reflects a reality which, while by no means omnipresent, infected most of Ireland to some degree:

> The proprietor . . . is often absentee; it often happens that he is unacquainted with his own estates; he knows vaguely that he possesses some hundred or hundred and fifty thousand acres in the county of Cork or Donegal . . . he is resolved not to spend a single farthing in improving their value. He or his ancestors [*sic*] obtained this vast tract by confiscation; who knows but some new revolution may take away what the preceding revolution has thrown into his family? . . . The resident landlord, though he touches the soil, rarely takes root in it, and Ireland is not the country to which he believes that his cares and sacrifices are due. (Beaumont, 1839, Vol. 1, p. 289)

The cooperative efforts of landlord and tenant, which were so indispensable if agricultural technology was to change, were simply not forthcoming. Without cooperation, the ability of the landlord to carry out his entrepreneurial duties was greatly curtailed even if he had the desire and the ability to do so. Without entrepreneurship, capital investment lost much of its attractiveness even if landlords had the resources to invest in farm improvement. The entire process of agricultural change was, if not wholly short-circuited, certainly greatly impeded. It is, of course, quite impossible to place a monetary value on the cost imposed on the Irish economy on account of the entire syndrome of entrepreneurial failure in agriculture. One contemporary, in a truly heroic calculation, estimated the cost inflicted upon the Irish economy by bad management at £89 million per annum (Kennedy, 1835, pp. 117–22). This sum is more than twice the total value of prefamine agricultural output as estimated by Ó Gráda (1980c). While the estimate is absurdly high, it illustrates the belief of informed and intelligent contemporaries that the inadequacies of the landlord class lay at the foundation of Ireland's economic backwardness.

Is "entrepreneurial failure" a valid explanation of the poor economic performance of an entire economy? The pendulum of the conventional wisdom on this issue has been swinging back and forth in recent years.

Most of the work carried out by New Economic Historians studying the Victorian economy in Britain has drawn conclusions which run counter to the entrepreneurship hypothesis. However, as pointed out at the start of this chapter, agriculture may have been quite different from the industries and services examined by those working on late nineteenth-century Britain. Moreover, a recent paper by Robert Allen (1981) makes clear that profit-maximization and entrepreneurial failure are not necessarily incompatible. Entrepreneurial failure, according to Allen, is not only possible when an industry adopts a "bad" equilibrium position, but can also characterize the speed at which the economy adjusts to disequilibria. T. W. Schultz (1975) has pointed out that coping with disequilibria is a basic entrepreneurial function, of central importance to the diffusion of technical progress in agriculture. Translating Allen's and Schultz's ideas into the issues of prefamine Ireland, we could blame Irish landlords and large-scale farmers and graziers for the slowness with which they introduced novel techniques into Irish agriculture, although within the confines of the traditional husbandry Irish agriculture may have been competitive, price-responsive, and even efficient. If the high rates of return reported in Chapter 6 are corroborated by further, more detailed, studies, we can conclude that the speed of adjustment to new techniques in crop rotation, drainage, fertilizer usage, and agricultural implements was exceedingly slow. It could then be concluded that one corner of the big puzzle of Irish poverty was conclusively solved.

When we ask the question what, in the final analysis, was the real cause, the true "external factor" in the dismal history of prefamine agriculture, it is reasonable to conclude that it was not just entrepreneurial failure, absenteeism, insufficient saving, incompetence, or even the complex set of factors leading to economic conflict between tenant and landlord. Ultimately, there is history to blame: the creation of the land-lord class from British and Scottish adventurers and mercenaries, a class of parvenus and foreigners. Elizabeth, Cromwell, and William III unwittingly set limits to both the quantity and the quality of the stock of entrepreneurship available to Irish agriculture in the nineteenth century.

Outside agriculture, the evidence for entrepreneurial failure is much weaker. There were some excellent native businessmen in Ireland, such as the Guinness family in brewing, Andrew Mulholland and William Barbour in the linen industry, and a host of successful bankers and merchants in Dublin. To the extent that local talent was not forthcoming, it was replaced—as it was everywhere in Europe—by foreigners. The most famous example was the Italian Charles Bianconi, who set up the first centralized system of stagecoaches in Ireland in the 1830s and 1840s. The Bianconi empire was unanimously commended for its efficient organization and excellent management. The Scotsman A. Buchanan established a woolen shawls factory in Limerick, in an attempt to exploit the cheap-labor resources available there (Great Britain, 1840, Vol. XXIII, pp. 500–1). After the famine, the Belfast shipping industry was built up by two English entrepreneurs, Edward

Harland and G. W. Wolff (Wolff was actually of German origin). The textile machinery and the iron foundries in the 1850s were dominated by immigrants from Scotland and Leeds (Lee, 1973a, p. 19).

(2) Employment and Labor Productivity

Labor problems and employment were uppermost on the minds of contemporary writers in search of causes for Ireland's economic distress. One of the most widespread complaints was unemployment. Weld (1832, p. 679), Lewis (1836a, pp. 57, 312), and Pim (1848, p. 128) were among the many writers to express their opinion that unemployment was one of the worst afflictions of the Irish economy. Depending on their political views, these authors attributed it either to laziness, or to insufficient capital and incentives. The problem was more complex than that, however, and some contemporaries instinctively felt the conceptual difficulties in assuming a long-run disequilibrium between the supply of and the demand for labor. Foster (1847), for instance, seems to have changed his mind during his visit to Ireland. Early on during his tour he could still write (p. 86) "the want most felt by its poor is the want of employment", later on he remarked that "employment abounds; there is the want of energy and the want of industry to set about finding employment" (p. 589). Of course, if "laziness" was the main source of unemployment, the resulting poverty was only apparent and what contemporaries saw as unemployment was in reality nothing but a massive "consumption of leisure". It seems unlikely, though, that the phenomenon can wholly be ascribed to leisure preference.

What was the nature of involuntary unemployment in prefamine Ireland? Some modern writers, influenced by the Keynesian tradition, seem to think of Ireland's distress primarily in terms of a "deflationary gap". Barrow, for example, interprets the somewhat eccentric writings of the Dublin banker T. Mooney (who thought that expanded banking was the answer to Ireland's problems) in Keynesian terms (Barrow, 1975, p. 119). Black (1960, p. 88 n.) distinguishes between "under-" and "unemployment" and cites "ample evidence that many 'landless men' were unemployed in the modern sense". By the "modern sense" Black presumably means Keynesian unemployment (cf. also ibid., p. 75).[3] A Keynesian interpretation of prefamine Irish history is not easy to accept. To some extent, such a view involves a confusion between short-run and long-run effects. Inadequate aggregate demand as a secular condition in any economy is not a likely occurrence. In the semi-monetized subsistence economy of the Irish countryside, where unemployment was especially widespread, the diagnosis of "secular stagnation" is even less plausible, since Keynesian economics breaks down in a barter economy. Even in so far as money was used, there seems to have been no reason why hoarding should have exceeded dis-hoarding for sustained periods. Barrow (1975, p. 194) pointed to the outflow of savings through landlords investing abroad, but this "leakage" must have been wholly offset in the long run by export surpluses. In short, the Keynesian view is as inapplicable to the Irish case as it was to other preindustrial economies (Mokyr, 1977, pp. 998–1003).

Unemployment in prefamine rural Ireland was largely seasonal in nature. During some periods of the year the country was fully employed and most unemployment resulted from fluctuations in the demand for labor due to the nature of agricultural work and the effect of weather on cottage industry. Seasonal unemployment may be regarded largely a result of friction and imperfect information in an economy. During the slack seasons workers in occupations affected by seasonality were un-employed, because it was too costly for them to seek employment in occupations which were not affected by seasonality or in which the seasonality pattern was different. The more backward an economy, the more severe seasonal unemployment could be expected to be not only because agricultural demand for labor was by its very nature more susceptible to seasonal fluctuations, but because backward economies lacked the facilities to shuttle workers back and forth. Seasonal migra-tion, both within Ireland and to Britain, was becoming increasingly commonplace in decades prior to the famine due to better transporta-tion and communications.

With this background it becomes understandable why some witnesses were "perplexed" when asked by the Poor Inquiry commissioners whether emigration would reduce the competition for land and allow steady wages. The witnesses replied that all employment was seasonal, with some periods of full employment, so that emigration would not alleviate unemployment (Great Britain, 1836b, Vol. XXXIII, p. 140). Some contemporary writers greatly overestimated the importance of seasonal unemployment. J. Gier, the author of an Ordnance Survey memoir for the parish of Killea, Co. Donegal, thought that the slack season lasted as long as eight months (OSM, box 21, file XV). Lewis (1836b, p. 312) estimated that only a third of the Irish laborforce were employed year-round, while the rest found work only at seasons of extraordinary demand. Otway provided similar figures in his report but restricted the phenomenon to occasional laborers. He estimated that, for thirty weeks per year, 300,000 laborers (about 25 percent of those who defined themselves as "labourers" in the 1841 Census) were out of work. While it is by no means the intention here to deny the severity of the problem of Irish unemployment, it seems that it ought to be kept in the proper perspective. The reports of the Poor Law commissioners provide us with two clues to the extent of seasonal unemployment among Irish laborers. One clue is contained in the data used in Chapter 2 to estimate the wage income figures. The Poor Law commissioners asked two separate questions, namely, what was the annual income that a laborer received on average in the respondent's district, and what was the daily wage paid in the district. If we take the daily wages to be the average between summer and winter wages and compute them without provisions (which often were supplied by the employer), the annual number of days worked implicitly believed by the witness can be obtained by dividing the annual income figure by the daily wage. This procedure is fraught with difficulties, the most serious of which is that in some cases the number of days implied in the witness's response exceeded 365. In other cases it was clear that the annual estimate was obtained by a multiplication by 360, which is absurd. For that reason, the estimates of the length of the working year provided in Table 7.3 have excluded all witnesses who implied a working year of more than 300 days. The estimates are therefore, if anything, too low, because they also exclude many witnesses who implied working years of 312 days (indicating full employment but correctly leaving out Sundays). An alternative is to use the data from baronial estimates provided by the commissioners themselves in appendix H, part I, to the third report of the Commission (Great Britain, 1836b, Vol. XXXIV, p. 652). The latter data, as can be verified from Table 7.3, are much lower. These figures are, however, useless and misleading. The appendix does not explain how and from what raw data they were computed (though the table identifies the baronies to which they pertain); the entries for Roscommon, Tipperary, and Waterford are missing, while for Co. Antrim the table says only that "majority employed great part of the year". For counties for which the tables provide more than one observation, they are sometimes too divergent to be taken seriously. For Sligo, for instance, the figures vary from twenty-four days a year to 120. It is clear moreover that, whatever the source of this table, it does not fully take into account the work performed by laborers on their own small plots and gardens. The data in column 1 in Table 7.3 show, on the other hand, that the Irish laborers worked in one way or another for forty weeks a year, and that there were only small variations between the different regions of Ireland with respect to seasonal unemployment.

Table 7.3   *Implicit Length of the Labor Year (in days)*

Province	(1) Computed from income data	(2) Baronial estimates
Ulster	234·3	166·9
Leinster	244·8	145·3
Munster	239·2	133·4
Connaught	225·2	97·8
Ireland	236·8	140·5

Sources: Column 1: computed from Great Britain, 1836b, Vol. XXXI (see Appendix to Chapter 2).
Column 2: Great Britain, 1836b, Vol. XXXIV, p. 652.

The second clue to the quantitative significance of seasonal unemployment is provided by the fact that the same data also distinguish between summer wages and winter wages. The difference between the two in virtually all cases was constant, namely, 2d. After the shorter working day in the winter is taken into account, the small gap seems to indicate that the difference in the demand for labor was less dramatic than some of the accounts cited above seem to indicate. Of course, it is possible that the supply of labor was highly elastic, so that the decline in demand manifested itself wholly in reduced employment. But even if such were the case, it would indicate that workers did have good alternatives to employment as hired laborers. A very elastic labor supply curve, indicating workers' unwillingness to work below a given minimum wage, means that at very low wages workers preferred to remain at home whether for leisure purposes or for home production. Such a supply curve is hardly consistent with an image of a mass of semi-starved peasants desperately searching for employment. The majority of Irish peasants, after all, were largely self-employed, grew their own potatoes, cut their own fuel, built and maintained their houses, and engaged in household production which could be postponed to the slack season. In other words, the Irish worker was seldom wholly unemployed in the full sense of the word; during the slack season many of them switched back to household production.

A special form of household production was cottage industry, in which the final output was sold rather than consumed by the peasant. The decline of most cottage industries in the last decades before the famine should not be allowed to obscure their role in absorbing seasonal unemployment. The seasonal pattern of the demand for labor of textile industry and agriculture was sufficiently different to allow this complementarity between the two sectors.[4] In the south and in the midlands there was less cottage industry, but seasonal unemployment seems to have been less severe there as well, in part because of the higher proportion of grazing farms which provided steadier employment. Seasonal unemployment was also alleviated by seasonal migration. The seasonal demand patterns in England differed significantly from Ireland, where late June, July, and early August were the weeks of the least employment, whereas in England these were the weeks of haymaking, hoeing of turnips, preparation of composts, and so on (Great Britain, 1836b, Vol. XXXIII, p. 140). Fishing, collecting and processing of seaweed, lime-burning, and the tending of pigs, chickens, and other farm animals, also occupied poor cottagers and laborers in the off-season. The length of the labor day varied with the season, but *extended* periods during which the marginal product of labor was zero seem to have been rare. Unemployment was likely to have been more severe in urban than in rural areas. The urban workers were to a lesser extent self-employed, and the opportunities for domestic production of either household or marketed goods were much more limited. Seasonal unemployment occurred in urban areas as well. In Dublin, workers in the silk and sailcloth manufactures were out of work for two to three and a half months a year (Great Britain, 1840, Vol. XXIII, pp. 457, 469). Evidence of long-term unemployment (to be distinguished from pauperism, which usually pertained to the unemployable) is hard to find. Even in Drogheda, where "the redundant population ... is as great if not greater than in almost any other part of Ireland", it was still observed that if "any of 60 (employers) were to attempt to reduce his rate of wages below what the demand would enable him to give, the other 59 would be glad to get his weavers" (Great Britain, 1840, Vol. XXIII, pp. 471–2). The latter statement, if accurate, implies no excess supply of labor, that is, no involuntary unemployment.

Schultz (1964) has pointed out that the doctrine of zero marginal product of labor or "disguised" unemployment is inapplicable to the cases he has studied.[5] As he emphasizes, it is "untidy" to mix seasonal unemployment with the broader concept of zero marginal product in agriculture (ibid., p. 53 n.). In prefamine Ireland there was no Keynesian, nor much "structural" unemployment. Seasonal unemployment was a serious problem, and probably considerably worse than in most other Western European economies. None the less, it was of a secondary factor in Ireland's economic plight. The true problem of Ireland was not that its laborers, cottagers, and farmers did not work, but that their productivity was so low when they did.

What could explain this low productivity? I have argued above that low capital–labor ratios and backward technology must be assigned most of the blame. It is quite possible that additional factors were at work which reduced the effectiveness of the Irish worker. The most widespread explanations of the low productivity of Irish workers were their poor diet and their laziness. We have seen that, on the whole, diets in prefamine Ireland were satisfactory. There were, however, notable exceptions, which we shall examine in detail below.

Another interesting possibility is that the seasonal fluctuations in work effort directly affected the worker's ability to devote himself systematically to one task and, thus, impaired his productivity throughout the entire year. One observer wrote in 1840 that "under strong exciting circumstances the Irish peasant will work harder than the labourer of any other country; but his toil is neither steady nor continuous . . . the character of the peasant is rendered all the worse by the striking magnitude of the vicissitude . . . were the amount of labour already required more equally divided over the year . . . these evils would, in a great measure, be avoided" (Great Britain, 1840, Vol. XXIII, p. 439). In the absence of evidence this suggestion must remain speculative. But given our deficient knowledge of human motivation and incentives, the idea that steadiness of employment is associated with a "work ethic" which affects productivity can by no means be ruled out.

A further topic that has to be dealt with is the widespread assertion that the Irish were averse to hard labor. It is beyond doubt that in many cases allegations of this nature reflect mere racial prejudice. Not all statements in this spirit can be brushed off in this manner, however. Ricardo (1952, Vol. 1, p. 100) claimed that emigration would not raise labor income by much because the positive effects of rising wages would be offset by a decline in the supply of labor resultant from increased leisure consumption. Regardless of how seriously one wants to take this suggestion, it is telling that Ricardo apparently believed in such a degree of leisure preference as to imply that the supply curve of labor was downward-sloped. In any event the identification of their clearly biased source does not amount to the refutation of the allegations that the Irish were lazy. Is it possible that nations differ from each other in their basic attitudes to work and in the degrees at which they value leisure relative to income? The "Protestant work ethic" may not have been confined to Protestants, and was probably found to a higher degree in Japan and Belgium than in some Protestant countries. Nevertheless it is often alleged that differences in work attitudes can go a long way in explaining the economic success of some nations. Could the laziness of the Irish people have been responsible for Ireland's poor economic performance? Contemporary observers made this point quite explicitly. Bishop Berkeley noted already in 1749 that "there still remains in the natives of this island a remarkable antipathy to labour" (Berkeley, 1953, p. 235). For examples in the nineteenth century, see Foster (1847, p. 168), Kohl (1844, p. 40), and Wakefield (1812, Vol. 1, p. 586). Muggeridge cited one informant who computed that the Irish year, after all holidays had been subtracted, contained only 200 working days (Great Britain, 1840, Vol. XXIII, p. 570). Closely related to the high preference of the Irish for leisure was their reported acquiescence in their poverty. Foster (1847) maintained that the Irish tenant, once he had the certainty of subsistence before him, often ceased making any exertion beyond what was requisite to pay the rent. "It is because the poor Celt is content to put up with bad fare and worse clothing and shelter that he is made to put up with them" (p. 42). For a further summary of contemporary views of this type, see Lebow (1977).

As Hutchinson (1970, p. 516) has pointed out, condemnation of laziness was by no means directed exclusively at the Irish, and a non-Anglo-Saxon nation which escaped such condemnation was fortunate indeed. Yet even the Frenchman Beaumont (1839, Vol. 2, pp. 19–20) joined the chorus blaming the Irishman's "repugnance to work, apathy, and carelessness". Interestingly enough, Hutchinson himself subscribes to the view that the Irish lacked the "Protestant ethic". According to him, social values in Ireland were different from those in many of the other societies with which it was often compared. For the Irish, the distinction between "industriousness" and "indolence" was not equivalent to a distinction between virtue and vice. The view that a man not working was doing nothing of importance is a value created by industrial society. In Ireland dancing, music-making, celebrating, conversing, and other forms of social contact, constituted the "main purpose of living, and hence of working" (Hutchinson, 1970, p. 517). There is no question that social attitudes of the kind Hutchinson is referring to *could* have been of major importance. However, what was observed could either have been a different leisure preference function, or a lower point on the same function. In other words, it may have been the case that even at the same wage the Irish would have worked less than the Scottish or the Belgians, but it is equally possible that the only reason why they worked less was that labor paid less in Ireland. Blacker (1845, p. xxxi) maintained that "there is no unwillingness in an Irishman to work where sufficient remuneration is held out—but he will not work for nothing and he would be a great fool if he did".

A further difficulty with accepting Hutchinson's apparently plausible arguments is that there is abundant evidence that the Irish liked to consume more and better "material" goods, and that dancing and celebrations were a poor substitute for food and clothing. Indeed, it could well be argued that quality clothing, alcoholic beverages, and good food were strongly complementary to those social activities which the Irish valued so highly. For the parish of Racavan (Co. Antrim), for example, we read that the people were consuming increasing amounts of baker's bread (instead of potatoes), and smoked a lot of tobacco. The women displayed a desire for dressing up on Sundays, while the young men desired watches (OSM, box 15, file IV). Weld (1832, pp. 327–8) described a similar situation in the market in Strokestown, Co. Roscommon.

Related to but actually quite different from the issue of leisure preference were the arguments made by contemporaries that the Irish were both able and willing to work hard, but that somehow the economic system did not provide them with adequate incentives to do so. Tighe (1802, p. 507) wrote that "the spirit of industry seems only to want excitement: for themselves the labouring poor can make great exertions; but for others or when not closely overlooked, they work in a manner most languid and indolent". Some authors argued that it was far more efficient to make the workers perform task work since that tended to make them exert themselves much more (for example, Thompson, 1802, p. 347). At least as far as agriculture is concerned, the "incentive" theory encounters one serious logical difficulty. Ireland, on the whole, was predominantly an economy of self-employed tenant farmers. Demesne agriculture, in which the landlords or their agents were in complete control and in which labor was hired, was rare. Farmers and graziers employed some workers, but there seems to be little evidence that somehow the way in which they supervised and monitored their labor force was radically different than in England. Task work in agriculture, except perhaps during harvesting, was never easy due to the difficulties involved in measuring the quality of output. In any event, the weakest part of the Irish economy was the mass of self-employed smallholders and the notion that they somehow had insufficient incentive to work hard is difficult to accept. If terms such as "exertion" and "industry" mean increasing output by increasing labor input, there is little reason to doubt that tenants would have been able to keep their additional earning whether they had leases or not.

The observation that Irish peasants seem to have had little incentive to work hard can, however, be rationalized in terms of the simple model in which agricultural output per acre is a function of three inputs: labor, capital, and something which we may call entrepreneurship, information, or managerial effort. If the three inputs are complementary, both the average and the marginal product of input i will be a positive function of the amount of input j. I have argued above that a scarce supply of "entrepreneurship" was a factor in reducing the rate of return on capital investment and, thus, in part responsible for a low capital–labor ratio. This resulted in a low *average* product of labor, which is for all practical purposes synonymous with low income per capita. In addition, however, it reduced the *marginal* product of labor. As decisions on effort and exertion are made at the margin, the conclusion we can draw is that the same factors which explained poverty in the Irish countryside could have led to the indolence and languor that so many observers noted. The lack of an incentive to work hard was thus not a *cause* of low income, nor a *result* of it; it would be more accurate to say that *both* phenomena were functions of other variables, such as the productivity of labor, the capital–labor ratio, and the technologies used.

Hutchinson (1970, pp. 521–3) has proposed an entirely different argument, based on the assertion that Irish agriculture was founded to a large degree on cooperation and mutual aid. Hutchinson argues that this form of organization was an impediment to economic growth:

> Mutual aid . . . has an essentially static character. Work that is shared must be work that is familiar to those collaborating in it . . . Technological improvement, and its adoption if suggested, will be rare features of an economic life organized on such a basis ... The economic life of such a community, susceptible for reasons of economic and social stability to the fear of nonconformity, discourages a man from seeking an economic surplus beyond what is usual. (ibid., p. 522)

The Irishman who wanted to pursue material progress, consequently, ended up having to emigrate. Hutchinson's theory is ingenious, but he produces little evidence to support his case as an explanation of Ireland's tardy economic development. Except for one citation from a famous Irish author, there is no evidence to support that the slowness of technical change in Irish agriculture was due to a socially induced fear of success.[6] Actually, for many peasant societies, this harmonious picture of mutually supportive and loyal neighbors is not very consistent with the facts. Rogers (1965, p. 115) and Banfield (1958, pp. 110–11) point to the mutual distrust and suspiciousness in personal relations in backward rural areas. Much of this attitude was based on the view of the world as a gigantic zero-sum game, in which one person's gain is another's loss. Daniel O'Connell pointed out to the 1825 Select Committee that in Ireland "the lower classes are harsh and unfeeling towards each other in pecuniary matters" (Great Britain, 1825b, Vol. VIII, p. 51). Cooperation and mutual aid were limited to occasions in which the gains were indisputable. In Ireland they were especially important in regions where the rundale system, in which holdings were fragmented into noncontiguous strips, was still in effect.[7] In these regions agriculture was, indeed, most backward, but the reasons cited were typically not the ones proposed by Hutchinson but rather the continuous quarreling, litigation, and mutual sabotage which the scattering of holdings caused. Neighborhood effects, trespassing, and collective responsibility for rent payment were said to have extinguished the opportunities and the incentives for improvement in areas where rundale was the practice (Weld, 1832, pp. 472–3; Tighe, 1802, p. 420; Mason, 1814–19, Vol. 1, p. 604; Vol. 2, pp. 163, 367; Kennedy, 1847, p. 419). Almquist has maintained that rundale and scattered plots were not as inefficient as was thought traditionally

(Almquist, 1977, ch. 3). In this he joins a venerable tradition, but his discussion does not deal adequately with the negative externalities which peasants imposed on each other in rundale agriculture. In any case, there is no evidence that fear of neighbors' jealousy stopped smallholders or farmers from introducing improvements. The only form in which neighbors' sentiments could affect agricultural practices was through the resistance to consolidation discussed above. That resistance was, however, based on rational fears for one's own livelihood, and had little to do with either cooperation, or an attempt to impose conformity *per se* on ambitious peasants.

Outside agriculture, arguments dealing with the quality of Irish labor bear a different character. Wages in Irish industry were low, and it seems unlikely that higher fuel costs or the absence of certain economies of agglomeration fully offset the cost advantages implied by cheaper labor. Low wages should have provided Ireland with an opportunity to accumulate capital in the modern sector at a rapid rate. What is not known is whether the lower wages in Ireland led, in fact, to cheaper production costs, or whether they were in part a demand-induced phenomenon reflecting the lower productivity of Irish workers. Kane, for one, was unequivocal on this issue:

> That human labour can be obtained in this country on lower terms than almost any other in Europe is too well-known to require example ... this nominal cheapness is, however, by no means necessarily economy in final cost ... British labourers ... would probably be paid at least twice as much money per day but in the end the work would not cost the employer more. (Kane, 1845, p. 397)

Kane attributed the lower productivity of Irish workers primarily to malnutrition, bad education, and lack of proper incentives. One case in point is the experience of the Scottish entrepreneur A. Buchanan, who established a textile factory in Limerick in the late 1830s. Buchanan explicitly pointed out to the Assistant Commissioner of the Handloom Weavers Commission that he settled in the south of Ireland for the single reason that labor there was even cheaper than in Belfast. His experience is a vivid illustration of the validity of Kane's argument that low wages did not necessarily imply cheap labor. Finding the weavers themselves totally unfit to weave any but the very coarsest work, he established a factory in which boys were indentured to learn shawl-weaving according to the most modern principles. Buchanan recounted that he brought over from Scotland the best weavers and mechanics to teach the local boys the trade and maintain the equipment. His supply of labor left much to be desired however:

> The weaving trade in this country being hitherto in such a low state, there is a great reluctance on the part of the respectable persons to bind their children to it. Some of the best weavers I have are boys who were taken almost naked out of the streets. The great difficulty as

regards the people, has been to create a spirit of industry amongst them. (Great Britain, 1840, Vol. XXIII, p. 501)

R. M. Muggeridge, in the same report, wrote that

the monotony of continuous labour is that against which the volatile spirit of the Irish seems most to rebel . . . much of the inertness or idleness may be ascribed to the low and inadequate rate of wages in Ireland . . . Hence it is, though paradoxical it may seem, that 'cheap labour is dear labour'. (ibid., p. 570)

In neoclassical economic models problems such as "cheap labour is dear labour" do not mean much. The competitive firm faces a wage at which it hires workers. If workers are "better", or have more capital to work with, the market demand curve for them will be higher, and in general wages will be higher and/or more people will be employed. The "quality" of labor, in other words, is incorporated in the shape of the marginal revenue product curve and thus affects only the demand for labor, whereas the "cheapness" of labor refers to the equilibrium price. What contemporaries meant was that Irish workers were cheap, but because they were less productive, profits in Ireland were not necessarily higher.

Kane and others repeatedly pointed out that "cheap labour was dear" because poorly paid workers were poorly fed workers and were less productive. That wages and productivity seemed closely related was an observation made by many contemporaries. Arthur Young, when comparing France and England in the late 1780s, pointed out that

the vast superiority of English manufactures, taken in the gross, to those of France, united with this higher price of labour, is a subject of great . . . curiosity and importance, for it shows clearly, that it is not the nominal cheapness of labour that favours manufactures . . . Perhaps they flourish on this account, since labour is generally *in reality* the cheapest where it is *nominally* the dearest; the quality of the work . . . must, on an average, depend very much on the state of ease in which the workman lives. If he be well nourished and clothed . . . he will perform his work incomparably better than a man whose poverty allows but a scanty nourishment. (Young, 1929, p. 311; emphasis in original)

For Ireland, Young repeatedly made the same observation. In his *Tour* (1892), first published in 1780, he summarized his views as follows: "There is nothing more mistaken than dearness and cheapness of labour. Artizans and manufacturers of all sorts are as well paid by the day as in England; but the *quantity* of work they give for it, and in many cases the *quality* differ exceedingly. Husbandry labour is very low priced, but by no means cheap" (Vol. 2, p. 278; emphasis in original). In his appendix, written in 1785, he added: "Upon the article of low wages I lay little stress . . . cheap labour to the master and the benefit of his fabric, is not to be discovered by the day per diem; for skill, goodness of work +c. come into the question . . . in this mode of enquiry, 10s. per week will generally be found to be cheaper than 8s" (Vol. 2, pp. 306–7). It is noteworthy, however, that Young was little inclined to a diet-induced efficiency wage model, since he clearly realized the advantages of the cheap and healthy potato diet (Vol. 2, p. 43). Instead, he opted for the following explanation:

> granting their food to be the cause [of their low labor productivity], it decides very little against potatoes, unless they were tried with good nourishing beer instead of their vile potations of whisky . . . If their bodies are weak, I attribute it to whisky, not potatoes; but it is still a question with me whether their miserable working arises from any such weakness or from an habitual laziness. (Vol. 2, p. 44)

Later sources, however, do seem to implicate the potato. The baronial examinations concerning the "Earnings of labourers" appended to the Poor Law Inquiry of 1836 stated in a number of places that inadequate nutrition was to blame for the quality of Irish labor. For instance, in Co. Louth:

> Irish labourers do not work with the same steadiness or skill as the English which [is] fully accounted for by their want of both instruction and example and by the inferior quality and sometimes insufficient quality of their food . . . A very intelligent agriculturalist in this barony, who has also farmed in England, thought there was a difference of 30 percent in the work performed by an English and an Irish labourer, but that it arose from want of industry and steadiness in the latter, and not from that of strength and skill. (Great Britain, 1836b, Vol. XXXI, p. 29)

Robert Kane (1845, p. 398) agreed that labor productivity in Ireland was impaired by bad diet. Modern historians have proposed similar ideas. For Ireland, poor nutrition has been pointed to by Ó Gráda (1980c, pp. 10–11), and for England, by Freudenberger and Cummins (1976). Support for the undernourishment of Irish laborers can be found in appendix D to the Poor Law Inquiry, where more than twenty witnesses confirmed that productivity was affected by insufficient food (Great Britain, 1836b, Vol. XXXI, pp. 4–75).

Modern economic theory has formalized the nexus between wages and productivity and drawn from it some important conclusions. These "efficiency-wage" models were first formulated by Leibenstein (1957). In a brilliant chapter entitled "The theory of underemployment in densely populated backward areas", he laid the foundation of a model which was further refined and expanded by Mirrlees (1975), Stiglitz (1976), and Bliss and Stern (1978). A formal presentation of the model is not necessary here, but its relevance to the Irish experience warrants a discussion of its implications.

The "efficiency-wage" model works as follows. Higher wages make workers more productive but at the same time more expensive. It can be shown that there is some "optimal" wage at which a slightly higher wage increases labor costs more than it increases revenues, while at a marginally lower wage costs decline by less than revenues. At that optimal wage the employer wishes to hire a certain number of workers. The important point is that there is no mechanism that sets the number of workers that employers want to hire equal to the number of workers offering themselves for work at that wage. Only by fluke would these two quantities be equal to each other. The model still holds if the labor market is "implicit", which was the case to a large extent in Ireland where workers bid for land and wages were determined residually after rents had been paid.

If the quantity of labor demanded exceeds the quantity supplied, the optimum wage is unfeasible, and the employers will bid the wage up, competing for scarce labor. However, if the number of workers willing to work at the "optimal" wage exceeds the number of workers demanded, the wage level will not be forced downward by competition. Economists have long realized that asymmetry in wage movements may lead to involuntary unemployment. The difficulty has always been to specify conditions under which such an asymmetry would occur, assuming rational behavior on all sides. The "efficiency-wage" model provides this condition.

The model, thus, reproduces three essential features observed for pre-famine Ireland. First, the model shows how a long-term equilibrium can persist, in which some workers are unemployed (or landless) although they are desperate to obtain employment (or occupy land), while at the same time other workers—who are otherwise similar—are employed (or occupy land). Secondly, the model provides one more mechanism leading to the emergence of a "poverty trap", as Stiglitz (1976, p. 193) points out: a family has a low income, so it has low productivity; and because it has low productivity, it has a low income. Thirdly, the model provides an explanation of the often-sounded charge that rents were somehow "too high", and that landlords would make themselves, as well as everybody else, better off by reducing rents (see, for instance, Wiggins, 1844, pp. 47–59).[8] The "efficiency-wage" model thus seems to solve neatly a number of puzzles in the prefamine Irish economy. However, as we have stressed before, an economic model should not be accepted on those grounds alone. Closer examination indicates that there is room to doubt the usefulness of this model as a description of the Irish prefamine economy.

First, it seems likely that many Irish entrepreneurs and landlords did not maximize their long-term profits and allowed the competitive pressures of underemployed workers to bid the wage down level below the "optimum" level.[9] Muggeridge pointed out in his report on the linen industry that

> the existence of a redundancy of labour ... manifests itself in ... a competition for employment quite ... disastrous in its effect on wages ... Masters seeking labour will search out the market where it can be

obtained at the cheapest rate . . . [making] poverty subservient to the still further extension of its attendant evils . . . [by getting] work done at, what the weavers not inappropriately term, starvation prices. (Great Britain, 1840, Vol. XXIII, p. 565)

The "efficiency-wage" model thus seems neatly to solve a number of puzzles in understanding the operation of the prefamine economy. The difficulty in relying on this model lies in the low marginal cost of energy. Consider a typical adult male aged 25, weighing 145 lb. The difference in energy requirements between very light work (2 cal/min) and very heavy work (10 cal/min) at ten hours per day and fifty minutes of actual labor per hour comes to at most 4,000 calories a day. This estimate is an upper bound of the difference, but even so, provided the individual was willing to obtain the calories from potatoes, the amount of food needed (about 1 stone of potatoes) could be purchased for about 2–2½d. This sum is less than a fifth of the average daily earnings of an adult male. In actuality, potatoes were even cheaper than this, because potatoes purchased at the market were priced higher than the implicit price of potatoes produced by smallholders or cottiers on their rented plots or conacre land.

It should be noted, moreover, that much of this evidence pertains to a very distinct group of the most disadvantaged workers in the economy, namely, the occasional laborers employed for short periods during the summer months. These occasional laborers or "spalpeens" were at the very bottom of the Irish income scale, and in much worse condition than the cottiers or "bound" agricultural laborers. It would be unwarranted to generalize from this group to wider classes of the Irish working class (Thompson, 1802, pp. 339–40; Coote, 1801b, p. 57). Furthermore, the seasons in which nutrition seemed to be a constraint on the physical energy of workers consisted of the months of August and early September, when the previous year's crop of potatoes had been exhausted and the new crop was not yet in. As it happened, these months were by comparison a slack season for most regions (Great Britain, 1836b, Vol. XXXI, p. 37). Furthermore, the witnesses asked whether nutrition affected work effort and thus productivity were by no means unanimous (see, for example, ibid., pp. 58, 65, 70, 75), and many of the witnesses who stated that undernourished workers were unable to perform arduous tasks qualified their statements by "sometimes" or "it has been observed". It is, thus, not easy to conclude how general the phenomenon was. Contemporaries, especially Englishmen, often failed to understand the structure of Irish diets and how it was possible for them to subsist on nothing but lumpers and skim milk.[10] It is interesting in this respect that poor nutrition was always thought of as a result, and not a cause, of low wages. In any event, there is little evidence that a large proportion of Irish workers were suffering from any long-term malnutrition. Evidence on this point was provided in Chapter 2. Health translated itself into high productivity, as was indicated by the demand for the seasonal workers from Ireland employed in the Scottish harvest, who were "welcomed by the Scottish farmers everywhere for their powerful frames, inexplicably nurtured on potatoes and milk, and their strong right arms were freely and cheerfully put at the disposal of their employers" (cited by Handley, 1945, p. 45). The seasonal migrants came usually from the poorest rural regions in Ireland. In spite of these qualifications, the "efficiency-wage" model is a useful tool to examine the Irish economy, even if it applies only to a comparatively small section of the economy. More research on the nutrition of the people of Ireland in the century before the famine is necessary before we can evaluate the aptness of this model to this period. Extending the research of Cullen (1981a, 1981b) to the diets of the masses along the lines indicated for example by the work of Crawford (1981) would be a promising research strategy.

Not all Irish labor was cheap. One recurrent complaint among entrepreneurs was of "combinations" or trade unions trying to set higher wages and extract concessions out of entrepreneurs. Writers in the *laissez-faire* tradition of political economy were quick to blame the failure of Irish industry on combinations. Otway, for example, held them responsible for halting technical progress in all of the Irish textiles, and especially blamed them for the troubles in the silk industry (Great Britain, 1840, Vol. XXIII, pp. 454, 512). A shipmaster told the Poor Law Commission that Ireland was the dearest country in the world for labor; every description of artisan demanded at least a third more than in England. The combinations in the Irish towns led to a situation in which there were 200,000 artisans earning 3s 6d a day and a million agricultural workers earning 10d a day (Great Britain, 1836b, Vol. XXX, p. 527). Other contemporary writers joined in the condemnation of unions (see Senior, 1868, Vol. 1, pp. 39–41, 120; Pim, 1848, p. 155; Foster, 1847, p. 600). A twentieth-century writer, Webb (1913, pp. 42–51), held the Dublin combinations and the violent way in which they conducted business responsible for the decay of Dublin's industries in the first half of the nineteenth century. "That any industry could be prosperous under such a 'Reign of Terror' would be a matter of wonder", he wrote (p. 49). Kane (1845, pp. 403–6) presented a more balanced analysis of trade unions in Ireland, sensibly pointing out that there was no more combination in Ireland than in Britain, and that Irish combinations were receiving undue publicity because of the sensitive political situation in Ireland. Kane added, however, that Ireland was more vulnerable than Britain to strikes, because employers had a tighter cash flow so that temporary interruptions in the circulation of working capital were more acutely felt. While it would definitely be specious to blame Ireland's slow industrialization on its unions, it seems plausible that unions may have helped negate some of the advantages that low wages provided.[11]

Skilled labor in Ireland was expensive, too. Systematic evidence on wages by occupation is lacking, but fragments of information strongly support that point. In the early 1820s, for instance, Dublin wages of skilled workers were as high or higher than in London, which by itself already had higher than average wages for England (Great Britain, 1822a, Vol. XIII, pp. 1225–1632; Green, 1969, p. 96). One businessman sighed that the wages of skilled artisans were "out of all proportion" in Ireland (Great Britain, 1830, Vol. VII, p. 196). Kane (1845, pp. 397–402) concluded from a considerable amount of evidence that "skilled labour . . . is certainly dearer in this country [Ireland] than in Great Britain, whilst unskilled labour is much cheaper". Kane wondered whether on balance labor costs in Ireland were lower than in Britain and, uncharacteristically, found it difficult to provide an unambiguous answer, contenting himself to remark that the differences in labor costs between the two countries were much less than was "popularly thought".

One reason why skilled labor was more expensive relative to unskilled labor is that better-paid laborers were more mobile (since transportation costs to and from Britain were a smaller proportion of their income), and Irish employers had therefore to compete with Britain for their skilled labor (Great Britain, 1822a, Vol. XIII, pp. 1530, 1544). Moreover, many of the more skill-intensive industries, such as silk and calico printing employed English and Scottish workers who had superior skills, and their employers had to pay them premium wages to get them to come to Ireland (ibid., p. 1533). One result of the scarcity of skilled labor in Ireland was that some Irish industries were unable to produce at the quality standards required by the British market. A printer pointed out in 1822 that paper and labor in Ireland were cheaper than in Britain, but that none the less there was little chance for the Irish to penetrate the British book market because the books would not look well; Irish printing quality was simply inferior (ibid., p. 1227).

A further argument raised by contemporaries in this context is the operation of the Poor Laws in Britain (Great Britain, 1822a, Vol. XIII, pp. 1483, 1531). The notion that outdoor relief subsidized labor and, thus, reduced wages in Britain is by now pretty much discarded. But in Ireland, where unskilled wages, especially in urban areas, were at times little above the minimum required for food and fuel, manufacturers maintained that they faced a dilemma during slumps in demand: reducing wages during a decline in demand might conceivably lead to starvation among workers and their families, as there was no formal poor-relief system in Ireland before 1838. In England, the Poor Laws permitted employers to lay off workers and reduce wages during depressions without further qualms. Irish manufacturers complained that their inability to reduce wages during depressions was tantamount to an additional cost. It is hard to believe that such humanitarian considerations were of substantial consequence on the cost structure of Irish manufacturing, since unskilled workers in Ireland were cheap and easy to come by. The testimonies before the Revenue Commission (Great Britain, 1822a, Vol. XIII) should be taken with more than the customary grain of salt. The Commissioners were, after all, investigating whether removal of a protective tariff was advisable or not. Manufacturers, thus, had an obvious incentive to overstate their costs and the difficulties of producing in Ireland.

Why was there no more industrialization in Ireland in spite of low wages? In the Irish case, low wages of unskilled laborers did not necessarily imply cheap labor. Accepting for the moment the hypothesis that Irish workers were indeed less efficient, there remains the further puzzle of why this was so. Nutrition does not, I believe, provide the whole answer. Even less persuasive are arguments about religion, social impediments to success, Irish love for alcohol, or the quarrelsome nature of Irish workers. Nor can we seriously argue that productivity was low because Ireland failed to undergo an industrial revolution. After all, it is the latter that has to be somehow explained. The best-practice technology in manufacturing could be imported from Britain, and this technology defined the potential productivity of the labor employed in utilizing it. If actual productivity fell short of what could have been achieved, it was because the labor force was inadequately trained, organized, disciplined, and motivated.

One possible reason why Irish nonagricultural workers were less successful in producing cheap and well-made goods is that Irish data reflect only the people who remained behind and did not emigrate. If emigrants were in some sense self-selected and if they were the people most likely to succeed in working in factories, it follows that those who were left behind represented a "truncated distribution". Otway reported from Limerick that "those who could not obtain jobs ... left the country; and the class of weavers who remained in Limerick are, generally speaking, aged or infirm persons, who were not fit to emigrate, or to look for, or obtain other employment" (Great Britain, 1840, Vol. XXIII, p. 501). It is, therefore, necessary to examine the contribution that emigration made to Ireland's poverty.

Notes: Chapter 7

1 Even T. W. Schultz, who is in general suspicious of entrepreneurial failure as an explanation of economic backwardness and poverty, notes that absentee arrangements are in general inefficient because absentee parties cannot become sufficiently informed about the current operating decisions which are subject to spatial, seasonal, mechanical, and biological subtleties that cannot be routinized (cf. Schultz, 1964, pp. 118–19).

2 The professional rent-collectors were often recruited from the ranks of the younger sons of poorer gentlemen, many of whom had served in the army and thus acquired experience in "the habits of command". If they had any agricultural experience, it was by "attempting to cultivate a farm and failing in the attempt" (Smyth, 1844–9, Vol. 3, p. 84).

3 Lynch and Vaisey (1960, pp. 33–4) also speak of slumps and deflations, but they confine their analysis explicitly to the "maritime" part of the Irish economy.

4 During the late summer and early autumn many of the water mills ran dry at the same time when agricultural demand for labor was at a peak (cf. OSM, box 35, file II).

5 The concepts of "disguised unemployment" and "structural unemployment" as commonly used are more or less equivalent. Neither is Keynesian or seasonal in nature, and both depend instead on the insufficiency of nonlabor inputs, which causes the productivity of labor to be very low.

6 The quotation is from Brendan Behan: "If there is one vice the Irish really abhor, it is that of success."

7 Beside rundale, interhousehold cooperation was rare in prefamine Ireland. In Roscommon horses were sometimes bought jointly by several families (Weld, 1832,

p. 274). Peasants helped each other in the construction of their cottages and sometimes in the digging of peat. On the whole, however, the Irish cottagers and smallholders were largely self-sufficient in their own labor demand, and the larger farmers and graziers hired the extra work they needed.

8   A fourth predicton of the "efficiency-wage" model is that employers would attempt to pay their workers in food rather than in money (since money would be spent in part on family members who did not work for the employers). The wage data presented in Chapter 2 amply bear this out. In many parts of Ireland some workers were paid "with diet", and usually received 2d less per day if they were paid in provisions. This phenomenon, too, could be explained in alternative ways, however, and does not necessarily confirm the "efficiency-wage" hypothesis. Bardhan (1979) has pointed out that the efficiency wage hypothesis can also lead to results in which the outside wage earned by occasional laborers is inversely correlated with the land–labor ratio. Although his regressions, which are carried out at a disaggregated level, cannot readily be compared with the analysis at the county level in Chapter 3, it is possible that the key to the perverse coefficient on the labor–land ratio may be found in the "efficiency-wage" hypothesis. It should be added, however, that Bardhan proposes an alternative model to explain his findings, and that some of these do not square with the "efficiency-wage" hypothesis.

9   The outcome depends on several factors. The optimal wage is only relevant if the firms fully perceive the nexus between wages and productivity. If firms do not fully perceive the connection, they will pay lower wages and employ more (but less-productive) workers. Secondly, there is a question of the response of the unemployed. The model does not specify their response, and it cannot be ruled out that they will react violently, trying to force the firm to employ them. The conflict thus arising is a special case of the "labor-demand effect" introduced in Chapter 5. A further complication can arise if the effect of wages on productivity operates with a timelag. In that case it is likely that firms will pay lower wages than optimal simply because the high wage is like a form of nonspecific human capital, which means that the firm should be concerned with the worker quitting it to work for another firm once he has attained a higher level of productivity.

10   Otway wrote in his report to the Handloom Weavers Commission in 1840 that "the health and strength of Irishmen are referred to as a proof of the wholesomeness of the potatoes as an article of food; but the Irishmen are strong and healthy, not by, but in spite of, their food; it is to air and exercise . . . to their ignorance of comfort that they owe their health" (Great Britain, 1840, Vol. XXIII, p. 444).

11   One example of how unions affected labor costs is the rule enforced by Dublin workers at the local shipyards which disallowed using apprentices in shipbuilding. Consequently, labor costs in Dublin exceeded those in Whitehaven (Great Britain, 1825b, Vol. VIII, pp. 137–8).

Chapter 8

Emigration and the Prefamine Economy

(1) Introduction

From the point of view of sheer numbers, Irish emigration was the most significant outflow from any European country before 1850. While the famine reinforced and enhanced the exodus from Ireland, it did not start it. Connell (1950a, p. 27) estimated that during 1780–1845 1·75 million Irishmen left their country. Connell's estimate is at best an informed guess, since usable data for the years before 1815 are unavailable. Adams's classic work on emigration before the famine (Adams, 1932) allows us, however, to estimate with some accuracy the dimensions of the phenomenon in the three decades between the end of the Napoleonic Wars and the famine. Total emigration to North America and the British colonies was estimated by Adams at about 1 million. Fairly reliable data for the years 1825–45 show the total number of emigrants to North America in these years to have been about 825,000.[1] In the late 1820s and early 1830s Canada accounted for two-thirds of the emigrants to North America, but after 1835 the USA became the preferred destination, and absorbing almost three-fifths of Irish overseas emigrants. The estimation of the magnitude of the Irish exodus is complicated by a large emigration to Britain. Irish emigrants to Britain were not registered in any port, and it is therefore difficult to form a precise idea on their numbers. The only figure available is the estimate of the British Census of 1841 of the number of persons born in Ireland residing in Great Britain. The British Census (Great Britain, 1843, Vol. XXIV, p. lxxxix) reported this number as 419,256. Since Irish emigrants lived predominantly in urban and thus high-mortality areas, the number of emigrants to Great Britain almost certainly exceeded 500,000. A lower-bound estimate of total emigration from Ireland between Waterloo and the famine would thus be around 1·5 million, or about 0·7 percent annually.[2]

What were the economic effects of Irish emigration? For the purpose of this study, the most pertinent question is what the effects of emigration were on those who remained behind. By 1845 the population of Ireland had already become what Verrière has aptly named a "residual population". The question we have to face is to what extent can we explain the failures of the Irish economy by the economic impact of a large outflow of population?

On a purely abstract level it is possible to answer that question with a certain degree of precision. In the simplest model in which output is produced by two factors of production one of which is mobile ("labor") and the other is not ("land"), emigration is tantamount to a decline in the input of the variable factor. While it is true that a decline in the quantity of labor will raise its marginal product and therefore presumably its price, it has been shown by Berry and Soligo (1969) that emigration under these assumptions typically leads to a decline to the average income received by those who do not emigrate. The intuitive explanation of this result lies in the fact that the income received by landlords declines as a result of emigration by more than the increase in income earned by those workers who remain behind. Thus the totality of the nonemigrants suffer a decline in income per capita, although that movement masks a further redistribution of income in favor of the non-emigrating workers.[3] A simple depiction of the model is presented in Figure 8.1. Consider the effect of the emigration of $L_1 - L_2$ workers. Before emigration, the income per capita of those who will not migrate is total income ($0KE_1L_1$) minus the rectangle $ME_1L_2L_1$ divided by $L_2 + H$, where H is the number of non-migrating landlords. After migration has taken place, the income earned by the same $L_2 + H$ non-emigrants is $0KE_2L_2$. Thus, there is a deadweight loss in income to the economy of E_2ME_1, which equals the profits or surplus value generated by the emigrants prior to their departure.

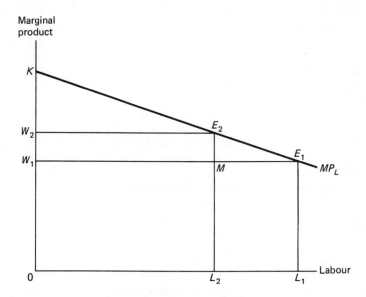

Figure 8.1   *Emigration and the income of non-emigrants*

The assumptions behind the simple model are rather restrictive. Berry and Soligo also analyze the model in which the emigrants own some of the "nonlabor factor". In this case the result depends on whether they take the nonlabor with them: if the nonlabor factor is capital and it is taken with the emigrants, the average income of those who remain behind will decline, unless the capital–labor ratio is by fluke unchanged. In that case, income is unchanged by considerations of constant returns to scale, since such an economy would be a perfect miniature replica of itself, and would therefore—in the absence of scale effects—not experience change in anybody's income. However, if the capital–labor ratio is altered (in either direction) due to the migration of "bundles" of capital and labor, income of nonemigrants will decline. If the emigrants leave the capital behind (but take the ownership of it with them), it is possible that the income of those remaining behind increases after emigration if the amount of capital owned by the emigrants is sufficiently large (see Berry and Soligo, 1969, pp. 783–4 for a precise demonstration).

Further elaborations show that as the simplifying assumptions of the model are relaxed, some of the unambiguous conclusions of Berry and Soligo lose their sharpness. Carlos Rodriguez (1975) demonstrated that in the life-cycle model of saving, the emigration of low-savers could lead to an increase in the incomes of those remaining. In a realistic life-cycle model, however, this is a minor quibble, since emigrants tend to be over-whelmingly in the age brackets in which life-cycle savings are high. The emigration of low-savers in a life-cycle model implies a massive outflow of infants and old people, which is not a realistic scenario. Usher (1977) qualified Berry and Soligo's conclusion from a different angle: since much of the property in any country is publicly owned, emigration, by increasing the demand for the services of public property in the country of destination and reducing them in the country of origin, has a negative effect on the welfare of the original inhabitants of the former and a positive effect on the nonemigrating inhabitants of the latter.

Perhaps the most effective argument against the adoption of the conclusions of the Berry–Soligo model in the context of prefamine emigration from Ireland is that while emigration may have reduced average income per capita in some cases, the eagerness with which some landlords supported emigration suggests that the simple one-product economy is not realistic in this context. Introducing complications such as the pasturage vs tillage conflict discussed in Chapter 5 forces us to abandon the static equilibrium model. Moreover, even on the Berry–Soligo assumptions it is not clear that emigration increases poverty defined as vulnerability to famines. While in their model emigration reduces total income per capita of the nonemigrants, it also involves a redistribution of income from landlords to workers. Such a redistribution implies a reduction in the inequality of income distribution and, thus, a decline in the danger of food scarcities. Clearly, income per capita is a misleading measure of the welfare of an economy in this context.

None the less, the effects of emigration on the Irish economy were far-reaching. Verrière (1979, p. 233) has stated flatly that "by the constant leakage which it exercised on the population, emigration has immiserized the country". This view, which was also held by some of the most perspicacious contemporaries (for example, Pim, 1848, p. 164;

Foster, 1847, pp. 275–84; Blacker, 1846, p. 7), requires both theoretical and empirical elaboration.

Perhaps it is useful to start with one mechanism which was probably *not* important here. Verrière suggests that emigration constituted a hemorrhage which kept demand at a low level, depriving the economy of an indispensable stimulus. It is not possible to rule out the operation of such "demand-side" mechanisms altogether, but the likelihood that they played an important role is small. A conclusion that a decline in demand caused a decline in income per capita must rest on unsubstantiated assumptions linking technological progress to local market size, or even more implausible assumptions about scale economies on the level of the (Irish) economy. Some of the problems involved in the role of demand are discussed—in the context of the British industrial revolution—in Mokyr (1977).

Three supply-related effects linking emigration to retarded economic development can be distinguished. Of the three, the *life-cycle effect* is probably the most readily measurable. The life-cycle effect is based on a simple but powerful model which views the economic history of a society as a series of intergenerational transfers. The youngest members of society are fed, clothed, and housed for years before they start producing. This transfer is a loan, not a gift, because when the children reach a certain age they start to repay their debt to society. They do this both by supporting in their turn their own children and by supporting their old parents, if these have survived. Finally, upon reaching old age, individuals may collect a "pension" from their own children.

Emigration will leave this process undisturbed only if the age distribution of emigrants is identical to that of the entire pre-emigration population, an assumption clearly violated in nineteenth-century emigration, which consisted predominantly of young men and women (Thomas, 1973, p. 57; Taylor, 1971, pp. 32, 36, 62). Economic historians have tried to explain US economic growth in the nineteenth century by the influx of "instant adults" from Europe. The earliest attempts to measure these effects were carried out by Friedrich Kapp in the 1860s (Kapp, 1870, pp. 144–7; Mayo-Smith, 1890, pp. 103–5). The most serious of the attempts to measure the benefits the American economy obtained from immigrants are contained in the seminal works of Paul J. Uselding (1971) and Neal and Uselding (1972). The precise measurement of these gains is hard, and the work has been criticized (Gallman, 1977). The important point to note here is that these gains were essentially a transfer payment from Europe to the USA and not a net world-wide improvement. For every adult worker whose cost of upbringing was not paid by the USA, there was a child reared in Europe who did not live his productive life there.[4] For postfamine Irish migration, the aggregate age distribution of the original population at the beginning of the decade and of the emigrants are presented in Table 8.1.

Table 8.1 demonstrates that during 1861–1911 Irish emigrants came predominantly from the 15–35 age brackets. Clearly, a high degree of clustering in these ages in the period before the famine would be a possible cause of failures in capital formation in the context of a life-cycle model. But how high is "high" here, and what kind of data exist that will allow us to estimate the cost of emigration to the prefamine economy? In Section 2 of this chapter a simple method of computing such costs is developed and then utilized to compute them for the period 1820–48.

Table 8.1   *Age Distribution of Emigrants and Total Population, 1861–1911 (Percentages)*

Decade	Under 15 In population	Emigrants	15–24 In population	Emigrants	25–34 In population	Emigrants	35 and over In population	Emigrants
1861–71	32·8	14·8	22·2	44·4	13·1	25·1	31·9	15·7
1871–81	35·4	14·4	18·3	46·3	13·5	26·8	32·8	12·5
1881–91	35·1	13·7	20·0	57·2	12·2	18·5	32·7	10·6
1891–1900	32·5	7·8	21·1	60·0	12·7	23·7	33·7	8·5
1901–11	30·4	8·9	20·6	59·2	14·7	24·1	34·3	7·8

Sources: Emigration: Thomas, 1973, p. 74; population: Vaughan and Fitzpatrick, 1978, pp. 78–81.

The second effect may be termed the *labor-quality effect*. Emigrants were different from the rest of the population in many respects other than their age. After all, the majority of young men and women in pre-famine Ireland did not emigrate. It is hard to believe that those who did emigrate were selected by a random process, so that on average they were not different in their personal characteristics from those who remained behind.

It seems reasonable to suppose that the labor force, rather than consisting of one homogeneous lump of labor, consisted of a number of "noncompeting groups" which were complementary in the production process. For instance, assume that the economy produced with the help of three factors of production, labor, capital, and entrepreneurship. The three factors are complementary, that is, an increase in any of the three raises the marginal product of the other two. The emigration of entre-preneurs, real or potential, could be a factor in the decline of the marginal product of labor, and thus in the impoverishment of Ireland. The same personal characteristics which made for successful entrepreneurs increased the chances for an individual to emigrate.

What were these characteristics? Emigration in the early nineteenth century involved considerable risk, a definite postponement of consumption in the present and the immediate future for the sake of higher earnings in the remote future (possibly only enjoyed by another generation), and in any event considerable physical and emotional effort. The emigrants were, thus, likely to be persons whose utility functions were different from the rest of the population in three crucial respects: they were less risk-averse, had a lower subjective rate of time preference, and a lower preference for leisure. This is precisely the stuff entrepreneurship is made of. By removing the resourceful, the ingenious, the energetic, the ambitious, and the most sophisticated members of the labor force, emigration could have removed a larger than proportional portion of the potential economic leadership. We can think of this leadership as a group complementary to the bulk of the labor force.

The hypothesis that emigration removed the "cream" of Irish society in this sense sounds plausible, but can we test it? The answer in general has to be negative, since utility functions are not directly observable. Looking at the degree of success Irish emigrants experienced in the countries of destination is not a completely fair test either, since it is not possible to isolate the effect of a different economic environment from the effects of the characteristics of the emigrants. Only in very indirect and approximate ways can we attempt to measure the ways in which the emigrants were different from the population at large. The techniques utilized for this measurement and some results are the subject of Section 3.

The third way in which emigration affects the economic condition may be termed the *human-capital effect*. In some respects it overlaps with the labor-quality effect, but it differs from it in that it looks only at the past investment embodied in the emigrants which is taken with them overseas (Grubel and Scott, 1977, ch. 3). Since human capital is complementary to unskilled labor, the emigration of skilled workers was likely to reduce the marginal product of the workers who stay behind. Moreover, to the extent that nonemigrants (parents and artisans) paid for the investment in the skills of the emigrants, they will in all likelihood sustain a loss. Direct information on the formal education and the literacy of emigrants is not available. Instead, occupational data will be used. A summary of the results of this test will be presented in Section 4.

All three of the above effects are based on the observation that emigrants differ in some crucial way from the rest of the population. In other words, if the characteristic x is positively correlated with the probability of emigrating, the residual population will experience a declining level of its average endowment of x. In principle, a declining level of a characteristic x in the population as a result of emigration could affect income (or any other variable measuring economic performance) in two ways. The first is the purely statistical fact that by looking at the "residual" population, we are observing a truncated distribution of x, that is, a distribution with more observations removed from the upper tail than from the rest. The mean value of x in the truncated distribution is, therefore, by definition lower than for the pre-emigration population. If x is correlated with income, emigration will reduce it. Secondly, the influence of x on income is not independent of the values of x. For example, positive externalities may cause the productivity of a "mediocre worker" to be higher if a "good worker" is present, so that the emigration of workers with high values of x would reduce the incomes of those who remained behind.

To see the differences among the three effects, consider the example of the emigration of a hypothetical 18-year-old cabinet-maker. At age 18 it is clear that the past consumption of the individual exceeds his past production. He still owes society a debt equal to the difference between the total value of his past consumption and his past production. If he was to live out his life in Ireland, the two sums would be equal over the lifetime of an average person who has survived to age 18. In general, the expected surplus which an individual aged i will produce over the rest of his expected lifetime equals the deficit he has accumulated by living up to age i. It is this surplus of which residual society is deprived when he emigrates that we define as the life-cycle effect. Secondly, assume that the dexterity required to become a cabinet-maker is distributed normally over the population, and that this individual was heavily endowed with this scarce talent. Society may thus be able to replace him, but if his replacement is not as well-endowed as he is with the natural abilities needed for cabinet-making, a loss is incurred. This is the labor-quality effect. Thirdly, if the individual has paid for his training himself, his emigration will not cause a long-term loss to society, but there will still be a short-run loss even if society can replace him with an equally able craftsman who will pay for his own training, because of the time-lag involved in training the replacement. During that lag the stock of human capital is below equilibrium level, so that the earnings of complementary factors of production are temporarily reduced. This loss is part of the human-capital effect. If the training is not paid for in full by the artisan himself during the apprenticeship period, the unpaid fraction of the training cost has to be added to the human-capital effect.[5]

(2) The Life-Cycle Effect

In what follows I shall try to develop a method by which to compute the economic costs of emigration incurred by the country of origin on account of the age distribution of the emigrants. Since the argument below is unavoidably somewhat technical, a brief verbal exposition may be useful here. In every society some people work and support those who are too young or too old to work (we ignore those who do not work for other reasons). Emigration removes proportionally more people who work than do not work. Consequently, there are fewer workers among those who remain and thus income per capita is lower. Because the labor participation rates are unknown, a slightly different but logically equivalent approach will be taken here. This "life-cycle" approach postulates that the family operates like a savings bank: before they reach working age, people "borrow". Once they begin to work, they repay these loans. Once the childhood loan has been fully paid back, they start to save for retirement.

To make this approach work, we have to assume that society is in a "steady state", so that each individual pays back into the bank an amount equal to the childhood loan he receives plus the pension he expects to draw later on. These sums have to be weighted by survival probabilities, of course, since not all children become working adults and not all working adults will live to enjoy retirement. For that reason, each person who reaches adulthood actually pays in more than he receives, because he has to pay for the many children who die before reaching working age. The "steady state" means, first, that if no emigration occurs, there is zero net accumulation per capita, and secondly, that the cost of emigration to those who remain behind is determined by the difference in age structure of the emigrants as a group and the original, pre-emigration, population. For example, the emigration of a group of 20-year-olds will impoverish those who stay behind. There are two alternative ways to see why this is so: one is to realize that the emigrants will not yet have fully repaid the loans they received while children (plus the "survival premium" which reflects the rearing costs of those members of their cohort who died before age 20). The other way is to note that the emigration of members of the prime working age leaves the others with a higher "dependency ratio".

Ages are easier to observe than participation ratios, and the "life-cycle approach" in general is numerically easier to deal with. The basic idea is to devise a function which I shall call β. This function translates ages into costs. For each emigrant aged x, there is a number $\beta(x)$ which is the cost of that person emigrating to some subset of those who remain behind. The function β is constructed in such a way that it is zero for a newborn, then starts to rise as the "debt" accumulates. At some age the individual joins the labor force and starts to pay back his debt. When the rearing costs are fully paid back, β is zero once again and then becomes negative. The negative value of β reflects the emigration of people who will not claim their pensions, although they have already contributed to the "pension fund". The functional form of β is of course arbitrary, and alternative forms of the life-cycle model could be experimented with.

The algorithm is based on a large number of simplifying assumptions, which are necessary if the exercise is to remain manageable. First, the difference between males and females will be ignored here, although there were clearly differences in the time-pattern of male and female life-cycle savings. Secondly, it will be assumed that prior to emigration, population was not growing and that there was no net accumulation of capital. Both these assumptions are obviously unrealistic, but relaxing them would greatly complicate the computations without significantly changing the overall results.

The assumption about the stationary state implies that the expected consumption and the expected value of output over a lifetime are equal at birth. Let A be the age of an individual in question, $C_A(A)$ his annual consumption during the year he is aged A, and $Q_A(A)$ his annual production during that year. The stationary state assumption thus implies:

$$\sum_{A=0}^{\infty} P_A (Q_A - C_A) = 0, \qquad (8.1)$$

where P_A is the probability that the individual will survive to age A. Note that we do not discount future consumption or production. It has been argued convincingly by David and Temin (1976, pp. 197–8) that discounting is not appropriate in this framework. The life-cycle model implies that net savings per year $Q_A - C_A$, are negative at first, then become positive, and finally become negative again. Now define $\beta_A(A)$, the cost incurred by society due to the emigration of an individual aged A as:

$$\beta_A = \sum_{i=A}^{\infty} P_i | A (Q_i - C_i).$$ (8.2)

Equations 8.1 and 8.2 jointly imply that $\beta(0) = 0$, while $\beta(1)$ is positive even though a 1-year-old consumes more than he produces. The reason for this is that a 1-year-old has consumed one year's worth of goods and not produced anything. Since the expected consumption flow and the expected production flow for his *entire* life are equal, his expected future savings are positive. It is this amount that society loses when he emigrates. Obviously, for a 2-year-old child this cost is higher, since not only has he consumed for two years instead of one, but his consumption in his second year is likely to be higher than in his first year. Thus:

$$\beta(1) = C_1$$ (8.3)
$$\beta(2) = C_1 + C_2.$$ (8.4)

Assume now that on average a person enters the labor force at age 15. Hence:

$$\beta(15) = \sum_{i=0}^{15} C_i.$$ (8.5)

The precise pattern of consumption over childhood is not known. The simplifying assumption employed here is:

$$C_i = i, \text{ and therefore } \beta(A) = C_1 + C_2 + \ldots C_A = \frac{A(A+1)}{2}.$$ (8.6)

The unit of measurement of β, thus, becomes the annual consumption of a 1-year-old. The cost of emigration of any individual aged less than 15 is thus:

$$\beta_A(A) = \sum_{i=0}^{A} i \text{ for } A \leq 15.$$ (8.7)

At age 15 the individual has accumulated a "debt" to society which can be calculated by substituting $A = 15$ into equation 8.7, which yields $\beta = 120$. If he were to emigrate at that age, the cost to society would be maximized. At age 15 he starts to pay off his debt by supporting his parents and/or raising his own children.[6] At some age A^* the debt is fully paid off. Keeping in mind that equation 8.1 means that the lifelong value of net savings is also zero, it follows that:

$$\sum_{i=A^*}^{\infty} P_i (Q_i - C_i) = 0.$$ (8.8)

In other words, A^* is defined in such a way that the expected future stream of production from A^* on is equal to the expected future stream of consumption from A^* on. Society incurs neither loss, nor benefit, from the emigration of an individual aged A^*. The emigration of an individual aged older than A^* constitutes a net benefit to society, although that individual may still be highly productive and frugal at the time of his emigration. What counts is that the *expected* value of his consumption for the rest of his life exceeds the *expected* value of his future production. The framework is conveniently summarized in Table 8.2.

Table 8.2   *Consumption, Production, and Savings in a Life-cycle Model*

Age	Current consumption (C_A)	Current production (Q_A)	Current savings $(Q_A - C_A)$	Expected value of future savings $\sum\limits_{i=A}^{\infty} P_i \mid A\,(Q_i - C_i)$
0	0	0	0	0
$0 < A \le 15$	+	0	–	+
$15 < A < A^*$	+	+	Probably +	+
A^*	+	+	+	0
$A^* < A$	+	+ or 0	?	–

In order actually to calculate β, we must make one further assumption, which is that after age 15 the "debt" to society (β) declines linearly from its peak of 120 units. Under that assumption, once we know the value of A^*, $\beta_A(A)$ can be computed readily for any given A. Write β as:

$$\beta_A(A) = Z - YA \text{ for } A > 15. \tag{8.9}$$

Then:

$$Y = \frac{120}{A^* - 15} \tag{8.10}$$

and

$$Z = \frac{120A^*}{A^* - 15}. \tag{8.11}$$

The value of A^* is obtained by regarding the Irish population of 1821 as a "pre-emigration" population with the properties stated earlier. Recall that we have assumed that this population is not growing, so that the only reason why cohort $i + 1$ is smaller than cohort i is mortality. Let n_0, $n_1 \ldots$ be the sizes of the cohorts. It can then readily be shown that:

$$\frac{\sum\limits_{A=0}^{\infty} n_A \beta_A}{\sum\limits_{A=0}^{\infty} n_A} = 0. \tag{8.12}$$

To prove 8.12, note that 8.2 and 8.1 jointly imply $\sum\limits_{A=0}^{\infty} P_A \beta_A = 0$, that is, the sum of the βs weighted by the corresponding survival probabilities equals 0. Since by definition the size of each cohort aged A, n_A, equals $n_0 P_A$, equation 8.12 becomes

$$\frac{n_0 \sum\limits_{A=0}^{\infty} P_A \beta_A}{\sum\limits_{A=0}^{\infty} n_A} = 0. \tag{8.13}$$

The intuition behind 8.12 is that if a sample from the population whose age structure is identical to that of the entire population emigrates, the cost imposed on those who remain behind is zero. Based on equation 8.12, and the data for the ns from the 1821 Census,[7] the values of Y and Z in equations 8.10 and 8.11 were calculated. $A*$ was estimated by an iterative procedure as that value of A which satisfies 8.12. This value of the "break-even" age turns out to be approximately 31.

How can we calculate the cost of Irish emigration before 1845? By construction, any random sample of individuals taken from a population similar to the Irish one as measured by the 1821 Census should have such an age structure as to set the expected value of $\sum_A \beta_A(A)$ equal to zero. Any nonrandom sample, such as Irish immigrants arriving in New York, could be tested for the hypothesis $\sum_A \beta_A = 0$. If we were to find that these values were in fact significantly different from zero (and positive), we could conclude that those who remained behind had sustained a social loss due to the emigration process (Figure 8.2).

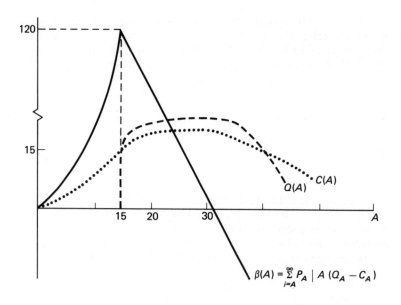

Figure 8.2   *The behavior of the main variables over an individual's lifetime*

The assumptions concerning the functional form of the $\beta(A)$ function may appear unnecessarily arbitrary. However, experiments with other forms show that as long as the constraints embodied in equation 8.12 are preserved, the estimates of the total social losses of emigration to those who stay behind are not very sensitive to the exact specification of the functional form. For instance, the loss function could be approximated by a fourth-degree polynomial, which produces similar orders of magnitude although some of the parameters, such as $A*$, differ to some extent (Mokyr and Ó Gráda, 1982b).

Before turning to the calculation, a rough computation can be carried out on the assumption that the only mechanism which changed the age distribution during 1821–41 was emigration. Since the aggregate group (emigrants plus nonemigrants) satisfies $\sum_A \beta_A = 0$, it must be true that if for the emigrating group $\sum_A \beta_A > 0$, then for the nonemigrating population, we should find $\sum_A \beta_A < 0$. Applying equations 8.2 and 8.9 to the entire population of Ireland in 1841 results in a value of $\Sigma\beta_A$ of about –29,000,000, or about –3·55 per capita. The negative sign implies that during 1821–41 Ireland lost resources.

We cannot, of course, be sure that the change in age structure during 1821–41 and the concomitant rise in the dependency rate, were entirely the result of emigration. The phenomenon observed could be explained by a decline in the age-specific mortality rate affecting especially those aged over 31. It is also conceivable that a sudden peak in birth rates at the end of the eighteenth century led to an abnormally large contingent of prime-aged workers by 1821, while 1841 represents a more normal age distribution. The abnormally large proportion of workers aged 15–30 in 1821 had by 1841 become the cohort 35–50, swelling the ranks of "dependents". In the absence of information about trends in birth or age-specific death rates, it is not possible to reject such objections against this simple calculation of the costs of emigration.

Values of β as well as other pertinent information about prefamine emigration can be obtained from the passenger lists of vessels arriving in New York harbor. From 1 January 1820 until mid-June 1897 the captain or master of each ship arriving in the USA was required by law to submit to the collector of customs in his port of destination a list of all passengers aboard his ship. Transcripts of the New York original lists were utilized to draw a sample of Irish emigrants arriving in New York. For each of the emigrants, the following information was provided: name, age, sex, occupation, and country of origin. The latter in most cases simply denoted "Ireland" but in some ships the captain noted the county and sometimes even the town or parish of origin. More details on the passenger lists and their value as a historical source can be found in Erickson (1981) and Mokyr and Ó Gráda (1982b).

The technique by which the Irish Emigrant Sample was constructed was as follows: every tenth ship listed in the passenger lists was included if it contained Irish emigrants. In addition, all ships containing Irish emigrants which listed the county of origin within Ireland were included in the sample. The years covered in the sample are 1820–48, containing a total of 30,535 emigrants. It is not easy to say how representative this sample is of Irish emigration as a whole. It seems reasonable to assume that it is representative of Irish emigration to the USA, but as noted above the USA absorbed only about a third of total Irish emigration. Of the emigrants who went to Canada, a large number ultimately ended up in the USA, but since most of these emigrants arrived by land, they could not be traced. The fare to Canada was considerably cheaper, which would imply that the New York emigrants were likely to have been better off than those who went to Canada. The same line of reasoning holds *a fortiori* for emigrants to Britain. There also seems to have been a regional differentiation with emigrants from Ulster tending more than others to prefer Canada as their destination.

Table 8.3   *Values of β, 1820–48 (All Emigrants)*

Period	Number of emigrants	Average value of β	Median age	%age aged 16–34
1820–4	628	41·07	21·3	70·0
1825–9	1,921	32·56	22·1	67·3
1830–4	3,968	38·75	21·4	71·6
1835–9	6,904	43·93	20·9	73·8
1840–4	7,657	38·42	21·3	70·2
1845–6	3,295	46·31	20·3	72·1
1847–8	6,162	38·97	21·3	66·7
Total	30,535	40·35	21·7	70·5

Source: New York port sample of Irish emigrants.

Some summary statistics about the age composition of Irish emigrants to New York are contained in Tables 8.3 and 8.4. The average value of β for the period as a whole was approximately 40. If we multiply this figure by the total emigration from Ireland, we arrive at a loss of 60 million units. This is twice as high as the 29 million estimate derived from the 1841 population age distribution. The cost imposed on Ireland by emigration on account of the life-cycle effect alone seems, thus, quite substantial.

Table 8.4   *Values of β by Province of Origin*

Province	Emigrants	Average value of β
Ulster	4,374	41·54
Leinster	3,417	41·89
Munster	1,648	38·00
Connaught	1,671	43·65
Not available	19,425	39·74
Total	30,535	40·35

Source: As Table 8.3.

How much was 60 million "units of β"? One way of determining that is by way of comparison. Applying the formula to the 1841 age distribution corrected for age-heaping, we observe that the cost which would be imposed on the economy through the life-cycle effect of *all* persons aged 20–24 was approximately 54 million units of β. Similarly, the values of β associated with all persons aged 15 and 16 was 49 million. Therefore, the drain upon the Irish economy in 1821–45 was roughly equivalent to the loss sustained if all persons aged 15–16 or all persons aged 20–24 had left on one day in 1841. A money value cannot be readily associated with this loss, but on the basis of a few heroic assumptions the orders of magnitude involved can be approximated. Income per capita before the famine was approximately £15. Infants and children consumed, however, much less than adults. Assume that over the first fifteen years of his life an average child consumes on average only one quarter of the national average. This would imply a cost of £60 per child. To that we should add the forgone earnings of the mother. All in all, a cost of £90 to rear a child to age 15 seems reasonable. The only estimate of child-rearing cost for a comparable society in this period is the figure cited by Kapp (1870, p. 146) from the studies of Ernst Engel. Engel estimated that in Prussia the cost of rearing a child from birth to age 15 was about 750 thaler, which comes to about £115. A gap of about a third between prefamine Ireland and Prussia in the 1860s seems not unrealistic. Since $\Sigma\beta = 120$ at age 15, the value of β is approximately 15s on these assumptions. This would set the cost of emigrants at around £40–£45 million over a period of twenty-five years, or $1\cdot5$–2 percent of personal income. The net drain from Ireland was somewhat smaller, because remittances from overseas partially offset the outflow of "life-cycle capital". Prefamine remittances were perhaps larger than is sometimes supposed and may have amounted to £100,000–£125,000 annually in the prefamine years (Ó Gráda, 1981, p. 22). Some proportion of these remittances were intended for the purpose of financing the crossing of relatives and thus cannot be considered as transfers to the Irish economy (for example, see Pim, 1848, p. 165). All in all, life-cycle effects of emigration imposed a not inconsiderable drain on Irish resources, especially toward the end of the period, when the number of emigrants increased rapidly and the average value of β exceeded 40.

(3) The Labor-Quality Effect

Were emigrants better workers than nonemigrants of equal age and skill? The best-informed and most insightful contemporary observers certainly thought so. William Blacker, a land agent and agricultural specialist, wrote that emigration

> far from being a remedy for the evils of Ireland [is] one direct and influential cause of their continuance. It is the wealthy, the industrious ... the young, the healthy and the strong who swell the emigrant list ... If these were located in this country instead of ... out of it, the result would be ... progress, comfort, content, manufactures, employed and improved agriculture. (Blacker, 1846, p. 7)

The Poor Law Commission in appendix F to their report (Great Britain, 1836b, Vol. XXXIII) included many remarks on the character and motives of emigrants. One witness remarked that "unfortunately for Ireland [the emigrants] have generally been the most industrious, well-behaved, and in most cases the most monied of their class, thus leaving the worst and all the riff-raff as an increased burden on the country" (p. 134). The emigrants included many of the Limerick Palatinates (p. 138), whose industriousness and well-being had astonished both Arthur

Young (1892, Vol. 2, pp. 378–9) and the Halls (1825–40, Vol. 2, pp. 250–4).[8] The replies to the standard questions distributed by the Poor Law commissioners are replete with remarks on the valuable qualities of the emigrants. The emigrants were "young men and women of industrious habits" (p. 500); "mostly labourers, tradesmen and young women . . . in a word, the labour and enterprise of the country" (p. 544); "generally exemplary for their industry and conduct" (p. 690). One witness, presumably better-informed about the character of the emigrants than about their fate in the countries of destination, remarked that "the best and most enterprising people are hasting away to cultivate the American wilderness" (p. 782). The Ordnance Survey memoirs remark similarly that the industrious and well-conducted emigrate while "able bodied idlers and disorderly characters are but rarely known to leave the country" (OSM, box 9, file VI, p. 88). The same conclusion is drawn by the author of the best book on Irish emigration before 1845 (Adams, 1932, p. 194).

Who were the Irish emigrants? The majority of Ireland's emigrants consisted of smallholders and cottiers. Many of the emigrants were farmers whose leases expired and who were replaced by tenants at will drawn from the cottier class. In the Ulster counties the decline of cottage industries led to massive displacement of workers. The suddenness of the decline, the absence of alternative nonagricultural employment opportunities, and the geographical location of the region all contributed to the unique rate of emigration of Ulster weavers and spinsters.

There is, thus, strong reason to believe that the labor-quality effect of importance in the emigration from prefamine Ireland. Can it be measured? Many of the properties which are thought to be sources of economic externalities, such as willingness to take risk, the subjective rate of time preference (willingness to delay gratification), or plain ambition, do not lend themselves to measurement without carefully controlled experiments. One quality, possibly correlated with some of the others, is what may be termed "quantitative sophistication". A possible measurement of the quantitative sophistication is through the degree of age-heaping in populations. The phenomenon of age-heaping is well known among all populations, and prefamine Ireland was no exception. A finding of consistently and significantly less age-heaping among the emigrants than among the 1841 population would suggest that emigrants were more sophisticated than those who stayed behind in the sense that they were able to recollect the exact date of their birth and perform the correct subtraction, or else knew their age exactly, thus indicating a more acute awareness of the concept of time.

The degree of age-heaping can be measured as follows. We shall confine the analysis to the cohort aged 15–34, since this group constituted the vast bulk of the emigrants. The true age distribution of the population can be approximated by "de-heaping" or smoothing. Sophisticated techniques for smoothing have been developed. The particular technique used here is Graybill's weighted moving average of the Sprague coefficients (Shryock and Siegel, 1973, pp. 700–2, 878). This technique results in drastic smoothing of the population and does not preserve the subtotals of each age group. For each age i ($i = 15, 16 \ldots$ 34) we calculated $\hat{n}_i/\Sigma\hat{n}_i$ and $n_i/\Sigma n_i$, the proportion of each age group in the smoothed and reported population, respectively. The degree of heaping γ is defined by

$$\gamma = \sum_i \left(\frac{\hat{n}_i}{\Sigma\hat{n}_i} - \frac{n_i}{\Sigma n_i} \right)^2.$$

An alternative measure which is independent of population size is λ, which is defined as

$$\lambda = \frac{\Sigma|n_i - \hat{n}_i|}{\Sigma\hat{n}_i}.$$

Before turning to the emigrant data, let us examine the severity of age-heaping in the reference population. Table 8.5 contains the values of γ and λ for the four Irish provinces as well as for three other populations, Mexico in 1960 (which is used by Shryock and Siegel as their illustrative example) and the USA in 1880 and 1970. In addition to the values of γ and λ, the table presents the values of δ, computed as

$$\sum_i \frac{(n_i - \hat{n}_i)^2}{\hat{n}_i}.$$

If the null-hypothesis of no age-heaping is true, δ is distributed χ^2 with 19 degrees of freedom. The critical value of χ^2 at the 99 percent level of confidence is 36·2. A value of δ in excess of this critical value indicates that we reject the hypothesis of no age-heaping in the population.[9]

Table 8.5 *Values of γ, λ, and δ for Selected Populations*

Population	Population size (ages 15–34 only)	γ	λ	δ
Ulster, 1841	792,094	54·53	0·238	4,745
Leinster, 1841	711,429	54·99	0·233	4,317
Munster, 1841	860,130	72·22	0·255	6,828
Connaught, 1841	483,717	98·94	0·296	5,261
Ireland, 1841	2,841,546	66·18	0·251	20,744
USA, 1880	17,548,751	10·20	0·111	396,200
USA, 1970	60,348,798	1·14	0·038	139,900
Mexico, 1960	11,038,864	23·64	0·177	595,400

Sources: Ireland: Great Britain, 1843, Vol. XXIV.
USA: Department of Commerce, 1970, p. 268.
Mexico: UN, 1962, p. 204.

Table 8.5 confirms the expectation that the values of γ and λ are negatively correlated with the degree of development of the economy. The ranking of the four Irish provinces by their values of λ is identical to their ranking by income, and the ranking by the values of γ differs only in that Leinster and Ulster have changed places. It is also clear that age-heaping is almost absent in the USA in 1970. The high level of δ demonstrates that the observed distribution is still significantly different from the smoothed one, but that is caused primarily by the inability of the smoothed population to preserve adequately the baby boom of 1946. In 1880, however, the USA was still subject to age-heaping, although somewhat less so than present-day less-developed economies like Mexico. In prefamine Ireland age-heaping was far more severe than in Mexico in 1960.

Table 8.6   *Values of γ and λ for the Emigrant Population*

Period	Number of persons included in calculation	Percentage of total population in sample	γ	λ
1820–4	440	70·0	107·4	0·408
1825–9	1,293	67·3	114·2	0·383
1830–4	2,843	71·6	96·75	0·384
1835–9	5,096	73·8	104·9	0·370
1840–4	5,374	70·2	103·8	0·374
1845–6	2,374	72·1	150·0	0·382
1847–8	4,106	66·7	239·9	0·472
Total	21,526	70·5	120·52	0·351

Source: See text.

The results of the application of these procedures to the emigrant sample are presented in Table 8.6. The conclusion that emerges from these results is that the hypothesis that emigrants were more quantitatively sophisticated than the population at large is resoundingly rejected. The values of γ and λ for the emigrants are consistently higher than for the enumerated population of Ireland in 1841. Emigrants tended to age-heap *more*, not less, than those who remained behind. It is also quite clear that the heaping phenomenon among the emigrants in the famine years (1847–8) was much worse than among earlier emigration waves.

To the extent, therefore, that the degree of age-heaping was correlated with other qualities such as arithmetical ability ("numeracy"), a respect for accuracy, or a more serious attitude toward time, age-heaping measures valuable human attributes which have the potential to create important economic externalities and to play an important role in development. The hypothesis that Ireland suffered from a constant hemorrhage of its entrepreneurial talents in the years before the famine is not confirmed under these assumptions.

It is, of course, possible that the correlation between age-heaping and genuinely important characteristics was weak. Willingness to bear risk and to postpone gratification—two qualities which seem necessary for economic development—may still have been present in doses larger than average among those who left Ireland. Although *a priori* plausible, these arguments are not likely to be tested directly and escape the realm of speculation.

Nor is it likely that we will ever be able to determine whether the Irish emigrants were really more industrious than average. The vast bulk (94·3 percent) of the Irish male population above age 15 was classified as "occupied" in the 1841 Census, with only a negligible fraction reported to be paupers. Comparing the proportions occupied population among other groups shows that among the emigrants a much higher percentage declared an occupation. For the emigrants who left Ireland in 1835–44, for instance, the percentage of females above 15 who were occupied was 47·15 percent, compared to 41·74 percent in the population at large. The proportion of children under 15 declaring an occupation was 11·53 percent among emigrants and 6·68 percent among the enumerated 1841 population. These differences are, however, to some extent misleading, because they reflect the higher proportion of unmarried women among emigrants and the different age structure of emigrant children.

(4) The Human-Capital Effect

Were the Irish emigrants on average better educated and more skilled than those who remained behind? Since Irish emigrants were not asked themselves to fill out any forms, there is no way of estimating the rate of literacy among them. There is some reason to believe, however, that literacy was of some importance in the process of emigration. The sailings and ships were advertised, and in order to obtain information about the various technical details concerning emigration, at least some members of the emigrating group had to be able to read (Adams, 1932, pp. 76–9). In the 1840s education seems to have been responsible for emigration originating from parishes from which there had never been emigration before (ibid., p. 218). Causality ran in both directions, however, since some people seem to have tried to educate themselves with the explicit goal of emigrating (OSM, box 21, file II). Americans often were impressed, however, by the high rate of illiteracy among the Irish emigrants (for example, Mayo-Smith, 1890, p. 163), but this does not rule out the possibility that the emigrants were more literate than the Irish population at large. Schrier (1958, pp. 22–3) notes the large numbers of letters sent home by the Irish emigrants. In any event, Ireland in 1841 was still a country with very low literacy rates. Of all males aged 15 and above, only 45·5 percent could read and write, 15·5 could read only, and 39·0 could do neither. Among females literacy was much lower, the respective percentages being 21·2, 23·7, and 55·1 (Great Britain, 1843, Vol. XXIV, pp. 438–9).

In any case, literacy may not have been a very good approximation of human capital embodied in emigrants. Skill, experience, and professional training in trades and crafts were the primary forms which human capital took. Hence, human capital can be measured approximately by occupational data. Comparing the occupational structure of the emigrating population with that of the entire nation, can provide some clues to the question of whether the emigrants differed significantly from those who remained behind. The data available are the occupations enumerated by the captains at the port of New York, and the occupational data in the 1841 Census.

Table 8.7 *Occupational Structure of Irish Population, 1841 (Percentages)*

Group number	Description	Adults		Children (under 15)		Total
		Males	Females	Males	Females	
1	Laborers	52·65	10·40	82·84	21·21	40·11
2	Servants	2·70	23·29	7·07	28·01	9·75
3	Farmers	20·69	1·92	0·16	0·04	13·73
4	Factory workers, miners, mechanics	0·59	0·03	0·16	0·03	0·39
5	Textile workers	7·08	59·93	5·59	49·95	24·16
6	Artisans processing leather	2·55	0·33	1·03	0·16	1·76
7	Carpenters	1·75	—	0·17	—	1·12
8	Other woodworkers	0·79	0·02	0·16	—	0·52
9	Construction workers	1·53	—	0·22	—	0·98
10	Metal workers	1·65	0·04	0·64	0·05	1·09
11	Artisans processing food	1·22	0·13	0·36	0·03	0·83
12	Other craftsmen and artisans	0·45	0·11	0·67	0·17	0·35
13	Merchants and commercial	2·37	2·80	0·49	0·30	2·38
14	White collar	2·54	0·63	0·10	0·01	1·81
15	Unclassified	1·45	0·35	0·34	0·04	1·04
Total		100	100	100	100	100

Source: Great Britain, 1843, Vol. XXIV, p. 440.

The standard of reference against which the occupational distribution of the emigrants is to be evaluated is the list of occupations in the 1841 Census. The occupational data in the Census were collected in a peculiar manner. The enumerators did not group the population into predetermined occupational classes. Rather, each person stated his own occupation, and was grouped together with other persons declaring the same profession. The result is a bewildering variety of no less than 435 different professions (Great Britain, 1843, Vol. XXIV, p. 440). Some of these occupations are rather esoteric: Ireland's only billiard-table maker occupies a line for himself, as does the only curled-hair manufacturer, the only rocket maker, and the four birdstuffers. The distinction between "different" occupations is therefore nonexistent in many cases: "salters" and "saltmakers" are separately listed, as are "veterinary surgeons", and "cow doctors". Of course, the more esoteric occupations do not appear among emigrants. It is doubtful whether the masters of the emigrant vessels would have known the fine distinction between "japanners" and "harnessplaters", or between "glass and delph dealers" and "delph and china dealers". For the comparison of the occupational distribution of the emigrants to that of the population of 1841, the hundreds of occupations listed in the Census were divided into fifteen major groups. The description of the groups and their proportion in the employed population are presented in Table 8.7.

The occupational structure of the emigrants should be expected to differ from the occupational structure of the population for a number of reasons. A major reason is that the classification of the emigrants into professions was not carried out by skilled enumerators who were familiar with Irish conditions. Furthermore, the emigrants differed from the general population in their age structure. A farmer's son was a laborer until he inherited the farm. A carpenter's apprentice could have been a servant if he was 17 years old, although that status was simply part of the training of becoming a carpenter. It is also apparent that language and customs varied from place to place, and that as the geographical composition of the emigration to New York changed, the occupational structure was subject to changes stemming not only from differences in the actual occupations of these emigrants, but from differences in terms used for similar types of labor and occupations. These complications compound the usual pitfalls of comparing the occupational structures of different populations.

Table 8.8   *Occupational Structure of Irish Emigrants Arriving in New York, 1820–48* (Percentages)*

Class	1820–4	1825–9	1830–4	1835–9	1840–4	1845–6	1847–8
1	25·56	44·71	43·38	44·87	45·71	50·75	51·80
2	5·43	4·25	11·52	9·42	14·15	30·22	13·00
3	28·44	19·64	15·45	16·55	14·48	4·79	12·09
4	—	—	0·33	1·61	1·19	0·23	0·14
5	16·29	16·11	13·49	13·30	12·78	5·25	14·10
6	5·75	3·07	2·26	2·13	2·03	2·51	1·29
7	4·47	1·81	2·05	2·46	1·86	0·70	1·20
8	0·64	1·63	1·29	0·82	0·68	0·61	0·59
9	0·95	2·09	1·63	2·58	1·00	1·04	1·27
10	0·31	0·81	2·22	1·54	1·21	0·81	0·79
11	0·95	1·35	2·01	0·99	1·51	0·70	0·88
12	0·95	0·72	0·71	0·86	1·23	0·85	0·69
13	5·75	2·09	1·97	1·46	0·70	0·20	0·98
14	4·47	1·72	1·71	1·41	1·45	1·35	1·17
Total	100	100	100	100	100	100	100

* For details on the occupational classification schedule, see Table 8.7.
Source: See text.

Table 8.8 presents the changing occupational structure of Irish emigrants of both sexes over the twenty-eight years covered by the sample. The figures refer only to those who declared a profession or occupation. While there was considerable volatility of the occupational structure over time, it is quite clear that, except perhaps for the 1820s, the proportion unskilled workers (classes 1 and 2) exceeded 50 percent and thus exceeded their proportion in the population at large. To some extent, however, looking at laborers and servants alone is misleading. A primary reason why the number of laborers is so high among the emigrants is that many women who classified themselves as textile workers or unoccupied in the 1841 Census listed themselves as laborers in New York. These women led triple lives: as wives and mothers, as occasional agricultural laborers, and as spinsters or seamstresses in cottage industry. Under different circumstances, faced with slightly different questions, the answers they gave regarding their occupation could have differed, and it is not surprising that a large shift in their nominal occupations appears.

Table 8.9   *Occupational Structure of Irish Emigrants Arriving in New York, 1820–48* (Percentages)*

| Occupational class | Adults | | Children | | |
	Males	Females	Males	Females	Total
1	56·84	26·11	52·70	34·65	46·86
2	2·75	36·78	13·18	28·72	14·03
3	15·68	9·18	19·09	12·01	13·73
4	0·94	0·42	0·17	—	0·73
5	6·95	24·42	6·25	18·54	12·49
6	2·80	0·61	3·04	1·06	2·10
7	2·44	0·45	1·18	0·46	1·74
8	1·17	0·17	0·17	0·30	0·81
9	2·23	0·23	0·68	0·61	1·53
10	1·71	0·24	0·68	0·15	1·19
11	1·70	0·35	0·84	0·61	1·24
12	1·21	0·28	—	0·76	0·89
13	1·50	0·52	1·35	0·46	1·17
14	2·09	0·23	0·68	1·37	1·47
Total	100	100	100	100	100

* For details on the occupational classification schedule, see Table 8.7.
Source: See text.

To clarify the impact of Irish emigration, the comparison should perhaps focus more on artisans and craftsmen rather than on such ill-defined classes as "servants", "laborers", or "farmers". Table 8.10 presents the values of what could be called the Occupational Difference Index (ODI). This index is simply equal to the ratio of the percentage emigrants in a given occupation to the percentage of the 1841 population in that occupation. An ODI value of larger than unity indicates that the country was losing a larger than proportional number of persons in any occupation.

Table 8.10 shows that emigration removed more skilled artisans from Ireland than if emigration had been truly "neutral". The differences between the proportions emigrating and the proportions in the population are statistically significant at the 1 percent level for all male adult artisans except textile workers and metal workers. Moreover, because the emigrating population contained proportionally more young adults, the impact of emigration was larger than Table 8.10 suggests. For instance, consider carpenters and other woodworkers, which jointly comprised 1·64 percent of the occupied population of Ireland in 1841, and accounted for 2·55 percent of the emigrating population. Since the proportion "occupied" among the emigrant population was 66·7 percent, while among the total 1841 population this percentage was only 42·5 percent, the proportion of woodworkers among the total emigrating population was 1·62 percent, while among the population at large it was 0·69 percent. Assuming that the proportion of carpenters and woodworkers in the entire emigrating population was not very different from those emigrating to New York, we can estimate that in the absence of emigration, the proportion woodworkers and carpenters in the total population of Ireland would have been 0·85 percent, which is 21 percent higher (Table 8.9). Similar counterfactual calculations can be carried out for other occupations.[10] In the absence of emigration the proportion of factory workers and mechanics in Ireland would have been 28 percent higher, that of leatherworkers 12 percent higher. The counterfactual decline in the proportion of construction workers was 21 percent, that of metal workers 10 percent, while in food processing the loss was 19 percent and in "other artisans" 44 percent. The proportion of merchants and other commercial workers in the population would have been lower by about 4 percent. For all nontextile artisans (classes 4 and 6–12), the loss calculated in this fashion amounted to 12 percent.

Table 8.10 *Values of the ODI for Irish Emigrants Arriving in New York*

| Occupation | Adults | | Children | | |
	Males	Females	Males	Females	Total
Laborers, Servants, and Farmers	0·99	2·02	0·94	1·53	1·17
Textile Workers	0·98	0·41	1·12	0·25	0·52
All other Artisans	1·35	4·17	1·98	8·98	1·45
White collar and Commercial	0·73	0·22	4·61	5·90	0·63

Source: As Table 8.8.

The loss of human capital due to emigration can also be illustrated from other sources. The agricultural seminary in Templemoyle, Co. Londonderry, which was one of the better institutions of its kind in prefamine Ireland, followed up on the careers of its alumnae, which allows us to compute the proportion of them which Ireland lost through emigration. The school was founded in 1828 (by the Northwest of Ireland Society). By 1834 twenty-one of the 126 graduates had left Ireland, which is 19 percent of total graduates whose fates were known (OSM, box 41, file 8). By 1843 this proportion had risen to 27 percent (ninety-three out of 341) and possibly more (since only overseas emigration was listed), implying a substantial loss of a very scarce and highly valuable form of human capital (Kennedy, 1847, p. 58).

While the data thus confirm that there was some loss of human capital due to emigration, it is also reasonably clear that as far as *measurable* quantitative information is concerned, we are dealing with a second-order effect. Over 60 percent of all emigrants were classified as laborers and servants, exceeding the corresponding percentage in the population at large which was only about 50 percent. Moreover, among adult male workers—the backbone of the labor force—the difference between the occupational composition of the emigrating population and that of the 1841 population is not very marked and can be accounted for by the different age composition of the emigrants. The high concentration of emigrants in the 16–25 age bracket explains the relatively large number of servants and small number of farmers in the emigrant population. Furthermore, among the emigrating artisans, there were in all likelihood some structurally unemployed workers whose livelihood in domestic industry was increasingly put under pressure by factory products. The emigration of such workers would not constitute a "loss" to the rest of the economy, since their human capital had already become obsolete (Mokyr and Ó Gráda, 1982b).

(5)   The Irish Abroad

Can we learn something about the effects of emigration on those who remained behind from the fate of the emigrants in their countries of destination? The main methodological difficulty with that approach is that it is not possible to separate between the effects of the personal qualities of the emigrants and the fact that they had moved into a new environment. Even if the emigrants represented, say, the top 5 percent of the Irish labor force with respect to willingness to bear risk, skill, or ingenuity, they might have ended up at the bottom of the social and economic ladder in Great Britain and the USA because of adjustment problems, prejudice, or simply because the average level of these qualities was much higher in the countries of destination than in Ireland. A second difficulty with inferring anything from data on the Irish abroad about the effect of prefamine emigration on Ireland is that most of the usable information which could be used for this purpose postdates the famine, and thus "dilutes" the early emigrants with those who left Ireland during the mass exodus of the late 1840s.

Irish immigrants, both in Great Britain and in North America, were found by and large in urban areas, working in low-skilled occupations. This description is undisputed for Irish emigration in the second half of the nineteenth century, and it also seems true of earlier Irish emigration. In 1841 two industrial counties in Great Britain, Lancashire and Lanarkshire, accounted for 38·6 percent of all Irish emigrants, Middlesex (London) for another 13·9 percent (Great Britain, 1843, Vol. XXIV, pp. lxxxviii, lxxxix). Lees (1979), working largely with 1851 and later Census data of Britain, concluded that "the Irish [in London] were heavily concentrated in a few trades, in occupations that placed most of them among the lowest social and economic groups". The same is true for Irish-born living in Britain in the 1830s. In a remarkable essay written as appendix G to the Poor Law Commissioners' Report (Great

Britain, 1836b, Vol. XXXIV, pp. 427–74), George Cornewall Lewis maintained that the bulk of the Irish population of Great Britain consisted of common laborers, especially in construction and transportation (for example, porters) and unskilled agricultural laborers. Farming and agriculture attracted a substantial number of Irishmen in Britain, to judge from the number of Irish-born residing in rural Britain.

In the USA the proportion of Irish in agriculture was not large. Adams (1932, p. 341) conjectured that the proportion Irish in American agriculture was at most 10 percent in the prefamine years. Of the total occupied population of Irish-born Americans in 1870, 14·6 percent were either farmers or agricultural laborers, as opposed to 47·4 percent of the entire American population. It is doubtful whether the percentage of Irish-born in US agriculture in 1845 was much higher than in 1870. The absence of an agricultural wage labor force in the USA and the high fixed cost of moving west and setting up a farm geared toward cash crops were in part responsible for this unexpected behavior of an essentially rural and agrarian population, of whom John Mitchel had said that "land was life". Possibly the agriculture that the Irish emigrants were used to, a comparatively small-scale, land-extensive subsistence agriculture, provided little background and experience to prepare them for the more commercialized, land-using agriculture which was spreading through the American midwest in the 1830s and 1840s. However, similar considerations ought to apply to other emigrants, such as Scandinavians or Germans, who settled on farms in far larger proportions. It may have been true, as Wittke (1956, p. 62) has suggested, that the gregarious Irish were "afraid of the lonely prairie, where there were neither neighbors, villages, or churches". For whatever reasons, the Irish emigrants were different. The vast majority were attracted to urban centers, where most of them became wage laborers.[11] Even in Canada, where cities were smaller and less attractive economically, "the mass of the immigrants became part of the urban working class" (Adams, 1932, p. 342).

The importance of the Irish immigrants for the Industrial Revolution in Britain has been emphasized by many scholars (for example, Clapham, 1964, Vol. 1, p. 61; Pollard, 1978, pp. 113–15). Lees (1979, p. 88) points out that although the Irish in London were at the bottom of the social and economic hierarchy, they kept alive a vast pool of casual labor essential to the transportation, construction, and food-distribution industries, and were therefore an essential component of the British urban economy. In Scotland Irish migrant laborers, or "navvies", took part in the digging of canals and the construction of railroads (Handley, 1945, pp. 58–79). In the USA the Irish were instrumental, and in some cases essential, in the construction of the first canals and railroads during 1820–40. In a somewhat tasteless metaphor Handlin has remarked that the Irish "were the guano of the American communications system . . . despised and robbed, downtrodden and poor, they made the railroads grow" (Handlin, 1977, p. 72). In the 1830s and early 1840s their presence began to be felt in the textile industries in Rhode Island and Massachusetts. As early as 1833 Lowell, "the city of spindles", had its "New Dublin" and "Irish Acres" (Wittke, 1956, p. 28). By 1860 more than half the factory operatives in New England were of Irish descent (Taylor, 1951, pp. 286–92).

It is, of course, quite impossible to infer much from the impressions and *obiter dicta* of contemporaries about the character of the Irish emigrants compared to those who did not emigrate. For instance, we cannot be sure that the Irish emigrants had different propensities to save than those who did not emigrate. We do know, however, that the Irish outside Ireland were considered to be low-savers compared to the native population. G. C. Lewis makes the interesting observation that Irish emigrants in Britain consisted of two distinct and very different groups. One group was industrious, clever, and honest; the other group was drunken and idle. The two classes shared, however, one quality: both were widely judged to be "improvident", spending money on immediate luxuries (especially clothing and drink) and "it is not a general characteristic for them to lay money up for the future" as one witness cited by him put it (Great Britain, 1836b, Vol. XXXIV, pp. 436–8). Lewis's report also provides little support for the hypothesis that emigrants were particularly ambitious and energetic. One manufacturer reported that he had to dismiss all but a few Irish workers because they did their work in a slovenly and untidy manner. The low quality of Irish labor was attributed to "satisfaction with their present condition" and unwillingness to exert themselves (ibid., p. 440). It is not easy to reconcile these opinions of Irish emigrants with the plausible idea that emigration required courage, patience, and perseverance. Lewis points out, however, that Irish emigrants came to England with very vague and confused notions concerning the English economy awaiting them, and were suffering from exaggerated notions of the chances of success in England (ibid., p. 431).

It is more difficult to find such explicit comparisons and judgements for the Irish in the USA without running the risk of confusing the true characteristics of the Irish immigrants with the perceived image, often distorted beyond recognition by xenophobia and contempt (Wittke, 1956, ch. 5). The facts presented by Oscar Handlin (1977) on the Irish in Boston indicate that the Irish did not come to America equipped to compete with native Americans or other emigrants. The Irish in Handlin's Boston were excluded from more desirable professions, not only by the prejudice and suspicion of others, but because of their lack of capital and training. Even the blacks, most similar to the Irish in occupational experience, did better than they did. "While their [the blacks of Boston] position shone chiefly by comparison with less fortunate members of their own race, it was clearly closer to that of the natives than the Irish. The latter unquestionably were lowest in the occupational hierarchy" (Handlin, 1977, p. 70). Even in peddling food and groceries to their own kinsmen the Irish seem to have done poorly in the USA in contrast with Britain (Great Britain, 1836b, Vol. XXXIV, p. 434; Handlin, 1977, p. 65), which is fully consistent with our finding that the percentage of overseas emigrants in commercial occupations was very low and that they were, on the whole, not very numerate.

(6) Emigration and Backwardness

Measuring the cost of emigration to those who remained behind is quite pertinent to an understanding of the troubles the Irish economy underwent in the three decades before the famine. The attempts to measure these costs in the previous sections allow us to derive three conclusions. First, the age distribution of the emigrants was sufficiently different from the rest of the population to impose a cost on the economy: 70 percent of the emigrants were in their economically most active years (15–34) as opposed to 34 percent in the population at large. The cost of this emigration was estimated at an annual siphoning off of 1·5–2 percent of personal income. Secondly, emigration constituted something of a "brain drain" from Ireland in the sense that it removed the skilled laborers in a somewhat higher proportion than their share in population. If the New York port sample used here is representative, we can conclude that Ireland lost a proportion of its trained craftsmen, but the damage was in all likelihood not devastating. Thirdly, no evidence was found that the emigrants were more "numerate", that is, more quantitatively sophisticated than those who stayed behind. As far as other important characteristics are concerned, there seems to be little evidence to support the plausible but unsubstantiated proposition that emigrants were, *ceteris paribus*, more thrifty or more diligent than those who remained behind. The results of the quantitative investigation into the effect of prefamine emigration on the economic condition of those who remained in Ireland are, thus, rather mixed.

The effect of emigration on Ireland is not wholly quantifiable. The aggregate data used here could be misleading in two respects. The first is that aggregation could conceal the loss of important qualities (for instance, entrepreneurship) if the persons endowed with those talents constituted a very small proportion of the population and if the distribution of these properties were not continuous. For instance, suppose that pre-emigration society consists of three disjoint classes, namely, "potential entrepreneurs", "skilled workers", and "unskilled workers". The classes differ in that they have very different endowment of a quality z, the entrepreneurs having the highest endowment of z and the unskilled having the lowest. Assume that all three classes are indispensable in the production process. Assume that in the pre-emigration population the entrepreneurs constituted 1 percent of the total, skilled workers 49 percent, and unskilled workers 50 percent. Suppose that a quarter of the population emigrates, removing *all* potential entrepreneurs and consisting for the rest of unskilled laborers. The potential entrepreneurs comprise only 4 percent of the emigrants, so that the average value of z for the emigrating population could well be *lower* for the emigrants than for the pre-emigrating population. None the less, the economy has lost all its "high-z" workers and under the assumptions stated will suffer a severe loss of output.

Is this a description of what happened to the Irish economy? There were very few highly successful entrepreneurs of Irish extraction in Britain and the USA, but it cannot be ruled out that some of these "potential entrepreneurs" who ended up in the British construction or USA railroad sectors as unskilled workers would have been extremely successful had they stayed home.[12] There were economic opportunities in Ireland, but significantly many of the entrepreneurs who were successful in Ireland were foreigners.

There is a further possible connection between emigration and the absence of an industrial revolution in Ireland. In England, Belgium, and other countries in which the Industrial Revolution was successful an important part of the laborforce employed in the "new" industries was recruited from the countryside, primarily from domestic industry. The rural weavers, nailors, spinners, frame-knitters and (perhaps more important) their children supplied the workers without which there would not and could not be an industrial revolution (Mokyr, 1976b). An impoverished and crowded countryside was often the mainspring of capital accumulation in nearby industrial centers. Workers who were absorbed in the modern sector had usually to migrate physically to new locations, but in most cases did not move over long distances. Hence, there is a well-documented spatial correlation between the centers of domestic industry and the emergence of modern manufacturing. In Ireland this link was largely short-circuited by emigration. The basic process of rural workers being gradually absorbed in a "modern" sector *did* occur in Ireland, in a way, just as it did elsewhere. The difference was that the relocation of displaced or dissatisfied workers occurred outside Irish borders. An example of this relocation is provided by Collins (1981) who describes the settlement of displaced workers from the Irish cottage industry in the Scottish Lowlands. The result of Irish emigration was that Ireland remained comparatively unindustrialized not only in the decades before the famine, but also in the century after.

There is a problem in the proper identification of cause and effect in the relation between emigration and the failure to industrialize. On the one hand, it could be maintained that the Irish emigrated overseas rather than to Drogheda or Waterford because there were better employment opportunities in Britain and the USA. On the other hand, it seems likely that if large amounts of suitable and cheap labor had accumulated in the Irish towns due to migration, perceptive entrepreneurs would have taken advantage of the opportunities, and the industrial revolution in Ireland might have been faster and more significant. These two interpretations are not mutually exclusive. The first requires the existence of other exogenous causes which prevented a more rapid accumulation of capital in the nonagricultural Irish economy, such as low savings propensities, worries about insecurity of property, poor entrepreneurship, and so forth. The second requires some further explanation of why the Irish migrated overseas rather than to their own urban centers. Had they stayed in Ireland, the factories and overhead projects in which they would have been employed would have ultimately benefited the economy as a whole.

A simple economic model can be used to speculate about the possible reasons for this difference between Irish emigrants in the first half of the nineteenth century and population movements in other economies during this period. Assume for the sake of simplicity that there is no uncertainty involved in emigration, so that every individual decides to emigrate when the present value of the returns to emigration exceeds the costs, both psychic and pecuniary. (If uncertainty is allowed for, the present values have to be replaced by expected present values, and a risk premium has to be added to the costs.) The costs of emigrating consist of two parts: a fixed cost, which is paid independent of the distance traveled, and a variable cost which is a (positive) function of the distance. The fixed cost is higher the more the languages, customs, social organization, and so on in the country of origin differ from those in potential countries of destination. It also depends on the ease with which emigrants can market nonmovable assets such as property rights in land, livestock, housing, and "goodwill". The variable cost reflects not only the transportation cost to the country of destination, but also the extent to which the emigrant has to separate himself from his community.

The cost structure for Irish emigrants differed considerably from that of other emigrants. The backwardness and isolated nature of Irish rural life made movement of any kind costly and painful. Many of the rights enjoyed by Irish peasants were customary (rights to turbaries, to collect seaweed, and so on), and could not be readily sold except perhaps where the "sale of tenant right" was practiced. The *fixed* cost was, therefore, likely to be high for the average Irish emigrant. On the other hand, Ireland was favorably located for lumber and raw-cotton carrying freighters on their way back to America (Hansen, 1961, pp. 181–3). Relative easy access to seaports set Ireland apart in the prerailroad era. The existence of Irish communities in places such as Boston and New York, as well as in Glasgow and Manchester, reduced the psychic cost of emigrating to a more remote location. *Variable* costs were therefore likely to be low in Ireland relative to other countries.

If we accept the hypothesis that the variable costs-fixed ratio was lower for Irish emigrants than for others, it becomes clear why the Irish went to Britain and North America rather than to their own urban centers. It can be shown that under the assumptions about differences in the cost structure of emigration, the Irish were more likely to emigrate long distances and to foreign countries. This behavior sets them apart from migrants in other countries who moved predominantly over small distances before 1850 (Deane and Cole, 1969, p. 121; Great Britain, 1836b, Vol. XXXIV, p. 453). Internal migration in Ireland was small compared with emigration.[13] Differences in the economic cost of emigration took a variety of forms, and recognizing them allows us to explain why the rural Irish left in such large numbers while the population of the non-industrializing English South, for instance, showed very little inclination to emigrate before 1850. One example of such differences in cost can be found in Poor Relief. In England, Poor Relief guaranteed at least subsistence whereas in Ireland no such relief could be relied upon. It has been maintained, in fact, that the Speenhamland system in the South of England was established to provide for agricultural workers in the slack season precisely to prevent their emigration and thus to ensure an adequate supply of labor during the peak season (Boyer, 1982).

One of the most intriguing questions in the history of migration is this: what made some men and women leave their rural cottages and go to cities, sometimes foreign, to work for other men in factories, shipyards, offices, or railroads, while others did not? Clearly, many factors counted in this decision-making process, fortune or "random noise" not being the least among them. But if we could observe all the characteristics of emigrants in the early nineteenth century and compare them to the characteristics of those who did not go, we would likely find that on average the emigrants were somewhat different from people with the same socioeconomic characteristics. I have already surmised that the emigrants were likely to have a lower risk-aversion and a lower subjective rate of time-preference. It is also possible that the emigrants differed from those who stayed behind in their willingness and ability to adapt to a different work regime. Irish peasants, whether employed exclusively in agriculture or part-time in domestic industry, were largely self-employed. Emigration required more than courage and effort in extracting oneself from the trusted neighborhood of one's hometown. It implied the almost certain transition into the work regime of discipline, supervision, order, and rigid schedules. It meant that the emigrant expected to be absorbed into a hierarchy in which he occupied the lowest ranks, with little chance of ever climbing up. Not all peasants were willing and able to subject themselves to such a change, and opted to stay. Among those who actually went, the willingness to work in factories or factory-like circumstances must have been on average higher.

While there were many contemporary complaints about the unruliness and pugnacity of the Irish, there is also evidence for the Irish willingness to work under tight discipline. In 1846 the Rhode Island mill owners were reported to prefer Irish workers because they were more "submissive" than native hands (Clark, 1929, p. 398). Irish women were much in demand in Boston because of their willingness to serve in households, being more docile and loyal than American women (Handlin, 1977, p. 61). In Scotland "there appeared ... a general preference of the Irish to the Highlanders as labourers on account of the superior diligence and pliability of the former though the latter were considered more orderly in their conduct". A Glasgow dyer noted that "no class of men are easier to manage than the Irish ... they have less pride and are less easily offended". The most valuable of the qualities of Irish workers were their "willingness, alacrity, and perseverance in the severest, most irksome, and most disagreeable kinds of coarse labour" (Great Britain, 1836b, Vol. XXXIV, pp. 455–6). William Dixon, the Scottish coal and iron master, described his Irish mineworkers as follows: "The Irish in the coal mines ... are fully more obedient and tractable than the natives, and are not so much given to combine ... An Irishman, who has never seen the mouth of a coalpit in his life, has no hesitation in going down" (cited by Handley, 1945, p. 119). In the sugar factories, in Scotland, the Irish workers were indispensable: the native workers refused to endure the working conditions and only the Irish could stand the heat (Great Britain, 1836b, Vol. XXXIV, p. 140). It is therefore quite plausible that while emigration may not have deprived Ireland of its potential entrepreneurs, it removed its potential industrial proletariat. All things considered, the loss of that part of the population from which the industrial laborforce was recruited was perhaps worse than the loss of potential entrepreneurs, since workers willing to work in factories were not and could not be replaced.

The question why Ireland failed to undergo an industrial revolution is central to the fate of the entire country both before and after the famine. In the 1820s many observers were highly optimistic about Ireland's ability to utilize its cheap labor force to create a manufacturing sector, successfully competing with Britain in labor-intensive products. One observer told a House of Lords Select Committee in 1825:

At present it is merely the profitable employment of the money and its immediate and speedy return that presents the temptation [to transfer English capital to Irish industry]. I conceive the actual transfer of capital will soon follow. I conceive that Lancashire and Louth will form as if it were one factory, each will take to itself the processes to which it is best fitted . . . whatever operations can be procured best by the human hand, I think, will be performed in Ireland, for the hand which is satisfied with the cheaper subsistence will necessarily under-sell the hand not so circumstanced. (Great Britain, 1825c, Vol. IX, pp. 49–50)

The reason why this prediction failed to materialize was one of the most puzzling of enigmas to contemporaries. Nassau Senior pointed out in 1843 that British capitalists invested overseas in alien countries "at the mercy of barbarous, unsettled, or fraudulent governments", whereas Ireland which had the same laws and government as Britain, received very little capital from Britain. "It is obvious", wrote Senior, "that there is something in the institutions of Ireland, or in the habits of her people, which deters British capital from one of its most natural and apparently one of its most productive employments" (Senior, 1868, vol. 1, p. 33). Senior pointed to his "three Is" (insecurity, ignorance, and indolence) as the factors responsible. What he, and many others, apparently over-looked, is that British capital did not have to come to cheap Irish labor because cheap Irish labor could come to British capital, both in Britain and in North America. The factors Senior points to, and especially the lawlessness of Irish life which he exaggerates absurdly (ibid., pp. 34–45), explain the cost of moving capital to labor. The net result, however, was determined by the cost of moving labor to capital as well as by the cost of moving capital to labor. The relative cheapness with which the Irish could emigrate was as much a factor in the absence of industrialization in Ireland as the real or perceived dangers to property or the low productivity of labor.

Notes: Chapter 8

1   The figure for 1836 was unavailable and estimated by interpolation.
2   Verrière (1979, p. 79) presents figures which imply a total emigration figure of 1,390,000 and Verrière cites as his source the Commission on Emigration (1954). I have been unable to reproduce his estimates from the sources he cites.
3   It should be made clear that in this analysis Irish population was in effect growing, so that the Berry–Soligo model should be interpreted to mean that workers' income declined by less than it would have in the absence of emigration.
4   The life-cycle effect focuses on a pure transfer from Europe to North America. It should not be concluded that emigration was a zero-sum game and that there was no overall improvement in global economic conditions as a result of emigration. Emigrants, by moving from a low wage to a high wage economy, improved their lot, and could have compensated their countries of origin by remittances overseas which would have left the latter indifferent while still improving the economic situation of the countries of destination.
5   Note that the training costs are not necessarily paid back in money terms. One could envisage an inter-generational model in which each apprentice repays the cost of his own training to society by training young apprentices after he becomes a skilled artisan. Emigration of an 18-year-old artisan who has completed his own training but has not had any apprentices of his own constitutes, therefore, a clear cost to society.
6   In actuality, people paid off their "debt" to society in more ways than the ones mentioned. For instance, people supported younger siblings, the children of deceased or incapacitated older siblings, and so on. Hence, the "debt" is owed to society and not only to one's immediate relatives.
7   Great Britain, 1824, Vol. XXII, pp. 816–17. The age structure for 1821 is not given year by year, but by groups of five years up to age 20 and ten years for older persons. This introduces an element of inaccuracy in the computation. It has to be remembered, however, that even when finer breakdowns of the population by age are given (as in 1841), an element of inaccuracy persists due to heaping. The specific use made of the age structure here is not particularly sensitive to small errors in ages, especially since most such errors would tend to cancel each other out.
8   For more details on the history and economic situation of the Palatine settlers, see Salaman (1949, pp. 339–42).
9   Note that δ is computed from the actual values of n and $\hat{n}$, and is thus sensitive to the size of the population and cannot be used directly for comparison purposes.
10 Note that it is incorrect to look at the increase in the absolute number of craftsmen which would have been in Ireland in the absence of emigration, because the entire population would then have been larger by 1·5 million.
11 In 1870, the earliest year for which such data exist, 38·3 percent of all Irish-born in the USA lived in towns of 50,000 inhabitants or more, compared to 12·7 percent of the entire population. The proportion Irish who were classified as "laborers" or "employees of companies, not specified" was 39·6 percent of all occupied persons aged 10 or more, as opposed to only 16·1 percent in the population. See US 9th Census (1872, pp. 698–715). In 1850 48 percent of the Irish in Boston were "laborers," another 15·7 percent "servants" (Handlin, 1977, pp. 250–1).
12 The only industry in which the Irish succeeded as independent entrepreneurs was "dispensaries of liquor" (Wittke, 1956, p. 25).
13 In 1841 405,000 Irishmen and women lived in Ireland in counties in which they were not born. Two-thirds of those were living in counties adjacent to their own. Not all of these were migrants in the usual sense of the word; many were women living in areas in the border region of two counties who happened to marry a man living across the county border. This suspicion is confirmed by the fact that women constituted a majority (51·5 percent) of the persons living in the county adjacent to the one in which they were born, while men constituted a majority of the other internal migrants (51·7 percent). While these differences between the emigration of males and females appear small, they are highly significant statistically. The appropriate χ^2 statistic equals 340 (while the critical value at the 1 percent significance is 7·88).

Chapter 9

The Great Famine: The Economics of Vulnerability

The prefamine history of Ireland inevitably will be interpreted and evaluated in terms of the famine. I have argued in Chapter 2 that one useful way to define poverty is in terms of the probability of subsistence crises. It could be argued, however, that the assessment of Ireland's prefamine economic performance as a "failure" just because it was followed by a disaster of unprecedented magnitude rests on a logical fallacy. The reliance on the potato as a staple food in the century before the famine had been almost complete. Although local scarcities occurred, they seldom lasted longer than the summer, and even the disastrous year of 1816 did little to signal to the Irish that their dependency on a single source of food was ill-advised. By the time they realized that the potato was not dependable after all, and that diversification in the food supply was advised, it was too late. Dependence on potatoes was "uncertain" but not "risky", in the sense that people were not aware of the true variance of the crop over long periods of time. It could be maintained, thus, that poverty had little to do with the famine. The "reason" for the famine was bad luck: the system emitted misleading signals, but the response to those signals was wholly rational given the information available at the time. The fungus that struck the Irish potato crops in the 1840s had never struck before and could not have been anticipated.

While this line of criticism has some merit, it is possible to set up two lines of defense. The first is that in the poorer regions of Ireland the dependence on potatoes did not disappear after 1850. In the west potato dependency continued almost undiminished after the famine. Realizing that potatoes were not reliable, the Irish remained nevertheless astonishingly loyal to their fickle staple food. Salaman (1949, pp. 318–321) noted with some surprise that "the economic lessons to be learnt from the potato famine may appear obvious enough to us, but it was not until thirty years later, that the majority of the people began seriously to realize the danger of building their social structure on so narrow and precarious a basis ... the supremacy of the potato was scarcely shaken for another thirty years". While Salaman's views apply more to the poor west than to the rest of the country, they raise the important issue of rationality: were Irish peasants, and especially the poorer ones, unable to shed the habit of eating potatoes, although it was apparent to all that the potato was more risky and thus more costly than had been supposed previously? Irrationality in the strict sense can never be ruled out, of course, but it squares poorly with evidence that post-famine peasants were responsive to changes in relative prices (Ó Gráda,

1973, pp. 39–63). It is disturbing, however, that the variability of potatoes was rising in the thirty years before the famine, although there were no indications that anything on the order of magnitude of the famine was imminent. In fact, there is some reason to believe that in the twenty years prior to the famine potatoes displayed a higher relative variability than other crops. Estimates based on French data support this hypothesis; time-series for prefamine Ireland do not exist (Mokyr, 1981b).

The dependency of the population on potatoes was a function of income per capita. Regression results reported in Mokyr (1981a) demonstrate that potatoes were grown more intensively in poor regions. The desire to diversify the diet existed even before the famine, but because of the amazing ability of the potato to provide large amounts of human food per acre, the Irish poor simply could not afford to eat a less cheap food.[1] Apparently, even after the famine raised the cost of potatoes by adding to it a new element reflecting the higher perceived probability of famine, the gap between potatoes and the next best source of food was not closed for large segments of the population. Even if the Irish had better realized the dangers of an overdependence on the potato diet, it is not quite clear whether they could have done much about it. Irish agriculture, after all, *was* diversified, potatoes accounting for perhaps a third of land under tillage and one seventh of the land under cultivation (inclusive of grazing lands). It was the consumption pattern of its lower classes that was insufficiently diversified.

The second line of defense has been discussed at some length in Chapter 6. Simply put, lower wealth per capita implies higher vulnerability to any kind of disaster. Private wealth can be converted into food for oneself or one's neighbors; overhead capital facilitates the relief of the worst-affected regions. It is clear, however, that both lines of defense cannot be accepted on *a priori* bases alone. What is necessary is to test for the factors which were responsible for the vulnerability of Ireland's society to the ravages of the *Phytophthora infestans*. In order to do this, it is necessary to discuss in some greater detail the quantitative dimensions of the famine.[2]

For historical demographers, the interest in the last great European natural disaster is self-evident. As far as economic historians are concerned, the famine has been traditionally the major watershed in Irish history. This view has been recently called into question. One author (Cullen, 1972, p. 132) has gone so far as to suggest that "the Famine was less a national disaster than a social and regional one . . . even if famine had not intervened, a decline in population was inevitable". Of course, it is not easy to test the hypothesis that the Great Famine was a major watershed in Irish economic history without defining properly what is meant exactly by a watershed. It is clear, however, that the vastness with which the potato failure looms over Irish history has not been significantly diminished by such revisionism.

The Irish famine has, of course, been viewed by Irish historians as an event of singular importance. Yet, it is rather astonishing how imprecisely historians have estimated the actual number of people who died during the famine as a result of the blight. The commissioners of the 1851 Census (Great Britain, 1856a, Vol. XXIX, pp. 509–10) carried out a simple calculation, extrapolating the 1841 population to the hypothetical level it would have reached in 1851 in the absence of the disaster. Rather than pursuing that computation in full, they followed by simply reporting a *total* mortality (instead of *excess* mortality) estimate of 985,366, which is the total number of persons reported to have died in 1846–50 on the forms of the 1851 Census, a number which is essentially useless. In 1874 O'Rourke (1902, p. 499) estimated the number at 1·24 million. Even among present-day historians, the range in the various estimates is surprisingly large. Green (1957, p. 126) implies that only slightly more than 500,000 died, but in the same volume O'Neill (1957, p. 255) cites 1 million as the number of famine deaths, and McArthur (1957, p. 312) thinks that excess mortality was "well over 500,000 [and] nearly a million . . . may not be far from the truth". In what appears to be the only careful computation of excess mortality during the famine Cousens (1960a) arrives at a figure of 800,645. This figure seems to have been uncritically adopted in some of the best work done on nineteenth-century Ireland (for example, Donnelly, 1973, p. 44; and Lee, 1973a, p. 1). A detailed critique of Cousens's estimates is presented below. The highest estimate among modern historians is that of Flinn (1977, p. 421), who suggests a possible death toll of 1·5 million. Verrière (1979, p. 64) has estimated famine mortality at 1·6 million, but this figure is apparently total and not excess mortality. Dupâquier (1980, pp. 172–3) utilizes Verrière's estimates to put excess mortality at 600,000.

The range of these estimates seems to bear out Edwards and Williams's statement (1957, p. vii) that "it is difficult to know how many men and women died in Ireland in the famine years between 1845 and 1852". Yet many economic historians will find themselves in disagreement with their subsequent statement that "perhaps all that matters is the certainty that many, many died". If possible, knowing with some precision how many people died is preferable to the vague notion that "many" died. As will be shown, existing data allow a fairly accurate estimate of the number of famine-related deaths in Ireland. These "excess" deaths are defined as those who died during the famine who would not have died otherwise. As is usually the case, the reconstruction of historical data from defective and incomplete information requires assumptions. These assumptions will be stated explicitly wherever employed, so that the reader has an opportunity to judge for himself the accuracy and reliability of the ensuing estimations. One such assumption is that up to the Great Famine the Irish population was "stable", that is, the birth and death rates computed for 1841 generally hold for the entire period 1821–45. Emigration became a major factor from the mid-1830s on. The direct effect of emigration is taken into account by the procedures used, but it is far more difficult to assess from the existing data what the secondary effects of emigration were on the demographic variables. While the assumption of a "prefamine steady state" is obviously an oversimplification, the sudden and catastrophic impact of the famine was of such an enormous order of magnitude that reality is not distorted too much by measuring the impact of the famine as a deviation from this steady state.

The demographic information available for the decade following the 1841 Census is of uneven quality. Until 1846 it may be assumed that, except for total emigration figures, the basic variables, such as death and birth rates, marriage age, and so on, did not change radically. However, the five years between 1846 and the 1851 Census were extremely disturbed from every point of view, and there is no justification for using the steady-state values of the prefamine period for these years. The decade can hence be conveniently divided into two subperiods of equal length, 1841–5 and 1846–50.

The death rates for the critical years 1846–50 can be estimated in two alternative ways. One procedure is to obtain the recorded death rates for the famine years from the 1851 Census. The other procedure is to estimate the death rates as a residual by comparing the 1846 and 1851 total populations after accounting for births, overseas migration, and internal migration. The latter procedure, described in detail below, will be adopted here. The former procedure constitutes the basis of the estimates of S. H. Cousens (1960a; 1960b), and its rejection here warrants some explanation. Cousens utilized the information provided in Great Britain, 1856b, Vol. XXX. This information contains the number of persons who were reported to have died in the decade 1841–51. Two separate sources of famine deaths were reported in the Census, namely, those reported on Census forms (that is, reported in 1851 by surviving family members to have died in the famine years) and those who were reported to have died in public institutions (workhouses, prisons, hospitals, and so on). Cousens simply added the two to obtain county-by-county death rates after correcting for the supposedly incorrect time-pattern of the deaths reported to have occurred during the decade. He then subtracted an annual normal death rate somewhat arbitrarily set equal to 22 per 1,000 for every county, and estimated excess death rates. The basic objection to Cousens's procedure is that they double-count those who died in institutions and were also reported by their relatives anyway, while they undercount those who were in neither group. The latter objection is probably by far the more important. Since entire families had been eliminated from Ireland, by death and/or emigration, deaths occurring in these families would never surface in the 1851 Census. Moreover, memories concerning deceased relatives—always a weak reed—were likely to have been especially blurred in those turbulent times. Not only are Cousens's figures therefore biased downward, but the bias differs from region to region. The conclusion is that the 1851 Census data cannot be used for the purpose of estimating the excess death rates during the Irish famine.

The only alternative to Cousens's procedure is to estimate the death rate as a residual. More complete details on the computation technique are provided in Mokyr (1980b, pp. 245–7). The calculation proceeded in the following stages: first, the population of each county was extrapolated to 1846 by assuming that the average prefamine birth and death rates computed in Chapter 3 held approximately for 1841–6, and subtracting emigration in those years. Secondly, the 1851 population was compared with the "counterfactual" population each county would have had if death and birth rates had remained the same during the years 1846–50, subtracting the famine emigrants. Thirdly, an upper bound of the famine death rate was obtained by assuming that birth rates were unaffected by the famine. In that case the famine death rate is simply that death rate which sets the "counterfactual" population equal to the actual population in 1851. Fourthly, a lower bound of the famine death rate was computed by assuming that the lower child/woman rates observed in 1851 compared to 1841 were wholly due to reduced birth rates (rather than partially due also to the fact that infant mortality rates rose proportionally more than death rates among women aged 17–45). Fifthly, the excess death rates were computed by subtracting the pre-famine death rates from the estimated famine death rates. Sixthly, the number of "famine casualties" was calculated by applying the excess death rates to the estimated 1846 population.

As already indicated, these calculations do not result in an unambiguous set of figures. First and foremost, we do not know what happened to birth rates during the famine years, so that we have to set upper and lower bounds to our estimates. The precise interpretation of the upper-bound estimates is that they represent the demographic deficit caused by the famine. If birth rates did not decline, of course, the deficit is wholly due to excess death rates. Since they obviously did decline, albeit to an unknown extent, part of the demographic deficit should be attributed to these "averted births" which, depending on one's philosophic outlook, may or may not be reckoned as famine casualties.[3] Two other ambiguities arise. One of them is due to the ambiguity of death rates already indicated in Chapter 3. Since there was no obvious way to choose between the two alternative procedures outlined there, both had to be tried. Furthermore, a serious problem emerged with respect to the county of origin of Irish emigrants during the famine decade. Data on the county of origin of Irish emigrants became available in 1851, and could be estimated for the period 1821–41 by survival techniques. But there is no obvious solution to the problem during the period 1841–51, and a number of alternative assumptions had to be experimented with.[4] For the estimate of the total number of famine casualties for Ireland as a whole, the last difficulty is, of course, unimportant. In Tables 9.1 and 9.2 the main results are presented. The numbers represent averages of the estimates implied by the various assumptions made about the geographical distribution of emigration in 1846–50. That this procedure is very approximate, hardly needs to be said. The average of three guesses is not necessarily better than the individual conjectures. Most of the results, however, do not seem sensitive to the assumptions employed. The two tables demonstrate that famine mortality was higher than most modern historians suppose. The upper-bound estimates, which include averted births as deaths, are close to 1·5 million, and the lower bounds are still well in excess of 1 million. These are, to repeat, *excess* death figures:

persons who died in the disaster years who would not otherwise have died. Thus, the 1851 Census commissioners were close to the mark when they perceived a gap of approximately 2·5 million people for which overseas emigration could account for only about 1 million. The gap thus calculated is somewhat too small, since the Census commissioners applied a natural rate of growth of 1·0036% (Great Britain, 1856a, Vol. XXIX, p. 509; also Great Britain, 1856c, Vol. XXXI, p. xvi), which understated the true rate by about 0·6 percent and, therefore, understated the gap by 250,000 people or so. This error is compensated for by their failure to include in the emigration figures those who went to Great Britain.

Table 9.1   *Average Annual Excess Death Rates and Total Excess Deaths,*
1846–51 (all rates in per 1,000)

Death Rate, Version I*	Ulster	Leinster	Munster	Connaught	Ireland
Excess Death Rate, Upper Bound	26·7	13·8	36·2	60·5	33·0
Excess Death Rate, Lower Bound	19·8	8·6	24·8	49·7	24·3
Total Excess Deaths, Upper Bound	345,264	140,088	489,779	516,468	1,491,599
Total Excess Deaths, Lower Bound	251,613	85,843	326,017	411,885	1,075,358
Death Rate, Version II*					
Excess Death Rate, Upper Bound	24·6	14·5	36·4	62·8	33·2
Excess Death Rate, Lower Bound	17·9	9·2	25·0	52·0	24·5
Total Excess Deaths, Upper Bound	315,277	147,342	492,546	542,623	1,497,788
Total Excess Deaths, Lower Bound	223,933	92,827	328,547	436,821	1,082,128

* Compare Table 3.2.
Source: Mokyr, 1980b, pp. 248–9 (slightly revised).

Furthermore, there are two reasons to believe that the estimates in Tables 9.1 and 9.2 are, in fact, biased *downward*, though the magnitudes of the biases are probably small. The first source of bias is technical in nature. The algorithm used treats emigration as one sudden event occurring in 1851 rather than as a constant continuous flow occurring continuously over the five years. This assumption tends to bias the estimates of famine mortality downward by a small amount.[5] The second source of downward bias is quantitatively more important. Until now, it has been assumed that mortality and emigration were mutually exclusive, so that excess mortality rates were computed by subtracting off all emigrants. The procedure employed completely ignores all those who died at sea or shortly after arrival due to famine-related causes. The number which theoretically should have been included in our estimate consists of two components. First, since emigration was always some-what risky as a result of conditions on board, the increase in emigration itself led to more mortality. Secondly, there is much evidence to support the contention that mortality rates en route to America rose dramatically during and because of the famine. Overcrowding, poor nutrition, and the already-emaciated condition of many emigrants, all compounded by the contagious diseases which raged in Ireland, led to many deaths of emigrants. Moreover, the season of travel was extended to cover the entire year, which meant that many emigrants arrived in the USA and Canada in the late autumn, hence reducing the probability of surviving the harsh winter. Furthermore, the sudden surge in demand for passage to America made many unseaworthy vessels participate in the emigrant trade, some of which sank.

Table 9.2 *Average Annual Excess Death Rates, 1846–51, by County (per 1,000, Average of Versions I and II)*

County	Upper bound	Lower bound	County	Upper bound	Lower bound
Antrim	20·3	15·0	Limerick	20·9	10·0
Armagh	22·2	15·3	Londonderry	10·1	5·7
Carlow	8·8	2·7	Longford	26·7	20·2
Cavan	51·8	42·7	Louth	14·6	8·2
Clare	46·5	31·5	Mayo	72·0	58·4
Cork	41·8	32·0	Meath	21·2	15·8
Donegal	18·7	10·7	Monaghan	36·0	28·6
Down	12·5	6·7	Queen's	29·1	21·6
Dublin	0·7	−2·1	Roscommon	57·4	49·5
Fermanagh	39·1	29·2	Sligo	61·1	52·1
Galway	58·0	46·1	Tipperary	35·0	23·8
Kerry	36·1	22·4	Tyrone	22·3	15·2
Kildare	12·0	73·4	Waterford	30·8	20·8
Kilkenny	18·1	12·5	Westmeath	26·3	20·0
King's	24·9	18·0	Wexford	6·6	1·7
Leitrim	50·2	42·9	Wicklow	14·6	10·8

Note: Minor inconsistencies between Tables 9.1 and 9.2 are due to rounding and averaging.
Source: As Table 9.1.

How many deaths should be added to our excess mortality figures to account for deaths among emigrants? Beyond doubt, the death rates on some "coffin ships" were staggering: on the *Ceylon,* almost 45 percent of the steerage passengers died on the way; on the *Loosthank,* 33 percent perished (McArthur, 1957, pp. 131–2). Many who arrived alive died shortly after. The *Agnes* arrived in 1847 with 427 passengers, of whom only 150 were alive after fifteen days (Woodham-Smith, 1962, p. 231). Yet these horror stories are not necessarily representative of the emigration movement during the entire period. The mortality on board emigration ships was unusually high in 1847, far higher than in any other year (Great Britain, 1847a, Vol. XIX, p. 467; Great Britain, 1851,

Vol. XIX, p. 4; Great Britain, 1854, Vol. XIII, p. 100). It is quite obvious, moreover, that there was large variability among emigrant ships, and that even in the fatal year 1847 the majority of ships arriving in Quebec contained passengers in good health, among whom death rates were minimal (Great Britain, 1847–8, Vol. XLVII, pp. 398 ff.). For the year 1847, the Government Emigration Office in Quebec reported that 98,125 persons embarked on ships or were born on board, the vast majority of these were Irish. Of these 5,282 (5·39 percent) died at sea, 3,389 (3·46 percent) died in quarantine on Grosse Isle, and 8,154 (8·3 percent) died in hospitals. Total mortality in 1847 to Canada was thus about 17 percent (MacDonagh, 1957, p. 371). However, the next year only 1·11 percent died on board or in quarantine. The voyage to the USA, which imposed tighter regulations on passenger ships, was generally less lethal than to Canada.

All in all, maybe 5 percent of total overseas migration at the most should be included in the total death rates. This addition would add at most about 46,000 to the overall death figures during the period 1846–51, and of course even less to the excess deaths. Thus, while the bias tends to make our estimates somewhat too small, it does not do so by an amount that could change any of the conclusions.

As Table 9.2 demonstrates, the famine was anything but uniform in its impact on Ireland. Some areas suffered far more than others. The breakdown of the death rates by province does not fully reflect these differences, since there was also considerable intraprovincial variation. As shown above, the excess death rates are somewhat sensitive to our assumptions concerning famine emigration rates and prefamine mortality rates. None the less, four groups of counties can be distinguished somewhat roughly according to the severity of the famine. First, low excess death rates are observed for East Leinster including Dublin, as well as in the northern and northeastern counties of Ulster. Moderate excess death rates occurred in central Ireland (West Leinster and Tipperary), as well as in central Ulster (Tyrone and Armagh). High excess mortality rates characterize most of Munster and the southern counties of Ulster. Finally, extremely high excess mortality occurred in most of Connaught, particularly Sligo, Galway, and, worst of all, Mayo.

What accounts for this pattern? A detailed theoretical analysis of factors that could be responsible for the extent of the excess mortality would be very difficult to attempt, but a brief list of possible candidates may prove useful. First, since the blight was first and foremost a reduction of the potato crop, the degree of dependency on potatoes would at first sight appear an obvious determinant of famine mortality. A second strong candidate is prefamine income. A peasant with a higher income facing the loss of his crop could feed his family by dis-saving or by borrowing with greater ease, and the obstacles to his emigration were less formidable. A third factor which is likely to be of major importance in explaining excess mortality rates is urbanization. Since urban areas were more commercialized, the absence of potatoes did not completely cut off the food supply, though it did raise the prices of necessities to dangerous and, at times, lethal levels. The absence of a food retail system in the more remote provinces in the west and south is often cited as a major cause of mortality. The degree of self-sufficiency in food supply (on the household level) cannot be readily measured, but it is likely to be negatively correlated with the level of urbanization. Finally, urbanized areas were likely to have had lower excess death rates simply because their prefamine death rates were already considerably higher.

Some socioeconomic characteristics of the population are also possible factors determining the impact of the famine. Literacy rates are one such factor. Literacy may have been correlated with other skills which were important for survival (for instance, personal hygiene, ability to adjust rapidly to unknown foods such as Indian corn, knowledge about emigration opportunities, and so on). The occupational structure of the population may also have mattered. Arguably, the larger the proportion of persons dependent on agriculture, all other things equal, the more vulnerable a society is to harvest failure. As a general rule, this relation is clearly false, but it seems to fit an economy dependent on a subsistence crop.

A standard argument has been that the size of landholding was a major element in the famine. The main victims of the famine were farm laborers, cottagers, and smallholders. But was farm size *as such* that crucial? Many cottagers and smallholders worked part-time in rural industry or on other farms, others migrated to England on a seasonal basis. Thus, they may have had comparatively more resources that were not associated with potatoes than someone whose farm was large enough to guarantee a comfortable existence on potatoes in ordinary years. A different variable is the quality of housing in Ireland. Housing quality is one proxy for private capital formation and wealth, although its precise relation with excess mortality is ambiguous (cf. Mokyr, 1980b, p. 253). There is no way of determining these issues *a priori*, and empirical tests are required to make further progress.

A further index of availability of capital which could be used for emergency food is livestock. In contrast to housing, this form of capital can be easily converted from capital goods to consumer goods. While ownership of livestock was heavily concentrated among the wealthier farmers, a large number of animals in a region might have made a difference for the poor farmers. Reports on livestock theft were, needless to say, common, and much livestock was sold off in anticipation thereof (Green, 1957, p. 124). But the actual data are very difficult to interpret. The puzzling and surprising fact is that during the 1840s the value of livestock increased in Ireland. According to the 1841 Census, the value of livestock in Ireland was £20·7 million (Great Britain, 1843, Vol. XXIV, p. 455), while in 1847 it was £22·5 million, and in 1848, £23·1 million (Great Britain, 1849a, Vol. XLIX, p. 6). In a country in which many millions were starving, livestock would be expected to be eaten or sold rather than maintained. Some of that, of course, did occur, as disaggregating the data will reveal. Pigs, a main consumer of potatoes, declined in number from 1,353,101 in 1841 to 517,446 in 1847. The proportion of their value to total livestock value fell from 8·1 to 2·8 percent. It is also telling that the proportion of livestock owned by large farms (above 30 acres) increased from 34·8 to 56·4 percent. In part, therefore, the difficulty is resolved by realizing that only a small part of the livestock was owned by the millions of laborers, cottagers, and sub-tenants, who were most vulnerable to a failure of the potato crop. A similar phenomenon was observed by Lefgren (1973, pp. 22–3) for the Finnish famine in 1867–8. Lefgren, too, is surprised that not more animals were slaughtered during the famine. One might conclude tentatively that there is not much *prima facie* evidence that the eating of livestock (except pigs) served as an effective defense against starvation. There are, however, other grounds for a defense of including the live-stock variable. For example, livestock per capita is a good proxy for the capital–labor ratio, which is strongly correlated with the technological development of agriculture and the diversification of crops. Moreover, cattle, sheep, and poultry produce dairy products which could have been an important complement to famine diets—as well as a good reason not to slaughter the animals.

Finally, one could argue that the amount of rent per capita should be used as an independent variable. One reason for the inclusion of this variable, as argued in a different context by Cousens (1963) and by Almquist (1977, pp. 161, 210), is that rent per capita is a good measure of population pressure. From a purely theoretical point of view, the assumption that rent per capita is inversely correlated with population pressure is not necessarily correct (Mokyr, 1980b, p. 275, n. 30). Perhaps more important is the fact that landlords paid poor rates, and poor rates were used for famine relief. While the British government passed emergency relief measures under Peel and Russell, and opened soup kitchens all over Ireland in the spring of 1847, it was decided in June 1847 that the Irish Poor Law system should be put in charge of any further assistance. With some understatement Woodham-Smith (1962, p. 310) notes that "from this point onwards the good intentions of the British Government became increasingly difficult to discern". In any event, the notion that the property of Ireland was to support the poverty of Ireland means for our purpose that the more the landowners could pay in poor rates, the better the chance of inhabitants to receive the much-needed emergency relief from the local Union. The financial condition of the vast majority of the Irish Unions was desperate, so that ability of landlords to pay the poor rates could be a matter of life and death (O'Neill, 1957). Ability to support the starving peasantry was as relevant as empathy with the victims of the famine. On both accounts it cannot be denied that the Irish upper class was far less helpful in absorb-ing the shocks caused by the disaster than their counterparts in Scotland and the continent. To be sure, a large number of Irish landlords, resident or absentee, were alienated from their peasantry, and were in bad financial straits. This difficulty was compounded, however, by the Irish Poor Law, imposed on Ireland by the British in 1838 and designed along lines similar to the British Poor Law of 1834. The Irish system was not designed to deal with emergencies and crumbled under the onslaught. The average Poor Law Union, the basic administrative unit of the system, was much larger in Ireland than in Britain. The average Poor

Law Union in Ireland contained 63,000 people, as opposed to 27,000 in England and Wales. This structure led to severe management and information problems, and also enhanced "free rider" effects. The individual voluntary efforts of landlords to employ or feed their tenants had little effect on their poor rates, thus diminishing the incentives to provide voluntary support (Central Relief Committee, 1852, pp. 16–17).

A sample of the regressions run to isolate the factors which contributed to excess mortality during the famine is presented in Table 9.3. A much larger number of equations can be found in Mokyr (1980b, pp. 256–66).[6] All regressions in Table 9.3 were run using generalized least-squares to eliminate possible heteroscedasticity of the error term due to the unequal size of the counties.

The regression results presented in Table 9.3 are suggestive but not entirely unambiguous due to the inevitable limitations of the data base. All of the regression equations are highly significant statistically with the lowest F-statistics still well beyond 10.00. The critical value of $F_{5,26}$ at the 1 percent level is 3.82. Broadly speaking, the overall explanatory power of the independent variables is fairly robust to the various assumptions used for computing the excess death rate. At the same time, however, some coefficients on individual variables change from significance to insignificance and back with changes in the assumptions made, weakening to some extent the results reported. The coefficients should, therefore, be interpreted with some caution.

Several independent variables were clearly unimportant in determining the vulnerability of a given county. First and foremost, the pre-famine acreage of potatoes fails to show any significance in any specification whether the variable is defined as acreage per capita, or acreage as a percentage of total land under cultivation. Surprising as this may seem, the tentative conclusion must be that the degree of dependency on potatoes seems to have mattered little in determining the distribution of the excess death rates within Ireland. How is that possible? One explanation is that the 1844–5 constable survey on which the data is based (Bourke, 1959–60) was deficient and cannot be trusted. More likely, however, is the possibility that the dependency on potatoes before the famine was so extensive and the destruction of the crops in 1846 so complete, that variations in the potato acreage per capita or per acre hardly mattered. The reduction in nutrition was so large that it possibly made little difference whether a county cultivated 0.46 acres per capita (as was the case in the county most dependent on potatoes, Waterford), or 0.17 acres per capita (in Co. Leitrim, the lowest besides Dublin). Finally, the independent variable used is potato acreage, not potato crops. Little is known about variations in prefamine productivity per acre, but if high yields per acre were associated with low acreage and vice versa (as would be the case if the potato consumption per capita were relatively constant), the acreage data are poor proxies for the "degree of dependency on potatoes".

Among the other variables which appear unrelated to a county's vulnerability to the blight, rent per capita appears to be the most

Table 9.3 *Average Annual Regressions of Excess Mortality Rates, Versions 1 and 2 of Prefamine Mortality Rates (t-values in parentheses)*

Regression number	1	2	3	4	5	6	7	8
Dependent variable*	Upper-bound excess mortality rate	Upper-bound excess mortality rate	Upper-bound excess mortality rate	Lower-bound excess mortality rate	Upper-bound excess mortality rate	Upper-bound excess mortality rate	Upper-bound excess mortality rate	Lower-bound excess mortality rate
Constant	0·0677 (3·76)	0·0985 (3·30)	0·0759 (3·52)	0·0598 (2·90)	0·0637 (1·78)	0·107 (3·36)	0·047 (2·57)	0·0853 (2·85)
Income, per capita		-0·0037 (-3·23)	-0·0043 (-3·41)	-0·0036 (-3·01)				-0·0028 (-2·46)
Labor Income, per capita	-0·0026 (-1·84)					-0·0034 (-2·80)		
Housing-Quality Index†					0·0415 (1·50)		0·0891 (3·29)	
Livestock, per capita					-0·0068 (-2·09)		-0·0095 (-2·21)	
Percentage Small Farms‡	0·0386 (1·63)	0·0263 (1·23)	0·0391 (2·19)	0·0412 (2·41)	0·0112 (0·47)	0·0336 (1·40)		0·0350 (1·55)
Average Farm Size × 100							0·000097 (0·20)	
Literacy Rate	-0·0824 (-1·82)	-0·1111 (-2·74)	-0·0972 (-2·39)	-0·0923 (-2·37)	-0·0864 (-2·36)	-0·0823 (-1·97)		-0·0768 (-1·96)
Percentage Urban		0·0577 (2·99)	0·0596 (3·03)	0·0541 (2·88)				
Percentage Nonagricultural					-0·488 (-1·73)		-0·0758 (-2·50)	
Rural Industry§	-0·0260 (-1·05)					-0·0590 (-2·67)		-0·0517 (-2·50)

	1	2	3	4	5	6	7	8
Potato Acreage, per capita		−0·017 (−0·45)				−0·0543 (−1·31)		−0·0534 (−1·38)
Percentage of acreage in potatoes			0·022 (0·47)	0·0013 (0·03)			−0·0314 (−0·514)	
Rents, per capita	−0·0012 (−0·35)							
F (d.f.)	11·64 (5,26)	16·82 (5,26)	18·46 (5,26)	14·81 (5,26)	15·57 (5,26)	15·54 (5,26)	13·12 (5,26)	13·11 (5,26)

* Dependent variables are average annual excess mortality rates, defined as follows:
  column 1: assumption I with respect to prefamine death rates; famine emigration computed from the mean of 1851 and prefamine emigration shares;
  columns 2, 3, and 4: assumption I with respect to prefamine death rates; famine emigration computed from the mean of 1851–5 and prefamine emigration shares;
  column 5: assumption II with respect to prefamine death rates; famine emigration computed from the mean of 1851 and prefamine shares;
  columns 6, 7, and 8: assumption II with respect to prefamine death rates; famine emigration computed from the mean of 1851–5 and prefamine shares.
† Measured as the proportion fourth-class (that is, worst) houses.
‡ Threshold size: 20 acres.
§ Defined as total rural male and female workers employed in textile production as a percentage of total rural employment.

unexpected for the reasons stated above. In spite of the *a priori* plausibility of a positive relation between rent per capita and the resilience of the economy, this hypothesis cannot be accepted at any level of statistical confidence. It also seems quite obvious that there is no evidence whatsoever to support the hypothesis that the degree of urbanization, or any variable strongly correlated with it, was in any way a protection against the famine. The results indicate quite clearly that the excess death rates tended to be higher in urbanized counties. Apparently, the effect of the cities' greater sensitivity to malnutrition and contagious disease was stronger than the combined effect of the alleged greater resilience of towns to harvest failure, and the higher prefamine death rates in cities (which tended to make excess death rates lower, *ceteris paribus*). The effect of rural industry is not clear. In some specifications the relation seems to be negative, in others positive. It has to be concluded that the coefficient of the rural industry variable depends on the particular assumption used, and that the data available cannot therefore determine the effect of rural industry on the magnitude of the famine.

The coefficient of income per capita (labor income or total income) is in most cases between -0.0015 and -0.0040. Thus, for each additional pound sterling of income per capita, the annual average excess death rate for five years would have been lower by something between 0.15 percent and 0.4 percent. Thus, 63,000–168,000 *fewer* people would have died in the entire period from famine-related causes (who would not have died otherwise) for each £1 increase in personal income per capita, all other factors held constant. If we assume, somewhat unreasonably, that the linearity assumption can be maintained even for nonmarginal changes, we could speculate what the net cost of relative backwardness was for Ireland. Income in Great Britain in 1841 was about £9 higher than in Ireland. Taking the lower bound of our estimate, it can thus be seen that poverty (in the narrow sense of low income) accounted for *at least* 600,000 famine deaths.

A second variable which seems to do well in accounting for the impact of the disaster is literacy. The coefficient on this variable is between -0.06 and -0.10, indicating that a 1 percent increase in the literacy rates would cause excess death rates to fall by 0.06–0.1 percent. Again, the magnitudes involved can best be clarified by means of a simple example. The average literacy rate (defined as the proportion of those aged 5 and over who could both read and write) in Ireland was 28.3 percent, according to the 1841 Census. If this rate had been half as high again (which would probably have brought Ireland up to British levels, though such comparisons remain extremely hazardous), and we take the lower coefficient of -0.06, the excess death rate would have fallen from 0.033 to about 0.024, implying approximately 500,000 *fewer* famine deaths.

The argument that farm size was a major determinant of excess mortality finds limited support in the data. Average farm size, as defined by total land under cultivation divided by the number of farms, displays no systematic association with excess death rates; and the relation is weak and highly sensitive to specifications and assumptions. More important is the result that excess death rates are positively correlated with the proportion of farms under a given level. The results suggest that the critical level was about 20 acres: the proportion of farms under that level is in general significantly and positively related to excess death rates. The livestock and housing-quality variables which serve as proxies for the overall capital stock (with the reservations noted) perform, on the whole, well and have the expected signs. It seems injudicious to analyze the magnitude of the coefficients, since the two variables are not unambiguous indicators of the ability of a county to cushion the impact of a disaster like the Great Famine. The housing-quality variable is the proportion of fourth-class houses, and as such it is an inaccurate proxy for the overall quality of housing even if we believe that the classification schemes used in the 1841 Census were consistently adhered to. The difficulties with the livestock variables have already been pointed out. Still, the overall size of the coefficients, 0·006–0·009, is consistent with our earlier findings. The value of livestock per capita in 1841 was about £2·5. Increasing this figure by £1 (or 40 percent) would have reduced the death toll by at least 250,000. Finally, the coefficient of the variable measuring the proportion of population engaged in nonagricultural activity has the expected sign, but its magnitude and level of significance are reduced if income variables are included. While the variable may have affected excess death rates in more than one way, at this stage it is not possible to distinguish meaningfully between other (and unobserved) variables for which the percentage in nonagricultural occupations may be a proxy, and the direct effect of industrialization on income.

To summarize, the Irish potato famine of 1846–51 was the last large-scale natural demographic disaster to strike Europe. It provides an opportunity to study in some detail the impact and the factors determining the magnitude of the excess mortality such disasters involved. While the information base for Ireland (both before and after the famine) is far better than for any comparable event in European history, the data should be interpreted with caution. The excess death figures were calculated, inevitably, on the basis of certain simplifying assumptions. The assumptions used for the present calculations are, however, superior to those implicit in previous attempts to estimate (or guess) the number of persons who perished due to famine-related causes.

The factors which made Ireland so vulnerable to the famine have been identified with some certainty. The actual acreage devoted to potatoes was statistically insignificant in explaining excess mortality. Far more important were general economic variables such as income, literacy, and capital–labor ratios. While farm size seems also to have played a role, it is clear that the famine struck down not only the smallest farmers (cottagers and landless laborers), but also those whose farms were somewhat larger, up to 20 acres. Rent per capita whether it reflected generally the pressure of labor on the land, or more specifically the ability of landowners to pay poor rates, were unimportant.

There is no single explanation of why the potato blight brought such a catastrophe to Ireland while its effects on other countries was relatively light by comparison with Ireland (although not when compared to anything that these countries had experienced in the decades before the famine). Excess mortality in the Netherlands amounted to about 2 percent of the population, in Belgium about 1·1 percent (Mokyr, 1980a, pp. 436–7). In Scotland the data do not permit a precise estimation of famine mortality, but figures presented in Flinn (1977, pp. 423–6) show that the rate of population growth in the decade 1841–51 was the same as the rate of growth in the previous decade. Flinn (1978, p. 56) points out that in the Scottish northwest "there seems to have been virtually no starvation" and cites one official in 1846 maintaining that "so healthy a season has seldom been known". The dependency on potatoes in Ireland was probably higher than in Flanders or in the Scottish Highlands. The finding that *within* Ireland the variation in potato cultivation does not explain the variation in excess mortality rates, does not warrant the conclusion that the same holds when we compare Ireland to other economies. None the less, it seems clear that a higher rate of overall development and industrialization in Scotland and Belgium made it possible for society to save their laboring poor from the fate of the Irish. Smout (1978, pp. 29–30) attributes the Scottish success in preventing the famine from becoming the demographic disaster it became in Ireland in part to the "general level of sophistication and wealth that Scotland had reached", and in part to the efficiency and generosity of those who had it in their power to relieve the famine. The record of Scottish landlords was also more positive than in Ireland, but in part this reflects ability and not just willingness. Similarly, in Belgium the stronger sectors of the economy were able to pull the starving peasants of Flanders through the worst stages of the famine. The Belgian government, in spite of its aversion to intervening directly by food purchases, departed from its principles and bought large amounts of food, provided free transportation for food shipments, organized public works, and like Britain removed all tariff barriers on food imports. Local authorities, in part subsidized by the Brussels government, supplemented these relief efforts. Soup kitchens, communal bakeries, and societies for the purchase of grain were established throughout Flanders (Jacquemyns, 1929, pp. 270–94). Private charity, too, made major contributions to famine relief. The resources of the Belgian economy made it possible to make up a large segment of the deficit caused by the failure of the potato and rye harvest through imports (Mokyr, 1976a, p. 252). Interestingly enough, in the Netherlands, which was much less industrialized than Belgium or Scotland, mortality rates were much higher, though they were still far removed from the cataclysmic order of magnitude reached in Ireland.

Marc Bloch once wrote: "Just as the progress of a disease shows a doctor the secret life of a body, so to the historian the progress of a great calamity yields valuable information about the nature of the society so stricken." Ireland's experience in the first half of the nineteenth century serves as a grim reminder of the cost of failing to industrialize. These costs are often neglected by adherents of the so-called "pessimist" school, which views the Industrial Revolution as at best a mixed blessing for those who lived through it and that economies which escaped it for one reason or another should have regarded themselves as fortunate. Industrialization was a costly process, as a long tradition of writers, from the Hammonds to Hobsbawm, have maintained in vivid detail. The Irish famine—and to a lesser extent the Dutch and Austrian experience in the 1840s and the Finnish in 1868—illustrates the risks and costs associated with the alternative.

Notes: Chapter 9

1   The witnesses before the Poor Law Inquiry commissioners repeatedly voiced their dissatisfaction with the monotony of the potato diet. A Co. Galway witness spoke for many when he exclaimed that "we would all prefer one meal of [oat] meal a day and the other of potatoes than the two meals of potatoes" (Great Britain, 1836b, Vol. XXXII, p. 2).

2   Much of the following is based on Mokyr (1980b).

3   Data for the Finnish famine of 1867–8 suggest that if the experience of Ireland was anything like that in Finland, the lower-bound figures are much closer to the truth. The Finnish experience is summarized by the following data (1860–5 = 100) (see Lefgren, 1973, p. 24):

year	birth rate	death rate	infant-mortality rate
1866	86·7	131·2	126·1
1867	87·5	148·8	128·3
1868	66·7	303·1	225·2
1869	91·3	98·4	79·6

4   The three assumptions are: (a) the share of each county in total emigration is an average of its share in 1851 and its share in 1821–41; (b) the share of each county is an average of its share in the five years 1851–5 and its prefamine share; (c) the share of each county is computed by extrapolating the 1851–5 trendline backward to the midpoint of the famine if the trend was significant, and equal to the mean share if the trendline was not significant.

5   Intuitively the source of the bias can be seen as follows. Let P_1 be population at the beginning of the famine, P_2 population at the end of the famine, and E emigration in the famine years. The rate of population decline has been estimated by assuming that all emigration occurred at the end of the period. Then the rate of population decline x is computed from

$$x = \log \frac{(P_2 + E)}{P_1}.$$

An alternative is to assume that all emigration occurred on the first day of the famine. In that case, the rate of population decline is

$$x' = \log \frac{(P_2)}{P_1 - E}.$$

The "correct" rate of decline is, of course, somewhere in between. Since $(P_2 + E)/P_1 > P_2/(P_1 - E)$, the absolute value of the rate of population decline $|x|$ is smaller than $|x'|$ and smaller than any value between x and x' including the "true" rate of population decline.

6   The results reported in Table 9.2 differ slightly from those reported in Mokyr (1980b, pp. 262–6), because of some minor adjustments in the computation of the potato acreage variable. The nature of these adjustments is reported in Mokyr (1981a). None of the conclusions has been revised due to these adjustments.

Chapter 10

Explaining Irish Poverty

Why did Ireland starve? To start with, it should be emphasized that Irish poverty was not really one single "event". Rather, we are dealing with a series of related but separate phenomena which did not necessarily share the same causal mechanisms. Irish agriculture was poor and backward. Ireland did not undergo an industrial revolution. The Irish potato crop failed in the 1840s. These three "events" were all part of Ireland's economic plight, but they were not necessarily caused by the same factors. Nor did they inexorably lead to each other, although feedback mechanisms no doubt existed. It should, then, come as no surprise that the question "Why Ireland Starved" cannot be answered in a single sentence.

What insights into the Big Question of Irish poverty have been provided here? First, the main negative results should be mentioned. Three influential theses have been put forward in the past to account for Ireland's poor economic performance. First, poverty, has been associated with overpopulation. I have shown in Chapter 3 that to the extent that this hypothesis is falsifiable at all, it is indeed not confirmed by the evidence. A second explanation related the slow pace of development of Irish agriculture to the land-tenure system. Chapter 4 has shown the limitations and difficulties inherent in that view. Thirdly, the importance of the absence of certain natural resources such as coal and iron has been shown to have been exaggerated. A fourth hypothesis links Irish poverty to emigration. This hypothesis has ranked less prominently than the other three in the literature, but its testing yielded less clear-cut results, due to the many unmeasurable aspects of emigration. None the less, as far as quantitative aspects are concerned, emigration—like the other three hypotheses—has to be relegated to the category of "also rans".

What, then, can be said about the causes of Irish poverty? It is perhaps useful to recast our model of causality, and to distinguish between two types of causal factors. One source of trouble was what one might call "transitory" or "cyclical" shocks, which were specific to these years and most of which were experienced elsewhere in Europe as well. The other source was the fundamental, long-term weakness peculiar to the Irish economy. To be sure, it is not possible to decompose the poverty of the country into these two types of causes in an exhaustive manner. Yet few will disagree that the ability of any economy to withstand short-term exogenous shocks depends very much on the "structural parameters" of its system. For instance, the ability of the Western economies to withstand the exogenous rise in energy prices in the 1970s was a function of variables which determined the resilience of their economies. While the German and Swiss economies were exposed in the same degree to rising oil prices as the Portuguese or Turkish economies, the results were very different.

The most violent and spectacular exogenous disturbance to affect the Irish economy was, of course, the potato famine itself. Two other external shocks greatly affected the Irish economy in the years 1790–1850, and while not as dramatic as the famine, they left a profound imprint on the economic well-being of Ireland. These two shocks were the changes in the price level (which rose during the French wars and fell subsequently) and the decline of cottage industries resulting from the mechanization of textile industries.

As the economy became more and more part of a larger economic unit, it became more susceptible to exogenous disturbances which emanated from events in foreign countries. After 1760, and especially after 1790, Ireland became increasingly integrated into a larger economic unit consisting of Great Britain and later the entire North Atlantic economy. The abolition of the Penal Codes and Cattle Acts, the Revolutionary and Napoleonic Wars, the Union and the subsequent gradual abolition of restrictions on Anglo-Irish trade, the merger of the two treasuries in 1817, and the complete commercial Union of 1824, all made Ireland increasingly a part of the British economy. The reduction in transportation costs due to the beginning of steamship service across the Irish Sea and the construction of railroad networks in Britain and the continental countries reinforced this trend after 1825. In the three-quarters of a century before the famine, Ireland was steadily becoming more and more what economists refer to as a "small open economy", that is, an economy which faces a set of prices given by the world market over which it has no control. World events affected the Irish economy through changes in these exogenously given prices.

Do these shocks "explain" Irish poverty? Before we discuss them in greater detail, it should be emphasized that Ireland was in no way unique being exposed to their effects. Indeed, the violence of the Napoleonic Wars and the continental blockade probably affected Ireland less than other European countries on whose soil the battles were fought or whose economies were even more dependent on international trade (for example, the Netherlands). Similar causes had dissimilar effects because Ireland's economy was more backward and more rigid than other Western European economies, and thus was more vulnerable to these disturbances.

Some examples illustrate the way in which Ireland's peculiar economic features amplified these shocks. Consider the potato, widely viewed as a blessing by contemporaries and a nutritional miracle by historians.[1] The potato, however, could not be stored for periods exceeding one year, so that there were no buffer stocks. Moreover, because of its high ratios of volume and weight to value, transportation costs were very high, and trade in potatoes was limited. Only about 2 percent of the potato crop was exported directly. It was, thus, difficult to convert bumper crops into a store of value to serve as a protection if the potato harvest were to fail. The only way to carry out this conversion was by raising pigs. The stock of pigs was, indeed, decimated during the famine years. Contemporaries realized the hazards of the potato economy: "Life or death depends on the potato crop . . . when the crop fails starvation must ensue for none of a former year's crop can be preserved . . . should the crop of any year fail, extreme distress is inevitable" (Great Britain, 1836b, Vol. XXXII, pp. 1–4). The situation with turf was similar: abundant for local use in households as well as in manufacturing, it was not traded on a large scale because its bulkiness and weight made inland transportation very costly. Irish potatoes and turf were fundamentally different from Newcastle coal or Saudi oil: the abundance of energy could not be transformed into liquid assets which would have served as a hedge against a "rainy day".

One result of the high transaction costs associated with trade in the most widely consumed goods was the low level of commercialization of the rural Irish economy. Commercialization implies that a larger proportion of agricultural produce is sold at the market and a larger proportion of consumption is bought. For purposes of exposition only, assume that prior to commercialization the farmer was completely self-sufficient in food. Compare a self-sufficient farmer to a farmer consuming a basket of products, most of which are purchased in the market. The variance of income of the self-sufficient farmer is by definition equal to the variance of agricultural output caused by external factors. For a typical farmer who sells most of his crop, this identity is no longer true. When output falls due to harvest failure, agricultural prices rise, offsetting partially or completely the fall in income due to harvest failure. In this way, the downward slope of the demand curve serves as an insurance policy. That is to say, when crops are small, agricultural prices are usually high, and the farmer may receive a higher money income than with good crops, although it is not obvious that he will be better off in real terms. It seems, however, that the risks of starvation in case of harvest failures are smaller for the commercial than for the self-sufficient farmer. Although that is likely, one cannot conclude that the rise of the market economy *necessarily* reduces the risk to which farmers are exposed. The reason for this ambiguity is that the farmer in a market economy is now also subject to fluctuations which have nothing to do with his crop, but which are caused by perturbations in the non-agricultural sector or by fluctuations of harvests half a globe away. Such fluctuations would be perceived by farmers as movements of (rather than along) the demand curve. None the less, it seems that these fluctuations typically were less disastrous than major harvest failures.

Another source of rigidity peculiar to Ireland was the land system. As was demonstrated in Chapter 4, most Irish land on the eve of the famine was held on long leases. While in general long leases encouraged agricultural improvement, the specification of the rent in nominal terms meant that movements in the price of agricultural goods transferred income from landlords to tenants over 1790–1814, and from tenants to landlords after 1814. In 1790–1813 agricultural prices (as well as the overall price level, of which agricultural prices were the main component) were high. In 1814 agricultural prices fell precipitously, and although they fluctuated afterwards with weather and other short-term random factors, the average price of agricultural goods did not recover. The average price level of agricultural goods averaged 125·52 in 1790–1814 and 107·36 in 1815–45 (1821–5 = 100), which with a standard error of the difference in means of 4·61, is significant at the 0·1 percent level.[2] As a result of rigid nominal rents, Irish agriculture adjusted to changing market conditions with long lags. Falling prices of agricultural goods after 1814 led to a rise in real rents, although population growth leading to an increased demand for land also pushed in the same direction. Price movements led to much confusion, uncertainty, and abuse. Arrears in rents were ubiquitous, of course. Many landlords had no choice but to forgive the arrears or to reduce nominal rents in some other way to bring the level of rents in line with the price level (Blacker, 1834, p. 5; Weld, 1832, p. 480; Great Britain, 1836b, Vol. XXXIII, pp. 287, 296; OSM, box 23, file XVIII; box 26, file I; Clark, 1979, pp. 28–33). Some landlords, however, insisted on the specified level of rents, thus exacerbating the already-tense relations with their tenants and possibly discouraging capital formation by "confiscating" the tenants' capital in this way. Taxes, too, did not decline in nominal terms. On the other hand, it is possible that some tenants took advantage of the willingness of landlords to forgive arrears and paid lower real rents. The movement of the price level, in short, raised the cost of transacting, especially between landlord and tenant, creating more uncertainty and more confusion because leases were long. Short leases would have resolved the problem of price movement, but opened the door to "predatory landlordship". The only efficient solution would have been long-term leases expressed in real (as opposed to nominal) terms with symmetric escalator clauses. In view of the fact that persistent inflation in many modern Western economies has not yet led to universal adoption of contracts specified in real terms, it is hardly surprising that this solution was not feasible in nineteenth-century Ireland. Other sources of inflexibility in the Irish agricultural economy have been identified and discussed in previous chapters. The most important examples are the factors which prevented the economy from shifting to mixed farming and pasturage, and the highly imperfect land market which made it all but impossible for land to accumulate in the hands of those who could manage it best.

The most painful and damaging shock before the Great Famine was the decline in the fortunes of Ireland's cottage industries. Domestic industries were an important part of the Irish rural economy; their rapid decay after 1825, though it did not originate from anything that happened in Ireland, severely affected it. The Industrial Revolution in Britain and—to a much lesser extent—in Ulster, had a devastating effect on the incomes of the hundreds of thousands of rural and semi-urban spinners, weavers, and other workers who made their living in part from domestic nonagricultural activities. Cottage industries in Ireland included the preparation, spinning, and weaving of linen, and for a while the weaving of cotton cloth. Other, less important, occupations which belong to this category were rural nailors, cutlers, buttonmakers, and so forth. While the demise of the textile industries was disastrous for hundreds of thousands of people, by itself it cannot explain all of Ireland's poverty. In most of the south and midlands, where cottage industries had never been very important, economic conditions were just as wretched. Had there never been any rural industry in Connaught, its history in the 1830s and 1840s would probably not have been dramatically different. Almquist (1977, p. 169) has maintained that rural industry led to an explosion of population which then became insupportable when the nonagricultural sources of income vanished. It is quite true that cottage industries had a positive effect on population growth. Had there been no cottage industry, however, population growth would still have been rather rapid. In Kerry, Wicklow, or King's county (in which rural industry was insubstantial) population growth was still substantial. The regression results reported in Table 3.10 and in Mokyr (1981a) tell a similar story.[3]

All the same, the misery caused by the precipitous decline in earnings of textile weavers and spinsters was real enough. The cottage-industry sector in Ireland was composed of two subsectors: the more backward industries in Connaught which specialized in coarse yarn and where spinning was far more important than weaving, and the more advanced fine linens, such as cambrics and damasks, in Ulster. This geographical division was unfortunate. As it happened, the Industrial Revolution affected spinning before weaving, and the coarser qualities before the finer qualities. Consequently, the shock-wave hit the most vulnerable areas first. In the 1830s the situation of the Ulster weavers was bad; in Mayo, Sligo, and Leitrim the entire industry had disintegrated. Describing Lurgan (Co. Armagh) in 1838 C. G. Otway could still write that "nearly the entire population . . . is composed of weavers; and the wages of agricultural labour during harvest and seed time are high. It is stated that . . . there is full employment for all the hand loom weavers and that many more young persons wove now than formerly, and that the females who used formerly to spin the hand spun yarn now in general weave" (Great Britain, 1840, Vol. XXIII, p. 488). In Sligo, by contrast, it was all over: "There was no hand-spun yarn coming in worth speaking of . . . the linen manufacture on the old system has died a natural death, and the new system . . . has become extinct" (ibid., p. 494). Spinning had expired even earlier. In the late 1820s wet spinning techniques allowed the mechanical production of the finer counts of linen yarn. By the late 1830s hand-spinning was completely ruined (Gill, 1925, pp. 322–3). The handloom weaver survived longer, although his income was declining and he was gradually losing the independent status he enjoyed while working "for his own account".

What was the role played by the decline of domestic industries in the overall situation of the Irish economy? The demise of cottage industries in the 1830s and 1840s was ubiquitous, causing shocking misery in half a dozen regions in Europe from Scotland to Silesia. Still, the modern sectors in most of these economies were able to absorb many of the rural workers and their children. In Ireland the weaver facing an ever-declining wage married to a spinster whose yarn could no longer be sold, had only two options. One of these was to emigrate. More than any-where else in the world, this solution was resorted to by the Irish in the years before the famine. Those who remained behind had to find their livelihood in full-time agriculture, and thus the ranks of those unfortunate persons whose existence depended utterly on potatoes were unnaturally swollen on the eve of the famine not only in Mayo and Donegal, but also in the better-off counties like Antrim, Down, and Londonderry (OSM, box 9, file VI, pp. 78–80; box 13, file I; box 36, file III; Great Britain, 1836b, Vol. XXXIII, p. 312).

Temporary disequilibria caused by exogenous shocks emanating from foreign countries or political events can thus be seen to have perturbed Ireland and to have resulted in increased impoverishment, but they do not go far enough in explaining why their effect on Ireland was so much more devastating than in other countries. A variety of causes for Ireland's lack of resilience have been identified, and most of them, in one way or another, directly led to increased poverty through the single mechanism of reduced capital formation. Whether we look at agriculture, manufacturing, fisheries, transportation, housing, or human capital, the same picture returns time and again: productivity was low because labor lacked the complementary nonlabor inputs it needed. By and large, these inputs were reproducible producer durables of one form or another, both tangible and intangible. The way in which the various causes led to retarded capital formation can be conveniently dichotomized between the demand and the supply sides of capital formation, although the terms of demand and supply should not be taken too literally in the present context.

The "demand" for capital depended primarily on its productivity. At first glance, it may seem that Ireland should have been blessed with very high rates of return on investment: cheap labor, vast opportunities in agricultural improvements, and overall reasonably favorable natural endowments. Realizable rates of return were likely to have been lower than what one would be led to expect. In agriculture the investment opportunities so amply illustrated by experiments and the success of a number of improving landlords and agents, required information, supervision, willingness to bear risk, and persistence on the part of landlords. Social impediments to progress and entrepreneurial failure in Irish agriculture meant not only that there were high rates of return which were not taken advantage of, but also that the rates of return in actuality were not nearly so high as was theoretically feasible under the best-practice techniques. The peculiar social and economic conditions created by "the potato economy", for instance, made the cost of any reorganization of agriculture much higher than the data obtained from experimental farms and drainage projects suggest. After all, in practice the cost of adopting new techniques included not only the price of implements, labor, fertilizer, buildings, and other expenditures on investment, but also often the cost of relocating displaced tenants, and the risk of agrarian violence and sabotage. Poor relations and lack of confidence between landlords and tenants led to a breakdown of information flows between proprietors and workers, greatly reducing the efficiency of cooperative investment efforts. In manufacturing wages were generally low, but by most accounts labor was not cheap. Skilled labor was expensive, labor unions imposed constraints on the freedom of decision of the entrepreneurs, and unskilled labor was often unproductive due to poor management, the emigration of the best workers to Britain and North America, and possibly poor nutrition and health. Investment in human capital in this mobile society, seemingly a high-return activity, may in actuality have been very dubious, in view of the fact that trained workers could and did emigrate. All these factors cooperated in reducing the realized productivity of investment.

Most of the factors which impeded capital formation should be classified as "supply-side" factors. In the absence of well-functioning capital markets, however, the distinction between demand and supply is blurred. Investment occurs because somebody, landlord, peasant, merchant, or manufacturer, devotes resources to purchase or create producer durables. There is no explicit price equating the quantities supplied and demanded. A number of causes responsible for inhibiting capital formation of this kind can be identified. The principal cause, however, was that Ireland was a peasant society, and one in which the poor were unable and most of the less poor unwilling to invest in agriculture. The lower classes of Irish society, cottiers and smallholders, were simply too destitute to undertake any serious improvement projects. The number of middle-class farmers was very small in Ireland. Less than a quarter of all farms were above 20 acres, and only about 30 percent of the rural population were farmers who could claim to belong to a class of capitalist farmers (cf. Tables 2.3 and 2.4). Even among the class of larger farmers, small as it was, the incentive to invest in productive projects was diminished significantly due to widespread violence and sabotage on the Irish countryside. We have seen in Chapter 5 those special features of the Irish economy which led to this situation. The result was that potentially improving farmers decided otherwise because of the impression—not always necessarily accurate—that property was "insecure" in Ireland. Emigration of young farmers and farmers' sons reduced savings by increasing the proportion of dependants (persons who consumed more than they produced). Landlords, the only element in Irish society with some access to capital markets, were rarely interested in agricultural progress, and as a class probably invested little.

Institutional barriers toward capital formation took a variety of forms. One of these forms was the malfunctioning of capital markets. In this, however, Ireland was far from unique, and surely the absence of investment banks in the first half of the nineteenth century cannot be relied upon as a convincing explanation of the slow development of the Irish economy. Ireland was different from the rest of Europe, however, in that until 1838 it had no formal Poor Law or any organized system of local or national poor relief. The effects of the absence of a formal system of poor relief in Ireland on such variables as capital formation, the wage level, and population growth, compared to countries such as Britain or Holland with well-organized welfare systems, are far from clear. In one respect, however, the impact of the absence of public poor relief before 1838 is clear: it increased the overall riskiness of the environment. In Ireland there was very little of a "fall-back" position if a risky venture failed. Applying a new and untried technique might mean starvation not only for the peasant himself, but also for those who depended on him. In England or Scotland such dependants could expect to become chargeable to the parish; in Ireland in all likelihood they would have to beg.

Another possibility is that the Irish saved less because they were on average less patient and less willing to postpone consumption. Although this hypothesis is based on little more than speculation, impressions about the high rate of time-preference among the Irish can be found in the literature. Foster, in an insightful passage, pointed out that it was difficult to understand why tenants did not improve, although they clearly derived a material advantage from the improvement even if the landlord raised the rent. All that the tenants see, wrote Foster, is that "the difficulty is at hand, the balance of the advantage is at a distance, and they therefore will not improve" (Foster, 1847, pp. 283–4; see also Great Britain, 1836b, Vol. XXXIV, p. 438). If true, what could explain this behavior on the part of the Irish? It is at least conceivable that poverty itself was responsible for a higher rate of subjective time-preference. Such a situation would occur if saving was a superior good, so that the savings rate rose with income.[4] At least for rather poor economies, this assumption seems reasonable, although the empirical evidence from underdeveloped economies is rather ambiguous (Mikesell and Zinser, 1973). Note that in societies in which the life expectancy is shorter, we should expect *ceteris paribus* people to display less willingness to postpone consumption and delay gratification. This model provides a theoretical basis for the concept of the poverty trap, in which poverty in some way begets itself. Note, however, that it is not necessary to make this assumption in order to produce the poverty trap, since very similar traps could be derived from the McKinnon type of models introduced in Chapter 6.

Models of "poverty traps" in which low income is the source of low income may appear to some to involve circular reasoning. In the present context, however, the logic is straightforward. Under a number of relatively reasonable assumptions, the simple growth models in the theoretical literature can be made to display such feedback effects. To choose a different example, Connell has argued that the rate of population growth was a negative function of income. Thus, the lower the level of income, the faster the rate of population growth, the slower the increase of the capital–labor ratio, the slower the rate of income growth, and the lower the level of income attained in the steady state. To be sure, quantitative evidence for the Connell hypothesis is not very strong (see Chapter 3) and the nexus between capital formation and income is based largely on speculation. None the less, such a model can have significant value as a pedagogical tool in helping us to think clearly about the various conditions under which poverty rather than growth emerges as the outcome of observed historical forces.

Economies in which the savings rate and/or the rate of population growth depend on the level of income can display a characteristic which economists refer to as "nonuniqueness" of equilibria. A formal presentation of this model will not be attempted here, but it can be found in the literature (Jones, 1976, pp. 88–90; Johnson, 1966, pp. 276–9; Leibenstein, 1957, ch. 3). The basic result from such models is that under certain assumptions, the capital–labor ratio can have more than one "steady state" or growth equilibrium. It can be shown that if there are three such equilibria, two of them are likely to be stable and one unstable. The unstable one, which is located between the high-income and the low-income steady state, is of little interest in and of itself, since the economy will not stay at it if the slightest disturbance occurs. It is important, however, because it represents an important demarcation line: it represents the boundary between the path that dooms the economy to a low-level equilibrium trap and the path that leads to capital accumulation and ultimate prosperity. The point is that the original differences which lead one economy in one direction and the other economies in another could be fairly small. Similarly, seemingly minor differences in the ways the savings and population growth functions depend on income could be decisive in determining the historical path of the economy. The historian is left with the unnerving conclusion that very important historical processes, which determined the material level of existence of many millions of persons for centuries need not necessarily have very profound reasons.

Of the noneconomic factors affecting the Irish economy, the most complex and controversial were those which originated in the political sphere. Irish economic historians such as O'Brien (1921) and Chart (1920) writing in the 1920s had little doubt that much or all of Ireland's economic woes could be laid at the door of British policies. Modern writers in the radical tradition, such as Gibbon (1975) and Hechter (1975), tend to blame British capitalism or industrialism rather than Britain's inherently anti-Irish tendencies. How much truth was there in these accusations? As O'Farrell has pointed out, most of the blame placed on England's domination of Ireland was little more than propaganda. Many of these arguments were "not based on economic research any more than could be the contention that [economic] retardation derived from the character and personality of Ireland, particularly its strong rural tradition" (O'Farrell, 1975, p. 119).

How does one test the hypothesis that Ireland was poor because of the perfidious policies of Albion? Conventional empirical tests are, of course, quite inapplicable to such an issue, but the issues at stake can be made somewhat clearer by disentangling a number of confusions. First, one ought to distinguish between the effects inadvertently caused by Britain just because it happened to be nearby and prosperous and the economic consequences of deliberate British policies. Secondly, one must differentiate between British policies toward Ireland over 1780–1845 and British policies in earlier periods. It is conceivable that the era of land confiscation and penal mercantilism during which Ireland's economic interests were flagrantly subjugated to the demands

of British pressure groups and during which Irish Catholics were ruth-
lessly dispossessed and persecuted, caused such irreparable damage to
the delicate basis of Irish economy that nothing could make Ireland
prosperous again after 1780. There is a kernel of truth in that line of
reasoning: the unprecedented change in landownership and the
emergence of a new class of parvenu proprietors lay at the heart of the
economic shortcomings of the rural upper class in eighteenth- and
nineteenth-century Ireland.

It is more difficult to evaluate such mercantilist measures as the
Woolen Acts and Cattle Acts and the economic effects of the Penal Acts.
Contemporaries had reasons to exaggerate the negative effects of these
laws, which in practice were widely evaded (Cullen, 1968a). Modern
historians of the eighteenth century agree that the Penal Codes were
rarely fully enforced and that British mercantilism was worse in theory
than in practice (Johnston, 1974, pp. 36, 78). Other activities, especially
linen and provisions exports, substituted for the industries which were
encumbered by mercantilist legislation. One historian has written that
the Cattle and Woolen Acts "deflected rather than destroyed Irish
economic development" (James, 1973, p. 203). Smuggling to some
extent reduced the damage which the English inflicted upon Ireland's
foreign trade (O'Brien, 1918, pp. 186–7; James, 1961). Perhaps the most
damning accusation against British repression before 1778 was that it
deliberately prevented the emergence of an Irish Catholic middle class
and destroyed the trade and manufactures of Ireland (Lecky, 1972, pp.
53–60; O'Brien, 1918, p. 22). It is difficult to determine the extent to
which this was the case. Linen-cloth exports, which hovered around
2–2·5 millions yards in the 1710s, reached 7 million yards in 1740, 15
million yards in 1762, and 25 million yards in the mid-1780s. Wall
(1958) has pointed to the unheralded but noteworthy rise of a Catholic
urban middle class in the second half of the eighteenth century and has
argued that by the end of the eighteenth century Catholics controlled a
large share of Irish commerce.

In any event, by 1780 most of the repressive legislation had been
suspended or repealed and the economy was in the midst of a period of
rapid expansion. The import statistics are perhaps more revealing about
what happened to the Irish economy in those years than the export
statistics. Imports of certain consumption goods, such as tobacco and
tea, as well as raw iron and hardware, rose rapidly between 1772 and the
early 1800s, and contemporary opinion supports the impression of
increasing economic activity and prosperity, a view supported by
modern historians (Wakefield, 1812, Vol. 2, pp. 38–45; Cullen, 1967,
pp. 11–13; James, 1973, pp. 200–12). From those years onward it
becomes increasingly difficult to detect the effects of any deliberate
economic exploitation in British policies toward Ireland. British
mercantilist policies after 1780 were dying, first in practice and later in
theory.

Equally indignant judgements were passed on the Act of the Union of
1800, by wide agreement an act of chicanery and political opportunism.
Is it possible that Ireland's economic problems can be attributed to the

fact that in 1800 it was forced to relinquish its economic independence and from 1824 on was completely integrated into a British common market? The conclusion is tempting. Almost immediately after the removal of the last tariff barriers, the Ulster cotton industry collapsed, and a few years later the rural textile industry entered a crisis from which it never recovered. Starting from Isaac Butt, leader of the Home Rule League, who as Professor of Political Economy at Trinity College staunchly defended protection, Irish nationalism and nationalist historiography has waved the banner of protection for Irish manufactures (Black, 1972, p. 201). The Union, it was argued, exposed the fragile Irish economy to the worst excesses of "imperialism of free trade". The economic unification with Britain forced Ireland into a nonoptimal specialization pattern, one that she would not have chosen for herself had she been self-governing. As Engels expressed it in his incomplete *History of Ireland*, written in 1869–70: "Today England needs grain quickly and dependably—Ireland is just perfect for wheat-growing. Tomorrow England needs meat—Ireland is only fit for cattle pastures" (Marx and Engels, 1972, p. 191).

That the Union Act of 1800, in contrast with the mercantilist acts of the seventeenth century, was not a calculated and odious act of economic selfishness on the part of the British is certain. MacDonagh (1977, pp. 16–17) concludes for example that "the Act of Union was, like much other legislation, an act of miscalculations . . . what perhaps ultimately determined the ruin of the Irish economy, the establishment of a free trade area within the British Isles . . . was altogether unanticipated in 1800". Whether intentional or not, the result was the same: Ireland became part of a large economic unit which also happened to contain the most advanced industrial nation in the world. One short-term consequence was the alleged depression of the economy after 1815, when Ireland revalued its currency prior to the merger with the British pound in 1826 (Lynch and Vaisey, 1960, pp. 32–5). The existence of this depression has been contested (Lee, 1971) and in any event belongs to the class of "temporary shocks" rather than "structural weaknesses".

Whether the Union itself can be blamed for the ever-tighter economic relations with Great Britain is meanwhile far from clear. The proportion of Ireland's trade with Britain shows a continuous rise from 1740, when Britain accounted for about half of Ireland's foreign trade, to 1800, when it accounted for 85 percent of its total exports and 79 percent of its imports (Cullen, 1968a, p. 45). The effects on the Irish economy of the economic integration with Britain can best be conceptualized when we envisage what would have happened in the absence of the Union. Michael Hechter, who has recently poured a new wine made of the Frank–Wallerstein notions of geographic segmentation into the old nationalist bottles, has defined the appropriate counterfactual: had Ireland not been forced to submit to the Union with England, it would have been able to encourage and maintain economic diversification (Hechter, 1975, p. 92). Hechter does not explain how such diversification would have been brought about, but he must have had in mind protective tariffs, since other effective mechanisms are hard to envisage. An explicit statement blaming the absence of protective tariffs for Ireland's slow industrialization is made by O'Malley (1981).

The intuitive response of most economists to the proposition that tariffs could have reduced Irish poverty is likely to be negative. If Irish manufactures could not compete with England and Scotland, they should not have. Wherever Ireland's industries withstood the test of competition, such as in linen and brewing, protection was unnecessary anyway. The "infant-industry" argument flaunted by contemporaries is frowned upon by conventional economic wisdom. Many of the objections raised by Baldwin (1969) are directly applicable here, and there is, moreover, no serious evidence for any "learning by doing effects" in Irish industry which could possibly serve as a justification for protection. While the intuition of the trained economist is often sensible, intricate historical situations require caution in its application. As Kafka (1962) has pointed out, in the absence of capital markets the rate of accumulation of capital is affected by tariffs, since the latter tend to redistribute income from consumers to capitalists and thus possibly from low-savers to entrepreneurs whose plowed-back profits laid the foundations for modern industry. Tariffs also could have reduced the uncertainty of investment and, thus, might have induced Irish business-men to reinvest larger portions in their enterprises rather than in safer assets such as government consols or land.

Whether protective tariffs would really have made a substantial difference in Ireland's economic fortune is, however, doubtful. It seems unlikely that government policies, of any type, could have brought about Ireland's much-desired industrialization. A more likely outcome of a high tariff policy would have been the prolongation of the life of the rural industries, which were the chief victims of Lancashire's mills. Such a prolongation might have provided some temporary relief to the Connaught and Ulster countryside, but the ultimate fate of Ireland's cottage industries would have been much the same, as the case of autonomous (and protected) Belgium demonstrates. Moreover, the implicit assumption that somehow specialization in agriculture was itself a cause of economic backwardness for the Irish economy misses the mark. It was not the specialization in agriculture which was the root of Ireland's poverty, but low agricultural productivity itself that was to blame. Even when it was doing what it did best, the Irish economy was not performing well. In the absence of the Union, Ireland probably still would have continued to export agricultural goods to Britain, and had such exports been stopped by some extreme government intervention, economic conditions on the Irish countryside would have been exacerbated gravely. Political domination may have been, in the final analysis, less important than sheer geographical proximity. Crotty (1979) has maintained that the process which he inelegantly terms "peripheralization" and which in his view started around 1820, was actually expedited by Ireland's independence in 1922.

All this is, of course, highly speculative. What is more certain is that British rule was not without its advantages for Ireland. British rule after

1800 provided an element of security and stability which may have appeared repugnant to Irish nationalists, but which was a beneficial background for the development of the economy. One modern historian (Beckett, 1972, p. 146) has pointed out that without the Union the constitutional changes which occurred in Ireland over 1800–1922 would have taken on a violent character, whereas in fact most of these changes were introduced peacefully by the British. As I have argued in Chapter 5, there surely was not enough "law and order" in Ireland. Things might have been even worse, however, had there been more organized political violence exacerbating the economic and social conflicts. Governing Ireland in the fifty years after the Union Act was a different proposition from governing Britain. The absence of an educated gentry with a large stake in local affairs made the "government by amateurs" as it was practiced in Britain impossible. In the years after the Union Irish government was centralized at a rapid rate. Long before Britain, Ireland was run by professional, well-trained, and generally conscientious administrators, among the finest of whom were John Burgoyne, Richard Griffith, Thomas Larcom, and Thomas Drummond. By the standards of the time, Ireland enjoyed a fine administration of education, public health, and police force. The Acts of 1828 and 1840 reformed municipal government, permitting the establishment of functional authorities to provide urban services and eliminating outdated urban "corporations". The Tithe Commutation Act of 1838 resolved once and for all a thorny problem which had bedeviled Ireland for generations. Ireland was also surveyed and mapped in great detail at the expense of the British treasury. Not all of these measures were carried out for altruistic reasons, of course. The reorganization of the constabulary was very much a result of the turbulent state of the Irish countryside. As for the Ordnance Survey, Lord Salisbury's words in 1883 say it best: "the most disagreeable part of the three kingdoms is Ireland, and therefore Ireland has a splendid map" (Andrews, 1975, p. v).

The only area in which British rule in Ireland failed was, significantly enough, poor relief. In spite of the unequivocal and heavily documented majority opinion of the Poor Inquiry Commission in 1836 advising against it, Parliament proceeded to implement the 1838 poor relief system in Ireland. The Irish Poor Law differed from the English one in two crucial aspects. First, in Ireland all relief was administered exclusively through workhouses, while in England and Wales only the able-bodied poor received exclusive indoor relief. Secondly, in England every destitute person had a *legal* right to relief, whereas in Ireland, even after 1838, nobody had a legal right to be supported, and when the workhouses were filled, further applicants were simply turned away. Since there was only one workhouse per Union (which meant, on average, one workhouse per 62,884 persons), the potential of the Irish Poor Law to relieve poverty was limited. It is hard to form an opinion on the consequences of the Irish Poor Law decision, because a few years after the system was introduced it collapsed under the avalanche of the Great Famine. As we have seen in Chapter 9, however, there is reason to believe that the Irish Poor Law might have made matters somewhat worse.

The real problem of Ireland's relations with Britain in the half-century before the famine was not that its willy-nilly integration into the British Empire seriously impaired its economy, but that the integration did not go far enough. The Union created a united Parliament and eventually a free-trade area. By the mid-1820s there was a free flow of goods, services, and labor between Ireland and Great Britain. But a single economy did not create a single nation, let alone a single society. Ireland and Britain in the decades between the Union and the famine were far more alien to each other than France, Germany, and the Netherlands are in today's Common Market. O'Farrell has remarked that "above all, it was the Industrial Revolution which drove England and Ireland irrevocably apart" (O'Farrell, 1975, p. 114). There is a sense in which this view is true, but Ireland and Britain were not driven "apart", since they had never been really together. The Industrial Revolution in Britain did not drive the English industrial counties "apart" from the southern parts, or separate the Scottish Lowlands from the Highlands. In general, peaceful and symbiotic relations between industrializing regions and those that remained agrarian were the rule, not the exception. The wedge between the two nations was not driven by Ireland's lack of an industrial sector, and not even by its poverty. The real problem was that Ireland was considered by Britain an alien and even hostile country.

The economic effects of this hostile attitude were important. English and Scottish capital shied away from Ireland. One contemporary stated that "as long as the statute law of the country treats four-fifths of the population as persons who are dangerous to the state and ought not to be trusted, there will exist a distrust on the part of English capitalists which will prevent them from investing capital [in Ireland]" (Great Britain, 1825b, Vol. VIII, p. 690). True, some British entrepreneurs did go to Ireland, but many more went to France, Belgium, and Prussia.

It has also been pointed out by Lebow (1977) that the British attitude to Irish poverty was quite different from British views toward their own poor. While in Britain poverty was considered the result of economic fluctuations and structural changes in the economy, Irish poverty was viewed as being caused by laziness, indifference, and ineptitude. Consequently, the British government did not bear the same responsibility toward the Irish poor as they did in Britain. Although Lebow's interpretation is somewhat oversimplified (he does not address the implementation of a British-type Poor Law in Ireland in 1838), it contains an important kernel of truth. Both the contemporary press and politicians seemed to believe, in Lebow's words (pp. 67, 71), that the Irish "unlike their British neighbours, did not really mind their penury" and thus "Britain's mission was not to alleviate Irish distress but to civilize her people and lead them to feel and act like human beings".

Most serious of all, when the chips were down in the frightful summer of 1847, the British simply abandoned the Irish and let them perish. There is no doubt that Britain could have saved Ireland. The British treasury spent a total of about £9·5 million on famine relief. While parts of the sum were considered a loan, most of it was never repaid (O'Neill, 1957, p. 241). Financed largely by advances from London, the soup kitchen program, despite its many inadequacies, saved many lives. When the last kitchens closed in October 1847, Lord Clarendon wrote in despair to the Prime Minister, Russell: "Ireland cannot be left to her own resources . . . we are not to let the people die of starvation." The reply was: "The state of Ireland for the next few months must be one of great suffering. Unhappily the agitation for Repeal has contrived to destroy nearly all sympathy in this country" (cited by Woodham-Smith, 1962, p. 317). A few years after the famine, the British government spent £69·3 million on an utterly futile adventure in the Crimea (Hughes, 1960, p. 26). Half that sum spent in Ireland in the critical years 1846–9 would have saved hundreds of thousands of lives. It is difficult to reconcile this lavishness with claims that British relief during the famine years was inadequate because the problem was "too huge for the British state to overcome" (Cullen and Smout, 1978, p. 11). The story of Poor Relief after June 1847 reads almost monotonously: Poor Union guardians or vice guardians (the latter being paid officials who replaced elected guardians when these were deemed incompetent or refused to serve further) desperately scrambling for funds, caught between the Scylla of starving hordes of inmates and the Charybdis of recalcitrant and overtaxed ratepayers, many of whom were facing financial ruin or even hunger themselves. The contribution of Westminster to the relief of this horror was a mere pittance. The guiding principle was that each Union should support itself from its poor rates. When the absurdity of this rigid rule was finally admitted, a rate-in-aid of 2d on the pound was levied in 1850, thus supporting the poorer regions somewhat at the expense of the stronger ones. As O'Neill (1957, p. 248) points out, if the political Union had been really complete, the rate-in-aid would have been levied not just in Ireland, but in all of Great Britain.

It is not unreasonable to surmise that had anything like the famine occurred in England or Wales, the British government would have overcome its theoretical scruples and would have come to the rescue of the starving at a much larger scale. Ireland was not considered part of the British community. Had it been, its income per capita may not have been much higher, perhaps, but mass starvation due to a subsistence crisis would have been averted, and in that sense Ireland might have been less poor, according to our earlier definition of poverty.

The economics of poverty should be at the forefront of interest to economists. As Theodore Schultz said in his Nobel Lecture: "Most of the people in the world are poor, so if we knew the economics of being poor we would know much of the economics that really matters" (Schultz, 1980, p. 639). Western Europe was, of course, the focal area of economic development in the nineteenth century. As long as people will ask why today Frenchmen, Swedes, Belgians, and Germans are prosperous whereas Indonesians and Bolivians are still struggling with hunger and want, we will inevitably find ourselves asking questions about the European experience. For people eager to see the "Very Big Picture", it is easy to gloss over the enormous variation that the European development process provides both within and among the different European economies. Easterlin (1981) has written, for example, that "the current preoccupation of Western scholars with American and European—largely northwestern European—economic history can only seem provincial, for the striking feature about these areas is the fundamental similarity in their experience". This statement is likely to be violently objected to by scholars of, say, French industrialization, who have made diversity of experience almost a trademark. It is less likely to be objected to by people who are also familiar with the economic history of Bihar or Gabon. Whether they industrialized slowly or rapidly, whether they emphasized steel or margarine, most of the European economies between the French Revolution and the beginning of World War I changed their economic environment and created the gap which currently exists between the "developed world" and the "fourth world". Within the European experience Ireland provided one of the most striking and noteworthy exceptions. Why was the Irish experience so unique? Or was it? Maybe what really ought to be explained is not the "unique" poverty of Ireland, but the unprecedented economic change in the rest of Western Europe? Certainly, if we take a global point of view, the Irish experience was the rule, while Belgium and Scotland were the exceptions. Europe's success was indeed miraculous, an aberration from the Eurasian continent of which it was part (Jones, 1981a). Part of the understanding of the miracle will have to come from those areas in Europe which failed to become part of it.

The causes for the wealth or poverty of nations are in some sense not only unknown, but unknowable, in the same way as the Origin of the Universe or what-the-prophet-Isaiah-really-meant are unknowable. One might speculate on the importance of the environment, education, or Western rationality as explanations of the "European miracle", but we will never be sure in the same way we are sure that, say, an epidemic outbreak of typhus is caused by *Rickettsia Prowazeki*. Knowledge of the micro-organism which causes typhus identifies an agent, but the micro-organism alone cannot be blamed for the deaths of tens of thousands who succumbed to typhus during wartime epidemics. The organism is one factor, but an equally valid "explanation" is the vulnerability of the population to it, which requires an entirely different set of factors for its explanation.

Needless to say, recognizing our inability to produce definitive and unequivocal answers to these questions is not tantamount to a defeatist attitude toward historical research into the causes of economic development. Many instructive lessons can be learned from the history of Ireland in the nineteenth century. Not all of them have been done justice to in the preceding pages. The poverty of prefamine Ireland had important ramifications which extend far beyond the shores of the Emerald Isle. Irish emigrants, fleeing the hopelessness of their homeland, filled the cities of Britain and North America. The Irish Question bedeviled British politics for more than half a century. Ireland was a principal reason why the young science of economics abandoned its steadfast adherence to the sanctity of private property and free enterprise and realized that under certain circumstances, Adam Smith's invisible hand transformed itself into a claw capable of holding the economy in a deadly grip of poverty. For modern economists, the Irish experience holds some important lessons. It was characterized by conflicts, poorly defined property rights, bargaining and transactions costs, inflexible contracts, imperfect information flows, and a variety of similar phenomena which economists regard as imperfections and failures of the market mechanism to allocate resources and to permit and generate economic growth. Finally, the Irish example serves as an important reminder that there never was anything warranted or automatic about the disappearance of poverty from the scene in the more fortunate European economies in the nineteenth century.

Notes: Chapter 10

1   The following is based on Hoffman and Mokyr (1981).
2   For details on the price-series used, see Appendix to Chapter 5.
3   Most of the regression coefficients of cottage industry with respect to the birth and population growth lie between 0·025 and 0·035. The variable measuring cottage industry (total rural workers employed in textile as a proportion of total rural employed inclusive of those not having specified occupations) for counties Mayo, Sligo, and Leitrim is between 0·18 and 0·25. Had the level of rural industry in Connaught been as low as it was in, say, Co. Limerick, the rate of natural population growth (births minus deaths) would have declined in Mayo from 2·1 to 1·9 percent; in Sligo from 2·2 to 2·0 percent; and in Leitrim from 1·5 to 1·1 percent, assuming the average value of the coefficients to be 0·030.
4   The formal condition for saving to be a superior good is that the expansion path in the standard Fisherian (two-period) diagram be not a straight line, but a convex curve. Interestingly enough, Irving Fisher himself explicitly stated that he believed that the rate of time-preference was not independent of income, an aspect of his work not pursued by his epigones in the modern theory of interest. In Fisher's words "other things equal, the smaller the income, the higher the preference for present over future income; that is, the greater the impatience to acquire income as early as possible . . . poverty bears down heavily on all portions of a man's expected life. But it increases the want for immediate income *even more* than it increases the want for future income . . . not only is a certain minimum of present income necessary to prevent starvation, but the nearer this minimum is approached, the more precious does present income appear relative to future income" (Fisher, 1930, pp. 72–3; italics in original).

Bibliography

Aalen, F. H. A., *Man and the Landscape in Ireland* (London: Academic Press, 1978).

Adams, Catherine F., *Nutritive Value of American Foods*, United States Department of Agriculture, Agricultural Research Service, Agriculture Handbook No. 456, Washington, DC, USA, 1975.

Adams, W. F., *Ireland and Irish Emigration to the New World from 1815 to the Famine* (New York: Russell, 1967; originally published in 1932).

Akenson, Donald H., *The Irish Education Experiment* (London: Routledge & Kegan Paul, 1970).

Allen, Robert C., "Entrepreneurship and technical progress in the northeast coast pig iron industry: 1850–1913", *Research in Economic History*, vol. 6 (1981), pp. 35–71.

Almquist, Eric, "Mayo and beyond: land, domestic industry, and rural transformation in the Irish west", unpublished Ph.D. dissertation, Boston University, Massachusetts, USA, 1977.

Almquist, Eric, "Prefamine Ireland and the theory of European proto-industrialization", *Journal of Economic History*, vol. XXXIX, no. 3 (September 1979), pp. 699–718.

Almquist, Eric, "Labor specialization and the Irish economy: an aggregate occupational analysis", unpublished manuscript, Boston, Mass., April 1980.

Anderson, Barbara, "Male age and fertility—results from Ireland prior to 1911", *Population Index*, vol. 41, no. 4 (October 1975), pp. 561–7.

Andrews, John H., *A Paper Landscape: The Ordnance Survey in the Nineteenth Century* (Oxford: Clarendon Press, 1975).

Andrews, John H., "Limits of agricultural settlement in prefamine Ireland", in L. M. Cullen and F. Furet (eds), *Ireland and France, 17th–20th Centuries: Towards a Comparative Study of Rural History* (Paris: Editions de l'Ecole des Hautes Etudes en Sciences Sociales, 1980, pp. 47–58).

Armstrong, D. L., "Social and economic conditions in the Belfast linen industry", *Irish Historical Studies*, vol. VII, no. 28 (September 1951), pp. 235–69.

Baldwin, Robert E., "The case against infant-industry tariff protection", *Journal of Political Economy*, vol. 77, no. 3 (May–June 1969), pp. 295–305.

Balfour, Graham, *The Educational Systems of Great Britain and Ireland* (Oxford: Clarendon Press, 1898).

Banfield, E. C., *The Moral Basis of a Backward Society* (New York: The Free Press, 1958).

Bardhan, Pranab K., "Wages and unemployment in a poor agrarian economy: a theoretical and empirical analysis", *Journal of Political Economy*, vol. 87, no. 3 (June 1979), pp. 479–500.

Barrow, G. L., *The Emergence of the Irish Banking System* (Dublin: Gill & MacMillan, 1975).

Barrow, G. L., "The use of money in mid-nineteenth century Ireland", *Studies*, vol. LIX, no. 233 (Spring 1970), pp. 81–8.

Beames, M. R., "Cottiers and conacre in pre-famine Ireland", *Journal of Peasant Studies*, vol. 2, no. 3 (April 1975), pp. 352–4.

Beames, Michael R., "Rural conflict in pre-famine Ireland: peasant assassinations in Tipperary, 1837–1847", *Past and Present*, no. 81 (November 1978), pp. 75–91.

Beaumont, Gustave de la Bonniniere (ed., W. C. Taylor), *Ireland, Social, Political, and Religious*, 2 vols (London: Bentley, 1839).

Beckett, J. C., "The eighteenth-century background", in T. W. Moody and J. C. Beckett (eds), *Ulster since 1800, a Political and Economic Survey* (London: BBC, 1954).

Beckett, J. C., *The Making of Modern Ireland* (London:Faber, 1966).

Beckett, J. C., "Ireland under the Union", in J. C. Beckett (ed.), *Confrontations: Studies in Irish History* (London: Faber, 1972, pp. 142–59).

Bergman, M., "The potato blight in the Netherlands and its social consequences (1845–1847)", *International Review of Social History*, vol. 17, pt 3 (1967), pp. 391–431.

Berkeley, George, "A word to the wise", in A. A. Luce and T. E. Jessup (eds), *The Works of George Berkeley, Bishop of Cloyne*, Vol. 6 (London: Nelson, 1953, pp. 235–49; originally published in 1749).

Berry, R. Albert, and Soligo, Ronald, "Some welfare aspects of international migration", *Journal of Political Economy*, vol. 77, no. 8 (September–October 1969), pp. 778–94.

Bicheno, J. E., *Ireland and its Economy* (London: Murray, 1830).

Black, R. D. Collison, *Economic Thought and the Irish Question, 1817–70* (Cambridge: Cambridge University Press, 1960).

Black, R. D. Collison, "Economic policy in Ireland and India in the time of J. S. Mill", *Economic History Review*, vol. XXI (2nd series) (1968), pp. 321–36.

Black, R. D. Collison, "The Irish experience in relation to the theory and policy of economic development", in A. J. Youngson (ed.), *Economic Development in the Long Run* (New York: St Martin's Press, 1972).

Blacker, William, *Prize Essay on the Management of Lorded Property in Ireland* (Dublin: Curry, 1834).

Blacker, William, *An Essay on the Improvement to be made in the Cultivation of Small Farms by the Introduction of Green Crops, and House-Feeding the Stock Thereon*, 6th edn (London: Groombridge, 1845).

Blacker, William, *An Essay on the Best Mode of Improving the Condition of the Labouring Classes of Ireland* (London: Groombridge, 1846).

Bliss, Christopher, and Stern, Nicholas, "Productivity, wages and nutrition", *Journal of Development Economics*, vol. 5, no. 4 (December 1978), pp. 331–98.

Bonn, Moritz J., *Modern Ireland and her Agrarian Problem* (trans., T. W. Rolleston) (Dublin: Hodges, Figgis, 1906).

Bourke, P. M. Austin, "The extent of the potato crop in Ireland at the time of the famine", *Journal of the Statistical and Social Inquiry Society of Ireland*, vol. XX, pt 3 (1959–60), pp. 1–35.

Bourke, P. M. Austin, "The scientific investigation of the potato blight in 1845–6", *Irish Historical Studies*, vol. XIII, no. 49 (March 1962), pp. 26–32.

Bourke, P. M. Austin, "Notes on some agricultural units of measurement in use in pre-famine Ireland", *Irish Historical Studies*, vol. XIV, no. 55 (March 1965a), pp. 236–45.

Bourke, P. M. Austin, "The agricultural statistics of the 1841 Census of Ireland, a critical review", *Economic History Review*, vol. XVIII, no. 2 (2nd series) (August 1965b), pp. 376–9.

Bourke, P. M. Austin, "The use of the potato crop in pre-famine Ireland", *Journal of the Statistical and Social Inquiry Society of Ireland*, vol. XII, pt 6 (1968), pp. 72–96.

Bourke, P. M. Austin," The average yields of food crops in Ireland on the eve of the Great Famine", *Journal of the Department of Agriculture (Ireland)*, vol. LXVI, no. 7 (1969), pp. 26–39.

Boyer, George, "The English Poor Law as an endogenous response to peak requirements for seasonal labor, 1795–1834", unpublished paper, Dept. of Economics, University of Wisconsin, Madison, Wisconsin, March 1982.

Boyle, Phelim, and Ó Gráda, Cormac, "Fertility trends, excess mortality, and the great Irish famine", unpublished discussion paper, University of British Columbia, Vancouver B.C. Canada, January 1982.

Brainard, William C., and Cooper, Richard N., "Uncertainty and diversification in international trade", *Stanford University Food Research Institute Studies in Agricultural Economics, Trade and Development*, vol. 8, no. 3 (1968), pp. 257–85.

Broeker, Galen, *Rural Disorder and Police Reform in Ireland, 1812–36* (London: Routledge & Kegan Paul, 1970).

Burke, John F., *Industrial and Economic History of Ireland* (Dublin: Fallon, c.1920).

Burton, W. G., *The Potato: A Survey of its History and of Factors Influencing its Yield, Nutritive Value, Quality and Storage*, 2nd rev. edn (Wageningen, Holland: Veenman & Zonen, 1968).

Carlyle, Thomas, "The present time", in *Latter Day Pamphlets*, Vol. 20 of T. Carlyle, *Complete Works* (Boston, Mass.: Estes & Larriat, 1884a, pp. 261–303).

Carlyle, Thomas, "Chartism", in *Critical and Miscellaneous Essays*, Vol. 16 of T. Carlyle, *Complete Works* (Boston, Mass.: Estes & Larriat, 1884b, pp. 36–117).

Carney, F. J., "Pre-famine Irish population: the evidence from the Trinity College estates", *Irish Economic and Social History*, vol. II (1975), pp. 35–45.

Central Relief Committee of the Society of Friends, *Transactions of the Central Relief Committee of the Society of Friends during the Famine in Ireland in 1846 and 1847* (Dublin: Hodges & Smith, 1852).

Chambers, J. D., and Mingay, Gordon, *The Agricultural Revolution, 1750–1880* (London: Batsford, 1966).

Chart, D. A., *An Economic History of Ireland* (Dublin: Talbot Press, 1920).

Clapham, John H., *An Economic History of Modern Britain* (Cambridge: Cambridge University Press, 1964).

Clark, Samuel, *Social Origins of the Irish Land War* (Princeton, NJ: Princeton University Press, 1979).

Clark, Victor S., *History of Manufactures in the United States, Volume I, 1607–1860* (New York: McGraw–Hill, 1929).

Clarkson, L. A., "The writing of Irish economic and social history since 1968", *Economic History Review*, vol. XXIII (2nd series) (February 1980), pp. 100–11.

Clarkson, L. A., "Irish population revisited, 1687–1821", in J. M. Goldstrom and L. A. Clarkson (eds), *Irish Population, Economy and Society, Essays in Honour of K. H. Connell* (Oxford: Clarendon Press, 1981, pp. 13–35).

Coale, Ansley J., "Factors associated with the development of low fertility: an historic summary", *Proceedings UN World Population Conference, 1965*, Vol. 2 (New York: United Nations, 1967, pp. 205–9).

Coale, Ansley J., "Age patterns of marriage", *Population Studies*, vol. 25, no. 2 (1971), pp. 193–214.

Coale, Ansley J., and McNeil, D. R., "The distribution of the frequency of first marriage in a female cohort", *Journal of the American Statistical Association*, vol. 67, no. 340 (December 1972), pp. 743–9.

Coe, W. E., *The Engineering Industry of the North of Ireland* (Newton Abbot: David & Charles, 1969).

Collins, Brenda, "Irish emigration to Dundee and Paisley during the first half of the nineteenth century", in J. M. Goldstrom and L. A. Clarkson (eds), *Irish Population, Economy, and Society, Essays in Honour of K. H. Connell* (Oxford: Clarendon Press, 1981, pp. 195–212).

Colquhoun, Patrick, *A Treatise on the Wealth, Power, and Resources of the British Empire* (London: Mawman, 1815).

Connell, K. H., *The Population of Ireland, 1750–1845* (Oxford: Clarendon Press, 1950a).

Connell, K. H., "The colonization of waste land in Ireland, 1780–1845", *Economic History Review*, vol. III, no. 7 (2nd series) (1950b), pp. 44–71.

Connell, K. H., "The history of the potato", *Economic History Review*, Essays in Bibliography and Criticism, vol. III, no. 3 (2nd series) (1951a), pp. 788–95.

Connell, K. H., "Some unsettled problems in English and Irish population history", *Irish Historical Studies*, vol. VII, no. 28 (September 1951b), pp. 225–34.

Connell, K. H., "Marriage in Ireland after the famine: the diffusion of the match", *Journal of the Statistical and Social Inquiry Society of Ireland*, vol. XIX (1955–6), pp. 82–103.

Connell, K. H., "Illicit distillation: an Irish peasant industry", *Historical Studies*, vol. 3 (1961), pp. 58–91.

Connell, K. H., "The potato in Ireland", *Past and Present*, vol. XXIII (November 1962), pp. 57–71.

Connell, K. H., "Illegitimacy before the famine", in K. H. Connell, *Irish Peasant Society: Four Historical Essays* (Oxford: Clarendon Press, 1968, pp. 51–86).

Connolly, S. J., "Illegitimacy and pre-nuptial pregnancy in Ireland before 1864: the evidence of some Catholic parish registers", *Irish Economic and Social History*, vol. VI (1979), pp. 5–23.

Coote, Charles, *General View of the Agriculture and Manufacturing of King's County* (Dublin: Graisberry & Campbell, 1801a).

Coote, Charles, *General View of the Agriculture and Manufacturing of Queen's County* (Dublin: Graisberry & Campbell, 1801b).

Coote, Charles, *Statistical Survey of the County of Armagh* (Dublin: Graisberry & Campbell, 1804).

Cousens, S. H., "Regional death rates in Ireland during the Great Famine from 1846 to 1851", *Population Studies*, vol. 14, no. 1 (July 1960a), pp. 55–74.

Cousens, S. H., "The regional pattern of emigration during the Great Irish Famine, 1846–51", *Institute of British Geographers, Transactions and Papers, 1960* (Publication no. 28) (1960b), pp. 119–34.

Cousens, S. H., "The regional variation in mortality during the Great Irish Famine", *Proceedings of the Royal Irish Academy*, vol. 63 (section C), no. 3 (February 1963), pp. 127–49.

Cousens, S. H., "The regional variations in emigration from Ireland between 1821 and 1841", *Institute of British Geographers, Transactions* no. 37 (December 1965), pp. 15–30.

Cousens, S. H., "The regional variations in population changes in Ireland, 1861–1881", *Economic History Review*, vol. XVII, no. 2 (2nd series) (December 1969), pp. 301–21.

Crawford, E. Margaret, "A nutritional analysis of diets in Ireland's workhouses, 1841–69", unpublished paper, Queen's University, Belfast, 1978.

Crawford, E. Margaret, "Indian meal and pellagra in nineteenth-century Ireland", in J. M. Goldstrom and L. A. Clarkson (eds), *Irish Population, Economy, and Society, Essays in Honour of K. H. Connell* (Oxford: Clarendon Press, 1981, pp. 113–33).

Crawford, W. H., "The rise of the linen industry", in L. M. Cullen (ed.), *The Formation of the Irish Economy* (Cork: Mercier Press, 1969, pp. 23–35).

Crawford, W. H., *Domestic Industry in Ireland* (Dublin: Gill & MacMillan, 1972).

Crawford, W. H., "Landlord–tenant relations in Ulster, 1609–1820", *Irish Economic and Social History*, vol. II (1975), pp. 5–21.

Crawford, W. S., *Depopulation Not Necessary: An Appeal to the Members of the Imperial Parliament against the Extermination of the Irish People* (London: Gilpin, 1850).

Cresswell, Robert, *Une Communaute Rurale de l'Irlande* (Paris: Institut d'Ethnologie, 1969).

Crotty, Raymond D., *Irish Agricultural Production: Its Volume and Structure* (Cork: Cork University Press, 1966).

Crotty, Raymond, "Capitalist colonialism and peripheralisation: the Irish case", in Dudley Seers, Bernard Schaffer, and Marja-Liisa Kiljunen (eds), *Underdeveloped Europe: Studies in Core-Periphery Relations* (Atlantic Highlands, New Jersey: Humanities Press, 1979, pp. 225–35).

Cullen, L. M., "Problems in the interpretation and revision of eighteenth century Irish economic history", *Transactions Royal Historical Society*, vol. 17 (5th series) (1967), pp. 1–22.

Cullen, L. M., *Anglo-Irish Trade, 1660–1800* (New York: Kelley, 1968a).

Cullen, L. M., "Irish history without the potato", *Past and Present*, vol. 40 (July 1968b), pp. 72–83.

Cullen, L. M., *Life in Ireland* (London: Batsford, 1968c).

Cullen, L. M., "Irish economic history: fact and myth", in L. M. Cullen (ed.), *The Formation of the Irish Economy* (Cork: Mercier Press, 1969, pp. 113–24).

Cullen, L. M., *An Economic History of Ireland from 1660* (London: Batsford, 1972).

Cullen, L. M., "The social and cultural modernization of rural Ireland, 1600–1900", in L. M. Cullen and F. Furet (eds), *Ireland and France, 17th–20th Centuries: Towards a Comparative Study of Rural History* (Paris: Editions de l'Ecole des Hautes Etudes en Sciences Sociales, 1980, pp. 195–212).

Cullen, L. M., *The Emergence of Modern Ireland, 1600–1900* (London: Batsford, 1981a).

Cullen, L. M., "Population growth and diet, 1600–1850", in J. M. Goldstrom and L. A. Clarkson (eds), *Irish Population, Economy and Society, Essays in Honour of K. H. Connell* (Oxford: Clarendon Press, 1981b, pp. 89–112).

Cullen, L. M., "Incomes, social classes and economic growth in Ireland and Scotland, 1600–1900", in David Dickson and T. M. Devine (eds), *Ireland and Scotland: Social and Economic Developments, 1650–1850* (Edinburgh: Donald, 1982; forthcoming).

Cullen, L. M., and Smout, T. C., "Economic growth in Scotland and Ireland", in L. M. Cullen and T. C. Smout (eds), *Comparative Aspects of Scottish and Irish Economic and Social History, 1600–1900* (Edinburgh: Donald, 1978, pp. 3–18).

Currie, E. A., "Land tenures, enclosures and field-patterns in Co. Derry in the eighteenth and nineteenth centuries", *Irish Geography*, vol. IX (1976), pp. 50–62.

Curtis, L. P., "Incumbered wealth: landed indebtedness in post-famine Ireland", *American Historical Review*, vol. 85, no. 2 (April 1980), pp. 332–67.

Daly, Mary, "The development of the National School System, 1831–4", in A. Cosgrove and Donal McCartney (eds), *Studies in Irish History Presented to R. Dudley Edwards* (Dublin: University College, 1979, pp. 150–63).

Daly, Mary E., *Social and Economic History of Ireland since 1800* (Dublin: Education Co., 1981).

Daultrey, Stuart, Dickson, David, and Ó Gráda, Cormac, "Eighteenth-century Irish population: new perspectives for old sources", *Journal of Economic History*, vol. XLI, no. 3 (September 1981), pp. 601–28.

David, Paul A., and Temin, Peter, "Slavery: the progressive institution", in Paul A. David, *et al.*, *Reckoning with Slavery* (New York: Oxford University Press, 1976).

Davidson, Stanley, and Passmore, R., *Human Nutrition and Dietetics*, 2nd edn (Baltimore, Md: Williams & Wilkins, 1965).

Davidson, W. D., "History of potato varieties", *Journal of the Department of Agriculture* (Ireland), vol. XXXIII, no. 1 (1935), pp. 57–81.

Davidson, W. D., "The history of the potato and its progress in Ireland", *Journal of the Department of Agriculture* (Ireland), vol. XXXIV, no. 2 (1937), pp. 286–307.

Deane, Phyllis, and Cole, W. A., *British Economic Growth, 1688–1959* (Cambridge: Cambridge University Press, 1969).

DeCanio, Stephen J., "Accumulation and discrimination in the postbellum South", *Explorations in Economic History*, vol. 16, no. 2 (April 1979a), pp. 182–206.

DeCanio, Stephen J., "Review of Ransom and Sutch, *One Kind of Freedom*", *Economic History Review*, vol. XXXII, no. 3 (August 1979b), pp. 455–57.

De Latocnaye, *A Frenchman's Walk through Ireland, 1796–7*, trans., John Sterensa (Belfast: McGaw, Stevenson & Orr, 1917).

Dickson, David, "Aspects of the rise and decline of the Irish cotton industry", in L. M. Cullen and T. C. Smout (eds), *Comparative Aspects of Scottish and Irish Economic and Social History* (Edinburgh: Donald, 1978, pp. 110–15).

Dickson, David, "Middlemen", in Thomas Bartlett and J. Hayton (eds), *Penal Era and Golden Age* (Belfast: Ulster Historical Foundation, 1979, pp. 162–85).

Donnelly, James S., *Landlord and Tenant in Nineteenth Century Ireland* (Dublin: Gill & MacMillan, 1973).

Donnelly, James S., *The Land and the People of Nineteenth Century Cork* (London/Boston, Mass.: Routledge & Kegan Paul, 1975).

Donnelly, James S., "The Whiteboy movement, 1761–5", *Irish Historical Studies*, vol. XXI, no. 81 (March 1978), pp. 20–54.

Drake, Michael, "Marriage and population growth in Ireland 1750–1845", *Economic History Review*, vol. XVI, no. 2 (2nd series) (December 1963), pp. 301–17.

Drake, Michael, "Population growth and the Irish economy", in L. M. Cullen (ed.), *The Formation of the Irish Economy* (Cork: Mercier Press, 1969, pp. 65–76).

Dubourdieu, John, *Statistical Survey of the County of Antrim* (Dublin: Graisberry & Campbell, 1812).

Dupâquier, Jacques, "Les aventures demographiques de la France et de l'Irlande (18e–20e siècles)" in L. M. Cullen and F. Furet (eds), *Ireland and France, 17th–20th Centuries: Towards a Comparative Study of Rural History* (Paris: Editions de l'Ecole des Hautes Etudes et Sciences Sociales, 1980, pp. 167–80).

Dutton, Hely, *Statistical Survey of the County of Clare* (Dublin: Graisberry & Campbell, 1808).

Dutton, Hely, *A Statistical and Agricultural Survey of the County of Galway* (Dublin: Graisberry, 1824).

Easterlin, Richard A., "Why isn't the whole world developed?" *Journal of Economic History*, vol. XLI, no. 1 (March 1981), pp. 1–19.

Eaton, Joseph W., and Mayer, Albert J., "The social biology of very high fertility among the Hutterites: the demography of a unique population", *Human Biology*, vol. 25, no. 3 (September 1953), pp. 201–64.

Edgeworth, Maria (ed., George Watson), *Castle Rackrent* (London: Oxford University Press, 1964).

Edwards, Ruth Dudley, *An Atlas of Irish History* (London: Methuen, 1973).

Edwards, R. Dudley and Williams, T. Desmond, "Foreword" in R. Dudley Edwards and T. Desmond Williams (eds), *The Great Famine* (New York: New York University Press, 1957, pp. vii–xvi).

Erickson, Charlotte, "Emigration from the British Isles to the U.S.A. in 1831", *Population Studies*, vol. XXXV, no. 2 (July 1981), pp. 175–97.

Feinstein, Charles, "Capital formation in Great Britain", in Peter Mathias and M. M. Postan (eds), *The Cambridge Economic History of Europe*, Vol. 7 (Cambridge: Cambridge University Press, 1978, pp. 28–96).

Fischer, Wolfram, "Rural industrialization and population change", *Comparative Studies in Society and History*, vol. 15, no. 2 (March 1973), pp. 158–70.

Fisher, Irving, *The Theory of Interest* (New York: Macmillan, 1930).

Flinn, Michael W., *Scottish Population History* (Cambridge: Cambridge University Press, 1977).

Flinn, Michael W., "Malthus, emigration and potatoes in the Scottish Northwest", in L. M. Cullen and T. C. Smout (eds), *Comparative Aspects of Scottish and Irish Economic History, 1600–1900* (Edinburgh: Donald, 1978, pp. 47–64).

Flinn, Michael W., *The European Demographic System, 1500–1820* (Baltimore, Md: Johns Hopkins University Press, 1981).

Foster, Thomas Campbell, *Letters on the Condition of the People of Ireland*, 2nd edn (London: Chapman & Hall, 1847).

Fraser, Robert, *General View of the Agriculture and Mineralogy, Present State and Circumstances of the County Wicklow* (Dublin: Graisberry & Campbell, 1801).

Fraser, Robert, *Statistical Survey of the County of Wexford* (Dublin: Graisberry & Campbell, 1807).

Freeman, T. W., *Pre-Famine Ireland* (Manchester: Manchester University Press, 1957).

Freudenberger, Herman, and Cummins, Gaylord, "Health, work and leisure before the Industrial Revolution", *Explorations in Economic History*, vol. 13, no. 1 (January 1976), pp. 1–12.

Gallman, Robert E., "Human capital in the first 80 years of the Republic: how much did America owe the rest of the world?", *American Economic Review*, vol. 67, no. 1 (February 1977), pp. 27–31.

Gaskin, Katherine, "Age at first marriage in Europe before 1850: a summary of family reconstitution data", *Journal of Family History*, vol. 3, no. 1 (Spring 1978), pp. 23–36.

Gayer, Arthur D., Rostow, W. W., and Schwartz, Anna J., *The Growth and Fluctuation of the British Economy, 1790–1850* (Oxford: Clarendon Press, 1953; reprinted edition, 1975).

Geary, F., "The rise and fall of the Belfast cotton industry: some problems", *Irish Economic and Social History*, vol. VIII (1981), pp. 30–49.

Gibbon, Peter, "Colonialism and the great starvation in Ireland, 1845–9", *Race and Class*, vol. XVII, no. 2 (Autumn 1975), pp. 131–9.

Gill, Conrad, *The Rise of the Irish Linen Industry* (Oxford: Clarendon Press, 1925).

Goldstrom, J. M., "The industrialization of the north-east", in L. M. Cullen (ed.), *The Formation of the Irish Economy* (Cork: Mercier Press, 1969, pp. 101–12).

Goldstrom, J. M., "Irish agriculture and the Great Famine", in J. M. Goldstrom and L. A. Clarkson (eds), *Irish Population, Economy and Society, Essays in Honour of K. H. Connell* (Oxford: Clarendon Press, 1981, pp. 155–71).

Grantham, George, "Scale and organization in French farming", in W. N. Parker and E. L. Jones (eds), *European Peasants and Their Markets* (Princeton, NJ: Princeton University Press, 1975, pp. 293–326).

Grantham, George, "The diffusion of the new husbandry in northern France, 1815–1840", *Journal of Economic History*, vol. XXXVIII, no. 2 (June 1978), pp. 311–37.

Great Britain, *Parliamentary Papers* (1819, Vol. VIII), "Reports from the Select Committee on the State of Disease and Condition of the Labouring Poor in Ireland".

Great Britain, *Parliamentary Papers* (1822a, Vol. XIII), "Reports of the Commissioners of Inquiry into the Collection and Management of the Revenue Arising in Ireland".

Great Britain, *Parliamentary Papers* (1822b, Vol. XIV), "Reports from the Commissioners and Miscellaneous Papers (Ireland)".

Great Britain, *Parliamentary Papers* (1823, Vol. VI), "Report from the Select Committee on the Employment of the Poor in Ireland".

Great Britain, *Parliamentary Papers* (1824, Vol. XXII), "Abstract of the Answers and Returns . . . (of the 1821 Census)".

Great Britain, *Parliamentary Papers* (1825a, Vol. V), "Report from the Select Committee on the Linen Trade of Ireland".

Great Britain, *Parliamentary Papers* (1825b, Vol. VIII), "Reports from the Select Committee on the State of Ireland".

Great Britain, *Parliamentary Papers*, (1825c, Vol. IX), "Minutes of Evidence taken before the Select Committee of the House of Lords, Appointed to Inquire into the State of Ireland".

Great Britain, *Parliamentary Papers* (1826, Vol. V), "Report from the Select Committee on the Butter Trade in Ireland".

Great Britain, *Parliamentary Papers* (1830, Vol. VII), "Report of the Select Committee on the State of the Poor in Ireland".

Great Britain, *Parliamentary Papers* (1833, Vol. XXXIX), "Abstract of the Answers and Returns . . . (of the 1831 Census)".

Great Britain, *Parliamentary Papers* (1835a, Vol. VIII, Pt I), "First and Second Reports from the Select Committee Appointed to Inquire into the State of Agriculture In Great Britain".

Great Britain, *Parliamentary Papers* (1835b, Vol. XX), "First and Second Reports from the Select Committee on Public Works in Ireland".

Great Britain, *Parliamentary Papers* (1835c, Vol. XXXI), "First Report from his Majesty's Commissioners for Inquiring into the Condition of the Poorer Classes in Ireland."

Great Britain, *Parliamentary Papers* (1835d, Vol. XXXIII), "First Report of the Commissioners of Public Instruction (Ireland)".

Great Britain, *Parliamentary Papers* (1836a, Vol. VIII, Pt II), "Third Report of the Select Committee Appointed to Inquire into the State of Agriculture".

Great Britain, *Parliamentary Papers* (1836b, Vols XXX–XXXIV), "Reports of the Commissioners for Inquiry into the Condition of the Poorer Classes In Ireland".

Great Britain, *Parliamentary Papers* (1837, Vol. XIV), "Report from the Secret Committee on Joint Stock Banks".

Great Britain, *Parliamentary Papers* (1837–8, Vol. XXXV), "Reports of the

Commissioners Appointed to Consider and Recommend a General System of Railways in Ireland".

Great Britain, *Parliamentary Papers* (1839a, House of Lords, Vols XVIII–XXI), "Report from the Select Committee of the House of Lords Appointed to Inquire into the State of Ireland in Respect to Crime (Wharncliffe Committee)".

Great Britain, *Parliamentary Papers* (1839b, Vol. XLII), "A Return of the Number of Persons Employed in Cotton, Woollen, Worsted, and Flax Factories in the United Kingdom".

Great Britain, *Parliamentary Papers* (1839a, Vols XI–XII), "Report from the Select Committee of the House of Lords Appointed to Inquire into the State of Ireland in Respect to Crime (Wharncliffe Committee)".

Great Britain, *Parliamentary Papers* (1840, Vol. XXIII), "Reports from the Assistant Handloom Weavers' Commissioners on the West Riding and Ireland".

Great Britain, *Parliamentary Papers* (1843, Vol. XXIV), "Reports of the Commissioners Appointed to Take the Census of Ireland for the Year 1841".

Great Britain, *Parliamentary Papers* (1844, Vol. VII), "Reports from the Select Committee on the Townland Evaluation of Ireland".

Great Britain, *Parliamentary Papers* (1845a, Vols XIX–XXII), "Report from Her Majesty's Commissioners of Inquiry into the State of the Law and Practice in Relation to the Occupation of Land in Ireland".

Great Britain, *Parliamentary Papers* (1845b, Vol. XXVI), "Third Annual Report from Commissioners Appointed . . . to Promote the Drainage of Land . . . in Ireland".

Great Britain, *Parliamentary Papers* (1846a, Vol. XXII), "Fourth Annual Report from Commissioners Appointed . . . to Promote the Drainage of Land . . . in Ireland".

Great Britain, *Parliamentary Papers* (1846b, Vol. XXXV), "A return of all aggravated assaults . . . in Ireland since Dec. 31, 1845".

Great Britain, *Parliamentary Papers* (1846c, Vol. XXXVII), "Correspondence Relating to the Measure Adopted by Her Majesty's Government for the Relief of Distress Arising from the Famine of the Potato Crop in Ireland".

Great Britain, *Parliamentary Papers* (1847a, Vol. XIX), "Report from the Select Committee of the House of Lords on Colonization from Ireland".

Great Britain, *Parliamentary Papers* (1847b, Vol. LI), "Accounts and Papers: Relief of the Distress in Ireland: Commissariat".

Great Britain, *Parliamentary Papers* (1847–8, Vol. XLVII), "Papers Relative to Emigration to the British Provinces in North America".

Great Britain, *Parliamentary Papers* (1849a, Vol. XLIX), "Returns of Agricultural Produce in Ireland in the Year 1848".

Great Britain, *Parliamentary Papers* (1849b, Vol. XLIX), "Different Works of Drainage in Ireland, Finished or in Progress . . .".

Great Britain, *Parliamentary Papers* (1851, Vol. XIX), "Report from the Select Committee on the Passenger Act".

Great Britain, *Parliamentary Papers* (1854, Vol. XIII), "Final Report from the Select Committee on Emigrant Ships".

Great Britain, *Parliamentary Papers* (1856a, Vol. XXIX), "The Census of Ireland for the Year (1851), Pt V: Tables of Death, Vol. 1".

Great Britain, *Parliamentary Papers* (1856b, Vol. XXX), "The Census of Ireland for the Year (1851), Pt V: Tables of Death, Vol. 2".

Great Britain, *Parliamentary Papers* (1856c, Vol. XXXI), "The Census of Ireland for the Year 1851, Pt VI: General Report".

Great Britain, *Parliamentary Papers* (1870, Vol. LVI), pp. 737–57, "Returns Showing the Number of Agricultural Holdings in Ireland".

Green, E. R. R., *The Lagan Valley, 1800–50: A Local History of the Industrial Revolution* (London: Faber, 1949).

Green, E. R. R., "The beginnings of Industrial Revolution", in T. W. Moody and J. C. Beckett (eds), *Ulster since 1800: A Political and Economic Survey* (London: BBC, 1954, pp. 28–38).

Green, E. R. R., "Agriculture", in R. Dudley Edwards and T. D. Williams (eds), *The Great Famine* (New York: New York University Press, 1957, pp. 89–128).

Green, E. R. R., "Industrial decline in the nineteenth century", in L. M. Cullen (ed.), *The Formation of the Irish Economy* (Cork: Mercier Press, 1969, pp. 89–100).

Greig, William, *General Report on the Gosford Estates in County Armagh, 1821* (Belfast: Public Record Office of Northern Ireland, 1976).

Gribbon, H. D., *The History of Water Power in Ulster* (Newton Abbot: David & Charles, 1969).

Grigg, David, *Population Growth and Agrarian Change: An Historical Perspective* (Cambridge; Cambridge University Press, 1980).

Grubel, Herbert G., and Scott, Anthony, *The Brain Drain: Determinants, Measurements, and Welfare Effects* (Waterloo, Ontario: Wilfred Laurier University Press, 1977).

Hajnal, John, "Age of marriage and proportions marrying", *Population Studies*, vol. 7, no. 2 (1953), pp. 111–36.

Hall, Mr and Mrs S. C., *Ireland, its Scenery, Character and History*, 6 vols (Boston, Mass.: Niccols, 1911; originally published, 1825–40).

Handley, James Edmund, *The Irish in Scotland, 1798–1845* (Cork: Cork University Press, 1945).

Handlin, Oscar, *Boston's Immigrants*, rev. edn (New York: Atheneum, 1977).

Hansen, Marcus Lee (ed., Arthur M. Schlesinger), *The Atlantic Migration, 1607–1860* (New York: Harper & Row, 1961; originally published, 1940).

Hechter, Michael, "Regional inequality and national integration: the case of the British Isles", *Journal of Social History*, vol. V, no. 1 (1971), pp. 96–117.

Hechter, Michael, *Internal Colonialism: The Celtic Fringe in British National Development, 1536–1966* (London: Routledge & Kegan Paul, 1975).

Heelan, J., and E. W. Henry, "Capital in Irish industry: financial and related aspects", *Journal of the Statistical and Social Inquiry Society of Ireland*, Vol. XXI, pt I, (1962–3), pp. 135–66.

Henry, Louis, "Some data on national fertility", *Eugenics Quarterly*, vol. 8, no. 1 (March 1961), pp. 81–91.

Herring, Ivor J., "Ulster roads on the eve of the railway age, *c.*1800–40", *Irish Historical Studies*, vol. II, no. 5 (March 1940), pp. 160–88.

Hobsbawm, Eric J., "The British standard of living, 1790–1850", in Arthur J. Taylor (ed.), *The Standard of Living in Britain in the Industrial Revolution* (London: Methuen, 1975, pp. 58–92).

Hobsbawm, Eric J., and Rudé, George, *Captain Swing: A Social History of the Great English Agricultural Uprising of 1830* (New York: Pantheon, 1968).

Hoffman, Elizabeth, and Mokyr, Joel, "Peasants, potatoes, and poverty: trans-actions costs in prefamine Ireland", Center for Mathematical Studies in Economics and Management Science, Discussion Paper No. 474, Northwestern University, Evanston, Illinois, USA, April 1981.

Hofstee, E. W., *De Demografische Ontwikkeling van Nederland in de Eerste Helft van de Negentiende Eeuw* (NIDI: Van Loghum Slaterus, 1978)

Hooker, Elizabeth R., *Readjustments of Agricultural Tenure in Ireland* (Chapel Hill; NC: University of North Carolina Press, 1938).

Hughes, Jonathan R. T., *Fluctuations in Trade, Industry and Finance: A Study of British Economic Development 1850–1860* (Oxford: Clarendon Press, 1960).

Huntingdon, Ellsworth, *Season of Birth* (New York: Wiley, 1938).

Hutchinson, Bertram, "On the study of non-economic factors in Irish economic development", *Economic and Social Review* (Dublin), vol. I, no. 3 (April 1970), pp. 509–29.

Hyman, Louis, *The Jews of Ireland* (Shannon: Irish University Press, 1972).

Hynes, Eugene, "The great hunger and Irish Catholicism", *Societas: A Review of Social History*, vol. 8 (Spring 1978), pp. 137–56.

Inglis, Henry D., *A Journey throughout Ireland during the Spring, Summer, and Autumn of 1834*, 2 vols (London: Whittaker, 1835).

Jacquemyns, G., "Histoire de la Crise Economique des Flanders, 1845–50", *Academie Royale de Belgique, Memoires*, vol. 26 (1929), pp. 11–472.

James, Francis G., "Irish smuggling in the eighteenth century", *Irish Historical Studies*, vol. XII, no. 48 (1961), pp. 299–317.

James, Francis G., *Ireland in the Empire, 1688–1770* (Cambridge, Mass.: Harvard University Press, 1973).

Johnson, Harry G., "The neoclassical one-sector growth model — a geometrical exposition and extension to a monetary economy", *Economica*, vol. 33, no. 131 (August 1966), pp. 265–87.

Johnson, James H., "The population of Londonderry during the Great Irish Famine", *Economic History Review*, vol. X, no. 2 (2nd series) (December 1957), pp. 273–85.

Johnson, James H., "Marriage and fertility in nineteenth century Londonderry", *Journal of the Statistical and Social Inquiry Society of Ireland*, vol. XX, no. 1 (1957–8), pp. 99–117.

Johnson, James H., "The two 'Irelands' at the beginning of the nineteenth century", in N. Stephens and R. W. Glasscock (eds), *Irish Geographical Studies in Honour of E. Estyn Evans* (Belfast: Queen's University of Belfast, 1970, pp. 224–43).

Johnston, Edith Marie, *Ireland in the Eighteenth Century* (Dublin: Gill & MacMillan, 1974).

Jones, Eric L., *Agriculture and the Industrial Revolution* (Oxford: Blackwell, 1974).

Jones, Eric L., *The European Miracle* (Cambridge: Cambridge University Press, 1981a).

Jones, Eric L., "Agriculture, 1700–80", in Roderick Floud and Donald McCloskey (eds), *The Economic History of Britain since 1700, Vol. I: 1700–1860* (Cambridge: Cambridge University Press, 1981b), pp. 66–86.

Jones, Hywel G., *An Introduction to Modern Theories of Economic Growth* (New York: McGraw-Hill, 1976).

Kafka, A., "An economic justification of protectionism: Further comments", *Quarterly Journal of Economics*, vol. 76, no. 1 (February 1962), pp. 163–6.

Kane, Robert, *The Industrial Resources of Ireland*, 2nd edn (Dublin: Hodges & Smith, 1845).

Kapp, Friedrich, *Immigration and the Commissioners of Emigration* (New York: Nation Press, 1870; reprinted, 1969).

Kennedy, Brian A., "Tenant right before 1870", in T. W. Moody and J. C. Beckett (eds), *Ulster since 1800: A Political and Economic Survey* (London: BBC, 1954, pp. 39–49).

Kennedy, J. P., *Instruct: Employ: Don't Hang Them: Ireland Tranquillized Without Soldiers and Without English Capital* (London: Boone, 1835).

Kennedy, J. P., *Digest of Evidence Taken Before Her Majesty's Commissioners of Inquiry into the State of the Law and Practice in Respect to the Occupation of Land in Ireland* (Devon Commission) (Dublin: Thom, 1847).

Kennedy, Liam, "The Roman Catholic Church and economic growth in nineteenth century Ireland", *Economic and Social Review* (Dublin), vol. 10, no. 1 (October 1978), pp. 45–60.

Kennedy, Liam, "Regional specialization, railway development, and Irish agriculture in the nineteenth century", in J. M. Goldstrom and L. A. Clarkson (eds), *Irish Population, Economy and Society, Essays in Honour of K. H. Connell* (Oxford: Clarendon Press, 1981, pp. 173–93).

Kennedy, Robert E. Jr., *The Irish: Emigration, Marriage and Fertility* (Berkeley, Calif.: University of California Press, 1973).

Kerr, Barbara M., "Irish seasonal migration to Great Britain, 1800–38", *Irish Historical Studies*, vol. III, no. 12 (September 1943), pp. 365–80.

Kindleberger, Charles P., *Economic Growth in France and Britain, 1851–1950* (New York: Simon & Schuster, 1964).

Kohl, J. G., *Ireland* (New York: Harper, 1844).

Kuznets, Simon, *Economic Growth of Nations* (Cambridge: Belknap Press, 1971).

Lane, Pádraig G., "An attempt at commercial farming in Ireland after the famine", *Studies*, vol. XLI, no. 241 (Spring 1972), pp. 54–66.

Large, David, "The wealth of the greater Irish landowners, 1750–1815", *Irish Historical Studies*, vol. XV, no. 57 (March 1966), pp. 21–47.

Larkin, Emmet, "Economic growth, capital investment and the Roman Catholic Church in nineteenth-century Ireland", *American Historical Review*, vol. LXXII, no. 3 (April 1967), pp. 853–84.

de Lavergne, Leonce, *The Rural Economy of England, Scotland and Ireland* (Edinburgh/London: Blackwood, 1855).

Leavitt, T. H., *Facts About Peat as an Article of Fuel* (Boston, Mass.: Lee & Shepard, 1867).

Lebergott, Stanley, *Wealth and Want* (Princeton, NJ: Princeton University Press, 1975).

Lebow, Richard Ned, "British images of poverty in pre-famine Ireland", in Daniel J. Casey and Robert E. Rhodes (eds), *Views of the Irish Peasantry, 1800–1916* (Hamden, Conn.: Anchor, 1977, pp. 57–85).

Lebow, Richard Ned (ed.), *John Stuart Mill on Ireland* (Philadelphia, Pa: Institute for Study of Human Issues, 1979).

Lecky, W. E. H., *A History of Ireland in the Eighteenth Century* (Chicago: University of Chicago Press, 1972; edited and abridged from 1892 edition by L. P. Curtis).

Lee, Joseph, "Money and beer in Ireland, 1790–1875", *Economic History Review*, vol. XIX, no. 1 (2nd series) (April 1966), pp. 183–90.

Lee, Joseph, "The construction costs of Irish railways, 1830–1853", *Business History*, vol. IX, no. 2 (July 1967), pp. 95–109.

Lee, Joseph, "Marriage and population in pre-famine Ireland", *Economic History Review*, vol. XXI (2nd series) (1968a), pp. 283–95.

Lee, Joseph, "The provision of capital for early Irish railways, 1830–53", *Irish Historical Studies*, vol. XVI, no. 6 (March 1968b), pp. 33–63.

Lee, Joseph, "Capital in the Irish economy", in L. M. Cullen (ed.), *The Formation of the Irish Economy* (Cork: Mercier Press, 1969a, pp. 53–63).

Lee, Joseph, "Irish agriculture", *Agricultural History Review*, vol. 17, pt 1 (1969b), pp. 64–76.

Lee, Joseph, "The railways in the Irish economy", in L. M. Cullen (ed.), *The Formation of the Irish Economy* (Cork: Mercier Press, 1969c, pp. 77–87).

Lee, Joseph, "The dual economy in Ireland, 1800–50", *Historical Studies*, vol. VIII (1971), pp. 191–201.

Lee, Joseph, *The Modernization of Irish Society* (Dublin: Gill & MacMillan, 1973a).

Lee, Joseph, "The ribbonmen", in T. Desmond Williams (ed.), *Secret Societies in Ireland* (Dublin: Gill & MacMillan, 1973b, pp. 26–35).

Lee, Joseph, "Patterns of rural unrest in nineteenth century Ireland: a preliminary survey", in L. M. Cullen and F. Furet (eds), *Ireland and France, 17th–20th Centuries: Towards a Comparative Study of Rural History* (Paris: Editions de l'Ecole des Hautes Etudes et Sciences Sociales, 1980, pp. 223–37).

Lee, Joseph, "Irish economic history since 1500", in Joseph Lee (ed.), *Irish Historiography, 1970–79* (Cork: Cork University Press, 1981a, pp. 173–224).

Lee, Joseph, "On the accuracy of the pre-famine Irish Censuses", in J. M. Goldstrom and L. A. Clarkson (eds), *Irish Population, Economy and Society, Essays in Honour of K. H. Connell* (Oxford: Clarendon Press, 1981b, pp. 37–56).

Lee, Ronald D., "Models of preindustrial population dynamics with application to England", in Charles Tilly (ed.), *Historical Studies of Changing Fertility* (Princeton, NJ: Princeton University Press, 1978, pp. 155–207).

Lees, Lynn Hollen, *Exiles of Erin: Irish Migrants in Victorian London* (Manchester: Manchester University Press, 1979).

Lefgren, John, "Famine in Finland", *Intermountain Economic Review*, vol. IV, no. 2 (Fall 1973), pp. 17–31.

Leibenstein, Harvey, *Economic Backwardness and Economic Growth* (New York: Wiley, 1957).

Lesthaeghe, Ron J., *The Decline of Belgian Fertility, 1800–1970* (Princeton, NJ: Princeton University Press, 1977).

Lewis, George Cornewall, *On Local Disturbances in Ireland* (London: Fellowes, 1836a).

Lewis, George Cornewall, "Report on the state of the Irish poor in Great Britain", *Parliamentary Papers*, 1836b, Vol. XXXIV, pp. 429–74 (Appendix G to the *Reports of the Commissioners for Inquiring into the Condition of the Poorer Classes in Ireland*).

Lewis, Samuel, *A Topographical Dictionary of Ireland*, 2 vols, 2nd edn (London: Lewis, 1840).

Lucas, A. T., "Paring and burning in Ireland", in Alan Gailey and Alexander Fenton (eds), *The Spade in Northern and Atlantic Europe* (Belfast: Ulster Folk Museum and Institute of Irish Studies, Queen's University, 1970, pp. 99–147).

Lynch, A. H., *Measures to be Adopted for the Employment of the Labouring Classes in Ireland* (London: Knight, 1839).

Lynch, Patrick, and Vaisey, John, *Guinness's Brewery in the Irish Economy, 1759–1876* (Cambridge: Cambridge University Press, 1960).

Lyons, F. S. L., "Vicissitudes of a middleman in county Leitrim, 1810–27", *Irish Historical Studies*, vol. IX, no. 35 (March 1955), pp. 300–18.

Lyons, F. S. L., *Ireland Since the Famine* (Glasgow: Collins/Fontana, 1973).

McArthur, William P., "Medical history of the famine", in R. Dudley Edwards and T. Desmond Williams (eds), *The Great Famine: Studies in Irish History, 1845–52* (New York: New York University Press, 1957, pp. 263–315).

McCloskey, Donald N., "The economics of enclosure: a market analysis", in William N. Parker and Eric L. Jones (eds), *European Peasants and Their Markets* (Princeton, NJ: Princeton University Press, 1975, pp. 123–60).

McCracken, Eileen, *The Irish Woods since Tudor Times: Distribution and Exploitation* (Newton Abbot: David & Charles, 1971).

McCulloch, J. R., *A Descriptive and Statistical Account of the British Empire*, 2 Vols 4th edn, (London: Longman, 1854; originally published, 1837).

McCulloch, J. R., *A Dictionary, Geographical, Statistical and Historical*, rev. edn (London: Longmans, Green, 1866).

McCutcheon, W. A., "The transportation revolution: Canals and river navigation", in Kevin B. Nowlan (ed.), *Travel and Transport in Ireland* (Dublin: Gill & MacMillan, 1973, pp. 64–81).

McCutcheon, Alan, *Wheel and Spindle: Aspects of Irish Industrial History* (Belfast: Blackstaff Press, 1977).

MacDonagh, Oliver, "Irish emigration to the United States of America and the British colonies during the famine", in R. Dudley Edwards and T. Desmond Williams (eds), *The Great Famine: Studies in Irish History, 1845–52* (New York: New York University Press, 1957, pp. 319–88).

MacDonagh, Oliver, *Ireland: The Union and its Aftermath* (London: Allen & Unwin, 1977).

McDowell, R. B., "From the Union to the famine", in T. W. Moody and J. C. Beckett (eds), *Ulster since 1800, Second Series: A Social Survey* (London: BBC, 1957a, pp. 25–34).

McDowell, R. B., "Ireland on the eve of the famine", in R. Dudley Edwards and T. Desmond Williams (eds), *The Great Famine, Studies in Irish History, 1845–52* (New York: New York University Press, 1957b, pp. 3–86).

McDowell, R. B., "The Irish courts of law", *Irish Historical Studies*, vol. X, no. 40 (September 1957c), pp. 363–91.

McEvoy, John, *Statistical Survey of the County of Tyrone* (Dublin: Graisberry & Campbell, 1802).

McHugh, Roger J., "The famine in Irish oral tradition", in R. Dudley Edwards and T. Desmond Williams (eds), *The Great Famine* (New York: New York University Press, 1957, pp. 391–436).

McKenna, Edward E., "Marriage and fertility in post-famine Ireland: a multivariate analysis", *American Journal of Sociology*, vol. 80, no. 3 (November 1974), pp. 688–705.

McKenna, Edward E., "Age, region and marriage in post-famine Ireland: an empirical examination", *Economic History Review*, vol. XXXI, no. 2 (2nd series) (May 1978), pp. 238–56.

McKinnon, Ronald I., *Money and Capital in Economic Development*, (Washington, DC: Brookings Institution, 1973).

McParlan, James, *Statistical Survey of the County of Donegal* (Dublin: Graisberry & Campbell, 1802a).

McParlan, James, *Statistical Survey of the County of Leitrim* (Dublin: Graisberry & Campbell, 1802b).

McParlan, James, *Statistical Survey of the County of Mayo* (Dublin: Graisberry & Campbell, 1802c).

McParlan, James, *Statistical Survey of the County of Sligo* (Dublin: Graisberry & Campbell, 1802d).

Magnusson, Magnus, *Landlord or Tenant? A View of Irish History* (London: Bodley Head, 1978).

Maguire, W. A., *The Downshire Estates in Ireland, 1801–1845* (Oxford: Clarendon Press, 1972).

Maguire, W. A., "Lord Donegal and the sale of Belfast: a case history from the encumbered estates court", *Economic History Review*, vol. XXIX, no. 4 (2nd series) (November 1976).

Malcomson, A. P. W., "Absenteeism in eighteenth century Ireland", *Irish Economic and Social History*, vol. I (1974), pp. 15–35.

Malthus, Thomas R., *An Essay on the Principle of Population*, 6th edn, 2 vols (London: Murray, 1826).

Malthus, Thomas R., *Principles of Political Economy*, 2nd edn (London: Pickering, 1836).

Mansergh, Nicholas, *The Irish Question, 1840–1921*, 3rd edn (London: Allen & Unwin, 1975).

Martin, R. Montgomery, *Ireland Before and After the Union with Great Britain* (London: Orr, 1843).

Marx, Karl, and Engels, Frederick, *Ireland and the Irish Question: A Collection of Writings* (New York: International, 1972).

Mason, William Shaw, *A Statistical Account or Parochial Survey of Ireland* (Dublin: Graisberry & Campbell, 1814, Vol. 1; 1816, vol. 2; 1819, vol. 3).

Maxwell, Constantia, *Country and Town in Ireland under the Georges* (Dundalk: Tempest, 1949).

Maxwell, Constantia, *The Stranger in Ireland* (London: Cape, 1954).

Mayo-Smith, Richmond, *Emigration and Immigration* (New York: Scribner's, 1890; reprinted, 1968).

Mikesell, Raymond F., and Zinser, James E., "The nature of the savings function in the developing countries: a survey of the theoretical and empirical literature", *Journal of Economic Literature*, vol. XI, no. 1 (March 1973), pp. 1–26.

Mill, John Stuart (ed., W. J. Ashley), *Principles of Political Economy* (London: Longman, 1929).

Miller, David W., "Irish Catholicism and the Great Famine", *Journal of Social History*, vol. IX, no. 7 (September 1975), pp. 81–104.

Milward, Alan S., and Saul, S. B., *The Development of the Economies of Continental Europe, 1850–1914* (London: Allen & Unwin, 1977).

Mingay, G. E., *English Landed Society in the Eighteenth Century* (London: Routledge & Kegan Paul, 1963).

Mirrlees, James A., "A pure theory of undeveloped economies", in Lloyd G. Reynolds (ed.), *Agriculture in Development Theory* (New Haven, Conn./London: Yale University, 1975, pp. 84–106).

Mitchell, Brian R., *European Historical Statistics, 1750–1970* (London: Macmillan, 1975).

Mitchell, Brian R., and Deane, Phyllis, *Abstract of British Historical Statistics* (Cambridge: Cambridge University Press, 1971).

Mokyr, Joel, "Capital, labor and the delay of the Industrial Revolution in the Netherlands", *Yearbook of Economic History* (Amsterdam), vol. XXXVII (1975), pp. 280–99.

Mokyr, Joel, *Industrialization in the Low Countries* (New Haven, Conn./London: Yale University Press, 1976a).

Mokyr, Joel, "Growing up and the Industrial Revolution in Europe", *Explorations in Economic History*, vol. 13, no. 4 (October 1976b), pp. 371–96.

Mokyr, Joel, "Demand vs supply in the Industrial Revolution", *Journal of Economic History*, vol. XXXVII, no. 4 (December 1977), pp. 981–1008.

Mokyr, Joel, "Industrialization and poverty in Ireland and the Netherlands: some notes toward a comparative case-study", *Journal of Interdisciplinary History*, vol. X, no. 3 (Winter 1980a), pp. 429–59.

Mokyr, Joel, "The deadly fungus: an econometric investigation into the short-term demographic impact of the Irish famine, 1846–1851", *Research in Population Economics*, vol. II, (1980b), pp. 237–77.

Mokyr, Joel, "Malthusian models and Irish history", *Journal of Economic History*, vol. XL, no. 1 (March 1980c), pp. 159–66.

Mokyr, Joel, "Irish history with the potato", *Irish Economic and Social History*, vol. VIII (1981a), pp. 3–29.

Mokyr, Joel, "Uncertainty and prefamine Irish agriculture", paper presented to 2nd International Conference on Comparative Irish-Scottish History, Glasgow, (September 1981b) in David Dickson and T. M. Devine, (eds), *Ireland and Scotland, Economic and Social Developments, 1650–1850* (Edinburgh: Donald,forthcoming).

Mokyr, Joel, and Ó Gráda, Cormac, "New developments in Irish population history, 1700–1850", paper presented to the conference on British Population History, Asilomar, California, March 7–9, 1982a (mimeo.).

Mokyr, Joel, and Ó Gráda, Cormac, "Emigration and poverty in prefamine Ireland", *Explorations in Economic History*, vol. 19, no. 4 (October 1982b), pp. 360–84.

Monaghan, John J., "The rise and fall of the Belfast cotton industry", *Irish Historical Studies*, vol. III, no. 9 (March 1942), pp. 1–17.

Morehouse, Frances, "The Irish migration of the 'forties", *American Historical Review*, vol. 33, no. 3 (April 1928), pp. 579–92.

Moyles, M. G., and dé Brun, Pádraig, "Charles O'Brien's agricultural survey of Kerry, 1800", *Journal of the Kerry Archaeological and Historical Society*, vol. I (1968), pp. 73–99; vol. II (1969), pp. 108–32.

Mulhall, Michael T., *The Dictionary of Statistics*, 4th edn (London: Routledge, 1899).

Murphy, John Nicholas, *Ireland, Industrial, Political, and Social* (London: Longmans, Green, 1870).

Neal, Larry, and Uselding, Paul, "Immigration, a neglected source of American economic growth, 1790–1912", *Oxford Economic Papers*, vol. 24 (March 1972), pp. 68–88.

Neher, Philip A., "Peasants, procreation and pensions", *American Economic Review*, vol. LXI, no. 3 (June 1971), pp. 380–9.

Nelson, Richard R., "A theory of the low-level equilibrium trap in under-developed economies", *American Economic Review*, vol. LVI, no. 5 (December 1956), pp. 894–908.

Nelson, Richard R., "Growth models and the escape from the equilibrium trap", *Economic Development and Cultural Change*, vol. VIII, no. 4, pt I (July 1960), pp. 378–88.

Nerlove, Marc, and Schultz, T. Paul, *Love and Life Between Censuses: A Model of Family Decision Making in Puerto Rico, 1950–1960* (Santa Monica, Calif., Rand Corporation, prepared for the Agency for International Development, September 1970).

Newenham, Thomas, *A View of the Natural, Political and Commercial Circumstances of Ireland* (London: Cadell, 1809).

Nicholls, George, *A History of the Irish Poor Law* (London: Murray, 1856).

Nicholson, Asenath, *Ireland's Welcome to the Stranger, or Excursions through Ireland in 1844 and 1845* (London: Gilpin, 1847).

O'Brien, George A. P., *The Economic History of Ireland in the Eighteenth Century* (Dublin/London: Maunsel, 1918; reprinted Porcupine Press, 1977).

O'Brien, George A. P., *The Economic History of Ireland from the Union to the Famine* (London: Longmans, Green, 1921).

O'Brien, W. P., *The Great Famine in Ireland* (London: Downey, 1896).

O'Donovan, John, *The Economic History of Livestock in Ireland* (Cork: Cork University Press, 1940).

O'Farrell, Patrick, *England and Ireland since 1800* (London: Oxford University Press, 1975).

Ó Gráda, Cormac, "Post-famine adjustment: essays in nineteenth century Irish economic history", unpublished Ph.D. dissertation, Columbia University, New York, USA, 1973a.

Ó Gráda, Cormac, "Seasonal adjustment and post-famine adjustment in the west of Ireland", *Studia Hibernica*, vol. 13 (1973b), pp. 48–76.

Ó Gráda, Cormac, "A note on nineteenth-century Irish emigration statistics", *Population Studies*, vol. 29, no. 7 (March 1975) pp. 143–9.

Ó Gráda, Cormac, "Some aspects of nineteenth-century Irish emigration", in L. M. Cullen and T. C. Smout (eds), *Comparative Aspects of Scottish and Irish Economic and Social History, 1600–1900* (Edinburgh: Donald, 1978, pp. 65–73).

Ó Gráda, Cormac, "Primogeniture and ultimogeniture in rural Ireland", *Journal of Interdisciplinary History*, vol. X, no. 3 (Winter 1980a), pp. 491–7.

Ó Gráda, Cormac, "Irish population trends, 1700–1900: a survey", unpublished manuscript, Northwestern University, Evanston, Illinois, USA, 1980b.

Ó Gráda, Cormac, "Irish agriculture before and after the Great Famine", unpublished manuscript, University College, Dublin, and Northwestern University, Evanston, Illinois, USA, June 1980c.

Ó Gráda, Cormac, "Demographic adjustment and seasonal migration in nineteenth century Ireland", in L. M. Cullen and F. Furet (eds), *Ireland and France, 17th–20th Centuries: Towards a Comparative Study of Rural History* (Paris: Editions de l'Ecole des Hautes Etudes en Sciences Sociales, 1980d, pp. 181–93).

Ó Gráda, Cormac, "Across the briny ocean: some thoughts on Irish emigration to America, 1800–50", paper presented to 2nd International Conference on Comparative Irish-Scottish History, Glasgow, September 1981 in David Dickson and T. M. Devine (eds), *Ireland and Scotland: Economic and Social Developments, 1650–1850* (Edinburgh: Donald, forthcoming).

Ó Gráda, Cormac, "Irish bogs", unpublished manuscript, private communication, n.d.

O'Malley, Eoin, "The decline of Irish industry in the nineteenth century", *Economic and Social Review*, vol. 13, no. 1 (October 1981), pp. 21–42.

O'Neill, Thomas P., "The scientific investigation of the failure of the potato crop in Ireland, 1845–6", *Irish Historical Studies*, vol. V, no. 18 (September 1946), pp. 123–38.

O'Neill, Thomas P., "Food problems during the Great Irish Famine", *Journal of the Royal Society of Antiquaries of Ireland*, vol. LXXXII (1952), pp. 99–108.

O'Neill, Thomas P., "The organization and administration of relief, 1845–52", in R. Dudley Edwards and T. Desmond Williams (eds), *The Great Famine* (New York: New York University Press, 1957, pp. 209–59).

O'Neill, Thomas P., "Bianconi and his cars", in Kevin B. Nowlan (ed.), *Travel and Transport in Ireland* (Dublin: Gill & MacMillan, 1973, pp. 82–95).

O'Rourke, John, *The History of the Great Irish Famine of 1847 with Notices of Earlier Irish Famines, 3rd edn (Dublin: Duffy, 1902).*

Ó Tuathaigh, Gearóid, *Ireland before the Famine, 1798–1848* (Dublin: Gill & MacMillan, 1972).

Ó Tuathaigh, Gearóid, "Ireland, 1800–1921", in Joseph Lee (ed.), *Irish Historiography, 1970–79* (Cork: Cork University Press, 1981, pp. 85–131).

Page, H. J., "Patterns underlying fertility schedules: a decomposition by both age and marriage duration", *Population Studies*, vol. 30, no. 3 (1978), pp. 85–106.

Parliamentary Gazetteer of Ireland, 3 vols (Dublin: Fullerton, 1846).

Petty, William, *The Political Anatomy of Ireland*, in C. H. Hull (ed.), *The Economic Writings of Sir William Petty* (Cambridge: Cambridge University Press, 1899; originally published, 1672).

Pigou, A. C., *The Economics of Welfare*, 4th edn (London: Macmillan, 1932).

Pim, Jonathan, *The Condition and Prospects of Ireland* (Dublin: Hodges & Smith, 1848).

Pollard, Sidney, "Labour in Great Britain", in Peter Mathias and M. M. Postan (eds), *The Cambridge Economic History of Europe*, Vol. 7 (Cambridge: Cambridge University Press, 1978, pp. 97–179).

Pollard, Sidney, *Peaceful Conquest: The Industrialization of Europe, 1760–1970* (Oxford: Oxford University Press, 1981).

Pomfret, John E., *The Struggle for Land in Ireland, 1800–1923* (Princeton, NJ: Princeton University Press, 1930).

Portlock, J. E., *Report on the Geology of the County of Londonderry and of Parts of Tyrone and Fermanagh* (Dublin: Milliken, 1843).

Ransom, Roger L., and Sutch, Richard, *One Kind of Freedom: The Economic Consequences of Emancipation* (Cambridge: Cambridge University Press, 1977).

Rawson, Thomas James, *Statistical Survey of the County of Kildare* (Dublin: Graisberry & Campbell, 1807).

Raymond, Raymond J., "Dublin: the Great Famine, 1845–1860", *Dublin Historical Record*, vol. 31, no. 3 (1979), pp. 98–105.

Razzell, Peter E., "Population growth and economic change in eighteenth and early nineteenth century England and Ireland", in E. L. Jones and G. E. Mingay (eds), *Land, Labour and Population in the Industrial Revolution* (London: Arnold, 1967, pp. 260–81).

Razzell, Peter E., *The Conquest of Smallpox* (Firle, Sussex: Caliban, 1977).

Reid, Joseph D., "Sharecropping and agricultural uncertainty", *Economic Development and Cultural Change*, vol. 24, no. 3 (April 1976), pp. 549–76.

Ricardo, David (ed., Piero Sraffa), *The Works and Correspondence of Ricardo*, 10 vols (Cambridge: Cambridge University Press, 1952).

Robinson, O., "The London companies as progressive landlords in nineteenth century Ireland", *Economic History Review*, vol. XV, no. 1 (2nd series), (August 1962), pp. 103–18.

Rodriguez, Carlos Alfredo, "On the welfare aspects of international migration", *Journal of Political Economy*, vol. 83, no. 5 (October 1975), pp. 1065–72.

Roebuck, Peter, "Landlord Indebtedness in Ulster in the seventeenth and eighteenth centuries", in J. M. Goldstrom and L. A. Clarkson (eds), *Irish Population, Economy and Society, Essays in Honour of K. H. Connell* (Oxford: Clarendon Press, 1981, pp. 135–54).

Rogers, Everett M., "Motivations, values, and attitudes of subsistence farmers: towards a subculture of peasantry", in Clifton R. Wharton (ed.), *Subsistence Agriculture and Economic Development* (Chicago: Aldine, 1965).

Royle, Stephen A., "Irish manuscript Census records: a neglected source of information", *Irish Geography*, vol. XI (1978), pp. 110–25.

Rudé, George, "English rural and urban disturbances on the eve of the first Reform Bill, 1830–31", *Past and Present*, no. 37 (July 1967), pp. 87–102.

Ryan, W. P., *The Irish Labor Movement* (New York: Huebsch, 1920).

Sadler, Michael Thomas, *Ireland, its Evils and Their Remedies*, 2nd edn (London: Murray, 1829).

Salaman, Redcliffe N., *The History and Social Influence of the Potato* (Cambridge: Cambridge University Press, 1949).

Sampson, George Vaughan, *Statistical Survey of the County of Londonderry* (Dublin: Graisberry & Campbell, 1802).

Schrier, Arnold, *Ireland and the American Emigration, 1850–1900* (Minneapolis, Minn.: University of Minnesota Press, 1958).

Schultz, Theodore W., *Transforming Traditional Agriculture* (New Haven, Conn./London: Yale University Press, 1964).

Schultz, Theodore W., "The value of the ability to deal with disequilibria", *Journal of Economic Literature*, vol. XIII, no. 3 (September 1975), pp. 823–46.

Schultz, Theodore W., "Nobel lecture: the economics of being poor", *Journal of Political Economy*, vol. 88, no. 4 (August 1980), pp. 639–51.

Scott, Sir Walter (ed., H. J. C. Grierson), *The Letters of Sir Walter Scott* (London: Constable, 1935).

Scrope, George Poulett, *Plan of a Poor Law for Ireland* (London: Ridgeway, 1833).

Scrope, George Poulett, *A Plea for the Rights of Industry in Ireland* (London: Ridgeway, 1848).

Sen, Amartya, *Poverty and Famines: An Essay on Entitlement and Deprivation* (Oxford: Clarendon Press, 1981).

Senior, Nassau William, *Journals, Conversations and Essays Relating to Ireland*, 2 vols, 2nd edn (London: Longmans, Green, 1868).

Shryock, Henry S., and Siegel, Jacob S., *The Methods and Materials of Demography*, 2 vols, (Washington, DC: US Department of Commerce, Bureau of the Census, 1973).

Simington, Robert C., "Title applotment books of 1834 — agricultural returns: produce and prices", *Journal of the Department of Agriculture* (Ireland), vol. XXXVII, no. 2 (1941), pp. 239–333.

Smith, Daniel Scott, "A homeostatic demographic regime: patterns in West European family reconstitution studies", in Ronald D. Lee (ed.), *Population Patterns in the Past* (New York: Academic Press, 1977, pp. 19–51).

Smout, T. C., "Famine and famine-relief in Scotland", in L. M. Cullen and T. C. Smout (eds), *Comparative Aspects of Scottish and Irish Economic History 1600–1900* (Edinburgh: Donald, 1978, pp. 21–31).

Smyth, George Lewis, *Ireland, Historical and Statistical*, 3 vols (London: Whittaker, 1844–9).

Solar, Peter M., "The agricultural trade statistics in the Irish railway commissioners' report", *Irish Economic and Social History*, vol. VI, (1979), pp. 24–40.

Solar, Peter M., "Agricultural productivity and economic development in Scotland and Ireland in the early nineteenth century", in T. M. Devine and D. Dickson (eds), *Ireland and Scotland, Social and Economic Developments, 1650–1850* (Edinburgh: Donald, 1982; forthcoming).

Solow, Barbara Lewis, *The Land Question and the Irish Economy, 1870–1903* (Cambridge, Mass.: Harvard University Press, 1971).

Solow, Barbara Lewis, "A new look at the Irish land question", *Economic and Social Review* (Dublin), vol. 12, no. 4 (July 1981), pp. 301–14.

Staehle, Hans, "Statistical notes on the economic history of Irish agriculture, 1847–1913", *Journal of the Statistical and Social Inquiry Society of Ireland*, vol. XVIII (1950–1), pp. 444–71.

Statistique Générale de la Belgique, *Exposé de la Situation du Royaume, 1841–1850* (Brussels; Ministère de l'Interieur, 1852).

Steele, J. H., "J. S. Mill and the Irish question: the principles of political economy, 1848–1865", *The Historical Journal*, vol. XIII, no. 2 (June 1970a), pp. 216–36.

Steele, J. H., "J. S. Mill and the Irish question: reform and the integrity of the empire, 1865–1870", *The Historical Journal*, vol. XIII, no. 3 (September 1970b), pp. 419–50.

Stiglitz, Joseph E., "The efficiency wage hypothesis, surplus labor, and the distribution of income in LDCs", *Oxford Economic Papers*, vol. 28, no. 2 (June 1976), pp. 185–207.

Swan, T. W., "Economic growth and capital accumulation", *Economic Record*, vol. XXXII, no. 63 (November 1956), pp. 334–61; reprinted in J. E. Stiglitz and H. Uzawa (eds), *Readings in the Modern Theory of Economic Growth* (Cambridge, Mass.: MIT Press, 1969).

Swift, Jonathan, *Irish Tracts, 1728–1733*, in Herbert Davis (ed.), *The Prose Works of Jonathan Swift*, Vol. 12 (Oxford: Blackwell, 1955).

Taylor, George Rogers, *The Transportation Revolution, 1815–1860* (New York: Holt, Rinehart & Winston, 1951).

Taylor, Philip, *The Distant Magnet: European Emigration to the US* (New York: Harper & Row, 1971).

Temin, Peter, "Freedom and coercion: notes on the analysis of debt peonage in *One Kind of Freedom*", *Explorations in Economic History*, vol. 16, no. 1 (January 1979), pp. 56–63.

Thackeray, William Makepeace, *The Irish Sketchbook (1843)* (London: Smith, Elder, 1901).

Thom's Directory of Ireland, 1847 and Subsequent Years (Dublin: Alexander Thom, 1848 and subsequent years).

Thomas, Brinley, *Migration and Economic Growth*, 2nd edn (Cambridge: Cambridge University Press, 1973).

Thompson, F. M. L., *English Landed Society in the Nineteenth Century* (London: Routledge & Kegan Paul, 1963).

Thompson, Robert, *Statistical Survey of the County of Meath* (Dublin: Graisberry & Campbell, 1802).

Tighe, William, *Statistical Observations Relative to the County of Kilkenny* (Dublin: Graisberry & Campbell, 1802).

Timmer, C. Peter, "The turnip, the new husbandry, and the English agricultural revolution", *Quarterly Journal of Economics*, vol. LXXXIII, no. 3 (August 1969), pp. 375–95.

de Tocqueville, Alexis (ed., J. P. Mayer), *Journeys to England and Ireland* (New Haven, Conn.: Yale University Press, 1958).

Townsend, Horatio, *A General and Statistical Survey of the County of Cork*, 2 vols (Cork: Edwards & Savage, 1815).

Trainor, Brian, *The Ordnance Survey Memoir for the Parish of Antrim (1830–40)* (Belfast: Northern Ireland Public Record Office, 1969).

Trimmer, Joshua Kirby, *A Brief Inquiry into the Present State of Agriculture in the Southern Part of Ireland* (London: Hatchard, 1809).

Trimmer, Joshua Kirby, *Further Observations on the Present State of Agriculture and Condition of the Lower Classes of the People in the Southern Part of Ireland* (London: Rivington, 1812).

Trussell, James, and Steckel, Richard, "The age of slaves of Menarche and their first birth", *Journal of Interdisciplinary History*, vol. VIII, no. 3 (Winter 1978), pp. 477–505.

Tucker, G. S. L., "Irish fertility ratios before the famine", *Economic History Review*, vol. XXIII, no. 2 (2nd series) (1970), pp. 267–84.

von Tunzelmann, G. N., *Steam Power and British Industrialization to 1860* (Oxford: Clarendon Press, 1978).

United Nations, *Demographic Yearbook, 1962*.

United States, *Ninth Census, Volume I: The Statistics of the Population of the United States* (Washington, DC: Government Printing Office, 1872).

United States, Department of Commerce, Bureau of the Census, *1970 Census of*

Population, Volume I: Characteristics of the Population (Washington, DC: Government Printing Office, 1972–3).

Uselding, Paul J., "Studies in the technological development of the American economy during the first half of the nineteenth century", unpublished Ph.D. dissertation, Northwestern University, Evanston, Illinois, USA, 1970.

Uselding, Paul J., "Conjectural estimates of gross human capital inflows to the American economy, 1790–1860", *Explorations in Economic History*, vol. 9, no. 1 (Fall 1971), pp. 50–61.

Usher, Dan, "Public property and the effects of migration upon other residents of the migrants' countries of origin and destination", *Journal of Political Economy*, vol. 85, no. 5 (October 1977), pp. 1001–21.

Van De Walle, Etienne, *The Female Population of France in the Nineteenth Century* (Princeton, NJ: Princeton University Press, 1974).

Vaughan, W. E., "Landlord and tenant relations in Ireland between the famine and the Land War, 1850–1878", in L. M. Cullen and T. C. Smout (eds), *Comparative Aspects of Scottish and Irish Economic and Social History, 1600–1900* (Edinburgh: Donald, 1978, pp. 216–26).

Vaughan, W. E., and Fitzpatrick, A. J., *Irish Historical Statistics: Population, 1821–1971* (Dublin: Royal Irish Academy, 1978).

Verrière, Jacques, *La Population de l'Irlande* (Paris: Mouton Editeur, 1979).

Wakefield, Edward, *An Account of Ireland, Statistical and Political,* 2 vols (London: Longman, 1812).

Wall, Maureen, "The Rise of a Catholic middle class in eighteenth-century Ireland", *Irish Historical Studies*, vol. XI, no. 42 (September 1958), pp. 91–115.

Wall, Maureen, "The Whiteboys", in T. Desmond Williams (ed.), *Secret Societies in Ireland* (Dublin: Gill & MacMillan, 1973, pp. 13–25).

Walsh, Brendan M., "A perspective on Irish population patterns", *Eire-Ireland*, vol. IV, no. 3 (Autumn 1969), pp. 3–21.

Webb, J. J., *Industrial Dublin since 1698 and the Silk Industry in Dublin* (Dublin/London: Mounsel, 1913).

Weiss, Andrew, "Job queues and layoffs in labor markets with flexible wages", *Journal of Political Economy*, vol. 88, no. 3 (June 1980), pp. 526–38.

Weld, Isaac, *Statistical Survey of the County of Roscommon* (Dublin: Graisberry, 1832).

Werly, John W., "The Irish in Manchester, 1832–49", *Irish Historical Studies*, vol. XVIII, no. 71 (March 1973), pp. 345–58.

Whyte, Ian D., "Written leases and their impact on Scottish agriculture in the seventeenth century", *Agricultural History Review*, vol. 27, pt I (1979), pp. 1–9.

Wiggins, John, *The "Monster" Misery of Ireland: A Practical Treatise on the Relation of Landlord and Tenant* (London: Bentley, 1844).

Wittke, Carl, *The Irish in America* (Baton Rouge, La: Louisiana State University Press, 1956).

Woodham-Smith, Cecil, *The Reason Why* (Harmondsworth: Penguin, 1958).

Woodham-Smith, Cecil, *The Great Hunger: Ireland, 1845–49* (London: Hamilton, 1962).

Wrigley, E. Anthony and Schofield, Roger, *The Population History of England, 1541–1871: A Reconstruction* (Cambridge, Mass.: Harvard University Press, 1891).

Young, Arthur (ed., A. W. Hutton), *Arthur Young's Tour in Ireland (1776–79),* 2 vols (London: Bell, 1892; originally published, 1780).

Young, Arthur (ed., Constantia Maxwell), *Travels in France during the Years 1787, 1788, and 1789* (Cambridge: Cambridge University Press, 1929; originally published, 1790).

Index

Aalen, F. H. A. 183
absenteeism 24, 189, 197-206
  consequences of 210-12
  economic costs of 198-201
  forms of 201-2
  index of 201
  and unemployment 198-9
acre
  different measures of 18
Adams, Catherine, F.
  on calorific value of turnips 165.
Adams, W. F. 244, 247, 253
  cited 253
  on emigration 230
adult population
  characteristics of 8-9
age-heaping
  as population characteristic 244, 246
  by province 245
agents
  estate 208-9
agrarian outrages 116, 283
  causes of 115-24, 128-9, 138, 146, 150
  consequences of 116, 146-7, 188
  and pasturage 144-5
  prevalence of 135
  regional patterns of 134-5, 137
  victims of 139
agricultural education
  extent of 207
agricultural schools 207, 251
Agriculture and Commercial Bank 186
agriculture
  employment in 11
  entrepreneurship in 199-201
  expertise and technological progress in 200, 206-8
  and national income 11
Akenson, Donald H.
  on National Schools attendance (enrollment) 184
Allen, Robert C. 212
Almquist, Eric 4, 270
  on prefamine population change 63
  on rundale 220
  on rural industry 282
Andrews, John H. 47, 175, 290
Antrim, co. 10, 24, 55, 127, 135, 219, 283
  industrialization 176-81
  landlord residency in 203
  peat reserves in 8
  rent-monetization index 24
  seasonal unemployment in 215
  tenant security in 90
arable
  increase in 114

Armagh, co. 158, 190, 206
  agrarian outrages in 135
  death rates in 268
  leases in 97
  Trinity College holdings in 202
arrears 281
  and consolidation 129
autarky effect
  and agrarian conflict 121-3

Baldwin, Robert E. 113, 289
Balfour, Graham
  on National Schools enrollment 184
Ballyclare, Antrim 177
Banbridge 177
Banfield, E. C. 220
banks 185-6
  and agricultural loans 186
Bank of Ireland 185
Barbour, William 212
Bardhan, Pranab
  on efficiency wage hypothesis 229
Barrow, G. L. 22, 213
  on banks, 185
  on savings outflow 213
barter
  extent of 24
Beames, Michael R. 125
  on agrarian crime 139
beans 164
Beaumont, Gustave de 127, 175, 210, 218
  cited 197-8, 211
  cited, on poverty and discontent in Ireland 8
  on Irish peasants and poverty 6
  on length of leases 82
  on middlemen 99
Beckett, J. C.
  on British policy 290
  on tithe war 124
Beecher, W. H. H. 208
Behan, Brendan
  cited 228
Belfast 13
  linen industry in 177, 178
  spinning industry in 176
Belgium
  famine in 276
Berkeley, George
  cited 218
  on Irish peasants and poverty 6
Berry, R. Albert and Soligo, Ronald 260
  on income effects of emigration 231-2
Bianconi, Charles 147, 193
  success of 212

Bicheno, J. E. 197
  cited 182
birth rate data
  in 1841 census 64-5
birth rates
  and age at marriage 78-9
  determinants of 57
  estimate of 33-4
  estimates of 61-8
  seasonal fluctuations in 66-7, 79
Black, R. D. C. 81, 109, 150, 198, 288
  on absenteeism 198
  on landlords 197
  on unemployment 213
Blacker, William 44, 164, 167-9, 175, 190,
    195, 199, 206, 208, 233, 281
  cited 165, 168, 207, 209, 218, 243
  on costs of reclamation 173
  on crop rotation 169
  on drainage 169
  on employment 110
  on fertilizer requirements 162-3
  on population 39
Bliss, Christopher and Stern, Nicholas 223
Bloch, Marc
  cited 276
Bonn, Moritz 110
  on population decline 78
Bourke, P. M. Austin 165, 173
  on acreage 18
  on calorific value of potato 7, 165
  on 1841 census 28
  on constable survey 271
  on land reclamation 173-4
  on potato consumption 7
  on potato output 165
  on potato yields 7
Bourke, Lt. Gen. 208
Boyer, George
  on poor relief 258
Broeker, Galen
  on Irish police 138
Bryan, J. B.
  on early marriage 79
Buchanan, A. 212, 221-2
Burgoyne, John 290
Burton, W. G. 165
  on prefamine diet 7
Butt, Isaac 288

Caledon, Lord 206
canals
  and social overhead investment 183
canting 126
capital
  agricultural 82, 162-72
  in manufacturing 180-1
  scarcity of 159-62
  social overhead 182-3
  working 185-6

capital accumulation
  see investment, capital formation
capital formation
  and poverty 283-6
  and agrarian outrages 194
  failure of 191
capital markets 107
  failure of 160-1, 171
  and investment 284
  and landlords 188-9
'Captain Swing' riots 145
Carlow, co. 19, 31
  monetization in 24
Carlyle, Thomas
  cited 43
Carney, Frank 202
  on population 32
Carrick on Shannon 185
Carrickfergus 177
"Cartel Hypothesis" 125-6
cash crops
  types of 21
cash economy
  operation of 22-3
Cattle Acts 279, 287
Cavan co. 31, 179
  agrarian outrages in 135
  monetization in 24
Celibacy
  Highest Celibacy Age (HCA) 71
Census, 1834 (religious)
  as source of population data 31
censuses
  reliability of 31-2
Central Relief Committee 271
Chambers, J. L. and Mingay, G. E. 82
  cited 205
Chart, D. A. 286
child labor
  rarity of 31
children
  desire for 60
  as form of investment 61
  as insurance 61
Clapham, John 253
Clare, co. 11, 55
  agrarian outrages in 137
  fishing in 172
  peat reserves in 8
Clarendon, Lord 292
Clark, Samuel 4, 123, 126-7, 281
  cited 17, 39, 113
  on definition of property rights 123
  on victims of outrage 125
  on violence 144
Clark, Victor 258
Clarkson, Leslie A. 4
  on population growth 32
clover 164
coal

as a factor in industrialization 154-8
  prices of 154
Coale, Ansley
  demographic measures of 35-6
  indices of Hutterite fertility 72
  nuptiality functions 71
Coe, W. E. 158, 187
  on industrialization 192
Collins, Brenda
  on Irish emigration to Scotland 256
Colquhoun, Patrick
  on housing in Great Britain 181-2
commercialization
  and resistance to shocks 280
  and subsistence crops 16-17
  relative to other countries 24
committals to prison
  regional patterns of 137
Committee on Public Works
  on land reclamation 174
conacre
  and agrarian outrages 125, 139
  definition of 21
Connaught 17, 41, 77, 134, 139, 282, 289
  agrarian outrages in 137
  compensation for consolidation in 134
  death rates in 268
  economic condition in 12
  ejectment in 133
  farm sizes in 19
  income estimates 26
  leases in 89
  monetization in 24
  primary school attendance 183
  reclamation in 174
  tenant security in 89-90
Connell, K. H. 30, 32-3, 64, 71, 78, 98, 110,
  114, 127, 150, 285
  cited 39, 148
  on contraception 60
  on diets 7
  on emigration 33, 230
  on land reclamation 173, 174
  on marriages 51
  on pre-1821 population 32
  on premarital sex 79
  on roads 182
  on schools 183
Connolly, Sean J.
  on illegitimacy 80
consolidation
  and agrarian outrages 128-9, 132, 141-4,
  150
  compensation for 133
  demand and supply 139-44
  and dispossession 134
  economic loss due to 146-7
  and economies of scale 206-7
  effects of 133
  and ejectment 125

and labor demand 125, 133
  prevalence of, regionally 129-32
  procedure of 132-3
  resisted by tenancy 116
  and scale economies 206
Constabulary Survey of 1846 5, 164, 271
consumption patterns 8
contraception 55, 60
conviction/committal
  rates of 150
cooperation
  in agriculture 220, 228
Coote, Charles, 83, 127, 168, 225
Cork, co. 5, 14, 31, 162, 179, 197
  monetization in 24
cottage industries 216, 244
  decline of 279, 282-3
  and demographic change 294
  and infant mortality rates 58
  and population growth 52
cottiers 21
cotton industry 176-7, 196
  employment in 176
  failure of 177, 179-81
county fairs 20
Cousens, S. H. 270
  on famine mortality 263-4
  on numbers of emigrants 68, 79
Crawford, Eleanor M. 7, 226
Crawford, William H.
  on leases 83
Crawford, William Sharman 175, 206
crime, agrarian
  see Agrarian outrages
crime, general
  comparison with England 138
  regional rates of 137
crop rotation
  practice of 164-6, 168
Crotty, Raymond 77, 82, 114, 150, 169
  on Anglo-Irish relations 289
  on fodder crops 165
  on relative prices 114
  on shift from arable to pasturage 115
  rent income, estimates of 26-8
  use of Devon Commission data 88
Cullen, Louis M. 22, 60, 99, 149, 159-60,
  198, 262, 287-8
  on diet 11, 123, 226
  on industrialization 13
  on monetization 29
Cullen and Smout 292
Curtis, L. Perry 189

Daultrey Stuart; Dickson, David and Ó
  Gráda, Cormac 32
David, Paul A. and Temin, Peter 237
Davidson, Stanley and Passmore, R. 7
  on nutritional value of potato 8

Deane, Phyllis and Cole, W. A. 10, 28, 195, 257
death rate data
   in 1841 census 68, 79
death rates
   by province 268-9
   estimated by 1851 census 267
   estimation of 33-5
   estimation procedure of 67-9, 264-8
   excess 265-8
   relative to other countries 33
   see also Mortality
DeCanio, S. J. 149
deforestation 171-2
demand
   and emigration 233
Devon Commission
   as historical source 88
   Digest of, *see* Kennedy, J. P.
Dickson, David 95, 179
   cited 196
diet
   nutritional value of prefamine 8-9
   and productivity 225-6
   see also Nutrition
Dixon, William
   cited 258
domestic industry
   correlation with economic change 12-13
   decline of 13
   see also Cottage industry
Donegal, co. 31, 179, 197, 202, 206, 283
   agrarian outrages in 135
   occupations in 29
Donegall, Lord 92
Donnelly, James, S. 5, 82-3, 95, 98, 110, 126, 209
   on famine mortality 263
   on landlord spending habits 190
Down, co. 10, 184, 283
   agrarian crime, in 135
Downshire, Lord 208
drainage 167
   costs of 170
   importance of 169-71
   rates of return in 171
Drake, Michael 71
Drogheda
   unemployment in 216
Drummond, Thomas 137, 290
dual economy 19-21
Dublin, city 14, 212
   labor unions in 229
   landlord residency in 203
   seasonal unemployment in 216
   wages in 226
   wool output in 14
Dublin, co. 24
   income per capita in 10
   percentage of cottiers and laborers 22

rent-monetization index in 24
   small farms in 18
Dublin Society
   statistical surveys 4
Dubourdieu, John 83, 176
   cited 172
Dupâquier, Jacques
   on famine mortality 263
Dutton, Hely
   on farming societies 207
   on peat reserves 8

Easterlin, Richard A.
   cited 293
   on education 184
Eaton Joseph W. and Mayer, Albert J. 36, 72, 80
economies of scale
   in agriculture 206-7
Edgeworth, Maria
   cited 196
education
   description of 183-5
Edwards, Robert Dudley and Williams, T. Desmond
   cited 263
efficiency-wage model 223-6
ejectment
   and agrarian outrages 138
ejectment, bills of 129, 132
Ely, Earls of 210
emigrants
   age distribution of 233-4, 242, 255
   characteristics of 234-5, 244, 255, 258-9
   deaths of 267
   excess mortality rates of 267-8
   literacy of 247
   occupational structure of 248-52
   occupations of 247
   quality of 234, 243-7
   work habits of 258-9
emigration, Ch. 8, *passim*
   between 1780-1845 33
   and consolidation 134
   costs of 242-4, 257-9
   and cottage industry 282
   data on 69
   effect of 230-2
   effects on industry 228
   effects on average income, and entrepreneurship 255
   extent of 230
   and income redistribution 232
   and industrialization 256
   and population growth 77-8
employment
   agricultural 29
   classifications of 13
   extent of annual 25
   frequency of 25

proportion in various types of 13
of women and children 25
structure of 11
see also Wage rates, Income, Labor
Encumbered Estates Act 91, 159
energy
and consumption patterns 8
sources of 7
supply of 154-8
Engel, Ernst
on child rearing costs 243
Engels, Friedrich
cited 288
entrepreneurial failure 211-12
Erickson, Charlotte 241
Ernle, Lord 204
excess mortality
determinants of 271-5
estimation of 264-8
see also Mortality, excess
export bounties 114
exports
regional specialization in 17
extra-marital sex 79

families
classification of 18
family settlement 189-90
famine
analysis of 261-77
effect on leases of 91
historiography of 262-3
rare before 1845 9
famine relief 292
farm buildings
neglect of 168
farming
commercial 20
farms
size distribution of 18-21
types of 21
farm size 109
agricultural census on 18
distribution of (bimodal) 21
minimum 175
and yield 206
fecundity
and potato diet 62
Feinstein, Charles 111
on value of residential housing 196
Fermanagh, co. 135, 211
consolidation in 130
landlord residency in 203
monetization in 24
fertility
determinants of 57-9
measures of 35
fertility, general 35
fertility, marital 35
and absence of Poor Law 61-2

and age at marriage 79
determinants of 60-2
fertilizer VI-76
scarcity of 162-3
sources of 163
Finland
famine in 270, 277
Fischer, Wolfram 63
Fisher, Irving 294
fishermen
numbers of 172
fishing industry 172-3
Fitzwilliam, Earl 189
Flinn, M. W. 38
on famine mortality 263
on Scottish famine 276
Fogel, Robert William 153
food supply
between 1740-1845 9
Foster, Thomas Campbell 4, 6, 25, 37, 85-6, 95, 116, 168, 171-2, 197, 209, 226, 233
cited 98, 218, 285
on bidding for land 126
on drainage costs 170
on land reclamation 173
on poverty, cited 8
on scale economies 207
on unemployment 213
on use of money 29
on work attitudes 218
freeholders 83
Freeman, T. W. 20, 78, 183, 195-6
cited 6
on fisheries 172
on green crops 169
Freudenberger, Herman and Cummings, G. 223
fuel
cost of 154-6

Gallman Robert E. 233
Galway, co. 11, 135, 168, 202, 207
death rates in 268
economic condition of 12
Gaskin, Katherine
on age at first marriage 37
Gayer, Arthur D., Rostow, W. W. and Schwartz, A. J.
as source for relative price data, 147-8
Geary, Frank 176, 179-80, 195
Gibbon, Peter 20, 286
Gier, J. 214
Gilford, co. Down 177
Gill, Conrad 81, 179, 282
Glengall, Earl of
cited 172
Goldstrom, J. M.
on industrialization 192
on use of trade data 115

Gombeen men 107, 186
good-will 100-1
Gosford, Lord 190
Government Emigration Office – Quebec 268
government valuation
  as source of rent income estimates 27
Grand Canal 183
Grantham, George 150
  on improved tillage 167
grass crops
  acreage under 164
Graybill
  deheaping technique 244
Great Britain
  attitudes toward Ireland 291
  investigations into Irish poverty 6
  Ireland's economic ties to 279
  policy toward Ireland 286-92
  trade with Ireland 288
Great Britain, Parliamentary Papers 4
  see specific documents
Green, E. R. R. 14, 176, 179-80, 226, 269
  on famine mortality 263
green crops 207
  see also New Husbandry
Gregory Clause 124
Greig, William 209
  on landlord consumption 190
  on middlemen 97
Gribbon, H. D.
  on water mills 157
  on water power 177
Griffith, Richard 173, 290
Grigg, David 78
  on overpopulation 38
Grubel, Herbert G. and Scott, Anthony 235
Guinness Brewery 193, 212

Hajnal, John 35
Hajnal's Singulate Mean (HSM) 35, 70-1
Hall, Mr. and Mrs. S. C. 4, 9, 171, 197, 244
Handley, James Edmund 226, 253, 258
Handlin, Oscar 253, 254, 258, 260
handloom weavers 177
Hansen, Marcus Lee 257
Harland, Edward 213
harvests
  failures of 9
health, of Irish 8-9
Hechter, Michael 113, 180, 286, 288
Heelan, J. and Henry, E. W.
  on industrial finance 187
Henry, Louis
  estimation of Hutterite fertility 72
Hill, Lord George 206
Hirschman, A. 145
Hobsbawm, Eric 29, 277
Hobsbawm, Eric and Rude, George
  on English unrest 145-6

Hoffman, Elizabeth and Mokyr, Joel 9, 294
  on commercialization 16
Hofstee, E. W. 79
housing
  data on 181-2
  and infant mortality 58
  investment in 180-2
  quality of, and population growth 52, 55
  value of residential 196
Hughes, Jonathan R. T. 292
human capital effect
  and emigration 235, 247-51
Huntingdon, Ellsworth 79
husbandry
  new 164-7
Hutchinson, Bertram 113
  on peasant society 220
  on work attitudes 218

immigrants
  in the U.S. 254, 260
  role in Industrial Revolution 253, 255
imports
  of consumption goods 289
improvements
  impediments to 284
  rate of return on 166-7
  responsibility for 83
  and security of tenure 103
incentives
  work 219-20
income
  annual personal 11
  from capital 27
  estimates of personal 10, 25-8
  from labor 25-6
  from land 26-8
  from livestock 28
  from self-employment 28
  per capita 10
  per capita, and poverty 15
  sources for estimates 10
  and wage rates 25-6
indivisibilities
  and capital formation 168
  and fisheries 172
industrialization 196
  and agricultural backwardness 192-3
  failure of 191-4
  lack of 12-14
  and profits 193-4
  and wage levels 227-8
industrial revolution
  absence of in Ireland 259
  see also Industrialization
industry
  food processing 14
  regional distribution of 17
  see also Manufacturing
    infant industry argument 288-9

infant mortality 35, 37-8
  and birth rate 60
  data on 37
  determinants of 58-60
  estimation of 72-5
  rates of 37-8
  relative to other countries 38
information, agricultural 206-7
Inglis, Henry D. 6, 99, 206, 209
  cited 110, 177
inheritance customs
  changes in 120
investment
  agricultural 159-61
  industrial 161-2
  by landlords 188-91
  and retained profits 187

Jacquemyns, G. 276
James, Francis G.
  cited 287
Johnson, Harry G. 286
Johnson, James H. 20, 21
  on seasonal emigration 21
Johnston, E. M. 287
Jones, Eric L. 204, 293
  on innovating landlords 205
Jones, Hywell G. 286

Kafka, A.
  on tariffs 289
Kane, Robert 4, 39, 153-4, 158, 165, 195,
  199
  cited 153, 187, 193, 221-3, 226-7
  on characteristics of population 9
  on coal prices 154
  on deforestation 171
  on diet 223
  on fuel costs 155
  on fuel usage 156
  on return to drainage 170
  on turf usage 158
  on unions 226
  on wages 155, 192, 221
  on water power 157
Kapp, Friedrich 233, 243
Kennedy, J. P. 4, 27, 83, 99, 100-1, 103,
  116, 125-6, 128, 134, 163, 167-9, 172,
  175, 186, 205, 207-8, 220, 251
  cited 205
  on agricultural school recruitment 207
  on costs of bad management 211
  on effect of uncertain tenure 81
Kennedy, Liam
  on regional specialization 17
Kerry, co. 142, 202, 282
  landlord residency in 203
Kildare, co. 10, 19
  absenteeism in 201
  agrarian crime in 135

Kilkenny, co. 133, 162, 164
  agrarian crime in 137
  monetization in 24
Kindleberger, Charles P. 199
Kings, co. (Offaly) 146, 206, 282
  agrarian crime in 135
Kingston, Earl of 92
Kohl, Johann Georg 218
  cited 6
  on roads 182
Kuznets, Simon 29

labor
  marginal product of 40
  payment for 23-4
  quality of 217-18, 221-2
labor demand
  and consolidation 133
  labor demand effect
  and agrarian outrages 118-19, 229
labor quality effect
  and emigration 234, 243-7
laborers 22
  types of payment of 23-4
land
  competition for 126-7
  cultivable and population 40-1
  monetization of market in 24
  proxies for quality of 75-7
  quality of 45, 48, 150
  quality of and overpopulation 41
  terms of holding 24
  uncultivated 173
land markets 200
land reclamation 173-5, 196
land stewards
  number of 208
  see also Agents
Land Tenure Hypothesis (LTH) 81-7
  as explanation of backwardness 99-103
  and types of leases 84-7
  see also Tenure
landholders
  definition of 17
landholding
  as determinant of welfare 18
  terms of 22-3
land/labor ratio
  and poverty 45
landlords 20
  absenteeism of 24, 189, 197-206
  consumption behavior 189-91
  financial distress of 190
  and investment 188-91
  number of 16
  predatory behavior of 86-7, 99-100, 111
  quality of 210
  role of 204-6
landlord-tenant conflicts
  causes of 116-24, 139-44, 208

landlord-tenant conflicts (*continued*)
  see also Agrarian outrages
Lane, Padraig 120, 168
Larcom, Thomas 31, 290
Large, David
  on family settlements 190
  on landlord behavior 189
Larkin, Emmet
  on national income 28
Larne, co. Antrim 177, 207
Lavergne, Leonce de 6
leases
  and agricultural investment 102-3, 105-9
  "at will" 86
  changes in 83-4
  distribution of 93-7
  effects of consolidation on 84
  frequency of 89
  for lives 103
  price level effects on 84
  and rent 109-10
  and security 83, 88-90
  tenant attitudes to 84, 90
  and underinvestment 90
Leavitt, T. H. 158
Lebergott, Stanley 60
Lebow, Richard Ned 218
  cited 291
Lecky, W. E. H. 287
Lee, Joseph J. 20, 22, 33, 44, 65, 71, 115, 125, 159, 187, 213, 288
  cited 159, 187
  on agrarian outrages 139
  on census accuracy 31-2
  on census of 1841 31
  on famine mortality 263
  on investment 193
  on roads 182
Lee, Ronald D.
  on Malthusian Models 43
Lees, Lynn H.
  on role of immigrants in London 253
Lefgren, John
  on Finnish famine 270, 277
Leibenstein, Harvey 286
  on efficiency wage hypothesis 223
Leinster province 17, 89, 147
  absenteeism in 202
  agrarian outrages in 136-7
  compensation for consolidation in 134
  consolidation 130
  death rates in 268
  ejectment in 133
  farm sizes in 19
  leases in 89
  monetization in 24
  primary school attendance in 183
  rural crime in 137
  small farms in 19

leisure 8
  consumption of 217, 218
Leitrim, co. 11, 158, 162, 185, 282, 294
  absenteeism in 201, 202
  agrarian outrages in 135
  consolidation in 130
  economic conditions in 12
  income estimates 26
  potato dependency in 271
Lesthaege, Ron J.
  on propensity to marry in Belgium 36
Lewis, Frank 111
Lewis, George Cornewall 213, 253
  cited 113, 194
  on agrarian outrages 116
  on causes of outrages 124
  on consolidation and unrest 128-9
  on Irish emigrants 254
  on seasonal unemployment 214
Lewis, Samuel 164
Life cycle effect 233-4, 236-43, 260
Limerick, co. 170, 208, 228
  peat reserves in 8
  rural crime in 137
Limerick, town 212, 221
linen exports
  level of 287
linen industry 177-80
  compared to cotton 179-80
  employment in 177-8
  success of 177-8
literacy 247, 274
  extent of 184-5
livestock
  value of 28, 269
loan fund 186
loans
  to peasants 185-6
London companies
  as absentee landlord 202, 209-10
Londonderry, co. 163, 202, 209, 283
  absenteeism in 202
  agrarian outrages in 135
  landlord residency in 203
Longford
  absenteeism in 201
  monetization in 24
  landlord residency in 203
  and Royal Canal 183
Louth, co. 135, 223
Lowell, Mass. 254
Lurgan, Armagh 282
Lynch, A. H.
  on Irish poverty, cited 6
Lynch, Patrick and Vaisey, John 24, 29, 193, 228, 288
  on dual structure of Ireland 20

MacDonagh, Oliver
  cited 288

MacDonagh, Oliver (*continued*)
  on emigrant mortality 268
Maguire, W. A. 82-3, 91-2, 98, 109
  on agent quality 208
  on landlord consumption 190
  on leaseholdings 91
Mahony, Pierce 186
Malcomson, A. P. W. 210, 211
  on absenteeism 202
Malthus, Thomas Robert
  on Irish economic prospects 39
  on overpopulation 39
Malthusian hypothesis 30, 38-40, 113
  testing of 40-60
Malthusian model
  intepretations of 43-4
mangel-wurzel 163
Mansergh, Nicholas 109
manufacturing
  capital formation in 191-2
  decline of 14
  see also Industrialization and individual
    industries
market failure 112-13
marriage
  neoclassical theory of 63-4
marriage age
  computation of 71-2
  data on 37, 71
  and income 51
  mean 36-7
  see also Propensity to marry
Marshall, William
  cited 168
Marx, Karl
  on Malthus 39
Mason, William Shaw (Parochial Surveys)
    61, 171, 172, 183, 220
  cited 47
  on diets 12
  on fishing 172-3
  on health of population 9
  on landlords 197
  and Parochial Surveys 4
Mayo, co. 11, 29, 135, 162, 170, 282-3, 294
  monetization in 24
  agrarian outrages in 135
  economic condition of 12
  excess death rates in 268
  percentage of "class III'" families 22
  tenant security in 90
Mayo-Smith, Richmond 233, 247
McArthur, William P.
  on famine mortality 263
  on emigrant mortality 267
McCloskey, Donald N. 140
McCulloch, J. R. 42, 168, 174, 205
  cited 82, 127
  on absenteeism 198
McCutcheon, W. A.

  on water mills 157
McDowell, R. B. 33
  cited 184
McKenna, Edward E. 80
McKinnon, Ronald I. 188
  on investment 160-1
McKinnon Syndrome 160, 167
Meath, co. 10, 170
mercantilism 287
middle class
  alleged absence of 99
  rise of in Eighteenth Century 287
middleman 121, 133
  extent of landholding 95-7, 110
  and improvement 98-9
  as improving landlords 110
  as social class 99
middleman, system 95-9
migration
  and equalization of incomes 44-5
  seasonal 214, 216
migration, internal 257
  extent of 44, 229
migration rates
  estimation of 68-9
  see also Emigration
Mikesell, Raymond F. and Zinser, James,
    E. 285
Mill, John Stuart
  on improvements 82
Miller, William, Lt. Col.
  on outrages 129
Milward, Alan S. and Saul, S. B. 205
mines 195
Mingay, Gordon E.
  on landlords 204
Mirrlees, James E.
  on efficiency wage models 223
Mitchel, John 253
Mitchell, Brian R. 38, 42, 79
Mitchell, Brian R. and Deane, Phyllis 36, 42
  on turnip output 165
Moate, co. Westmeath 185
Mokyr, Joel 6-7, 9, 29, 100-1, 149, 153-4,
    158, 162, 164, 187, 192-3, 195, 204,
    214, 233, 256, 262, 264, 270, 271,
    276-7, 282
Mokyr, Joel and Ó Gráda, Cormac 240-1
    252
Monaghan, co. 179
  agrarian crime in 135
  landlord residency in 203
  monetization in 24
Monaghan, John J. 176, 180
monetization, (cash) 29
  in Irish economy 20-3
Mooney, T. 213
mortality data
  in 1841 census 37
  in 1851 census 264

mortality, excess 263-8
  in Belgium 276
  causes of 268-70
  determinants of 268-70
  in the Netherlands 276
  in Scotland 276
mortality, famine 263-8
  causes of 275-7
  see also Excess Mortality
mortality rates, prefamine
  calculation of 68-9
Muggeridge, R. M. 179, 218
  cited 222, 224
Mulhall, Michael 42
  on housing value 182, 196
Mulholland, Andrew 212
Mulholland flax mill 155
municipal government
  acts of Reform 290
Munster, province 17, 147
  agrarian outrages 131, 137
  compensation for consolidation in 134
  economic condition in 12
  ejectments in 133
  farm sizes in 19
  leases in 89
  monetization in 24

National Board of Education
  and agricultural information 207
  influence of 183
natural resources
  and industrialization 153-4
  wealth and 152-8
Natural Resources Hypothesis (NRH)
  153-8
Neal, Larry and Uselding, Paul 233
Neher, Philip
  on children as insurance 62
Nelson, Richard R. 113
new husbandry
  profitability of 166-7
New York
  emigration to 241-2
New York Habor Passenger Lists 5
  see also passenger lists
Nicholls, George 27, 61
Norfolk rotation 166
numeracy 246
nutrition
  and productivity 222-6
  see also Diet, Efficiency wage hypothesis

O'Brien, George A. P. 1, 14, 29, 39, 78,
    109, 113, 171, 180, 196, 286-7
  cited 127
  on land reclamation 173
  on Malthus 39
O'Brien Rentals 5
  as source of lease data 91-9

occupational difference index 249-50
occupational distribution 17
occupations
  data on 248-51
O'Connell, Daniel 109
  cited 220
O'Donovan, John 114-15
O'Farrell, Patrick
  cited 286, 291
Ó Gráda, Cormac 4, 20, 118, 120, 195,
    211, 223, 261
  cited 31
  on agricultural output 11
  on effect of famine 78
  on income between 1850-1875 41
  on marginal product of labor 40
  on overseas remittances 243
  on potato yields 7
  on soil quality 152
  as source of agricultural output data 148
  on total factor productivity 175
O'Malley, Eoin 289
  on Irish backwardness 196
O'Neill, Thomas P. 270, 292
  cited 193
  on famine mortality 263
Ordinance Survey manuscripts 5
O'Rourke, John
  on famine mortality 263
Ó Tuathaigh, Gearóid 82, 183
  cited 152, 185
  on relative prices 144
Otway, C. G. 180, 191, 226
  cited 228-9, 282
  on unemployment 214
overpopulation
  and capital/labor ratio 48, 51
  controversy on 38-42
  definitions of 38
  and famine 42-4
  famine as consequence of 6
  relative to other countries 41
  see also Malthsusian Hypothesis

Page, H. J. 57
palatinates 244, 260
parish records 5
  as source of birth rate data 66-7
Parliamentary Gazetteer 195
  on landlords 205
parochial surveys
  see Mason, W. S.
passenger lists 241-2
pasturage
  attempts to revive 115
  and consolidation 206
  reduction in 114-15
  relative profitability of 114-15
  scale economies of 206
  versus arable farming 116-23

peas 164
peasant society
  social characteristics of 220
peat
  area under 195
  availability of 195
  as fuel source 8, 157-8
  in manufacturing 158
Peel, Sir Robert 270
Penal Acts 279, 287
Perroux, Francois 196
Petty, William
  on underpopulation and poverty 78
Pigou, Alfred 84
Pim, Jonathan 37, 82, 85, 99, 168, 189,
    197, 213, 226, 232, 243
  on landlords 16, 210
Pollard, Sidney 57, 253
Poor Law commission 22, 290
  on economic change since 1815 12
  on effects of agrarian outrages 147
  income data in 10, 25-6
  valuation 27-8
Poor Law inquiry
  see Poor Law commission
Poor Laws 146, 270-1, 284
  effect on wages 227
poor relief 16, 177
  as cause for emigration 257-8
  demographic effects of 61
poor relief system 284
  reform of 290-1
population 30
  growth rate of 31-3
  proportion in rural areas 16
  see also Overpopulation, Malthusian
    hypothesis, birth, mortality, etc
population growth
  determinants of 52-3
  and potato dependency 55
potatoes
  acreage per capita 271
  acreage under 7
  adoption as food source 149
  calories provided by 7
  consumption of 7
  dependence on 12, 17
  dietary value of 7-9, 62, 225-6, 262, 277
  energy value of 7-8
  fertilizer requirements of 162
  as means of payment 22
  over-dependence on 6
  reliability of 261-2
  and resistance to shock 280
  scarcities of 9
  storage of 186
  supplements in diet 11-12
  varieties of 12
  yields of 7
poverty

and agricultural employment 11
definition of 15-16
and discontent 8
explanation of 112-13
famine as consequence of 6
reduces resilience of economy 6
relative to other countries 11
as "voluntary" condition 113
"poverty trap" 166, 188, 224, 285-6
predatory landlords
  definition of 86-7, 104-9
  see also Landlord, Land Tenure
    Hypothesis (LTH)
  changes in 279
prices
  of arable and pasturage products 114, 147-9
prices, agricultural
  movement of 280-1
prices, industrial
  decline of 13
prices, relative
  index of 147-9
productivity
  determinants of 228
profits
  low rate of 193
propensity to marry 34-5, 78-9
  and birth rate 55-6
  capital/labor ratio 55
  compared to other countries 35-6
  determinants of 55-7
  estimates of 69-72
  and fertility rates 52
  and "price" of marriage 64
property rights 123-4
  poorly defined 86

Queen's co. (Laois) 19
  agrarian crime in 136
  landlords residency in 203
  monetization 24

rackrents 128
  see also Rents
Radford, Ebenezer
  rent data of 127
railroad
  investment in 187
Ransom, Roger and Sutch, Richard
    113-14, 149
rates of return 283-4
  on agricultural investment 111, 165-6,
    168
  on drainage projects 169-70
  on land reclamation projects 173
  on forestation 172
Razzell, Peter
  on smallpox mortality 78
reclamation land
  extent of 173-4

reclamation land (*continued*)
  methods of 174-5
  see also Land reclamation
Reid, Joseph D. 203
rent collectors 228
rental "drag" 109-10
rents 224
  and agrarian outrages 126-8
  data on 27-8
  level of 125-8
  maximization of 127
  and price movements 280-1
  terms of payment 22-4
  and underinvestment 85-7
residency
  index of 202-3
  technical progress 204
  see also Absenteeism
retail trade 20
Reynolds, John 185
Ricardo, David 85, 217
Rightboy movement 150
roads, 182-3
Robinson, Olive 202
  cited 209
  on London companies 209-10
Rodriguez, Carlos
  on income effects of emigration 232
Roe, Robert
  cited 180
Roebuck, Peter 188
  on landlord consumption behavior 190
Rogers, Everett M. 220
root crops
  acreage under 164
Roscommon, co. 11, 219, 229
  agrarian outrage in 135
  conflict in 139
Royal Canal 183
Royle, Stephen A. 30
Rude, George 146
Rundale 125, 206
  practice of 220-1
rural unrest
  in England 145-6
  see also Agrarian outrages
Russell, Lord John 270, 292

Sadler, Michael Thomas 61, 78
  cited 39
Salaman, Radcliffe, N. 260
  cited 261
  on Malthus 39
Salisbury, Lord
  cited 290
saving
  by capitalists 194
  incentive to 285
  propensity to 159-61

scale effect
  and agrarian outrages 119-21
school enrollment 183-4
Schrier, Arnold 247
Schultz, Theodore W. 149, 212
  cited 292
  on absenteeism 228
  on seasonal unemployment 217
Scotland
  Irish immigrants in 227
Scott, Sir Walter
  cited 11
  on Irish peasants and poverty 6
Scrope, Poulett
  cited 40, 132
  on landlords 210
seasonal emigration
  due to decline of industry 21
seasonal unemployment 214-16
self-employment
  farming 219
self-sufficiency
  and class structure 22
Sen, Amartiya
  on poverty 15-16
Senior, Edward
  on tenant right 100-1
Senior, Nassau 226
  on failue to industrialize 259
sharecropping 203
Shryock, Henry S. and Siegel, Jacob S. 244
Simington, Robert C. 127
skills
  lack of 258
Sligo, co. 11, 282, 294
  death rates in 268
  income estimates 26
  seasonal unemployment in 215
smallpox
  impact on population growth 78
Smith, Adam
  cited 9
Smith, Daniel Scott 79
Smout, T. Christopher
  on Scottish famine 276
smuggling 287
Smyth, George Lewis 9
  cited 200
  on rent collectors 228
society
  class structure of 17
Solar, Peter
  on total factor productivity 175-6
Solow, Barbara L. 78, 82, 99, 101, 109, 128
  cited 126, 127
  on leases 87
spalpeens 225
Spenser, Edmund
  cited 171
spinning

spinning (*continued*)
decline of 282
see also Cottage industries
stamp duty
on leases 109
standards of living 10
Steuart, James 178
Stiglitz, Joseph E. 223
subletting
between tenants 17
and scale economies of 121
see also Middlemen
subsistence crises 15
and mortality rates 16
subsistence economy
operation of 22-3
structure of 21
Swan, T. W. 78
Swift, Jonathan
on underpopulation and poverty 78

tariffs 289
Taylor, George Rogers 254
Taylor, Philip 233
Temin, Peter 149
Templemoyle agricultural school 251
tenant farms
régional distribution of 17
tenant right 133-4
as "good-will" payment 101
and improvements 81-2, 100-2
as "key-money" 100-1
and LTH 101
tenure
"at will" 85-6, 91, 109
insecurity of 99-102
see also Land Tenure Hypothesis
Thomas, Brinley 233-4
Thompson, F. M. L. 205, 209
Thompson, Robert 83, 206, 219, 225
on laborers 22
Thom's directory 138
Tighe, William 95, 103, 154, 162, 164, 168, 220
cited 219
on potato's dietary value 9
tillage
scale economies in 206
Timmer, Peter 168
on turnip cultivation 166
Tipperary, co. 127-8, 135, 139, 146
agrarian outrages in 135-6
death rates in 268
rural crime in 137
Tithe Commutation Act 290
tithes
and unrest 124, 149
Tocqueville, Alexis, De 6, 92, 189
total factor productivity 175-6
Townsend, Horatio 61, 127, 168, 171
cited 158

on fertilizer 162
on poverty and discontent in Ireland 8
on utility of children 60
transactions costs 123
transportation costs
decline of 279
trees 171-2
Trimmer, Joshua Kirby 163, 196
Trinity College
as absentee landlord 202
Tucker, G. S. L. 31, 65, 79
on 1841 census 33
Tunzelmann, G. N., Von 153, 156, 158
on coal prices 154
on fuel costs 155
on water power 157
turf
as means of payment 22
self-sufficiency in 280
see also Peat
Turnips 164
compared to potatoes 165
cultivation of 164-5
and landlord-tenant relation 168
Tyrone, co. 179
death rates in 268

Ulster, province 17, 89, 133-5, 158, 176, 202, 244, 281, 289
agrarian outrages in 137
child labor in 61
compensation for consolidation in 134
consolidation in 130
death rates in 268
economic change in 12
farm sizes in 19
leases in 89, 101-2
monetization in 24
weaving industry in 282
Ulster custom 89
and bidding for land 127
see also Tenant right
unemployment 228
extent of 213-17
long term 224
seasonal 25, 29, 214-17
urban 216
Union (with Great Britain) 279
Act of 287-8
Unions, labor
effect on wages 226, 229
U.S. Ninth Census 260
urban areas
and fertility rates 57
Uselding, Paul J. 233
Usher, Dan
effects of emigration on 232

valuation
of land 27-8, 125

Van De Walle, Etienne
  on propensity to marry in France 36
Vaughan, W. E. and Fitzpatrick, A. J. 234
  cited 149
Verrière, Jacques 77, 81, 230, 233
  cited 232
  on emigration 260
  on famine mortality 263
violence
  and agricultural investment 188
  and backwardness 283
  see also Agrarian outrages, crime
vulnerability
  and commercial development 24
  determinants of 16
  and wealth 262

wages
  and industrialization 193
  in industry 221-2
  in kind 22-3
  level of 155-6, 221, 226-7, 283
  paid with diet 229
  and productivity 222-5
  seasonality of 215-16
  of skilled labor 226-7
Wakefield, Edward 4, 103, 183, 208, 218, 287
  on absenteeism 198
  cited 171, 182
  on children as investment 61
  on drainage 169
  on family settlements 190
  on fishery 173
  on peat 8
Wall, Maureen 149
  on rise of middle class 287
wars
  French 279
Waterford 146
  potato dependency in 271
waterpower 228
  in industry 156-7
wealth
  and capital 151
  and resilience to disasters 152
weavers
  numbers of 17
  see also Cottage industry

Webb, J. J.
  on manufacturing 14
  on unions 226
Weld, Isaac 95, 162, 213, 219-20, 228, 281
  on peat as fuel source 8
Westmeath, co. 19, 185, 197
  absenteeism in 201
  consolidation in 130
Wexford, co. 10, 12, 110, 146, 193, 211
  laborers and cottiers in 22
  occupations in 29
Wharncliffe Commission 128
  on general crime statistics 137
Whiteboy movement 132
Whitehaven, shipyards 229
Whyte, Ian D. 82
  cited 103
Wicklow, co. 10, 12, 184, 193, 282
  agrarian outrages in 135
  cottiers and laborers in 22
Wiggins, John 126, 205, 209, 224
  cited 189, 210
  on agents 208
  on London companies 210
Wittke, Carl 254, 260
  cited 253
Wolff, G. W. 213
Woodham-Smith, Cecil 202, 292
  cited 270
  on census of 1841 30
  on emigrant mortality 267
Woolen Acts 114, 287
woolen industry 14, 179
work ethic
  in Ireland 217-19
working year
  length of 215
workhouses 290
Wrigley, E. A. and Schofield, Roger 79

Young, Arthur 95, 244
  cited 110, 197, 222-3
  on absenteeism 198
  on agricultural investment 167
  on animal fodder 165
  on health of population 9
  on road quality 182
  on soil quality 195
  on utility of children 60